THE RUSSIAN REVOLUTION

LEON TROTSKY, whose original name was Lev Davidovich Bronstein, was born in 1879. An early convert to Marxism, he spent much of the time between 1902 and 1917 abroad as a propagandist, agitator, and journalist and was repeatedly exiled to Siberia. In 1917 he took a major part in the Bolshevik October Revolution and became commissar for foreign affairs under Lenin. He negotiated the Treaty of Brest-Litovsk and organized the victorious Red Army in the civil war of 1918–1920. After Lenin's death, Trotsky led the leftist opposition against Stalin, but in 1927 he was expelled from the party, exiled, and, in 1929, ordered to leave the USSR. He found asylum first in Turkey, then France, and later Norway until 1937 when the Soviet government obtained his expulsion, his name having been linked with plots against Stalin in the Moscow treason trials of the 1930's. Trotsky hurled countercharges at Stalin, moved to Mexico, and founded the Fourth International, a minor but highly articulate group of intellectuals dedicated to the establishment of pure communism. He was murdered at his home on August 21, 1940, leaving behind numerous political and polemical works in addition to *The History of the Russian Revolution.*

THE RUSSIAN REVOLUTION

The Overthrow of Tzarism

and

The Triumph of the Soviets

Selected and Edited by

F. W. DUPEE

from

The History of the
Russian Revolution

by

LEON TROTSKY

Translated from the Russian by

MAX EASTMAN

ANCHOR BOOKS
DOUBLEDAY
NEW YORK LONDON TORONTO SYDNEY AUCKLAND

AN ANCHOR BOOK
PUBLISHED BY DOUBLEDAY
a division of Bantam Doubleday Dell Publishing Group, Inc.
666 Fifth Avenue, New York, New York 10103

ANCHOR BOOKS, DOUBLEDAY, and the portrayal of an anchor are trademarks of Doubleday, a division of Bantam Doubleday Dell Publishing Group, Inc.

Library of Congress Cataloging in Publication Data
Trotsky, Leon, 1879–1940.
[Istoriiâ russkoĭ revoliûtŝii. English. Selections]
The Russian revolution: the overthrow of tzarism and the triumph of the Soviets/selected and edited by F. W. Dupee from The History of the Russian revolution by Leon Trotsky; translated from the Russian by Max Eastman.
p. cm.
Translation of: Istoriiâ russkoĭ revoliûtŝii.
Includes index.
1. Soviet Union—History—Revolution, 1917–1921.
I. Dupee, F. W. (Frederick Wilcox), 1904– . II. Title.
DK265.T7722513 1989 59–6990 88-36760
947.084'1—dc19 CIP

ISBN 0-385-09398-5

PRINTED IN THE UNITED STATES OF AMERICA
FIRST ANCHOR BOOKS EDITION 1959
16 18 20 22 24 25 23 21 19 17

CONTENTS

Volume Three

THE TRIUMPH OF THE SOVIETS

EDITOR'S NOTE

Written during the early years of his enforced exile from Soviet Russia, Trotsky's *History of the Russian Revolution* quickly established itself as one of the great books of the twentieth century. Like Thucydides' *The Peloponnesian War* and Caesar's *Commentaries,* it is the work of an individual who was himself a major participant in the experience he describes and who, in addition, was equally the man of letters and the man of action. Trotsky's historical theses are challenging; his judgments of other leaders intransigent. We are all the more free to accept, reject, or modify his ideas because he presents them with such proud and lucid candor. Beneath them lies the author's radical humanism and his vision of the events of 1917 in Russia as a decisive stage in the liberation of man's consciousness. If, he writes, Proust could devote many finely wrought pages to the despairing thoughts of his characters, "it would seem that one might, at least with equal justice, demand attention to a series of collective historic dramas which lifted hundreds of millions of human beings out of non-existence, transforming the character of nations and intruding forever into the life of all mankind."

In making the following selections from the *History,* I have tried to preserve as much as possible of that impassioned sense of continuity which is perhaps its outstanding literary virtue. I have therefore represented in full, and in their original sequence, the chapters dealing with the principal events of the revolutions of February and October, 1917, the two high points of that momentous year, and have provided brief summaries of the omitted chapters, with the exception of Chapter XXIII, Volume One, which is itself a brief summarizing conclusion to the contents of that volume. No such abridgments can do entire justice to the intricacy of Trotsky's reasoning and the abundance of his dramatic detail. But the task of summarizing was made easier, and the results probably more reliable, by Trotsky's genius for clear, orderly, and vivid formulation. Wherever possible, the language of my summaries is Trotsky's language. Or Trotsky's *and* Max Eastman's, for Eastman's admirable translation has made *The History of the Russian Revolution* an English classic.

F. W. D.

PREFACE

During the first two months of 1917 Russia was still a Romanov monarchy. Eight months later the Bolsheviks stood at the helm. They were little known to anybody when the year began, and their leaders were still under indictment for state treason when they came to power. You will not find another such sharp turn in history—especially if you remember that it involves a nation of 150 million people. It is clear that the events of 1917, whatever you think of them, deserve study.

The history of a revolution, like every other history, ought first of all to tell what happened and how. That, however, is little enough. From the very telling it ought to become clear why it happened thus and not otherwise. Events can neither be regarded as a series of adventures, nor strung on the thread of some preconceived moral. They must obey their own laws. The discovery of these laws is the author's task.

The most indubitable feature of a revolution is the direct interference of the masses in historic events. In ordinary times the state, be it monarchical or democratic, elevates itself above the nation, and history is made by specialists in that line of business—kings, ministers, bureaucrats, parliamentarians, journalists. But at those crucial moments when the old order becomes no longer endurable to the masses, they break over the barriers excluding them from the political arena, sweep aside their traditional representatives, and create by their own interference the initial groundwork for a new régime. Whether this is good or bad we leave to the judgment of moralists. We ourselves will take the facts as they are given by the objective course of development. The history of a revolution is for us first of all a history of the forcible entrance of the masses into the realm of rulership over their own destiny.

In a society that is seized by revolution classes are in conflict. It is perfectly clear, however, that the changes introduced between the beginning and the end of a revolution in the economic bases of the society and its social substratum of classes, are not sufficient to explain the course of the revolution itself, which can overthrow in a short interval age-old institutions, create new ones, and again overthrow them. The dynamic of revolutionary events is *directly* determined by swift, intense and passionate changes in the psychology of classes which have already formed themselves before the revolution.

The point is that society does not change its institutions as need arises, the way a mechanic changes his instruments. On the contrary, society actually takes the institutions which hang upon it as given once for all. For decades the oppositional criticism is nothing more than a safety valve for mass dissatisfaction, a condition of the stability of the social structure. Such in principle, for example, was the significance acquired by the social-democratic criticism. Entirely exceptional conditions, independent of the will of persons or parties, are necessary in order to tear off from discontent the fetters of conservatism, and bring the masses to insurrection.

The swift changes of mass views and moods in an epoch of revolution thus derive, not from the flexibility and mobility of man's mind, but just the opposite, from its deep conservatism. The chronic lag of ideas and relations behind new objective conditions, right up to the moment when the latter crash over people in the form of a catastrophe, is what creates in a period of revolution that leaping movement of ideas and passions which seems to the police mind a mere result of the activities of "demagogues."

The masses go into a revolution not with a prepared plan of social reconstruction, but with a sharp feeling that they cannot endure the old régime. Only the guiding layers of a class have a political program, and even this still requires the test of events, and the approval of the masses. The fundamental political process of the revolution thus consists in the gradual comprehension by a class of the problems arising from the social crisis—the active orientation of the masses by a method of successive approximations. The different stages of a revolutionary process, certified by a change of parties in which the more extreme always supersedes the less, express the growing pressure to the left of the masses—so long as the swing of the movement does not run into objective obstacles. When it does, there begins a reaction: disappointments of the different layers of the revolutionary class, growth of indifferentism, and therewith a strengthening of the position of the counter-revolutionary forces. Such, at least, is the general outline of the old revolutions.

Only on the basis of a study of political processes in the masses themselves, can we understand the rôle of parties and leaders, whom we least of all are inclined to ignore. They constitute not an independent, but nevertheless a very important, element in the process. Without a guiding organization the energy of the masses would dissipate like steam not enclosed in a piston-box. But nevertheless what moves things is not the piston or the box, but the steam.

The difficulties which stand in the way of studying the changes of mass consciousness in a revolutionary epoch are quite obvious. The oppressed classes make history in the factories, in the barracks, in the villages, on the streets of the cities. Moreover, they are least of all accustomed to write things down. Periods of high tension in social passions leave little room for contemplation and reflection. All the muses—even the plebeian muse of journalism, in spite of her sturdy hips—have hard sledding in times of revolution. Still the historian's situation is by no means hopeless. The records are incomplete, scattered, accidental. But in the light of the events themselves these fragments often permit a guess as to the direction and rhythm of the hidden process. For better or worse, a revolutionary party bases its tactics upon a calculation of the changes of mass consciousness. The historic course of Bolshevism demonstrates that such a calculation, at least in its rough features, can be made. If it can be made by a revolutionary leader in the whirlpool of the struggle, why not by the historian afterwards?

However, the processes taking place in the consciousness of the masses are not unrelated and independent. No matter how the idealists and eclectics rage, consciousness is nevertheless determined by conditions. In the historic conditions which formed Russia, her economy, her classes, her State, in the action upon her of other states, we ought to be able to find the premises both of the February revolution and of the October revolution which replaced it. Since the greatest enigma is the fact that a backward country was the *first* to place the proletariat in power, it behooves us to seek the solution of that enigma in the *peculiarities* of that backward country—that is, in its differences from other countries.

The historic peculiarities of Russia and their relative weight will be characterized by us in the early chapters of this book, which give a short outline of the development of Russian society and its inner forces. We venture to hope that the inevitable schematism of these chapters will not repel the reader. In the further development of the book he will meet these same forces in living action.

This work will not rely in any degree upon personal recollections. The circumstance that the author was a participant in the events does not free him from the obligation to base his exposition upon strictly verified documents. The author speaks of himself, in so far as that is demanded by the course of events, in the third person. And that is not a mere literary form: the subjective tone, inevitable in autobiographies or memoirs, is not permissible in a work of history.

However, the fact that the author did participate in the struggle naturally makes easier his understanding, not only of the psychology of the forces in action, both individual and collective, but also of the inner connection of events. This advantage will give positive results only if one condition is observed: that he does not rely upon the testimony of his own memory either in trivial details or in important matters, either in questions of fact or questions of motive and mood. The author believes that in so far as in him lies he has fulfilled this condition.

There remains the question of the political position of the author, who stands as a historian upon the same viewpoint upon which he stood as a participant in the events. The reader, of course, is not obliged to share the political views of the author, which the latter on his side has no reason to conceal. But the reader does have the right to demand that a historical work should not be the defense of a political position, but an internally well-founded portrayal of the actual process of the revolution. A historical work only then completely fulfills its mission when events unfold upon its pages in their full natural necessity.

For this, is it necessary to have the so-called historian's "impartiality"? Nobody has yet clearly explained what this impartiality consists of. The often quoted words of Clemenceau that it is necessary to take a revolution "en bloc," as a whole—are at the best a clever evasion. How can you take as a whole a thing whose essence consists in a split? Clemenceau's aphorism was dictated partly by shame for his too resolute ancestors, partly by embarrassment before their shades.

One of the reactionary and therefore fashionable historians of contemporary France, L. Madelin, slandering in his drawing-room fashion the great revolution—that is, the birth of his own nation—asserts that "the historian ought to stand upon the wall of a threatened city and behold at the same time the besiegers and the besieged": only in this way, it seems, can he achieve a "conciliatory justice." However, the words of Madelin himself testify that if he climbs out on the wall dividing the two camps, it is only in the character of a reconnoiterer for the reaction. It is well that he is concerned only with war camps of the past: in a time of revolution standing on the wall involves great danger. Moreover, in times of alarm the priests of "conciliatory justice" are usually found sitting on the inside of four walls waiting to see which side will win.

The serious and critical reader will not want a treacherous impartiality, which offers him a cup of conciliation with a well-settled poison of reactionary hate at the bottom, but a scientific conscientiousness, which for its sympathies and antipathies—open and undisguised—seeks support in an honest study of the facts, a determination of their real connections, an exposure of the causal laws of their movement. That is the only possible historic objectivism, and moreover it is amply sufficient, for it is verified and attested not by the good intentions of the historian, for which only he himself can vouch, but by the natural laws revealed by him of the historic process itself.

The sources of this book are innumerable periodical publications, newspapers and journals, memoirs, reports, and other material, partly in manuscript, but the greater part published by the Institute of the History of the Revolution in Moscow and Leningrad. We have considered it superfluous to make reference in the text to particular publications, since that would only bother the reader. Among the books which have the character of collective historical works we have particularly used the two-volume *Essays on the History of the October Revolution* (Moscow-Leningrad, 1927). Written by different authors, the various parts of this book are unequal in value, but they contain at any rate abundant factual material.

The dates in our book are everywhere indicated according to the old style—that is, they are 13 days behind the international and the present Soviet calendar. The author felt obliged to use the calendar which was in use at the time of the revolution. It would have been no labor of course to translate the dates into the new style. But this operation in removing one difficulty would have created others more essential. The overthrow of the monarchy has gone into history as the February revolution; according to the Western calendar, however, it occurred in March. The armed demonstration against the imperialist policy of the Provisional Government has gone into history under the name of the "April Days," whereas according to the Western calendar it happened in May. Not to mention other intervening events and dates, we remark only that the October revolution happened according to European reckoning in November. The calendar itself, we see, is tinted by the events, and the historian cannot handle revolutionary chronology by mere arithmetic. The reader will be kind enough to remember that before overthrowing the Byzantine calendar, the revolution had to overthrow the institutions that clung to it.

L. TROTSKY

Prinkipo
November 14, 1930

Volume One

THE OVERTHROW OF TZARISM

Chapter I

PECULIARITIES OF RUSSIA'S DEVELOPMENT

The fundamental and most stable feature of Russian history is the slow tempo of her development, with the economic backwardness, primitiveness of social forms and low level of culture resulting from it.

The population of this gigantic and austere plain, open to eastern winds and Asiatic migrations, was condemned by nature itself to a long backwardness. The struggle with nomads lasted almost up to the end of the seventeenth century; the struggle with winds, bringing winter cold and summer drought, continues still. Agriculture, the basis of the whole development, advanced by extensive methods. In the north they cut down and burned up the forests, in the south they ravished the virgin steppes. The conquest of nature went wide and not deep.

While the western barbarians settled in the ruins of Roman culture, where many an old stone lay ready as building material, the Slavs in the East found no inheritance upon their desolate plain: their predecessors had been on even a lower level of culture than they. The western European peoples, soon finding their natural boundaries, created those economic and cultural clusters, the commercial cities. The population of the eastern plain, at the first sign of crowding, would go deeper into the forest or spread out over the steppe. The more aggressive and enterprising elements of the peasantry in the west became burghers, craftsmen, merchants. The more active and bold in the east became, some of them, traders, but most of them Cossacks, frontiersmen, pioneers. The process of social differentiation, intensive in the west, was delayed in the east and diluted by the process of expansion. "The Tzar of Muscovia, although a Christian, rules a lazy-minded people," wrote Vico, a contemporary of Peter I. That "lazy" mind of the Muscovites was a reflection of the slow tempo of economic development, the formlessness of class relations, the meagerness of inner history.

The ancient civilizations of Egypt, India and China had a character self-sufficient enough, and they had time enough at their disposal, to bring their social relations, in spite of low productive powers, almost to the same detailed completion to which their craftsmen brought the products of their craft. Russia stood not only geographically, but also socially and historically, between Europe and Asia. She was marked off from the European West, but also from the Asiatic East, approaching at different periods and in different features now one, now the other. The East gave her the Tartar yoke, which entered as an important element into the structure of the Russian state. The West was a still more threatening foe—but at the same time a teacher. Russia was unable to settle in the forms of the East because she was continually having to adapt herself to military and economic pressure from the West. The existence of feudal relations in Russia, denied by former historians, may be considered unconditionally established by later investigation. Furthermore, the fundamental elements of Russian feudalism were the same as in the West. But the mere fact that the existence of the feudal epoch had to be established by means of extended scientific arguments sufficiently testifies to the incompleteness of Russian feudalism, its formlessness, its poverty of cultural monuments.

A backward country assimilates the material and intellectual conquests of the advanced countries. But this does not mean that it follows them slavishly, reproduces all the stages of their past. The theory of the repetition of historic cycles—Vico and his more recent followers—rests upon an observation of the orbits of old pre-capitalistic cultures, and in part upon the first experiments of capitalist development. A certain repetition of cultural stages in ever new settlements was in fact bound up with the provincial and episodic character of that whole process. Capitalism means, however, an overcoming of those conditions. It prepares and in a certain sense realizes the universality and permanence of man's development. By this a repetition of the forms of development by different nations is ruled out. Although compelled to follow after the advanced countries, a backward country does not take things in the same order. The privilege of historic backwardness—and such a privilege exists—permits, or rather compels, the adoption of whatever is ready in advance of any specified date, skipping a whole series of intermediate stages. Savages throw away their bows and arrows for rifles all at once, without traveling the road which lay between those two weapons in the past. The European colonists in America did not begin history all over again from the beginning. The fact that Germany and the United States have now economically outstripped England was made possible by the very backwardness of their capitalist development. On the other hand, the conservative anarchy in the British coal industry—as also in the heads of MacDonald and his friends—is a paying-up for the past when England played too long the rôle of capitalist pathfinder. The development of historically backward nations leads necessarily to a peculiar combination of different stages in the historic process. Their development as a whole acquires a planless, complex, combined character.

The possibility of skipping over intermediate steps is of course by no means absolute. Its degree is determined in the long run by the economic and cultural capacities of the country. The backward nation, moreover, not infrequently debases the achievements borrowed from outside in the process of adapting them to its own more primitive culture. In this the very process of assimilation acquires a self-contradictory character. Thus the introduction of certain elements of Western technique and training, above all military and industrial, under Peter I, led to a strengthening of serfdom as the fundamental form of labor organization. European armament and European loans—both indubitable products of a higher culture—led to a strengthening of tzarism, which delayed in its turn the development of the country.

The laws of history have nothing in common with a pedantic schematism. Unevenness, the most general law of the historic process, reveals itself most sharply and complexly in the destiny of the backward countries. Under the whip of external necessity their backward culture is compelled to make leaps. From the universal law of unevenness thus derives another law which, for the lack of a better name, we may call the law of *combined development*—by which we mean a drawing together of the different stages of the journey, a combining of separate steps, an amalgam of archaic with more contemporary forms. Without this law, to be taken of course in its whole material content, it is impossible to understand the history of Russia, and indeed of any country of the second, third or tenth cultural class.

Under pressure from richer Europe the Russian State swallowed up a far greater relative part of the people's wealth than in the West, and thereby not only condemned the people to a twofold poverty, but also weakened the foundations of the possessing classes. Being at the same time in need of support from the latter, it forced and regimented their growth. As a result the bureaucratized privileged classes never rose to their full height, and the Russian state thus still more approached an Asiatic despotism. The Byzantine autocratism, officially adopted by the Muscovite tzars at the beginning of the sixteenth century, subdued the feudal Boyars with the help of the nobility, and then gained the subjection of the nobility by making the peasantry their slaves, and upon this foundation created the St. Petersburg imperial absolutism. The backwardness of the whole process is sufficiently indicated in the fact that serfdom, born at the end of the sixteenth century, took form in the seventeenth, flowered in the eighteenth, and was juridically annulled only in 1861.

The clergy, following after the nobility, played no small rôle in the formation of the tzarist autocracy, but nevertheless a servile rôle. The church never rose in Russia to that commanding height which it attained in the Catholic West; it was satisfied with the rôle of spiritual servant of the autocracy, and counted this a recompense for its humility. The bishops and metropolitans enjoyed authority merely as deputies of the temporal power. The patriarchs were changed along with the tzars. In the Petersburg period the dependence of the church upon the state became still more servile. Two hundred thousand priests and monks were in all essentials a part of the bureaucracy, a sort of police of the gospel. In return for this the monopoly of the orthodox clergy in matters of faith, land and income was defended by a more regular kind of police.

Slavophilism, the messianism of backwardness, has based its philosophy upon the assumption that the Russian people and their church are democratic through and through, whereas official Russia is a German bureaucracy imposed upon them by Peter the Great. Marx remarked upon this theme: "In the same way the Teutonic jackasses blamed the despotism of Frederick the Second upon the French, as though backward slaves were not always in need of civilized slaves to train them." This brief comment completely finishes off not only the old philosophy of the Slavophiles, but also the latest revelations of the "Racists."

The meagerness not only of Russian feudalism, but of all the old Russian history, finds its most depressing expression in the absence of real medieval cities as centers of commerce and craft. Handicraft did not succeed in Russia in separating itself from agriculture, but preserved its character of home industry. The old Russian cities were commercial, administrative, military and manorial—centers of consumption, consequently, not of production. Even Novgorod, similar to Hansa and not subdued by the Tartars, was only a commercial, and not an industrial city. True, the distribution of the peasant industries over various districts created a demand for trade mediation on a large scale. But nomad traders could not possibly occupy that place in social life which belonged in the West to the craft-guild and merchant-industrial petty and middle bourgeoisie, inseparably bound up with its peasant environment. The chief roads of Russian trade, moreover, led across the border, thus from time immemorial giving the leadership to foreign commercial capital, and imparting a semi-colonial character to the whole process, in which the Russian trader was a mediator between the Western cities and the Russian villages. This kind of economic relation developed further during the epoch of Russian capitalism and found its extreme expression in the imperialist war.

The insignificance of the Russian cities, which more than anything else promoted the development of an Asiatic state, also made impossible a Reformation—that is, a replacement of the feudal-bureaucratic orthodoxy by some sort of modernized kind of Christianity adapted to the demands of a bourgeois society. The struggle against the state church did not go farther than the creation of peasant sects, the faction of the Old Believers being the most powerful among them.

Fifteen years before the great French revolution there developed in Russia a movement of the Cossacks, peasants and worker-serfs of the Urals, known as the Pugachev Rebellion. What was lacking to this menacing popular uprising in order to convert it into a revolution? A Third Estate. Without the industrial democracy of the cities a peasant war could not develop into a revolution, just as the peasant sects could not rise to the height of a Reformation. The result of the Pugachev Rebellion was just the opposite—a strengthening of bureaucratic absolutism as the guardian of the interests of the nobility, a guardian which had again justified itself in the hour of danger.

The Europeanization of the country, formally begun in the time of Peter, became during the following century more and more a demand of the ruling class itself, the nobility. In 1825 the aristocratic intelligentsia, generalizing this demand politically, went to the point of a military conspiracy to limit the powers of the autocracy. Thus, under pressure from the European bourgeois development, the progressive nobility attempted to take the place of the lacking Third Estate. But nevertheless they wished to combine their liberal régime with the security of their own caste domination, and therefore feared most of all to arouse the peasantry. It is thus not surprising that the conspiracy remained a mere attempt on the part of a brilliant but isolated officer caste which gave up the sponge almost without a struggle. Such was the significance of the Dekabrist uprising.

The landlords who owned factories were the first among their caste to favor replacing serfdom by wage labor. The growing export of Russian grain gave an impulse in the same direction. In 1861 the noble bureaucracy, relying upon the liberal landlords, carried out its peasant reform. The impotent bourgeois liberalism during this operation played the rôle of humble chorus. It is needless to remark that tzarism solved the fundamental problem of Russia, the agrarian problem, in a more niggardly and thieving fashion than that in which the Prussian monarchy during the next decade was to solve the fundamental problem of Germany, its national consolidation. The solution of the problems of one class by another is one of those combined methods natural to backward countries.

The law of combined development reveals itself most indubitably, however, in the history and character of Russian industry. Arising late, Russian industry did not repeat the development of the advanced countries, but inserted itself into this development, adapting their latest achievements to its own backwardness. Just as the economic evolution of Russia as a whole skipped over the epoch of craft-guilds and manufacture, so also the separate branches of industry made a series of special leaps over technical productive stages that had been measured in the West by decades. Thanks to this, Russian industry developed at certain periods with extraordinary speed. Between the first revolution and the war, industrial production in Russia approximately doubled. This has seemed to certain Russian historians a sufficient basis for concluding that "we must abandon the legend of backwardness and slow growth."[1] In reality the possibility of this swift growth was determined by that very backwardness which, alas, continued not only up to the moment of liquidation of the old Russia, but as her legacy up to the present day.

The basic criterion of the economic level of a nation is the productivity of labor, which in its turn depends upon the relative weight of the industries in the general economy of the country. On the eve of the war, when tzarist Russia had attained the highest point of its prosperity, the national income per capita was 8 to 10 times less than in the United States—a fact which is not surprising when you consider that 4/5 of the self-supporting population of Russia was occupied with agriculture, while in the United States, for every one engaged

[1] The assertion is made by Professor M. N. Pokrovsky.

in agriculture, 2½ were engaged in industry. We must add that for every one hundred square kilometers of land, Russia had, on the eve of the war, 0.4 kilometers of railroads, Germany 11.7, Austria-Hungary 7. Other comparative coefficients are of the same type.

But it is just in the sphere of economy, as we have said, that the law of combined development most forcibly emerges. At the same time that peasant land-cultivation as a whole remained, right up to the revolution, at the level of the seventeenth century, Russian industry in its technique and capitalist structure stood at the level of the advanced countries, and in certain respects even outstripped them. Small enterprises, involving less than 100 workers, employed in the United States, in 1914, 35 per cent of the total of industrial workers, but in Russia only 17.8 per cent. The two countries had an approximately identical relative quantity of enterprises involving 100 to 1000 workers. But the giant enterprises, above 1000 workers each, employed in the United States 17.8 per cent of the workers and in Russia 41.4 per cent! For the most important industrial districts the latter percentage is still higher: for the Petrograd district 44.4 per cent, for the Moscow district even 57.3 per cent. We get a like result if we compare Russian with British or German industry. This fact—first established by the author in 1908—hardly accords with the banal idea of the economic backwardness of Russia. However, it does not disprove this backwardness, but dialectically completes it.

The confluence of industrial with bank capital was also accomplished in Russia with a completeness you might not find in any other country. But the subjection of the industries to the banks meant, for the same reasons, their subjection to the western European money market. Heavy industry (metal, coal, oil) was almost wholly under the control of foreign finance capital, which had created for itself an auxiliary and intermediate system of banks in Russia. Light industry was following the same road. Foreigners owned in general about 40 per cent of all the stock capital of Russia, but in the leading branches of industry that percentage was still higher. We can say without exaggeration that the controlling shares of stock in the Russian banks, plants and factories were to be found abroad, the amount held in England, France and Belgium being almost double that in Germany.

The social character of the Russian bourgeoisie and its political physiognomy were determined by the condition of origin and the structure of Russian industry. The extreme concentration of this industry alone meant that between the capitalist leaders and the popular masses there was no hierarchy of transitional layers. To this we must add that the proprietors of the principal industrial, banking, and transport enterprises were foreigners, who realized on their investment not only the profits drawn from Russia, but also a political influence in foreign parliaments, and so not only did not forward the struggle for Russian parliamentarism, but often opposed it: it is sufficient to recall the shameful rôle played by official France. Such are the elementary and irremovable causes of the political isolation and anti-popular character of the Russian bourgeoisie. Whereas in the dawn of its history it was too unripe to accomplish a Reformation, when the time came for leading a revolution it was overripe.

In correspondence with this general course of development of the country, the reservoir from which the Russian working class formed itself was not the craft-guild, but agriculture, not the city, but the country. Moreover, in Russia the proletariat did not arise gradually through the ages, carrying with itself the burden of the past as in England, but in leaps involving sharp changes of environment, ties, relations, and a sharp break with the past. It is just this fact—combined with the concentrated oppressions of tzarism—that made the Russian workers hospitable to the boldest conclusions of revolutionary thought—just as the backward industries were hospitable to the last word in capitalist organization.

The Russian proletariat was forever repeating the short history of its origin. While in the metal industry, especially in Petrograd, a layer of hereditary proletarians was crystallized out, having made a complete break with the country, in the Urals the prevailing type was half-proletarian, half-peasant. A yearly inflow of fresh labor forces from the country in all the industrial districts kept renewing the bonds of the proletariat with its fundamental social reservoir.

The incapacity of the bourgeoisie for political action was

immediately caused by its relation to the proletariat and the peasantry. It could not lead after it workers who stood hostile in their everyday life, and had so early learned to generalize their problems. But it was likewise incapable of leading after it the peasantry, because it was entangled in a web of interests with the landlords, and dreaded a shake-up of property relations in any form. The belatedness of the Russian revolution was thus not only a matter of chronology, but also of the social structure of the nation.

England achieved her Puritan revolution when her whole population was not more than 5½ millions, of whom half a million were to be found in London. France, in the epoch of her revolution, had in Paris also only half a million out of a population of 25 million. Russia at the beginning of the twentieth century had a population of about 150 million, of whom more than 3 million were in Petrograd and Moscow. Behind these comparative figures lurk enormous social differences. Not only England of the seventeenth century, but also France of the eighteenth, had no proletariat in the modern sense. In Russia, however, the working class in all branches of labor, both city and village, numbered in 1905 no less than 10 million, which with their families amounts to more than 25 million—that is to say, more than the whole population of France in the epoch of the great revolution. Advancing from the sturdy artisans and independent peasants of the army of Cromwell—through the Sansculottes of Paris—to the industrial proletarians of St. Petersburg, the revolution had deeply changed its social mechanism, its methods, and therewith its aims.

The events of 1905 were a prologue to the two revolutions of 1917, that of February and that of October. In the prologue all the elements of the drama were included, but not carried through. The Russo-Japanese war had made tzarism totter. Against the background of a mass movement the liberal bourgeoisie had frightened the monarchy with its opposition. The workers had organized independently of the bourgeoisie, and in opposition to it, in soviets, a form of organization then first called into being. Peasant uprisings to seize the land occurred throughout vast stretches of the country. Not only the peasants, but also the revolutionary parts of the army tended toward the soviets, which at the moment of highest tension openly disputed the power with the monarchy. However, all the revolutionary forces were then going into action for the first time, lacking experience and confidence. The liberals demonstratively backed away from the revolution exactly at the moment when it became clear that to shake tzarism would not be enough, it must be overthrown. This sharp break of the bourgeoisie with the people, in which the bourgeoisie carried with it considerable circles of the democratic intelligentsia, made it easier for the monarchy to differentiate within the army, separating out the loyal units, and to make a bloody settlement with the workers and peasants. Although with a few broken ribs, tzarism came out of the experience of 1905 alive and strong enough.

What changes in the correlation of forces were introduced by the eleven years' historical development dividing the prologue from the drama? Tzarism during this period came into still sharper conflict with the demands of historic development. The bourgeoisie became economically more powerful, but as we have seen its power rested on a higher concentration of industry and an increased predominance of foreign capital. Impressed by the lessons of 1905, the bourgeoisie had become more conservative and suspicious. The relative weight of the petty and middle bourgeoisie, insignificant before, had fallen still lower. The democratic intelligentsia generally speaking had no firm social support whatever. It could have a transitional political influence, but could play no independent rôle: its dependence upon bourgeois liberalism had grown enormously. In these circumstances only the youthful proletariat could give the peasantry a program, a banner and leadership. The gigantic tasks thus presented to the proletariat gave rise to an urgent necessity for a special revolutionary organization capable of quickly getting hold of the popular masses and making them ready for revolutionary action under the leadership of the workers. Thus the soviets of 1905 developed gigantically in 1917. That the soviets, we may remark here, are not a mere child of the historic backwardness of Russia, but a product of her combined development, is indicated by the fact that the proletariat of the most industrial country, Germany, at the time of its revolutionary high point—1918 to 1919—could find no other form of organization.

The revolution of 1917 still had as its immediate task the overthrow of the bureaucratic monarchy, but in distinction from the older bourgeois revolutions, the decisive force now was a new class formed on the basis of a concentrated industry, and armed with new organizations, new methods of struggle. The law of combined development here emerges in its extreme expression: starting with the overthrow of a decayed medieval structure, the revolution in the course of a few months placed the proletariat and the Communist Party in power.

In its initial task the Russian revolution was thus a democratic revolution. But it posed the problem of political democracy in a new way. While the workers were covering the whole country with soviets, including in them the soldiers and part of the peasantry, the bourgeoisie still continued to dicker—shall we summon or not summon a Constituent Assembly? In the course of our exposition this question will rise before us in full completeness. Here we wish only to mark the place of the soviets in the historic succession of revolutionary ideas and forms.

In the middle of the seventeenth century the bourgeois revolution in England developed under the guise of a religious reformation. A struggle for the right to pray according to one's own prayer book was identified with the struggle against the king, the aristocracy, the princes of the church, and Rome. The Presbyterians and Puritans were deeply convinced that they were placing their earthly interests under the unshakable protection of the divine Providence. The goals for which the new classes were struggling commingled inseparably in their consciousness with texts from the Bible and the forms of churchly ritual. Emigrants carried with them across the ocean this tradition sealed with blood. Hence the extraordinary virility of the Anglo-Saxon interpretation of Christianity. We see even today how the minister "socialists" of Great Britain back up their cowardice with these same magic texts with which the people of the seventeenth century sought to justify their courage.

In France, which stepped across the Reformation, the Catholic Church survived as a state institution until the revolution, which found its expression and justification for the tasks of the bourgeois society, not in texts from the Bible, but in the abstractions of democracy. Whatever the hatred of the present rulers of France for Jacobinism, the fact is that only thanks to the austere labor of Robespierre are they still able to cover their conservative rulership with those formulas with the help of which the old society was exploded.

Each of the great revolutions marked off a new stage of the bourgeois society, and new forms of consciousness for its classes. Just as France stepped over the Reformation, so Russia stepped over the formal democracy. The Russian revolutionary party, which was to place its stamp upon a whole epoch, sought an expression for the tasks of the revolution neither in the Bible nor in that secularized Christianity called "pure" democracy, but in the material relations of the social classes. The soviet system gave to these relations their simplest, most undisguised and transparent expression. The rule of the toilers has for the first time been realized in the soviet system, which, whatever its immediate historic vicissitudes, has penetrated as irrevocably into the consciousness of the masses as did in its day the system of the Reformation or of pure democracy.

Chapter II

TZARIST RUSSIA IN THE WAR

Russia's participation in the war was self-contradictory both in motives and in aims. That bloody struggle was waged essentially for world domination. In this sense it was beyond Russia's scope. The war aims of Russia herself (the Turkish Straits, Galicia, Armenia) were provincial in character, and to be decided only incidentally according to the degree in which they answered the interests of the principal contestants.

At the same time Russia, as one of the great powers, could not help participating in the scramble of the advanced capitalist countries, just as in the preceding epoch she could not help introducing shops, factories, railroads, rapid-fire guns and airplanes. The not infrequent disputes among Russian historians of the newest school as to how far Russia was ripe for present-day imperialist policies often fall into mere scholasticism, because they look upon Russia in the international arena as isolated, as an independent factor, whereas she was but one link in a system.

India participated in the war both essentially and formally as a colony of England. The participation of China, though in a formal sense "voluntary," was in reality the interference of a slave in the fight of his masters. The participation of Russia falls somewhere halfway between the participation of France and that of China. Russia paid in this way for her right to be an ally of advanced countries, to import capital and pay interest on it—that is, essentially, for her right to be a privileged colony of her allies—but at the same time for her right to oppress and rob Turkey, Persia, Galicia, and in general the countries weaker and more backward than herself. The twofold imperialism of the Russian bourgeoisie had basically the character of an agency for other mightier world powers.

The Chinese compradors are the classic type of the national bourgeoisie, a kind of mediating agency between foreign finance capital and the economy of their own country. In the world hierarchy of the powers, Russia occupied before the war a considerably higher position than China. What position she would have occupied after the war, if there had been no revolution, is a different question. But the Russian autocracy on the one hand, the Russian bourgeoisie on the other, contained features of compradorism, ever more and more clearly expressed. They lived and nourished themselves upon their connections with foreign imperialism, served it, and without its support could not have survived. To be sure, they did not survive in the long run even with its support. The semi-comprador Russian bourgeoisie had world-imperialistic interests in the same sense in which an agent working on percentages lives by the interests of his employer.

The instrument of war is the army. Inasmuch as every army is considered unconquerable in the national mythology, the ruling classes of Russia saw no reason for making an exception of the army of the tzar. In reality, however, this army was a serious force only against semi-barbaric peoples, small neighbors and disintegrating states; on the European arena it could act only as part of a coalition; in the matter of defense it could fulfill its task only by the help of the vastness of spaces, the sparsity of population, and the impassability of the roads. The virtuoso of this army of serfs had been Suvorov. The French revolution in breaking open the doors to the new society and the new military art, had pronounced a death-sentence on the Suvorov type of army. The semi-annulment of serfdom and the introduction of universal military service had modernized the army only as far as it had the country—that is, it introduced into the army all the contradictions proper to a nation which still has its bourgeois revolution to accomplish. It is true that the tzar's army was constructed and armed upon Western models; but this was more form than essence. There was no correspondence between the cultural level of the peasant-soldier and modern military technique. In the commanding staff, the ignorance, light-mindedness, and thievery of the ruling classes found their expression. Industry and transport continually revealed their bankruptcy before the concentrated demands of war time. Although appropriately armed, as it seemed, on the first day of the war, the troops soon turned out to have neither weapons nor even shoes. In the Russo-Japanese war the tzarist army had shown what it was worth. In the epoch of counter-revolution the monarchy, with the aid of the Duma, had filled up the military stores and put many new patches on the army, especially upon its reputation for invincibility. In 1914 came a new and far heavier test.

In the matter of military supplies and finances, Russia at war suddenly finds herself in slavish dependence upon her allies. This is merely a military expression of her general dependence upon advanced capitalist countries. But help from the Allies does not save the situation. The lack of munitions, the small number of factories for their production, the sparseness of railroad lines for their transportation, soon translated the backwardness of Russia into the familiar language of defeat—which served to remind the Russian national liberals that their ancestors had not accomplished the bourgeois revolution and that the descendants, therefore, owed a debt to history.

The first days of war were the first days of disgrace. After a series of partial catastrophes, in the spring of 1915 came the general retreat. The generals took out their own criminal incapacity on the peaceful population. Enormous tracts of land were violently laid waste. Clouds of human locusts were driven to the rear with whips. The external rout was completed with an internal one.

In answer to alarmed questions from his colleagues as to the situation at the front, the War Minister Polivanov answered in these words: "I place my trust in the impenetrable spaces, impassable mud, and the mercy of Saint Nicholas Mirlikisky, Protector of Holy Russia" (Session of August 4, 1915). A week later General Ruszky confessed to the same ministers: "The present-day demands of military technique are beyond us. At any rate we can't keep up with the Germans." That was not the mood of a moment. Officer Stankevich reports the words of an engineer of the corps: "It is hopeless to fight with the Germans, for we are in no condition to do anything; even the new methods of fighting become the causes of our failure." There is a cloud of such testimony. The one thing the Russian generals did with a flourish was to drag human meat out of the country. Beef and pork are handled with incomparably more economy. Gray staff-nonentities, like Yanushkevich under Nikolai Nikolaievich, and Alexeiev under the tzar, would stop up all cracks with new mobilizations, and comfort themselves and the Allies with columns of figures when columns of fighters were wanted. About fifteen million men were mobilized, and they brimmed the depots, barracks, points of transit, crowded, stamped, stepped on each other's feet, getting harsh and cursing. If these human masses were an imaginary magnitude for the front, for the rear they were a very real factor of destruction. About five and a half million were counted as killed, wounded and captured. The number of deserters kept growing. Already in July 1915 the ministers chanted: "Poor Russia! Even her army, which in past ages filled the world with the thunder of its victories . . . Even her army turns out to consist only of cowards and deserters."

The ministers themselves, with a gallows joke at the "bravery in retreat" of their generals, wasted hours in those days discussing such problems as whether to remove or not to remove the bones of the saints from Kiev. The tzar submitted that it was not necessary, since "the Germans would not risk touching them, and if they did touch them, so much the worse for the Germans." But the Synod had already started to remove them. "When we leave," they said, "we will take with us what is most precious." This happened not in the epoch of the Crusades, but in the twentieth century when the news of the Russian defeats came over the wireless.

The Russian successes against Austria-Hungary had their roots rather in Austria-Hungary than in Russia. The disintegrating Hapsburg monarchy had long ago hung out a sign for an undertaker, not demanding any high qualifications of him. In the past Russia had been successful against inwardly decomposing states like Turkey, Poland, Persia. The southwestern front of the Russian army, facing Austria, celebrated immense victories which made it very different from the other fronts. Here there emerged a few generals, who to be sure demonstrated no military gifts, but were at least thoroughly imbued with the fatalism of steadily-beaten commanders. From this milieu there arose subsequently several white "heroes" of the civil war.

Everybody was looking for someone upon whom to lay the blame. They accused the Jews wholesale of espionage. They set upon people with German names. The staff of the Grand Duke Nikolai Nikolaievich gave orders to shoot a colonel of gendarmes, Myasoyedov, as a German spy, which he obviously was not. They arrested Sukhomlinov, the War Minister, an empty and slovenly man, accusing him—possibly not without foundation—of treason. The British Minister of Foreign Affairs, Grey, said to the president of the Russian Parliamentary Delegation: Your government is very bold if it dares in time of war indict its War Minister for treason. The staff and the Duma accused the court of Germanophilism. All of them together envied the Allies and hated them. The French command spared its army by putting in Russian soldiers. England warmed up slowly. In the drawing rooms of Petrograd and the headquarters at the front they gently joked: "England has sworn to fight to the last drop of blood . . . of the Russian soldier." These jokes seeped down and reached the trenches. "Everything for the war!" said the ministers, deputies, generals, journalists. "Yes," the soldier began to think in the trenches, "they are all ready to fight to the last drop . . . of my blood."

The Russian army lost in the whole war more men than any army which ever participated in a national war—approximately two and a half million killed, or forty per cent of all the losses of the Entente. In the first months the soldiers fell under shell fire unthinkingly or thinking little; but from day to day they gathered experience—bitter experience of the lower ranks who are ignorantly commanded. They measured the confusion of the generals by the number of purposeless maneuvers on soleless shoes, the numbers of dinners not eaten. From the bloody mash of people and things emerged a generalized word: "the mess," which in the soldiers' jargon was replaced by a still juicier term.

The swiftest of all to disintegrate was the peasant infantry. As a general rule, the artillery with its high percentage of industrial workers, is distinguished by an incomparably greater hospitality to revolutionary ideas: this was clearly evident in 1905. If in 1917, on the contrary, the artillery showed more conservatism than the infantry, the cause lies in the fact that through the infantry divisions, as through a sieve, there passed ever new and less and less trained human masses. The artillery, moreover, suffering infinitely fewer losses, retained its original *cadres.* The same thing was observed in other specialized troops. But in the long run the artillery yielded too. During the retreat from Galicia a secret order was issued by the commander-in-chief: flog the soldiers for desertion and other crimes. The soldier Pireiko relates: "They began to flog soldiers for the most trivial offenses; for example, for a few hours' absence without leave. And sometimes they flogged them in order to rouse their fighting spirit." As early as September 17, 1915, Kuropatkin wrote, citing Guchkov: "The lower orders began the war with enthusiasm; but now they are weary, and with the continual retreats have lost faith in a victory." At about the same time the Minister of the Interior spoke of the presence in Moscow of 30,000 convalescent soldiers: "That's a wild crowd of libertines knowing no discipline, rough-housing, getting into fights with the police (not long ago a policeman was killed by soldiers), rescuing arrested men, etc. Undoubtedly, in case of disorders this entire horde will take the side of the mob." The same soldier, Pireiko, writes: "Everyone, to the last man, was interested in nothing but peace . . . Who should win and what kind of peace it would be, that was of small interest to the army. It wanted peace at any cost, for it was weary of war."

An observant woman, Feodorchenko, serving as sister of mercy, listened to the conversations of the soldiers, almost to their thoughts, and cleverly wrote them down on scattered slips of paper. The little book thus produced, *The People at War,* permits us to look in that laboratory where bombs, barbed-wire entanglements, suffocating gases, and the baseness of those in power, had been fashioning for long months the consciousness of several million Russian peasants, and where along with human bones age-old prejudices were cracking. In many of the self-made aphorisms of the soldiers appear already the slogans of the coming civil war.

General Ruszky complained in December 1916 that Riga

was the misfortune of the northern front. This is a "nest of propaganda, and so is Dvinsk." General Brussilov confirmed this: From the Riga district troops arrive demoralized; soldiers refuse to attack. They lifted one company commander on the points of their bayonets. It was necessary to shoot several men, etc., etc. "The ground for the final disintegration of the army was prepared long before the revolution," concedes Rodzianko, who was in close association with the officers and visited the front.

The revolutionary elements, scattered at first, were drowned in the army almost without a trace, but with the growth of the general discontent they rose to the surface. The sending of striking workers to the front as a punishment increased the ranks of the agitators and the retreat gave them a favorable audience. "The army in the rear and especially at the front," reports a secret service agent, "is full of elements of which some are capable of becoming active forces of insurrection, and others may merely refuse to engage in punitive activities." The Gendarme Administration of the Petrograd province declares in October 1916, on the basis of a report made by a representative of the Land Union, that "the mood in the army is alarming, the relation between officers and soldiers is extremely tense, even bloody encounters are taking place. Deserters are to be met everywhere by the thousands. Everyone who comes near the army must carry away a complete and convincing impression of the utter moral disintegration of the troops." Out of caution the report adds that although much in these communications seems hardly probable, nevertheless it must be believed, since many physicians returning from the active army have made reports to the same effect. The mood of the rear corresponded to that of the front. At a conference of the Kadet party in October 1916, a majority of the delegates remarked upon the apathy and lack of faith in the victorious outcome of the war "in all layers of the population, but especially in the villages and among the city poor." On October 30, 1916, the director of the Police Department wrote, in a summary of his report, of "the weariness of war to be observed everywhere, and the longing for a swift peace, regardless of the conditions upon which it is concluded." In a few months all these gentlemen—deputies, police, generals and land representatives, physicians and former gendarmes—will nevertheless assert that the revolution killed patriotism in the army, and that the Bolsheviks snatched a sure victory out of their hands.

The place of coryphées, in the chorus of military patriotism, undoubtedly belonged to the Constitutional Democrats (Kadets). Having already in 1905 broken its dubious ties with the revolution, liberalism at the beginning of the counter-revolutionary period had raised the banner of imperialism. One thing flowed from another: once it proved impossible to purge the country of the feudal rubbish in order to assure to the bourgeoisie a dominant position, it remained to form a union with the monarchy and the nobility in order to assure to capital the best position in the world market. If it is true that the world catastrophe was prepared in various quarters, so that it arrived to a certain degree unexpectedly even to its most responsible organizers, it is equally indubitable that Russian liberalism, as the inspirer of the foreign policy of the monarchy, did not occupy the last place in its preparation. The war of 1914 was quite rightly greeted by the leaders of the Russian bourgeoisie as their war. In a solemn session of the State Duma on July 26, 1914, the president of the Kadet faction announced: "We will make no conditions or demands. We will simply throw in the scales our firm determination to conquer the enemy." In Russia, too, national unity became the official doctrine. During a patriotic manifestation in Moscow the master of ceremonies, Count Benkendorff, cried to the diplomats: "Look! There is your revolution which they were prophesying in Berlin!" "A similar thought," explained the French minister Paléologue, "was evidently in the minds of all." People considered it their duty to nourish and propagate illusions in a situation which, it would seem, absolutely forbade illusions.

They did not wait long for sobering lessons. Very soon after the beginning of the war one of the more expansive Kadets, a lawyer and landlord, Rodichev, exclaimed at a session of the Central Committee of his party: "Do you really think we can conquer with those fools?" Events proved that it was not possible to conquer with fools. Liberalism, having more than half lost faith in the victory, tried to employ the momentum of the war in order to carry out a purgation of the camarilla and compel the monarchy to a compromise. The chief implement towards this end was to accuse the court party of Germanophilism and of preparing a separate peace.

In the spring of 1915, while the weaponless soldiers were retreating along the whole front, it was decided in governmental circles, not without pressure from the Allies, to recruit the initiative of private industry for work in behalf of the army. The Special Conference called for this end included, along with bureaucrats, the more influential industrialists. The Land and City unions which had arisen at the beginning of the war, and the Military-Industrial Committees created in the spring of 1915, became the points of support of the bourgeoisie in the struggle for victory and for power. The State Duma, backed by these organizations, was induced to intercede more confidently between the bourgeoisie and the monarchy.

These broad political perspectives did not, however, distract attention from the important problems of the day. Out of the Special Conference as out of a central reservoir tens of hundreds of millions, mounting up to billions, flowed down through distributing canals, abundantly irrigating the industries and incidentally nourishing numberless appetites. In the State Duma and in the press a few of the war profits for 1914 and 1915 were published. The Moscow textile company of the Riabushinskys showed a net profit of 75 per cent; the Tver Company, 111 per cent; the copper-works of Kolchugin netted over 12 million on a basic capital of 10 million. In this sector patriotic virtue was rewarded generously, and moreover immediately.

Speculation of all kinds and gambling on the market went to the point of paroxysm. Enormous fortunes arose out of the bloody foam. The lack of bread and fuel in the capital did not prevent the court jeweler Faberget from boasting that he had never before done such a flourishing business. Lady-in-waiting Vyrubova says that in no other season were such gowns to be seen as in the winter of 1915–16, and never were so many diamonds purchased. The night clubs were brimful of heroes of the rear, legal deserters, and simply respectable people too old for the front but sufficiently young for the joys of life. The grand dukes were not among the last to enjoy this feast in times of plague. Nobody had any fear of spending too much. A continual shower of gold fell from above. "Society" held out its hands and pockets, aristocratic ladies spread their skirts high, everybody splashed about in the bloody mud —bankers, heads of the commissariat, industrialists, ballerinas of the tzar and the grand dukes, orthodox prelates, ladies-in-waiting, liberal deputies, generals of the front and rear, radical lawyers, illustrious mandarins of both sexes, innumerable nephews, and more particularly nieces. All came running to grab and gobble, in fear lest the blessed rain should stop. And all rejected with indignation the shameful idea of a premature peace.

Common gains, external defeats, and internal dangers, drew together the parties of the ruling classes. The Duma, divided on the eve of the war, achieved in 1915 its patriotic oppositional majority which received the name of "Progressive Bloc." The official aim of this bloc was of course declared to be "a satisfaction of the needs created by the war." On the left the social-democrats and Trudoviks did not enter the bloc; on the right the notorious Black Hundred groups. All the other factions of the Duma—the Kadets, Progressives, three groups of Octobrists, the Center and a part of the Nationalists, entered the bloc or adhered to it—as also the national groups: Poles, Lithuanians, Mussulmans, Jews, etc. In order not to frighten the tzar with the formula of a responsible ministry, the bloc demanded "a united government composed of men enjoying the confidence of the country." The Minister of the Interior, Prince Sherbatov, at that time characterized the bloc as a temporary "union called forth by the danger of social revolution." It required no great penetration to realize this. Miliukov, the leader of the Kadets, and thus also of the oppositional bloc, said at a conference of his party: "We are treading a volcano. . . . The tension has reached its extreme limit. . . . A carelessly dropped match will be enough to start a terrible conflagration. . . . Whatever the government—whether good or bad—a strong government is needed now more than ever before."

The hope that the tzar, under the burden of defeat, would grant concessions, was so great that in the liberal press there appeared in August the slate of a proposed "Cabinet of confidence" with the president of the Duma, Rodzianko, as premier (according to another version, the president of the Land Union, Prince Lvov, was indicated for that office), Guchkov as Minister of the Interior, Miliukov, Foreign Minister, etc. A majority of these men who here nominated themselves for a union with the tzar against the revolution, turned up a year later as members of the "Revolutionary Government." History has permitted herself such antics more than once. This time the joke was at least a brief one.

A majority of the ministers of Goremykin's cabinet were no less frightened than the Kadets by the course things were taking, and therefore inclined towards an agreement with the Progressive Bloc. "A government which has not behind it the confidence of the supreme ruler, nor the army, nor the cities, nor the zemstvos, nor the nobles, nor the merchants, nor the workers, not only cannot function, but cannot even exist—the thing is obviously absurd." In these words, Prince Sherbatov in August 1915 appraised the government in which he himself was Minister of the Interior. "If you only arrange the scene properly and offer a loophole," said the Foreign Minister Sazonov, "the Kadets will be the first to propose a compromise. Miliukov is the greatest possible bourgeois and fears a social revolution above everything. Besides, a majority of the Kadets are trembling for their own capital." Miliukov on his side considered that the Progressive Bloc "would have to give in somewhat." Both sides were ready to bargain, and everything seemed thoroughly oiled. But on August 29 the Premier, Goremykin, a bureaucrat weighed down with years and honors, an old cynic playing politics between two games of *grand-patience* and defending himself against all complaints by remarking that the war is "not my business," journeyed out to the tzar at headquarters and returned with the information that all and everybody should remain in their places, except the rambunctious Duma, which was to be dissolved on the 3rd of September. The reading of the tzar's order dissolving the Duma was heard without a single word of protest: the deputies gave a "hurrah" for the tzar, and dispersed.

How did the tzar's government, supported according to its own confession by nobody at all, survive for over a year and a half after that? A temporary success of the Russian troops undoubtedly exerted its influence and this was reënforced by the good golden rain. The successes at the front soon ceased, to be sure, but the profits at the rear continued. However, the chief cause of the successful propping up of the monarchy for twelve months before its fall, was to be found in a sharp division in the popular discontent. The chief of the Moscow Secret Service Department reported a rightward tendency of the bourgeoisie under the influence of "a fear of possible revolutionary excesses after the war." During the war, we note, a revolution was still considered impossible. The industrialists were alarmed, over and above that, by "a coquetting of certain leaders of the Military Industrial Committee with the proletariat." The general conclusion of this colonel of gendarmes, Martynov—in whom a professional reading of Marxist literature had left some traces—announced as the cause of a certain improvement in the political situation "the steadily growing differentiation of social classes concealing a sharp contradiction in their interests, a contradiction felt especially keenly in the times we are living through."

The dissolution of the Duma in September 1915 was a direct challenge to the bourgeoisie, not to the workers. But while the liberals were dispersing with cries of "Hurrah!"—to be sure, not very enthusiastic cries—the workers of Petrograd and Moscow responded with strikes of protest. That cooled off the liberals still more. They feared worst of all the intrusion of an uninvited third party in their family discussion with the monarchy. But what further step was to be taken? Accompanied by a slight growl from the left wing, liberalism cast its vote for a well-tried recipe: to stand exclusively on legal grounds, and render the bureaucracy "as it were, unnecessary" in the course of a mere fulfillment of our patriotic functions. The ministerial slate at any rate would have to be laid aside for a time.

The situation in those days was getting worse automatically. In May 1916 the Duma was again convoked, but nobody knew exactly what for. The Duma, in any case, had no intention of summoning a revolution, and aside from that there was nothing for it to say. "At that session"—Rodzianko remembers—"the proceedings were languid; the deputies attended irregularly. . . . The continual struggle seemed fruitless, the government would listen to nothing, irregularities were increasing, and the country was headed for ruin." In the bourgeoisie's fear of revolution and its impotence without revolution, the monarchy found, during the year 1916, a simulacrum of social support.

By autumn the situation was still worse. The hopelessness of the war had become evident to all. The indignation of the popular masses threatened any moment to flow over the brim. While attacking the court party as before for Germanophilism, the liberals now deemed it necessary to feel out the chances of peace themselves, preparing their own future. Only in this way can you explain the negotiations of one of the leaders of the Progressive Bloc, the deputy Protopopov, with the German diplomat, Warburg, in Stockholm in the autumn of 1916. The Duma delegation, making friendly visits to the French and English, could easily convince itself in Paris and London that the dear Allies intended in the course of the war to squeeze all the live juice out of Russia, in order after the victory to make this backward country their chief field of economic exploitation. A defeated Russia in tow to a victorious Entente would have meant a colonial Russia. The Russian possessing classes had no other course but to try to free themselves from the too close embraces of the Entente, and find an independent road to peace, making use of the antagonism of the two more powerful camps. The meeting of the Duma deputy with the German diplomat, as a first step on this road, was both a threat in the direction of the Allies with a view to gaining concessions, and a feeling out of the actual possibilities of rapprochement with Germany. Protopopov was acting in agreement not only with the tzarist diplomats—the meeting occurred in the presence of the Russian ambassador in Sweden—but also with the whole delegation of the State Duma. Incidentally the liberals by means of this reconnoiter were pursuing a not unimportant domestic goal. "Rely on us"—they were hinting to the tzar—"and we will make you a separate peace better and more reliable than Stürmer[1] can." According to Protopopov's scheme—that is, the scheme of his backers—the Russian government

[1] Prime Minister from January to November 1916. [Trans.]

was to inform the Allies "several months in advance" that she would be compelled to end the war, and that if the Allies refused to institute peace negotiations, Russia would have to conclude a separate peace with Germany. In his confession written after the revolution, Protopopov speaks as of something which goes without saying of the fact that "all reasonable people in Russia, among them probably all the leaders of the party of 'the People's Freedom' (Kadets), were convinced that Russia was unable to continue the war."

The tzar, to whom Protopopov upon his return reported his journey and negotiations, treated the idea of a separate peace with complete sympathy. He merely did not see the necessity of drawing the liberals into the business. The fact that Protopopov himself was included incidentally in the staff of the court camarilla, having broken with the Progressive Bloc, is explained by the personal character of this fop, who had fallen in love, according to his own words, with the tzar and the tzarina—and at the same time, we may add, with an expected portfolio as Minister of the Interior. But this episode of Protopopov's treason to liberalism does not alter the general content of the liberal foreign policy—a mixture of greed, cowardice and treachery.

The Duma again assembled on November 1. The tension in the country had become unbearable. Decisive steps were expected of the Duma. It was necessary to do something, or at the very least say something. The Progressive Bloc found itself again compelled to resort to parliamentary exposures. Counting over from the tribune the chief steps taken by the government, Miliukov asked after each one: "Was this stupidity or treason?" High notes were sounded also by other deputies. The government was almost without defenders. It answered in its usual way: the speeches of the Duma orators were forbidden publication. The speeches therefore circulated by the million. There was not a government department, not only in the rear but at the front, where the forbidden speeches were not transcribed—frequently with additions corresponding to the temperament of the transcriber. The reverberation of the debate of November 1 was such that terror seized the very authors of the arraignment.

A group of extreme rights, sturdy bureaucrats inspired by

Durnovo, who had put down the revolution of 1905, took that moment to present to the tzar a proposed program. The eye of these experienced officials, trained in a serious police school, saw not badly and pretty far, and if their prescription was no good, it is only because no medicine existed for the sickness of the old régime. The authors of the program speak against any concessions whatever to the bourgeois opposition, not because the liberals want to go too far, as think the vulgar Black Hundreds—upon whom these official reactionaries look with some scorn—no, the trouble is that the liberals are "so weak, so disunited and, to speak frankly, so mediocre, that their triumph would be as brief as it would be unstable." The weakness of the principal opposition party, the "Constitutional Democrats" (Kadets), is indicated, they point out, by its very name. It is called democratic, when it is in essence bourgeois. Although to a considerable degree a party of liberal landlords, it has signed a program of compulsory land redemption. "Without these trumps from a deck not their own"—write these secret counselors, using the images to which they are accustomed—"the Kadets are nothing more than a numerous association of liberal lawyers, professors and officials of various departments—nothing more." A revolutionist, they point out, is a different thing. They accompany their recognition of the significance of the revolutionary parties with a grinding of teeth: "The danger and strength of these parties lies in the fact that they have an idea, they have money (!), they have a crowd ready and well organized." The revolutionary parties "can count on the sympathy of an overwhelming majority of the peasantry, which will follow the proletariat the very moment the revolutionary leaders point a finger to other people's land." What would a responsible ministry yield in these circumstances? "A complete and final destruction of the right parties, a gradual swallowing of the intermediate parties—the Center, the Liberal-Conservatives, the Octobrists and the Progressives of the Kadet party—which at the beginning would have a decisive importance. But the same fate would menace the Kadets . . . and afterwards would come the revolutionary mob, the Commune, destruction of the dynasty, pogroms of the possessing classes, and finally the peasant-brigand." It is impossible to deny that the police anger here rises to a certain kind of historic vision.

The positive part of their program was not new, but consistent: a government of ruthless partisans of the autocracy; abolition of the Duma; martial law in both capitals; preparation of forces for putting down a rebellion. This program did in its essentials become the basis of the government policy of the last pre-revolutionary months. But its success presupposed a power which Durnovo had had in his hands in the winter of 1905, but which by the autumn of 1917 no longer existed. The monarchy tried, therefore, to strangle the country stealthily and in sections. Ministers were shifted upon the principle of "our people"—meaning those unconditionally devoted to the tzar and tzarina. But these "our people"—especially the renegade Protopopov—were insignificant and pitiful. The Duma was not abolished, but again dissolved. The declaration of martial law in Petrograd was saved for a moment when the revolution had already triumphed. And the military forces prepared for putting down the rebellion were themselves seized by rebellion. All this became evident after two or three months.

Liberalism in those days was making its last efforts to save the situation. All the organizations of the enfranchised bourgeoisie supported the November speeches of the Duma opposition with a series of new declarations. The most impudent of these was the resolution of the Union of Cities on December 9: "Irresponsible criminals, fanatics, are preparing for Russia's defeat, shame and slavery." The State Duma was urged "not to disperse until the formation of a responsible government is attained." Even the State Council, organ of the bureaucracy and of the vast properties, expressed itself in favor of calling to power people who enjoyed the confidence of the country. A similar intercession was made by a session of the united nobility: even the moss-covered stones cried out. But nothing was changed. The monarchy would not let the last shreds of power slip out of its hands.

The last session of the last Duma was convoked, after waverings and delays, on February 14, 1917. Only two weeks remained before the coming of revolution. Demonstrations were expected. In the Kadet organ *Rech*, alongside an announcement by the chief of the Petrograd Military District, General Khabalov, forbidding demonstrations, was printed a letter from Miliukov warning the workers against "dangerous and bad counsel" issuing from "dark sources." In spite of strikes, the opening of the Duma was sufficiently peaceful. Pretending that the question of power no longer interested it, the Duma occupied itself with a critical, but still strictly business question: food supplies. The mood was languid, as Rodzianko subsequently remembered: "We felt the impotence of the Duma, weariness of a futile struggle." Miliukov kept repeating that the Progressive Bloc "will act with words and with words only." Such was the Duma that entered the whirlpool of the February revolution.

Chapter III

THE PROLETARIAT AND THE PEASANTRY

The Russian proletariat learned its first steps in the political circumstances created by a despotic state. Strikes forbidden by law, underground circles, illegal proclamations, street demonstrations, encounters with the police and with troops—such was the school created by the combination of a swiftly developing capitalism with an absolutism slowly surrendering its positions. The concentration of the workers in colossal enterprises, the intense character of governmental persecution, and finally the impulsiveness of a young and fresh proletariat, brought it about that the political strike, so rare in western Europe, became in Russia the fundamental method of struggle. The figures of strikes from the beginning of the present century are a most impressive index of the political history of Russia. With every desire not to burden our text with figures, we cannot refrain from introducing a table of political strikes in Russia for the period 1903 to 1917. The figures, reduced to their simplest expression, relate only to enterprises undergoing factory inspection. The railroads, mining industries, mechanical and small enterprises in general, to say nothing of agriculture, for various reasons do not enter into the count. But the changes in the strike curve in the different periods emerge no less clearly for this.

We have before us a curve—the only one of its kind—of the political temperature of a nation carrying in its womb a great revolution. In a backward country with a small proletariat—for in all the enterprises undergoing factory inspection there were only about 1½ million workers in 1905, about 2 million in 1917—the strike movement attains such dimensions as it never knew before anywhere in the world. With the weakness of the petty bourgeois democracy, the scatteredness and political blindness of the peasant movement, the revolutionary strike of the workers becomes the battering ram which the awakening nation directs against the walls of absolutism. Participants in political strikes in 1905 numbering 1,843,000—workers participating in several strikes are here, of course counted twice—that number alone would permit us to put our finger on the revolutionary year in our table, if we knew nothing else about the Russian political calendar.

Year	*Number in thousands of participants in political strikes*
1903	87*
1904	25*
1905	1,843
1906	651
1907	540
1908	93
1909	8
1910	4
1911	8
1912	550
1913	502
1914 (first half)	1,059
1915	156
1916	310
1917 (January–February)	575

For 1904, the first year of the Russo-Japanese war, the factory inspection indicates in all only 25,000 strikers. In 1905, political and economic strikes together involved 2,863,000 men—115 times more than in the previous year. This remarkable fact by itself would suggest the thought that a proletariat,

* The figures for 1903 and 1904 refer to all strikes, the economic undoubtedly predominating.

impelled by the course of events to improvise such unheard-of revolutionary activities, must at whatever cost produce from its depths an organization corresponding to the dimensions of the struggle and the colossal tasks. This organization was the soviets—brought into being by the first revolution, and made the instrument of the general strike and the struggle for power.

Beaten in the December uprising of 1905, the proletariat during the next two years makes heroic efforts to defend a part of the conquered positions. These years, as our strike figures show, still belong directly to the revolution, but they are the years of ebb. The four following years (1908–11) emerge in our mirror of strike statistics as the years of victorious counter-revolution. An industrial crisis coincident with this still further exhausts the proletariat, already bled white. The depth of the fall is symmetrical with the height of the rise. National convulsions find their reflection in these simple figures.

The industrial boom beginning in 1910 lifted the workers to their feet, and gave a new impulse to their energy. The figures for 1912–14 almost repeat those for 1905–07, but in the opposite order: not from above downwards, but from below up. On a new and higher historical basis—there are more workers now, and they have more experience—a new revolutionary offensive begins. The first half-year of 1914 clearly approaches in the number of political strikes the culminating point of the year of the first revolution. But war breaks out and sharply interrupts this process. The first war months are marked by political inertness in the working class, but already in the spring of 1915 the numbness begins to pass. A new cycle of political strikes opens, a cycle which in February 1917 will culminate in the insurrection of soldiers and workers.

The sharp ebbs and flows of the mass struggle had left the Russian proletariat after a few years almost unrecognizable. Factories which two or three years ago would strike unanimously over some single arbitrary police action, today have completely lost their revolutionary color, and accept the most monstrous crimes of the authorities without resistance. Great defeats discourage people for a long time. The consciously revolutionary elements lose their power over the masses. Prejudices and superstitions not yet burnt out come back to life. Gray immigrants from the village during these times dilute the workers' ranks. Sceptics ironically shake their heads. So it was in the years 1907–11. But molecular processes in the masses are healing the psychological wounds of defeat. A new turn of events, or an underlying economic impulse, opens a new political cycle. The revolutionary elements again find their audience. The struggle reopens on a higher level.

In order to understand the two chief tendencies in the Russian working class, it is important to have in mind that Menshevism finally took shape in the years of ebb and reaction. It relied chiefly upon a thin layer of workers who had broken with the revolution. Whereas Bolshevism, cruelly shattered in the period of the reaction, began to rise swiftly on the crest of a new revolutionary tide in the years before the war. "The most energetic and audacious element, ready for tireless struggle, for resistance and continual organization, is that element, those organizations, and those people who are concentrated around Lenin." In these words the Police Department estimated the work of the Bolsheviks during the years preceding the war.

In July 1914, while the diplomats were driving the last nail into the cross designed for the crucifixion of Europe, Petrograd was boiling like a revolutionary cauldron. The President of the French Republic, Poincaré, had to lay his wreath on the tomb of Alexander III amid the last echoes of a street fight and the first murmurs of a patriotic demonstration.

Would the mass offensive of 1912–14 have led directly to an overthrow of tzarism if the war had not broken out? It is hardly possible to answer that question with certainty. The process would inexorably have led to a revolution, but through what stages would the revolution in those circumstances have had to go? Would it not have experienced another defeat? How much time would have been needed by the workers in order to arouse the peasantry and win the army? In all these directions only guesses are possible. The war, at any rate, gave the process at first a backward movement, but only to accelerate it more powerfully in the next period and guarantee its overwhelming victory.

At the first sound of the drum the revolutionary movement died down. The more active layers of the workers were mobilized. The revolutionary elements were thrown from the factories to the front. Severe penalties were imposed for striking. The workers' press was swept away. Trade unions were strangled. Hundreds of thousands of women, boys, peasants, poured into the workshops. The war—combined with the wreck of the International—greatly disoriented the workers politically, and made it possible for the factory administration, then just lifting its head, to speak patriotically in the name of the factories, carrying with it a considerable part of the workers, and compelling the more bold and resolute to keep still and wait. The revolutionary ideas were barely kept glowing in small and hushed circles. In the factories in those days nobody dared to call himself "Bolshevik" for fear not only of arrest, but of a beating from the backward workers.

The Bolshevik faction in the Duma, weak in its personnel, had not risen at the outbreak of the war to the height of its task. Along with the Menshevik deputies, it introduced a declaration in which it promised "to defend the cultural weal of the people against all attacks wheresoever originating." The Duma underlined with applause this yielding of a position. Not one of the Russian organizations or groups of the party took the openly defeatist position which Lenin came out for abroad. The percentage of patriots among the Bolsheviks, however, was insignificant. In contrast to the Narodniks[1] and Mensheviks, the Bolsheviks began in 1914 to develop among the masses a printed and oral agitation against the war. The Duma deputies soon recovered their poise and renewed their revolutionary work—about which the authorities were very closely informed, thanks to a highly developed system of provocation. It is sufficient to remark that out of seven members of the Petersburg committee of the party, three, on the eve of the war, were in the employ of the Secret Service. Thus tzarism played blindman's buff with the revolution. In November the Bolshevik deputies were arrested. There began a general smash-up of the party throughout the country. In

[1] *Narodnik* is a general name for those non-Marxians who had originally hoped to accomplish the regeneration of Russia by "going to the people (*narod*)," and out of whom developed the Social Revolutionary party. The Mensheviks were the right, or so-called "moderate," wing of the Marxian or Social Democratic party, whom Lenin abandoned in 1903. [Trans.]

February 1915 the case of the Duma faction was called in the courts. The deputies conducted themselves cautiously. Kamenev, theoretical instigator of the faction, stood apart from the defeatist position of Lenin; so did Petrovsky, the present president of the Central Committee in the Ukraine. The Police Department remarked with satisfaction that the severe sentences dealt out to the deputies did not evoke any movement of protest among the workers.

It seemed as though the war had produced a new working class. To a considerable extent this was the fact: in Petrograd the personnel of the workers had been renewed almost forty per cent. The revolutionary succession had been abruptly broken. All that existed before the war, including the Duma faction of the Bolsheviks, had suddenly retired to the background and almost disappeared in oblivion. But under cover of this quietness and patriotism—and to some extent even monarchism—the moods of a new explosion were gradually accumulating in the masses.

In August 1915 the tzarist ministers were telling each other that the workers "are everywhere hunting out treason, betrayal and sabotage in behalf of the Germans, and are enthusiastic in the search for those guilty of our unsuccesses at the front." It is true that in that period the awakening mass-criticism—in part sincerely and in part for the sake of defensive coloration—often adopted the standpoint of "defense of the fatherland." But that idea was only a point of departure. The discontent of the workers was digging a deeper and deeper course, silencing the masters, the Black Hundred workers, the servants of the administration, permitting the worker-Bolsheviks to raise their heads.

From criticism the masses pass over to action. Their indignation finds expression first of all in food disturbances, sometimes rising to the height of local riots. Women, old men and boys, in the market or on the open square, feel bolder and more independent than the workers on military duty in the factories. In Moscow in May the movement turns into a pogrom of Germans, although the participants in this are chiefly the scum of the town armed under police protection. Nevertheless, the very possibility of such a pogrom in industrial Moscow proves that the workers are not yet sufficiently awakened to impose their slogans and their discipline upon the disturbed small-town people. These food disorders, spreading over the whole country, broke the war hypnosis and laid the road to strikes.

The inflow of raw labor power to the factories and the greedy scramble for war-profits, brought everywhere a lowering of the conditions of labor, and gave rise to the crudest methods of exploitation. The rise in the cost of living automatically lowered wages. Economic strikes were the inevitable mass reflection—stormy in proportion as they had been delayed. The strikes were accompanied by meetings, adoption of political resolutions, scrimmages with the police, not infrequently by shots and casualties.

The struggle arose chiefly in the central textile district. On June 5 the police fire a volley at the weavers in Kostroma: 4 killed, 9 wounded. On August 10 the troops fire on the Ivanovo-Voznesensk workers: 16 killed, 30 wounded. In the movement of the textile workers some soldiers of a local battalion are involved. Protest strikes in various parts of the country give answer to the shootings at Ivanovo-Voznesensk. Parallel to this goes the economic struggle. The textile workers often march in the front rank.

In comparison with the first half of 1914 this movement, as regards strength of pressure and clarity of slogans, represents a big step backward. This is not surprising, since raw masses are to a large extent being drawn into the struggle, and there has been a complete disintegration of the guiding layer of the workers. Nevertheless even in these first strikes of the war the approach of great battles can be heard. The Minister of Justice, Khvostov, said on the 16th of August: "If there are at present no armed demonstrations of the workers, it is only because they have as yet no organization." Goremykin expressed himself more concisely: "The trouble among the workers' leaders is that they have no organization, since it was broken up by the arrest of the five members of the Duma." The Minister of the Interior added: "We must not amnesty the members of the Duma (Bolsheviks)—they are the organizing center of the movement in its most dangerous form." These people at least made no mistake as to who was the real enemy.

While the ministry, even at the moment of its greatest dismay and readiness for liberal concessions, deemed it necessary as before to pound the workers' revolution on the head—i.e. on the Bolsheviks—the big bourgeoisie was trying to fix up a coöperation with the Mensheviks. Frightened by the scope of the strike movement, the liberal industrialists made an attempt to impose patriotic discipline upon the workers by including their elected representatives in the staff of the Military Industrial Committees. The Minister of the Interior complained that it was very difficult to oppose this scheme, fathered by Guchkov. "The whole enterprise," he said, "is being carried out under a patriotic flag, and in the interests of the defense." We must remark, however, that even the police avoided arresting the social-patriots, seeing in them a side partner in the struggle against strikes and revolutionary "excesses." It was indeed upon their too great confidence in the strength of patriotic socialism, that the Secret Service based their conviction that no insurrection would occur while the war lasted.

In the elections to the Military-Industrial Committees the defensists, headed by an energetic metal worker, Gvozdev—we shall meet him later as Minister of Labor in the Coalition Government of the revolution—turned out to be a minority. They enjoyed the support, however, not only of the liberal bourgeoisie, but of the bureaucracy, in getting the better of those who, led by the Bolsheviks, wished to boycott the committees. They succeeded in imposing a representation in these organs of industrial patriotism upon the Petersburg proletariat. The position of the Mensheviks was clearly expressed in a speech one of their representatives later made to the industrialists in the Committee: "You ought to demand that the existing bureaucratic power retire from the scene, yielding its place to you as the inheritors of the present social structure." This young political friendship was growing by leaps and bounds. After the revolution it will bring forth its ripe fruit.

The war produced a dreadful desolation in the underground movement. After the arrest of the Duma faction the Bolsheviks had no centralized party organization at all. The local committees had an episodic existence, and often had no connections with the workers districts. Only scattered groups, circles and solitary individuals did anything. However, the reviving strike movement gave them some spirit and some strength in the factories. They gradually began to find each other and build up the district connections. The underground work revived. In the Police Department they wrote later: "Ever since the beginning of the war, the Leninists, who have behind them in Russia an overwhelming majority of the underground social-democratic organizations, have in their larger centers (such as Petrograd, Moscow, Kharkov, Kiev, Tula, Kostroma, Vladimir Province, Samara) been issuing in considerable numbers revolutionary appeals with a demand to stop the war, overthrow the existing government, and found a republic. And this work has had its palpable result in workers' strikes and disorders."

The traditional anniversary of the march of the workers to the Winter Palace, which had passed almost unnoticed the year before, produces a widespread strike on January 9, 1916. The strike movement doubles during this year. Encounters with the police accompany every big and prolonged strike. In contact with the troops, the workers conduct themselves with demonstrative friendliness, and the Secret Police more than once notice this alarming fact.

The war industries swelled out, devouring all resources around them and undermining their own foundation. The peacetime branches of production began to die away. In spite of all plannings, nothing came of the regulation of industry. The bureaucracy, incapable of taking this business in hand against the opposition of the powerful Military-Industrial Committees, at the same time refused to turn over the regulating rôle to the bourgeoisie. The chaos increased. Skilled workers were replaced by unskilled. The coal mines, shops and factories of Poland were soon lost. In the course of the first year of the war a fifth part of the industrial strength of the country was cut off. As much as 50 per cent of production went to supply the needs of the army and the war—including about 75 per cent of the textile production of the country. The overloaded transport proved incapable of supplying factories with the necessary quantity of fuel and raw material. The war not only swallowed up the whole current national income, but seriously began to cut into the basic capital of the country.

The industrialists grew less and less willing to grant anything to the workers, and the government, as usual, answered every strike with severe repressions. All this pushed the minds of the workers from the particular to the general, from economics to politics: "We must all strike at once." Thus arose the idea of the general strike. The process of radicalization of the masses is most convincingly reflected in the strike statistics. In 1915, two and a half times fewer workers participated in political strikes than in economic conflicts. In 1916, twice as few. In the first months of 1917, political strikes involved six times as many workers as economic. The rôle of Petrograd is portrayed in one figure: 72 per cent of the political strikers during the years of the war fall to her lot!

Many of the old beliefs are burned up in the fires of this struggle. The Secret Service reports, "with pain," that if they should react according to the dictates of the law to "every instance of insolence and open insult to His Majesty, the number of trials under Article 103 would reach an unheard-of figure." Nevertheless the consciousness of the masses is far behind their action. The terrible pressure of the war and the national ruin is accelerating the process of struggle to such a degree that broad masses of the workers, right up to the very revolution, have not freed themselves from many opinions and prejudices brought with them from the village or from the petty bourgeois family-circle in the town. This fact will set its stamp on the first stage of the February revolution.

By the end of 1916 prices are rising by leaps and bounds. To the inflation and the breakdown of transport, there is added an actual lack of goods. The demands of the population have been cut down by this time to one-half. The curve of the workers' movement rises sharply. In October the struggle enters its decisive phase, uniting all forms of discontent in one. Petrograd draws back for the February leap. A wave of meetings runs through the factories. The topics: food supplies, high cost of living, war, government. Bolshevik leaflets are distributed; political strikes begin; improvised demonstrations occur at factory gates; cases of fraternization between certain factories and the soldiers are observed; a stormy protest-strike flares up over the trial of the revolutionary sailors of the Baltic Fleet. The French ambassador calls Premier Stürmer's attention to the fact, become known to him, that some soldiers have shot at the police. Stürmer quiets the ambassador: "The repressions will be ruthless." In November a good-sized group of workers on military duty are removed from the Petrograd factories and sent to the front. The year ends in storm and thunder.

Comparing the situation with that in 1905, the director of the Police Department, Vassiliev, reaches a very uncomforting conclusion: "The mood of opposition has gone very far—far beyond anything to be seen in the broad masses during the above-mentioned period of disturbance." Vassiliev rests no hope in the garrison; even the police officers are not entirely reliable. The Intelligence Department reports a revival of the slogan of the general strike, the danger of a resurrection of the terror. Soldiers and officers arriving from the front say of the present situation: "What is there to wait for?—Why don't you take and bump off such-and-such a scoundrel? If we were here, we wouldn't waste much time thinking," etc. Shliapnikov, a member of the Bolshevik Central Committee, himself a former metal worker, describes how nervous the workers were in those days: "Sometimes a whistle would be enough, or any kind of noise—the workers would take it for a signal to stop the factory." This detail is equally remarkable both as a political symptom and as a psychological fact: the revolution is there in the nerves before it comes out on the street.

The provinces are passing through the same stages, only more slowly. The growth in massiveness of the movement and in fighting spirit shifts the center of gravity from the textile to the metal workers, from economic strikes to political, from the provinces to Petrograd. The first two months of 1917 show 575,000 political strikers, the lion's share of them in the capital. In spite of new raids carried out by the police on the eve of January 9, 150,000 workers went on strike in the capital on that anniversary of blood. The mood was tense. The metal workers were in the lead. The workers all felt that no retreat was possible. In every factory an active nucleus was forming, oftenest around the Bolsheviks. Strikes and meetings went on continuously throughout the first two weeks of February. On the 8th, at the Putilov factory, the police received "a hail of slag and old iron." On the 14th, the day the Duma opened, about 90,000 were on strike in Petrograd. Several plants also stopped work in Moscow. On the 16th, the authorities decided to introduce bread cards in Petrograd. This novelty rasped the nerves. On the 19th, a mass of people gathered around the food shops, especially women, all demanding bread. A day later bakeries were sacked in several parts of the city. These were the heat lightnings of the revolution, coming in a few days.

The Russian proletariat found its revolutionary audacity not only in itself. Its very position as minority of the nation suggests that it could not have given its struggle a sufficient scope—certainly not enough to take its place at the head of the state—if it had not found a mighty support in the thick of the people. Such a support was guaranteed to it by the agrarian problem.

The belated half-liberation of the peasants in 1861 had found agricultural industry almost on the same level as two hundred years before. The preservation of the old area of communal land—somewhat filched from during the reform—together with the archaic methods of land culture, automatically sharpened a crisis caused by the rural excess population, which was at the same time a crisis in the three-field system. The peasantry felt still more caught in a trap because the process was not taking place in the seventeenth but in the nineteenth century—that is, in the conditions of an advanced money economy which made demands upon the wooden plow that could only be met by a tractor. Here too we see a drawing together of separate stages of the historic process, and as a result an extreme sharpening of contradictions. The learned agronomes and economists had been preaching that the old area with rational cultivation would be amply sufficient—that is to say, they proposed to the peasant to make a jump to a higher level of technique and culture without disturbing the landlord, the bailiff, or the tzar. But no economic régime, least of all an agricultural régime, the most tardy of all, has ever disappeared before exhausting all its possibilities. Before feeling compelled to pass over to a more intensive economic culture, the peasant had to make a last attempt to broaden his three fields. This could obviously be achieved only at the expense of non-peasant lands. Choking in the narrowness of his land area, under the smarting whip of the treasury and the market, the muzhik was inexorably forced to attempt to get rid of the landlord once for all.

On the eve of the first revolution the whole stretch of arable land within the limits of European Russia was estimated at 280 million dessiatins.[2] The communal allotments constituted about 140 million. The crown lands, above 5 million. Church and monastery lands, about 2½ million. Of the privately owned land, 70 million dessiatins belonged to the 30,000 great landlords, each of whom owned above 500 dessiatins. This 70 million was about what would have belonged to 10 million peasant families. These land statistics constitute the finished program of a peasant war.

The landlords were not settled with in the first revolution. Not all the peasants rose. The movement in the country did not coincide with that in the cities. The peasant army wavered, and finally supplied sufficient forces for putting down the workers. As soon as the Semenovsky Guard regiment had settled with the Moscow insurrection, the monarchy abandoned all thought of cutting down the landed estates, as also its own autocratic rights.

However, the defeated revolution did not pass without leaving traces in the village. The government abolished the old land redemption payments and opened the way to a broader colonization of Siberia. The frightened landlords not only made considerable concessions in the matter of rentals, but also began a large-scale selling of their landed estates. These fruits of the revolution were enjoyed by the better-off peasants, who were able to rent and buy the landlords' land.

However, the broadest gates were opened for the emerging of capitalist farmers from the peasant class by the law of November 9, 1906, the chief reform introduced by the victorious counter-revolution. Giving the right even to a small minority of the peasants of any commune, against the will of the majority, to cut out from the communal land a section to be

[2] A dessiatin is 2.702 English acres. [Trans.]

owned independently, the law of November 9 constituted an explosive capitalist shell directed against the commune. The president of the Council of Ministers, Stolypin, described the essence of this governmental policy towards the peasants as "banking on the strong ones." This meant: encourage the upper circles of the peasantry to get hold of the communal land by buying up these "liberated" sections, and convert these new capitalist farmers into a support for the existing régime. It was easier to propose such a task, however, than to achieve it. In this attempt to substitute the kulak[3] problem for the peasant problem, the counter-revolution was destined to break its neck.

By January 1, 1916, 2½ million home-owners had made good their personal possession of 17 million dessiatins. Two more million home-owners were demanding the allotment to them of 14 million dessiatins. This looked like a colossal success for the reform. But the majority of the homesteads were completely incapable of sustaining life, and represented only material for natural selection. At that time when the more backward landlords and small peasants were selling on a large scale—the former their estates, the latter their bits of land—there emerged in the capacity of principal purchaser a new peasant bourgeoisie. Agriculture entered upon a state of indubitable capitalist boom. The export of agricultural products from Russia rose between 1908 and 1912 from 1 billion roubles to 1½ billion. This meant that broad masses of the peasantry had been proletarianized, and the upper circles of the village were throwing on the market more and more grain.

To replace the compulsory communal ties of the peasantry, there developed very swiftly a voluntary coöperation, which succeeded in penetrating quite deeply into the peasant masses in the course of a few years, and immediately became a subject of liberal and democratic idealization. Real power in the coöperatives belonged, however, only to the rich peasants, whose interests in the last analysis they served. The Narodnik intelligentsia, by concentrating its chief forces in peasant coöperation, finally succeeded in shifting its love for the people on to good solid bourgeois rails. In this way was prepared,

[3] *Kulak*, the Russian word for fist, is a nickname for rich peasants —"land-grabbers," as we might say. [Trans.]

partially at least, the political bloc of the "anti-capitalist" party of the Social Revolutionaries with the Kadets, the capitalist party *par excellence.*

Liberalism, although preserving the appearance of opposition to the agrarian policy of the reaction, nevertheless looked with great hopes upon this capitalist destruction of the communes. "In the country a very powerful petty bourgeoisie is arising," wrote the liberal Prince Troubetskoy, "in its whole make and essence alien alike to the ideals of the united nobility and to the socialist dreams."

But this admirable medal had its other side. There was arising from the destroyed communes not only a "very powerful bourgeoisie," but also its antithesis. The number of peasants selling tracts of land they could not live on had risen by the beginning of the war to a million, which means no less than five million souls added to the proletarian population. A sufficiently explosive material was also supplied by the millions of peasant-paupers to whom nothing remained but to hang on to their hungry allotments. In consequence those contradictions kept reproducing themselves among the peasants which had so early undermined the development of bourgeois society as a whole in Russia. The new rural bourgeoisie which was to create a support for the old and more powerful proprietors, turned out to be as hostilely opposed to the fundamental masses of the peasantry as the old proprietors had been to the people as a whole. Before it could become a support to the existing order, this peasant bourgeoisie had need of some order of its own wherewith to cling to its conquered positions. In these circumstances it is no wonder that the agrarian problem continued a sharp one in all the State Dumas. Everyone felt that the last word had not yet been spoken. The peasant deputy Petrichenko once declared from the tribune of the Duma: "No matter how long you debate you won't create a new planet—that means that you will have to give us the land." This peasant was neither a Bolshevik, nor a Social Revolutionary. On the contrary, he was a Right deputy, a monarchist.

The agrarian movement, having, like the strike movement of the workers, died down toward the end of 1907, partially revives in 1908, and grows stronger during the following years.

The struggle, to be sure, is transferred to a considerable degree within the commune: that is just what the reaction had figured on politically. There are not infrequent armed conflicts among peasants during the division of the communal land. But the struggle against the landlord also does not disappear. The peasants are more frequently setting fire to the landlord's manors, harvests, haystacks, seizing on the way also those individual tracts which had been cut off against the will of the communal peasants.

The war found the peasantry in this condition. The government carried away from the country about 10 million workers and about 2 million horses. The weak homesteads grew still weaker. The number of peasants who could not sow their fields increased. But in the second year of the war the middle peasants also began to go under. Peasant hostility toward the war sharpened from month to month. In October 1916, the Petrograd Gendarme Administration reported that in the villages they had already ceased to believe in the success of the war—the report being based on the words of insurance agents, teachers, traders, etc. "All are waiting and impatiently demanding: When will this cursed war finally end?" And that is not all: "Political questions are being talked about everywhere and resolutions adopted directed against the landlords and merchants. Nuclei of various organizations are being formed. . . . As yet there is no uniting center, but there is reason to suppose that the peasants will unite by way of the coöperatives which are daily growing throughout all Russia." There is some exaggeration here. In some things the gendarme has run ahead a little, but the fundamentals are indubitably correct.

The possessing classes could not but foresee that the village was going to present its bill. But they drove away these black thoughts, hoping to wriggle out of it somehow. On this theme the inquisitive French ambassador Paléologue had a chat during the war days with the former Minister of Agriculture Krivoshein, the former Premier Kokovtsev, the great landlord Count Bobrinsky, the President of the State Duma Rodzianko, the great industrialist Putilov, and other distinguished people. Here is what was unveiled before him in this conversation: In order to carry into action a radical land reform it would require the work of a standing army of 300,000 surveyors for no less than fifteen years; but during this time the number of homesteads would increase to 30 million, and consequently all these preliminary calculations by the time they were made would prove invalid. To introduce a land reform thus seemed in the eyes of these landlords, officials and bankers something like squaring the circle. It is hardly necessary to say that a like mathematical scrupulousness was completely alien to the peasant. He thought that first of all the thing to do was to smoke out the landlord, and then see.

If the village nevertheless remained comparatively peaceful during the war, that was because its active forces were at the front. The soldiers did not forget about the land—whenever at least they were not thinking about death—and in the trenches the muzhik's thoughts about the future were saturated with the smell of powder. But all the same the peasantry, even after learning to handle firearms, could never of its own force have achieved the agrarian democratic revolution—that is, its own revolution. It had to have leadership. For the first time in world history the peasant was destined to find a leader in the person of the worker. In that lies the fundamental, and you may say the whole, difference between the Russian revolution and all those preceding it.

In England serfdom had disappeared in actual fact by the end of the fourteenth century—that is, two centuries before it arose in Russia, and four and a half centuries before it was abolished. The expropriation of the landed property of the peasants dragged along in England through one Reformation and two revolutions to the nineteenth century. The capitalist development, not forced from the outside, thus had sufficient time to liquidate the independent peasant long before the proletariat awoke to political life.

In France the struggle with royal absolutism, the aristocracy, and the princes of the church, compelled the bourgeoisie in various of its layers, and in several installments, to achieve a radical agrarian revolution at the beginning of the eighteenth century. For long after that an independent peasantry constituted the support of the bourgeois order, and in 1871 it helped the bourgeoisie put down the Paris Commune.

In Germany the bourgeoisie proved incapable of a revolutionary solution of the agrarian problem, and in 1848 betrayed the peasants to the landlords, just as Luther some three centuries before in the peasant wars had betrayed them to the princes. On the other hand, the German proletariat was still too weak in the middle of the nineteenth century to take the leadership of the peasantry. As a result the capitalist development of Germany got sufficient time, although not so long a period as in England, to subordinate agriculture, as it emerged from the uncompleted bourgeois revolution, to its own interests.

The peasant reform of 1861 was carried out in Russia by an aristocratic and bureaucratic monarchy under pressure of the demands of a bourgeois society, but with the bourgeoisie completely powerless politically. The character of this peasant emancipation was such that the forced capitalistic transformation of the country inevitably converted the agrarian problem into a problem of revolution. The Russian bourgeois dreamed of an agrarian evolution on the French plan, or the Danish, or the American—anything you want, only not the Russian. He neglected, however, to supply himself in good season with a French history or an American social structure. The democratic intelligentsia, notwithstanding its revolutionary past, took its stand in the decisive hour with the liberal bourgeoisie and the landlord, and not with the revolutionary village. In these circumstances only the working class could stand at the head of the peasant revolution.

The law of combined development of backward countries —in the sense of a peculiar mixture of backward elements with the most modern factors—here rises before us in its most finished form, and offers a key to the fundamental riddle of the Russian revolution. If the agrarian problem, as a heritage from the barbarism of the old Russian history, had been solved by the bourgeoisie, if it could have been solved by them, the Russian proletariat could not possibly have come to power in 1917. In order to realize the Soviet state, there was required a drawing together and mutual penetration of two factors belonging to completely different historic species: a peasant war —that is, a movement characteristic of the dawn of bourgeois development—and a proletarian insurrection, the movement signalizing its decline. That is the essence of 1917.

Chapter IV

THE TZAR AND THE TZARINA

This book will concern itself least of all with those unrelated psychological researches which are now so often substituted for social and historical analysis. Foremost in our field of vision will stand the great, moving forces of history, which are superpersonal in character. Monarchy is one of them. But all these forces operate through people. And monarchy is by its very principle bound up with the personal. This in itself justifies an interest in the personality of that monarch whom the process of social development brought face to face with a revolution. Moreover, we hope to show in what follows, partially at least, just where in a personality the strictly personal ends—often much sooner than we think—and how frequently the "distinguishing traits" of a person are merely individual scratches made by a higher law of development.

Nicholas II inherited from his ancestors not only a giant empire, but also a revolution. And they did not bequeath him one quality which would have made him capable of governing an empire or even a province or a county. To that historic flood which was rolling its billows each one closer to the gates of his palace, the last Romanov opposed only a dumb indifference. It seemed as though between his consciousness and his epoch there stood some transparent but absolutely impenetrable medium.

People surrounding the tzar often recalled after the revolution that in the most tragic moments of his reign—at the time of the surrender of Port Arthur and the sinking of the fleet at Tsu-shima, and ten years later at the time of the retreat of the Russian troops from Galicia, and then two years later during the days preceding his abdication when all those around him were depressed, alarmed, shaken—Nicholas alone preserved his tranquillity. He would inquire as usual how many versts he had covered in his journeys about Russia, would recall episodes of hunting expeditions in the past, anecdotes of official meetings, would interest himself generally in the little rubbish of the day's doings, while thunders roared over him and lightnings flashed. "What is this?" asked one of his attendant generals, "a gigantic, almost unbelievable self-restraint, the product of breeding, of a belief in the divine predetermination of events? Or is it inadequate consciousness?" The answer is more than half included in the question. The so-called "breeding" of the tzar, his ability to control himself in the most extraordinary circumstances, cannot be explained by a mere external training; its essence was an inner indifference, a poverty of spiritual forces, a weakness of the impulses of the will. That mask of indifference which was called breeding in certain circles, was a natural part of Nicholas at birth.

The tzar's diary is the best of all testimony. From day to day and from year to year drags along upon its pages the depressing record of spiritual emptiness. "Walked long and killed two crows. Drank tea by daylight." Promenades on foot, rides in a boat. And then again crows, and again tea. All on the very borderline of physiology. Recollections of church ceremonies are jotted down in the same tone as a drinking party.

In the days preceding the opening of the State Duma, when the whole country was shaking with convulsions, Nicholas wrote: "April 14. Took a walk in a thin shirt and took up paddling again. Had tea in the balcony. Stana dined and took a ride with us. Read." Not a word as to the subject of his reading. Some sentimental English romance? Or a report from the Police Department? "April 15: Accepted Witte's resignation. Marie and Dmitri to dinner. Drove them home to the palace."

On the day of the decision to dissolve the Duma, when the court as well as the liberal circles were going through a paroxysm of fright, the tzar wrote in his diary: "July 7. Friday. Very busy morning. Half hour late to breakfast with the officers. . . . A storm came up and it was very muggy. We walked together. Received Goremykin. Signed a decree dissolving the Duma! Dined with Olga and Petia. Read all evening." An exclamation point after the coming dissolution of the Duma is the highest expression of his emotions. The deputies of the dispersed Duma summoned the people to refuse to pay taxes. A series of military uprisings followed: in Sveaborg, Kronstadt, on ships, in army units. The revolutionary terror against high officials was renewed on an unheard-of scale. The tzar writes: "July 9. Sunday. It has happened! The Duma was closed today. At breakfast after Mass long faces were noticeable among many. . . . The weather was fine. On our walk we met Uncle Misha who came over yesterday from Gatchina. Was quietly busy until dinner and all evening. Went paddling in a canoe." It was in a canoe he went paddling—that is told. But with what he was busy all evening is not indicated. So it was always.

And further in those same fatal days: "July 14. Got dressed and rode a bicycle to the bathing beach and bathed enjoyably in the sea." "July 15. Bathed twice. It was very hot. Only us two at dinner. A storm passed over." "July 19. Bathed in the morning. Received at the farm. Uncle Vladimir and Chagin lunched with us." An insurrection and explosions of dynamite are barely touched upon with a single phrase, "Pretty doings!"—astonishing in its imperturbable indifference, which never rose to conscious cynicism.

"At 9:30 in the morning we rode out to the Caspian regiment . . . walked for a long time. The weather was wonderful. Bathed in the sea. After tea received Lvov and Guchkov." Not a word of the fact that this unexpected reception of the two liberals was brought about by the attempt of Stolypin to include opposition leaders in his ministry. Prince Lvov, the future head of the Provisional Government, said of that reception at the time: "I expected to see the sovereign stricken with grief, but instead of that there came out to meet me a jolly, sprightly fellow in a raspberry-colored shirt." The tzar's outlook was not broader than that of a minor police official—with this difference, that the latter would have a better knowledge of reality and be less burdened with superstitions. The sole paper which Nicholas read for years, and from which he derived his ideas, was a weekly published on state revenue by

Prince Meshchersky, a vile, bribed journalist of the reactionary bureaucratic clique, despised even in his own circle. The tzar kept his outlook unchanged through two wars and two revolutions. Between his consciousness and events stood always that impenetrable medium—indifference. Nicholas was called, not without foundation, a fatalist. It is only necessary to add that his fatalism was the exact opposite of an active belief in his "star." Nicholas indeed considered himself unlucky. His fatalism was only a form of passive self-defense against historic evolution, and went hand in hand with an arbitrariness, trivial in psychological motivation, but monstrous in its consequences.

"I wish it and therefore it must be—" writes Count Witte. "That motto appeared in all the activities of this weak ruler, who only through weakness did all the things which characterized his reign—a wholesale shedding of more or less innocent blood, for the most part without aim."

Nicholas is sometimes compared with his half-crazy great-great-grandfather Paul, who was strangled by a camarilla acting in agreement with his own son, Alexander "the Blessed." These two Romanovs were actually alike in their distrust of everybody due to a distrust of themselves, their touchiness as of omnipotent nobodies, their feeling of abnegation, their consciousness, as you might say, of being crowned pariahs. But Paul was incomparably more colorful; there was an element of fancy in his rantings, however irresponsible. In his descendant everything was dim; there was not one sharp trait.

Nicholas was not only unstable, but treacherous. Flatterers called him a charmer, bewitcher, because of his gentle way with the courtiers. But the tzar reserved his special caresses for just those officials whom he had decided to dismiss. Charmed beyond measure at a reception, the minister would go home and find a letter requesting his resignation. That was a kind of revenge on the tzar's part for his own nonentity.

Nicholas recoiled in hostility before everything gifted and significant. He felt at ease only among completely mediocre and brainless people, saintly fakirs, holy men, to whom he did not have to look up. He had his *amour propre*—indeed it was rather keen. But it was not active, not possessed of a grain of initiative, enviously defensive. He selected his ministers on a principle of continual deterioration. Men of brain and character he summoned only in extreme situations when there was no other way out, just as we call in a surgeon to save our lives. It was so with Witte, and afterwards with Stolypin. The tzar treated both with ill-concealed hostility. As soon as the crisis had passed, he hastened to part with these counselors who were too tall for him. This selection operated so systematically that the president of the last Duma, Rodzianko, on the 7th of January 1917, with the revolution already knocking at the doors, ventured to say to the tzar: "Your Majesty, there is not one reliable or honest man left around you; all the best men have been removed or have retired. There remain only those of ill repute."

All the efforts of the liberal bourgeoisie to find a common language with the court came to nothing. The tireless and noisy Rodzianko tried to shake up the tzar with his reports, but in vain. The latter gave no answer either to argument or to impudence, but quietly made ready to dissolve the Duma. Grand Duke Dmitri, a former favorite of the tzar, and future accomplice in the murder of Rasputin, complained to his colleague, Prince Yussupov, that the tzar at headquarters was becoming every day more indifferent to everything around him. In Dmitri's opinion the tzar was being fed some kind of dope which had a benumbing action upon his spiritual faculties. "Rumors went round," writes the liberal historian Miliukov, "that this condition of mental and moral apathy was sustained in the tzar by an increased use of alcohol." This was all fancy or exaggeration. The tzar had no need of narcotics: the fatal "dope" was in his blood. Its symptoms merely seemed especially striking on the background of those great events of war and domestic crisis which led up to the revolution. Rasputin, who was a psychologist, said briefly of the tzar that he "lacked insides."

This dim, equable and "well-bred" man was cruel—not with the active cruelty of Ivan the Terrible or of Peter, in the pursuit of historic aims—What had Nicholas the Second in common with them?—but with the cowardly cruelty of the late born, frightened at his own doom. At the very dawn of his reign Nicholas praised the Phanagoritsy regiment as "fine fellows" for shooting down workers. He always "read with satisfaction" how they flogged with whips the bob-haired girl-students, or cracked the heads of defenseless people during Jewish pogroms. This crowned black sheep gravitated with all his soul to the very dregs of society, the Black Hundred hooligans. He not only paid them generously from the state treasury, but loved to chat with them about their exploits, and would pardon them when they accidentally got mixed up in the murder of an opposition deputy. Witte, who stood at the head of the government during the putting down of the first revolution, has written in his memoirs: "When news of the useless cruel antics of the chiefs of these detachments reached the sovereign, they met with his approval, or in any case his defense." In answer to the demand of the governor-general of the Baltic States that he stop a certain lieutenant-captain, Richter, who was "executing on his own authority and without trial non-resistant persons," the tzar wrote on the report: "Ah, what a fine fellow!" Such encouragements are innumerable. This "charmer," without will, without aim, without imagination, was more awful than all the tyrants of ancient and modern history.

The tzar was mightily under the influence of the tzarina, an influence which increased with the years and the difficulties. Together they constituted a kind of unit—and that combination shows already to what an extent the personal, under pressure of circumstances, is supplemented by the group. But first we must speak of the tzarina herself.

Maurice Paléologue, the French ambassador at Petrograd during the war, a refined psychologist for French academicians and janitresses, offers a meticulously licked portrait of the last tzarina: "Moral restlessness, a chronic sadness, infinite longing, intermittent ups and downs of strength, anguishing thoughts of the invisible other world, superstitions—are not all these traits, so clearly apparent in the personality of the empress, the characteristic traits of the Russian people?" Strange as it may seem, there is in this saccharine lie just a grain of truth. The Russian satirist Saltykov, with some justification, called the ministers and governors from among the Baltic barons "Germans with a Russian soul." It is indubitable that aliens, in no way connected with the people, developed the most pure culture of the "genuine Russian" administrator.

But why did the people repay with such open hatred a tzarina who, in the words of Paléologue, had so completely assimilated their soul? The answer is simple. In order to justify her new situation, this German woman adopted with a kind of cold fury all the traditions and nuances of Russian medievalism, the most meager and crude of all medievalisms, in that very period when the people were making mighty efforts to free themselves from it. This Hessian princess was literally possessed by the demon of autocracy. Having risen from her rural corner to the heights of Byzantine despotism, she would not for anything take a step down. In the orthodox religion she found a mysticism and a magic adapted to her new lot. She believed the more inflexibly in her vocation, the more naked became the foulness of the old régime. With a strong character and a gift for dry and hard exaltations, the tzarina supplemented the weak-willed tzar, ruling over him.

On March 17, 1916, a year before the revolution, when the tortured country was already writhing in the grip of defeat and ruin, the tzarina wrote to her husband at military headquarters: "You must not give indulgences, a responsible ministry, etc. . . . or anything that *they* want. This must be your war and your peace, and the honor yours and our fatherland's, and not by any means the Duma's. They have not the right to say a single word in these matters." This was at any rate a thoroughgoing program. And it was in just this way that she always had the whip hand over the continually vacillating tzar.

After Nicholas' departure to the army in the capacity of fictitious commander-in-chief, the tzarina began openly to take charge of internal affairs. The ministers came to her with reports as to a regent. She entered into a conspiracy with a small camarilla against the Duma, against the ministers, against the staff-generals, against the whole world—to some extent indeed against the tzar. On December 6, 1916, the tzarina wrote to the tzar: ". . . Once you have said that you want to keep Protopopov, how does he (Premier Trepov) go against you? Bring down your fist on the table. Don't yield. Be the boss. Obey your firm little wife and our Friend. Believe in us." Again three days later: "You know you are right. Carry your head high. Command Trepov to work with him.

. . . Strike your fist on the table." Those phrases sound as though they were made up, but they are taken from authentic letters. Besides, you cannot make up things like that.

On December 13 the tzarina suggests to the tzar: "Anything but this responsible ministry about which everybody has gone crazy Everything is getting quiet and better, but people want to feel your hand. How long they have been saying to me, for whole years, the same thing: 'Russia loves to feel the whip.' That is *their* nature!" This orthodox Hessian, with a Windsor upbringing and a Byzantine crown on her head, not only "incarnates" the Russian soul, but also organically despises it. *Their* nature demands the whip—writes the Russian tzarina to the Russian tzar about the Russian people, just two months and a half before the monarchy tips over into the abyss.

In contrast to her force of character, the intellectual force of the tzarina is not higher, but rather lower than her husband's. Even more than he, she craves the society of simpletons. The close and long-lasting friendship of the tzar and tzarina with their lady-in-waiting Vyrubova gives a measure of the spiritual stature of this autocratic pair. Vyrubova has described herself as a fool, and this is not modesty. Witte, to whom one cannot deny an accurate eye, characterized her as "a most commonplace, stupid, Petersburg young lady, homely as a bubble in the biscuit dough." In the society of this person, with whom elderly officials, ambassadors and financiers obsequiously flirted, and who had just enough brains not to forget about her own pockets, the tzar and tzarina would pass many hours, consulting her about affairs, corresponding with her and about her. She was more influential than the State Duma, and even than the ministry.

But Vyrubova herself was only an instrument of "The Friend," whose authority superseded all three. ". . . This is my *private* opinion," writes the tzarina to the tzar, "I will find out what our Friend thinks." The opinion of the "Friend" is not private, it decides. ". . . I am firm," insists the tzarina a few weeks later, "but listen to me, *i.e. this means* our Friend, and trust us in everything. . . . I suffer for you as for a gentle soft-hearted child—who needs guidance, but listens to bad counselors, while a man sent by God is telling him what he should do."

The Friend sent by God was Gregory Rasputin.

". . . The prayers and the help of our Friend—then all will be well."

"If we did not have Him, all would have been over long ago. I am absolutely convinced of that."

Throughout the whole reign of Nicholas and Alexandra soothsayers and hysterics were imported for the court not only from all over Russia, but from other countries. Special official purveyors arose, who would gather around the momentary oracle, forming a powerful Upper Chamber attached to the monarch. There was no lack of bigoted old women with the title of countess, nor of functionaries weary of doing nothing, nor of financiers who had entire ministries in their hire. With a jealous eye on the unchartered competition of mesmerists and sorcerers, the high priesthood of the Orthodox Church would hasten to pry their way into the holy of holies of the intrigue. Witte called this ruling circle, against which he himself twice stubbed his toe, "the leprous court camarilla."

The more isolated the dynasty became, and the more unsheltered the autocrat felt, the more he needed some help from the other world. Certain savages, in order to bring good weather, wave in the air a shingle on a string. The tzar and tzarina used shingles for the greatest variety of purposes. In the tzar's train there was a whole chapel full of large and small images, and all sorts of fetiches, which were brought to bear, first against the Japanese, then against the German artillery.

The level of the court circle really had not changed much from generation to generation. Under Alexander II, called the "Liberator," the grand dukes had sincerely believed in house spirits and witches. Under Alexander III it was no better, only quieter. The "leprous camarilla" had existed always, changing only its personnel and its method. Nicholas II did not create, but inherited from his ancestors, this court atmosphere of savage medievalism. But the country during these same decades had been changing, its problems growing more complex, its culture rising to a higher level. The court circle was thus left far behind.

Although the monarchy did under compulsion make concessions to the new forces, nevertheless inwardly it completely failed to become modernized. On the contrary it withdrew into itself. Its spirit of medievalism thickened under the pressure of hostility and fear, until it acquired the character of a disgusting nightmare overhanging the country.

Towards November 1905—that is, at the most critical moment of the first revolution—the tzar writes in his diary: "We got acquainted with a man of God, Gregory, from the Tobolsk province." That was Rasputin—a Siberian peasant with a bald scar on his head, the result of a beating for horse-stealing. Put forward at an appropriate moment, this "Man of God" soon found official helpers—or rather they found him—and thus was formed a new ruling circle which got a firm hold of the tzarina, and through her of the tzar.

From the winter of 1913–14 it was openly said in Petersburg society that all high appointments, posts and contracts depended upon the Rasputin clique. The "Elder" himself gradually turned into a state institution. He was carefully guarded, and no less carefully sought after by the competing ministers. Spies of the Police Department kept a diary of his life by hours, and did not fail to report how on a visit to his home village of Pokrovsky he got into a drunken and bloody fight with his own father on the street. On the same day that this happened—September 9, 1915—Rasputin sent two friendly telegrams, one to Tzarskoe Selo to the tzarina, the other to headquarters to the tzar. In epic language the police spies registered from day to day the revels of the Friend. "He returned today 5 o'clock in the morning completely drunk." "On the night of the 25–26th the actress V. spent the night with Rasputin." "He arrived with Princess D. (the wife of a gentleman of the bedchamber of the Tzar's court) at the Hotel Astoria." . . . And right beside this: "Came home from Tzarskoe Selo about 11 o'clock in the evening." "Rasputin came home with Princess Sh— very drunk and together they went out immediately." In the morning or evening of the following day a trip to Tzarskoe Selo. To a sympathetic question from the spy as to why the Elder was thoughtful, the answer came: "Can't decide whether to convoke the Duma or not." And then again: "He came home at 5 in the morning pretty drunk." Thus for months and years the melody was played on three keys: "Pretty drunk," "Very drunk," and "Completely drunk." These communications of state importance were brought together and countersigned by the general of gendarmes, Gorbachev.

The bloom of Rasputin's influence lasted six years, the last years of the monarchy. "His life in Petrograd," says Prince Yussupov, who participated to some extent in that life, and afterward killed Rasputin, "became a continual revel, the drunken debauch of a galley slave who had come into an unexpected fortune." "I had at my disposition," wrote the president of the Duma, Rodzianko, "a whole mass of letters from mothers whose daughters had been dishonored by this insolent rake." Nevertheless the Petrograd metropolitan, Pitirim, owed his position to Rasputin, as also the almost illiterate Archbishop Varnava. The Procuror of the Holy Synod, Sabler, was long sustained by Rasputin; and Premier Kokovtsev was removed at his wish, having refused to receive the "Elder." Rasputin appointed Stürmer President of the Council of Ministers, Protopopov Minister of the Interior, the new Procuror of the Synod, Raev, and many others. The ambassador of the French Republic, Paléologue, sought an interview with Rasputin, embraced him and cried, "*Voilà, un véritable illuminé!*" hoping in this way to win the heart of the tzarina to the cause of France. The Jew Simanovich, financial agent of the "Elder," himself under the eye of the Secret Police as a night club gambler and usurer—introduced into the Ministry of Justice through Rasputin the completely dishonest creature Dobrovolsky.

"Keep by you the little list," writes the tzarina to the tzar, in regard to new appointments. "Our friend has asked that you talk all this over with Protopopov." Two days later: "Our friend says that Stürmer may remain a few days longer as President of the Council of Ministers." And again: "Protopopov venerates our friend and will be blessed."

On one of those days when the police spies were counting up the number of bottles and women, the tzarina grieved in a letter to the tzar: "They accuse Rasputin of kissing women, etc. Read the apostles; they kissed everybody as a form of greeting." This reference to the apostles would hardly convince the police spies. In another letter the tzarina goes still farther. "During vespers I thought so much about our friend," she writes, "how the Scribes and Pharisees are persecuting Christ pretending that they are so perfect . . . yes, in truth no man is a prophet in his own country."

The comparison of Rasputin and Christ was customary in that circle, and by no means accidental. The alarm of the royal couple before the menacing forces of history was too sharp to be satisfied with an impersonal God and the futile shadow of a Biblical Christ. They needed a second coming of "the Son of Man." In Rasputin the rejected and agonizing monarchy found a Christ in its own image.

"If there had been no Rasputin," said Senator Tagantsev, a man of the old régime, "it would have been necessary to invent one." There is a good deal more in these words than their author imagined. If by the word *hooliganism* we understand the extreme expression of those anti-social parasite elements at the bottom of society, we may define Rasputinism as a crowned hooliganism at its very top.

Chapter V

THE IDEA OF A PALACE REVOLUTION

Why did not the ruling classes, who were trying to save themselves from a revolution, attempt to get rid of the tzar and his circle? They wanted to, but they did not dare. They lacked both resolution and belief in their cause. The idea of a palace revolution was in the air up to the very moment when it was swallowed up in a state revolution. We must pause upon this in order to get a clearer idea of the interrelations, just before the explosion, of the monarchy, the upper circles of the nobility, the bureaucracy and the bourgeoisie.

The possessing classes were completely monarchist, by virtue of interests, habits and cowardice. But they wanted a monarchy without Rasputin. The monarchy answered them: Take me as I am. In response to demands for a decent ministry, the tzarina sent to the tzar at headquarters an apple from the hands of Rasputin, urging that he eat it in order to strengthen his will. "Remember," she adjured, "that even Monsieur Philippe (a French charlatan-hypnotist) said that you must not grant a constitution, as that would mean ruin to you and Russia. . . ." "Be Peter the Great, Ivan the Terrible, Emperor Paul—crush them all under your feet!"

What a disgusting mixture of fright, superstition and malicious alienation from the country! To be sure, it might seem that on the summits the tzar's family could not be quite alone. Rasputin indeed was always surrounded with a galaxy of grand ladies, and in general shamanism flourishes in an aristocracy. But this mysticism of fear does not unite people, it divides them. Each saves himself in his own way. Many aristocratic houses have their competing saints. Even on the summits of Petrograd society the tzar's family was surrounded as though plague-stricken, with a quarantine of distrust and hostility. Lady-in-waiting Vyrubova remembers: "I was aware and felt deeply in all those around us a malice toward those whom I revered, and I felt that this malice would assume terrible dimensions."

Against the purple background of the war, with the roar of underground tremors clearly audible, the privileged did not for one moment renounce the joys of life; on the contrary, they devoured them greedily. Yet more and more often a skeleton would appear at their banquets and shake the little bones of his fingers. It began to seem to them that all their misery lay in the disgusting character of "Alix," in the treacherous weakness of the tzar, in that greedy fool Vyrubova, and in the Siberian Christ with a scar on his skull. Waves of unendurable foreboding swept over the ruling class, contracting it with spasms from the periphery to the center, and more and more isolating the hated upper circle at Tzarskoe Selo. Vyrubova has pretty clearly expressed the feelings of the upper circle at that time in her, generally speaking, very lying reminiscences: ". . . For the hundredth time I asked myself what has happened to Petrograd society. Are they all spiritually sick, or have they contracted some epidemic which rages in war time? It is hard to understand, but the fact is, all were in an abnormally excited condition." To the number of those out of their heads belonged the whole copious family of the Romanovs, the whole greedy, insolent and universally hated pack of grand dukes and grand duchesses. Frightened to death, they were trying to wriggle out of the ring narrowing around them. They kowtowed to the critical aristocracy, gossiped about the royal pair, and egged on both each other and all those around them. The august uncles addressed the tzar with letters of advice in which between the lines of respect was to be heard a snarl and a grinding of teeth.

Protopopov, some time after the October revolution, colorfully if not very learnedly characterized the mood of the upper circles: "Even the very highest classes became *frondeurs* before the revolution; in the grand salons and clubs the policy of the government received harsh and unfriendly criticism. The relations which had been formed in the tzar's family were analyzed and talked over. Little anecdotes were passed around about the head of the state. Verses were composed. Many grand dukes openly attended these meetings, and their presence gave a special authority in the eyes of the public to tales that were caricatures and to malicious exaggerations. A sense of the danger of this sport did not awaken till the last moment."

These rumors about the court camarilla were especially sharpened by the accusation of Germanophilism and even of direct connections with the enemy. The noisy and not very deep Rodzianko definitely stated: "The connection and the analogy of aspirations is so logically obvious that I at least have no doubt of the coöperation of the German Staff and the Rasputin circle: nobody can doubt it." The bare reference to a "logical" obviousness greatly weakens the categorical tone of this testimony. No evidence of a connection between the Rasputinists and the German Staff was discovered after the revolution. It was otherwise with the so-called "Germanophilism." This was not a question, of course, of the national sympathies and antipathies of the German tzarina, Premier Stürmer, Countess Kleinmichel, Minister of the Court Count Frederiks, and other gentlemen with German names. The cynical memoirs of the old *intriguante* Kleinmichel demonstrate with remarkable clearness how a supernational character distinguished the aristocratic summits of all the countries of Europe, bound together as they were by ties of birth, inheritance, scorn for all those beneath them, and last but not least, cosmopolitan adultery in ancient castles, at fashionable watering places, and in the courts of Europe. Considerably more real were the organic antipathies of the court household to the obsequious lawyers of the French Republic, and the sympathy of the reactionaries—whether bearing Teuton or Slavic family names—for the genuine Russian soul of the Berlin régime which had so often impressed them with its waxed mustachios, its sergeant-major manner and self-confident stupidity.

But that was not the decisive factor. The danger arose from the very logic of the situation, for the court could not help seeking salvation in a separate peace, and this the more insistently the more dangerous the situation became. Liberalism in the person of its leaders was trying, as we shall see, to reserve for itself the chance of making a separate peace in connection with the prospect of its own coming to power. But for just this reason it carried on a furious chauvinist agitation, deceiving the people and terrorizing the court. The camarilla did not dare show its real face prematurely in so ticklish a matter, and was even compelled to counterfeit the general patriotic tone, at the same time feeling out the ground for a separate peace.

General Kurlov, a former chief of police belonging to the Rasputin camarilla, denies, of course, in his reminiscences any German connection or sympathies on the part of his protector, but immediately adds: "We cannot blame Stürmer for his opinion that the war with Germany was the greatest possible misfortune for Russia and that it had no serious political justification." It is hardly possible to forget that while holding this interesting opinion Stürmer was the head of the government of a country waging war against Germany. The last tzarist Minister of the Interior, Protopopov, just before he entered the government, had been conducting negotiations in Stockholm with the German diplomat Warburg and had reported them to the tzar. Rasputin himself, according to the same Kurlov, "considered the war with Germany a colossal misfortune for Russia." And finally the empress wrote to the tzar on April 5, 1916: ". . . They dare not say that He has anything in common with the Germans. He is good and magnanimous toward all, like Christ. No matter to what religion a man may belong: that is the way a good Christian ought to be." To be sure, this good Christian who was almost always intoxicated might quite possibly have been made up to, not only by sharpers, usurers and aristocratic procuresses, but by actual spies of the enemy. "Connections" of this kind are not inconceivable. But the oppositional patriots posed the matter more directly and broadly: they directly accused the tzarina of treason. In his memoirs, written considerably later, General Denikin testifies: "In the army there was loud talk, unconstrained both in time and place, as to the insistent demands of the empress for a separate peace, her treachery in the matter of Field-Marshal Kitchener, of whose journey she was supposed to have told the Germans, etc. . . . This circumstance played a colossal rôle in determining the mood of the army in its attitude to the dynasty and the revolution." The same Denikin relates how after the revolution General Alexeiev, to a direct question about the treason of the empress, answered, "vaguely and reluctantly," that in going over the papers they had found in the possession of the tzarina a chart with a detailed designation of troops on the whole front, and that upon him, Alexeiev, this had produced a depressing effect. "Not another word," significantly adds Denikin. "He changed the subject." Whether the tzarina had the mysterious chart or not, the luckless generals were obviously not unwilling to shoulder off upon her the responsibility for their own defeat. The accusation of treason against the court undoubtedly crept through the army chiefly from above downward—starting with that incapable staff.

But if the tzarina herself, to whom the tzar submitted in everything, was betraying to Wilhelm the military secrets and even the heads of the Allied chieftains, what remained but to make an end of the royal pair? And since the head of the army and of the anti-German party was the Grand Duke Nikolai Nikolaievich, was he not as a matter of duty chosen for the rôle of supreme patron of a palace revolution? That was the reason why the tzar, upon the insistence of Rasputin and the tzarina, removed the grand duke and took the chief command into his own hands. But the tzarina was afraid even of a meeting between the nephew and the uncle in turning over the command. "Sweetheart, try to be cautious," she writes to the tzar at headquarters, "and don't let Nikolasha catch you in any kind of promises or anything else—remember that Gregory saved you from him and from his bad people . . . remember in the name of Russia what they wanted to do, oust you (this is not gossip—Orloff had all the papers ready), and put me in a monastery."

The tzar's brother Michael said to Rodzianko: "The whole family knows how harmful Alexandra Feodorovna is. Nothing but traitors surround her and my brother. All honest people have left. But what's to be done in such a situation?" That is it exactly: what is to be done?

The Grand Duchess Maria Pavlovna insisted in the presence of her sons that Rodzianko should take the initiative in "removing the tzarina." Rodzianko suggested that they consider the conversation as not having taken place, as otherwise in loyalty to his oath he should be obliged to report to the tzar that the grand duchess had suggested to the President of the Duma that he destroy the tzarina. Thus the ready-witted Lord Chamberlain reduced the question of murdering the tzarina to a pleasantry of the drawing room.

At times the ministry itself came into sharp opposition to the tzar. As early as 1915, a year and a half before the revolution, at the sittings of the government, talk went on openly which even now seems unbelievable. The War Minister Polivanov: "Only a policy of conciliation toward society can save the situation. The present shaky dykes will not avert a catastrophe." The Minister of Marine Grigorovich: "It's no secret that the army does not trust us and is awaiting a change." The Minister of Foreign Affairs Sazonov: "The popularity of the tzar and his authority in the eyes of the popular mass is considerably shaken." The Minister of the Interior Prince Sherbatov: "All of us together are unfit for governing Russia in the situation that is forming. . . . We must have either a dictatorship or a conciliatory policy" (Session of August 21, 1915). Neither of these measures could now be of help; neither was now attainable. The tzar could not make up his mind to a dictatorship; he rejected a conciliatory policy, and did not accept the resignation of the ministers who considered themselves unfit. The high official who kept the record makes a short commentary upon these ministerial speeches: evidently we shall have to hang from a lamp-post.

With such feelings prevailing it is no wonder that even in bureaucratic circles they talked of the necessity of a palace uprising as the sole means of preventing the advancing revolution. "If I had shut my eyes," remembers one of the participants of these conversations, "I might have thought that I was in the company of desperate revolutionists."

A colonel of gendarmes making a special investigation of the army in the south of Russia painted a dark picture in his report: Thanks to propaganda chiefly relating to the Germanophilism of the empress and the tzar, the army is prepared for the idea of a palace revolution. "Conversations to this effect are openly carried on in officers' meetings and have not met the necessary opposition on the part of the high command."

Protopopov on his part testifies that "a considerable number of people in the high commanding staff sympathized with the idea of a coup d'état: certain individuals were in touch with and under the influence of the chief leaders of the so-called Progressive Bloc."

The subsequently notorious Admiral Kolchak testified before the Soviet Investigation Commission after his troops were routed by the Red Army that he had connections with many oppositional members of the Duma whose speeches he welcomed, since "his attitude to the powers existing before the revolution was adverse." As to the plan for a palace revolution, however, Kolchak was not informed.

After the murder of Rasputin and the subsequent banishment of grand dukes, high society talked still louder of the necessity of a palace revolution. Prince Yussupov tells how when the Grand Duke Dmitri was arrested at the palace the officers of several regiments came up and proposed plans for decisive action, "to which he, of course, could not agree."

The Allied diplomats—in any case, the British ambassador—were considered accessories to the plot. The latter, doubtless upon the initiative of the Russian liberals, made an attempt in January 1917 to influence Nicholas, having secured the preliminary sanction of his government. Nicholas attentively and politely listened to the ambassador, thanked him, and—spoke of other matters. Protopopov reported to Nicholas the relations between Buchanan and the chief leaders of the Progressive Bloc, and suggested that the British Ambassador be placed under observation. Nicholas did not seem to approve of the proposal, finding the watching of an ambassador "inconsistent with international tradition." Meanwhile Kurlov has no hesitation in stating that "the Intelligence Service remarks daily the relations between the leader of the Kadet Party Miliukov and the British Ambassador." International traditions, then, had not stood in the way at all. But their transgression helped little: even so, a palace conspiracy was never discovered.

Did it in reality exist? There is nothing to prove this. It was a little too broad, that "conspiracy." It included too many and too various circles to *be* a conspiracy. It merely hung in the air as a mood of the upper circles of Petrograd society, as a confused idea of salvation, or a slogan of despair. But it did not thicken down to the point of becoming a practical plan.

The upper nobility in the eighteenth century had more than once introduced practical corrections into the succession by imprisoning or strangling inconvenient emperors: this operation was carried out for the last time on Paul in 1801. It is impossible to say, therefore, that a palace revolution would have transgressed the traditions of the Russian monarchy. On the contrary, it had been a steady element in those traditions. But the aristocracy had long ceased to feel strong at heart. It surrendered the honor of strangling the tzar and the tzarina to the bourgeoisie. But the leaders of the latter showed little more resolution.

Since the revolution references have been made more than once to the liberal capitalists Guchkov and Tereshchenko, and to General Krymov who was close to them, as the nucleus of the conspirators. Guchkov and Tereshchenko themselves have confirmed this, but indefinitely. The former volunteer in the army of the Boers against England, the duelist Guchkov, a liberal with spurs, must have seemed to "social opinion" in a general way the most suitable figure for a conspiracy. Surely not the wordy Professor Miliukov! Guchkov undoubtedly recurred more than once in his thoughts to the short and sharp blow in which one regiment of the guard would replace and forestall the revolution. Witte in his memoirs had already told on Guchkov, whom he hated, as an admirer of the Young Turk methods of disposing of an inconvenient sultan. But Guchkov, having never succeeded in his youth in displaying his young Turkish audacity, had had time to grow much older. And more important, this henchman of Stolypin could not help but see the difference between Russian conditions and the old Turkish conditions, could not fail to ask himself: Will not the palace revolution, instead of a means for preventing a real revolution, turn out to be the last jar that loosens the avalanche? May not the cure prove more ruinous than the disease?

In the literature devoted to the February revolution the preparation of a palace revolution is spoken of as a firmly established fact. Miliukov puts it thus: "Its realization was already on the way in February." Denikin transfers its realization to March. Both mention a "plan" to stop the tzar's train in transit, demand an abdication, and in case of refusal, which was considered inevitable, carry out a "physical removal" of the tzar. Miliukov adds that, foreseeing a possible revolution, the heads of the Progressive Bloc, who did not participate in the plot, and were not "accurately" informed of its preparation, talked over in a narrow circle how best to make use of the coup d'état in case of success. Certain Marxian investigations of recent years also take on faith the story of the practical preparation of a coup d'état. By that example we may learn how easily and firmly legends win a place in historical science.

As chief evidence of the plot they not infrequently advance a certain colorful tale of Rodzianko, which testifies to the very fact that there was no plot. In January 1917 General Krymov arrived from the front and complained before members of the Duma that things could not continue longer as they were: "If you decide upon this extreme measure (replacement of the tzar) we will support you." *If* you decide! The Octobrist Shidlovsky angrily exclaimed: "There is no need to pity or spare him when he is ruining Russia." In the noisy argument these real or imaginary words of Brussilov are also reported: "If it is necessary to choose between the tzar and Russia, I side with Russia." *If* it is necessary! The young millionaire Tereshchenko spoke as an inflexible tzaricide. The Kadet Shingarev spoke: "The General is right, an overturn is necessary . . . *but who will resolve upon it?*" That is just the question: who will resolve upon it? Such is the essence of the testimony of Rodzianko, who himself spoke against an overturn. In the course of the few following weeks the plan apparently did not move forward an inch. They conversed about stopping the tzar's train, but it is quite unknown who was to carry out that operation.

Russian liberalism, when it was younger, had supported the revolutionary terrorists with money and sympathy in the hope that they would drive the monarchy into its arms with their bombs. None of those respected gentlemen was accustomed to risk his own head. But all the same the chief rôle was played not by personal but by class fear: Things are bad now —they reasoned—but they might get worse. In any case, if Guchkov, Tereshchenko and Krymov had seriously moved toward a coup d'état—that is, practically prepared it, mobilizing the necessary forces and means—that would have been established definitely and accurately after the revolution. For the participants, especially the active young men of whom not a few would have been needed, would have had no reason to keep mum about the "almost" accomplished deed. After February this would only have assured them a career. However, there were no revelations. It is quite obvious that the affair never went any farther with Krymov and Guchkov than patriotic sighs over wine and cigars. The light-minded *frondeurs* of the aristocracy, like the heavy-weight oppositionists of the plutocracy, could not find the heart to amend by action the course of an unpropitious providence.

In May 1917 one of the most eloquent and empty liberals, Maklakov, will cry out at a private conference of that Duma which the revolution will sweep away along with the monarchy: "If posterity curses this revolution they will curse us for having been unable to prevent it in time with a revolution from above!" Still later, when he is already in exile, Kerensky, following Maklakov, will lament: "Yes, enfranchised Russia was too slow with its timely coup d'état from above (of which they talked so much, and for which they prepared [?] so much)—she was too slow to forestall the spontaneous explosion of the state."

These two exclamations complete the picture of how, even after the revolution had unleashed its inconquerable forces, educated nincompoops continued to think that it could have been forestalled by a "timely" change of dynastic figure-heads.

The determination was lacking for a "big" palace revolution. But out of it there arose a plan for a small one. The liberal conspirators did not dare to remove the chief actor of the monarchy, but the grand dukes decided to remove its prompter. In the murder of Rasputin they saw the last means of saving the dynasty.

Prince Yussupov, who was married to a Romanov, drew into the affair the Grand Duke Dmitri Pavlovich and the monarchist deputy Purishkevich. They also tried to involve the liberal Maklakov, obviously to give the murder an "all-national" character. The celebrated lawyer wisely declined, supplying the conspirators however with poison—a rather stylistic distinction! The conspirators judged, not without foundation, that a Romanov automobile would facilitate the removal of the body after the murder. The grand ducal coat-of-arms had found its use at last. The rest was carried out in the manner of a moving picture scenario designed for people of bad taste. On the night of the 16–17th of December, Rasputin, coaxed in to a little party, was murdered in Yussupov's maisonette.

The ruling classes, with the exception of a narrow camarilla and the mystic worshipers, greeted the murder of Rasputin as an act of salvation. The grand duke, placed under house arrest, his hands, according to the tzar's expression, stained with the blood of a muzhik—although a Christ, still a muzhik!—was visited with sympathy by all the members of the imperial household then in Petersburg. The tzarina's own sister, widow of the Grand Duke Sergei, telegraphed that she was praying for the murderers and calling down blessings on their patriotic act. The newspapers, until they were forbidden to mention Rasputin, printed ecstatic articles. In the theaters people tried to demonstrate in honor of the murderers. Passers-by congratulated one another in the streets. "In private houses, in officers' meetings, in restaurants," relates Prince Yussupov, "they drank to our health; the workers in the factories cried *Hurrah* for us." We may well concede that the workers did not grieve when they learned of the murder of Rasputin, but their cries of Hurrah! had nothing in common with the hope for a rebirth of the dynasty. The Rasputin camarilla dropped out of sight and waited. They buried Rasputin in secrecy from the whole world—the tzar, the tzarina, the tzar's daughters and Vyrubova. Around the body of the Holy Friend, the former horse thief murdered by grand dukes, the tzar's family must have seemed outcast even to themselves. However, even after he was buried Rasputin did not find peace. Later on, when Nicholas and Alexandra Romanov were under house arrest, the soldiers of Tzarskoe Selo dug up the grave and opened the coffin. At the head of the murdered man lay an icon with the signatures: Alexandra, Olga, Tatiana, Maria, Anastasia, Ania. The Provisional Government for some reason sent an emissary to bring the body to Petrograd. A crowd resisted, and the emissary was compelled to burn the body on the spot.

After the murder of its "Friend" the monarchy survived in all ten weeks. But this short space of time was still its own. Rasputin was no longer, but his shadow continued to rule. Contrary to all the expectations of the conspirators, the royal pair began after the murder to promote with special determination the most scorned members of the Rasputin clique. In revenge for Rasputin, a notorious scoundrel was named Minister of Justice. A number of grand dukes were banished from the capital. It was rumored that Protopopov took up spiritualism, calling up the ghost of Rasputin. The noose of hopelessness was drawing tighter.

The murder of Rasputin played a colossal rôle, but a very different one from that upon which its perpetrators and inspirers had counted. It did not weaken the crisis, but sharpened it. People talked of the murder everywhere: in the palaces, in the staffs, at the factories, and in the peasants' huts. The inference drew itself: even the grand dukes have no other recourse against the leprous camarilla except poison and the revolver. The poet Blok wrote of the murder of Rasputin: "The bullet which killed him reached the very heart of the ruling dynasty."

Robespierre once reminded the Legislative Assembly that the opposition of the nobility, by weakening the monarchy, had roused the bourgeoisie, and after them the popular masses. Robespierre gave warning at the same time that in the rest of Europe the revolution could not develop so swiftly as in France, for the privileged classes of other countries, taught by the experience of the French nobility, would not take the revolutionary initiative. In giving this admirable analysis, Robespierre was mistaken only in his assumption that with its oppositional recklessness the French nobility had given a lesson once for all to other countries. Russia proved again, both in 1905 and yet more in 1917, that a revolution directed against an autocratic and half-feudal régime, and consequently against a nobility, meets in its first step an unsystematic and inconsistent but nevertheless very real coöperation not only from the rank and file nobility, but also from its most privileged upper circles, including here even members of the dynasty. This remarkable historic phenomenon may seem to contradict the class theory of society, but in reality it contradicts only its vulgar interpretation.

A revolution breaks out when all the antagonisms of a society have reached their highest tension. But this makes the situation unbearable even for the classes of the old society—that is, those who are doomed to break up. Although I do not want to give a biological analogy more weight than it deserves, it is worth remarking that the natural act of birth becomes at a certain moment equally unavoidable both for the maternal organism and for the offspring. The opposition put up by the privileged classes expresses the incompatibility of their traditional social position with the demands of the further existence of society. Everything seems to slip out of the hands of the ruling bureaucracy. The aristocracy finding itself in the focus of a general hostility lays the blame upon the bureaucracy, the latter blames the aristocracy, and then together, or separately, they direct their discontent against the monarchical summit of their power.

Prince Sherbatov, summoned into the ministry for a time from his service in the hereditary institutions of the nobility, said: "Both Samarin and I are former heads of the nobility in our provinces. Up till now nobody has ever considered us as Lefts and we do not consider ourselves so. But we can neither of us understand a situation in a state where the monarch and his government find themselves in radical disagreement with all reasonable (we are not talking here of revolutionary intrigue) society—with the nobility, the merchants, the cities, the zemstvos, and even the army. If those above do not want to listen to our opinion, it is our duty to withdraw."

The nobility sees the cause of all its misfortunes in the fact that the monarchy is blind or has lost its reason. The privileged caste cannot believe that no policy whatever is possible which would reconcile the old society with the new. In other words, the nobility cannot accept its own doom and converts its death-weariness into opposition against the most sacred power of the old régime, that is, the monarchy. The sharpness and irresponsibility of the aristocratic opposition is explained by history's having made spoiled children of the upper circles of the nobility, and by the unbearableness to them of their own fears in face of revolution. The unsystematic and inconsistent character of the noble discontent is explained by the fact that it is the opposition of a class which has no future. But as a lamp before it goes out flares up with a bright although smoky light, so the nobility before disappearing gives out an oppositional flash, which performs a mighty service for its mortal enemy. Such is the dialectic of this process, which is not only consistent with the class theory of society, but can only by this theory be explained.

Chapter VI

THE DEATH AGONY OF THE MONARCHY

The dynasty fell by shaking, like rotten fruit, before the revolution even had time to approach its first problems. Our portrayal of the old ruling class would remain incomplete if we did not try to show how the monarchy met the hour of its fall.

The tzar was at headquarters at Moghilev, having gone there not because he was needed, but in flight from the Petrograd disorders. The court chronicler, General Dubensky, with the tzar at headquarters, noted in his diary: "A quiet life begins here. Everything will remain as before. Nothing will come of his (the tzar's) presence. Only accidental external causes will change anything. . . ." On February 24, the tzarina wrote Nicholas at headquarters, in English as always: "I hope that Duma man Kedrinsky (she means Kerensky) will be hung for his horrible speeches—it is necessary (war time law) and it will be an example. All are thirsting and beseeching that you show your firmness." On February 25, a telegram came from the Minister of War that strikes were occurring in the capital, disorders beginning among the workers, but measures had been taken and there was nothing serious. In a word: "It isn't the first time, and won't be the last!"

The tzarina, who had always taught the tzar not to yield, here too tried to remain firm. On the 26th, with an obvious desire to hold up the shaky courage of Nicholas, she telegraphs him: "It is calm in the city." But in her evening telegram she has to confess: "Things are not going at all well in the city." In a letter she says: "You must say to the workers that they must not declare strikes, if they do, they will be sent to the front as a punishment. There is no need at all of shooting. Only order is needed, and not to let them cross the bridges." Yes, only a little thing is needed, *only* order! But the chief thing is not to admit the workers into the city—let them choke in the raging impotence of their suburbs.

On the morning of the 27th, General Ivanov moves from the front with the Battalion of St. George, entrusted with dictatorial powers—which he is to make public, however, only upon occupying Tzarskoe Selo. "It would be hard to imagine a more unsuitable person," General Denikin will recall later, himself having taken a turn at military dictatorship, "a flabby old man, meagerly grasping the political situation, possessing neither strength, nor energy, nor will, nor austerity." The choice fell upon Ivanov through memories of the first revolution. Eleven years before that he had subdued Kronstadt. But those years had left their traces; the subduers had grown flabby, the subdued, strong. The northern and western fronts were ordered to get ready troops for the march on Petrograd; evidently everybody thought there was plenty of time ahead. Ivanov himself assumed that the affair would be ended soon and successfully; he even remembered to send out an adjutant to buy provisions in Moghilev for his friends in Petrograd.

On the morning of February 27, Rodzianko sent the tzar a new telegram, which ended with the words: "The last hour has come when the fate of the fatherland and the dynasty is being decided." The tzar said to his Minister of the Court, Frederiks: "Again that fat-bellied Rodzianko has written me a lot of nonsense, which I won't even bother to answer." But no. It was not nonsense. He will have to answer.

About noon of the 27th, headquarters received a report from Khabalov of the mutiny of the Pavlovsky, Volynsky, Litovsky and Preobrazhensky regiments, and the necessity of sending reliable troops from the front. An hour later from the War Ministry came a most reassuring telegram: "The disorders which began this morning in certain military units are being firmly and energetically put down by companies and battalions loyal to their duty. . . . I am firmly convinced of an early restoration of tranquillity." However, a little after seven in the evening, the same minister, Belyaev, is reporting that

"We are not succeeding in putting down the military rebellion with the few detachments that remain loyal to their duty," and requesting a speedy despatch of really reliable troops—and that too in sufficient numbers "for simultaneous activity in different parts of the city."

The Council of Ministers deemed this a suitable day to remove from their midst the presumed cause of all misfortunes—the half-crazy Minister of the Interior Protopopov. At the same time General Khabalov issued an edict—prepared in secrecy from the government—declaring Petrograd, on His Majesty's orders, under martial law. So here too was an attempt to mix hot with cold—hardly intentional, however, and anyway of no use. They did not even succeed in pasting up the declaration of martial law through the city: the burgomaster, Balka, could find neither paste nor brushes. Nothing would stick together for those functionaries any longer; they already belonged to the kingdom of shades.

The principal shade of the last tzarist ministry was the seventy-year old Prince Golytsin, who had formerly conducted some sort of eleemosynary institutions of the tzarina, and had been advanced by her to the post of head of the government in a period of war and revolution. When friends asked this "good-natured Russian squire, this old weakling"—as the liberal Baron Nolde described him—why he accepted such a troublesome position, Golytsin answered: "So as to have one more pleasant recollection." This aim, at any rate, he did not achieve. How the last tzarist government felt in those hours is attested by Rodzianko in the following tale: With the first news of the movement of a crowd toward the Mariinsky Palace, where the Ministry was in session, all the lights in the building were immediately put out. (The government wanted only one thing—that the revolution should not notice it.) The rumor, however, proved false; the attack did not take place; and when the lights were turned on, one of the members of the tzarist government was found "to his own surprise" under the table. What kind of recollections he was accumulating there has not been established.

But Rodzianko's own feelings apparently were not at their highest point. After a long but vain hunt for the government by telephone, the President of the Duma tries again to ring up Prince Golytsin. The latter answers him: "I beg you not to come to me with anything further, I have resigned." Hearing this news, Rodzianko, according to his loyal secretary, sank heavily in an armchair and covered his face with both hands. . . . "My God, how horrible! . . . Without a government . . . Anarchy . . . Blood . . ." and softly wept. At the expiring of the senile ghost of the tzarist power Rodzianko felt unhappy, desolate, orphaned. How far he was at that moment from the thought that tomorrow he would have to "head" a revolution!

The telephone answer of Golytsin is explained by the fact that on the evening of the 27th the Council of Ministers had definitely acknowledged itself incapable of handling the situation, and proposed to the tzar to place at the head of the government a man enjoying general confidence. The tzar answered Golytsin: "In regard to changes in the personal staff in the present circumstances, I consider that inadmissible. Nicholas." Just what circumstances was he waiting for? At the same time the tzar demanded that they adopt "the most decisive measures" for putting down the rebellion. That was easier said than done.

On the next day, the 28th, even the untamable tzarina at last loses heart. "Concessions are necessary," she telegraphs Nicholas. "The strikes continue; many troops have gone over to the side of the revolution. Alix."

It required an insurrection of the whole guard, the entire garrison, to compel this Hessian zealot of autocracy to agree that "concessions are necessary." Now the tzar also begins to suspect that the "fat-bellied Rodzianko" had not telegraphed nonsense. Nicholas decides to join his family. It is possible that he is a little gently pushed from behind by the generals of the staff, too, who are not feeling quite comfortable.

The tzar's train traveled at first without mishap. Local chiefs and governors came out as usual to meet him. Far from the revolutionary whirlpool, in his accustomed royal car, surrounded by the usual suite, the tzar apparently again lost a sense of the close coming crisis. At three o'clock on the 28th, when the events had already settled his fate, he sent a telegram to the tzarina from Vyazma: "Wonderful weather. Hope you are well and calm. Many troops sent from the front. With tender love. Niki." Instead of the concessions, upon which even the tzarina is insisting, the tenderly loving tzar is sending troops from the front. But in spite of that "wonderful weather," in just a few hours the tzar will stand face to face with the revolutionary storm. His train went as far as the Visher station. The railroad workers would not let it go farther: "The bridge is damaged." Most likely this pretext was invented by the courtiers themselves in order to soften the situation. Nicholas tried to make his way, or they tried to get him through, by way of Bologoe on the Nikolaevsk railroad; but here too the workers would not let the train pass. This was far more palpable than all the Petrograd telegrams. The tzar had broken away from headquarters, and could not make his way to the capital. With its simple railroad "pawns" the revolution had cried "check" to the king!

The court historian Dubensky, who accompanied the tzar in his train, writes in his diary: "Everybody realizes that this midnight turn at Visher is a historical night . . . To me it is perfectly clear that the question of a constitution is settled; it will surely be introduced. . . . Everybody is saying that it is only necessary to strike a bargain with them, with the members of the Provisional Government." Facing a lowered semaphore, behind which mortal danger is thickening, Count Frederiks, Prince Dolgoruky, Count Leuchtenberg, all of them, all those high lords, are now for a constitution. They no longer think of struggling. It is only necessary to strike a bargain, that is, try to fool them again as in 1905.

While the train was wandering and finding no road, the tzarina was sending the tzar telegram after telegram, appealing to him to return as soon as possible. But her telegrams came back to her from the office with the inscription in blue pencil: "Whereabouts of the addressee unknown." The telegraph clerks were unable to locate the Russian tzar.

The regiments marched with music and banners to the Tauride Palace. A company of the Guards marched under the command of Cyril Vladimirovich, who had quite suddenly, according to Countess Kleinmichel, developed a revolutionary streak. The sentries disappeared. The intimates were abandoning the palace. "Everybody was saving himself who could," relates Vyrubova. Bands of revolutionary soldiers wandered about the palace and with eager curiosity looked over everything. Before they had decided up above what should be done, the lower ranks were converting the palace of the tzar into a museum.

The tzar—his location unknown—turns back to Pskov, to the headquarters of the northern front, commanded by the old General Ruszky. In the tzar's suite one suggestion follows another. The tzar procrastinates. He is still reckoning in days and weeks, while the revolution is keeping its count in minutes.

The poet Blok characterized the tzar during the last months of the monarchy as follows: "Stubborn, but without will; nervous, but insensitive to everything; distrustful of people, taut and cautious in speech, he was no longer master of himself. He had ceased to understand the situation, and did not take one clearly conscious step, but gave himself over completely into the hands of those whom he himself had placed in power." And how much these traits of tautness and lack of will, cautiousness and distrust, were to increase during the last days of February and first days of March!

Nicholas finally decided to send—and nevertheless evidently did not send—a telegram to the hated Rodzianko stating that for the salvation of the fatherland he appointed him to form a new ministry, reserving, however, the ministries of foreign affairs, war and marine for himself. The tzar still hoped to bargain with "them": the "many troops," after all, were on their way to Petrograd.

General Ivanov actually arrived without hindrance at Tzarskoe Selo: evidently the railroad workers did not care to come in conflict with the Battalion of St. George. The general confessed later that he had three or four times found it necessary on the march to use fatherly influence with the lower ranks, who were impudent to him: he made them get down on their knees. Immediately upon the arrival of the "dictator" in Tzarskoe Selo, the local authorities informed him that an encounter between the Battalion of St. George and the troops would mean danger to the tzar's family. They were simply afraid for themselves, and advised the dictator to go back without detraining.

General Ivanov telegraphed to the other "dictator," Khabalov, in Petrograd ten questions, to which he received succinct answers. We will quote them in full, for they deserve it:

Ivanov's questions:	*Khabalov's replies:*
1. How many troops are in order and how many are misbehaving?	1. I have at my disposal in the Admiralty building four companies of the Guard, five squadrons of cavalry and Cossacks, and two batteries; the rest of the troops have gone over to the revolutionists, or by agreement with them are remaining neutral. Soldiers are wandering through the town singly or in bands disarming officers.
2. Which railroad stations are guarded?	2. All the stations are in the hands of the revolutionists and strictly guarded by them.
3. In what parts of the city is order preserved?	3. The whole city is in the hands of the revolutionists. The telephone is not working, there is no communication between different parts of the city.
4. What authorities are governing the different parts of the city?	4. I cannot answer this question.
5. Are all the ministries functioning properly?	5. The ministers have been arrested by the revolutionists.
6. What police forces are at your disposal at the present moment?	6. None whatever.

Ivanov's questions:	*Khabalov's replies:*
7. What technical and supply institutions of the War Department are now in your control?	7. I have none.
8. What quantity of provisions is at your disposal?	8. There are no provisions at my disposal. In the city on February 5 there were 5,600,000 poods of flour in store.
9. Have many weapons, artillery and military stores fallen into the hands of the mutineers?	9. All the artillery establishments are in the hands of the revolutionists.
10. What military forces and staffs are in your control?	10. The chief of the Staff of the District is in my personal control. With the other district administrations I have no connections.

Having received this unequivocal illumination as to the situation, General Ivanov "agreed" to turn back his echelon without detraining to the station "Dno."[1] "Thus," concludes one of the chief personages of the staff, General Lukomsky, "nothing came of the expedition of General Ivanov with dictatorial powers but a public disgrace."

That disgrace, incidentally, was a very quiet one, sinking unnoticed in the billowing events. The dictator, we may suppose, delivered the provisions to his friends in Petrograd, and had a long chat with the tzarina. She referred to her self-sacrificing work in the hospitals, and complained of the ingratitude of the army and the people.

During this time news was arriving at Pskov by way of Moghilev, blacker and blacker. His Majesty's own bodyguard, in which every soldier was known by name and coddled by the

[1] The name of this station is also the Russian word meaning "bottom." [Trans.]

royal family, turned up at the State Duma asking permission to arrest those officers who had refused to take part in the insurrection. Vice-Admiral Kurosh reported that he found it impossible to take any measures to put down the insurrection at Kronstadt, since he could not vouch for the loyalty of a single detachment. Admiral Nepenin telegraphed that the Baltic Fleet had recognized the Provisional Committee of the State Duma. The Moscow commander-in-chief, Mrozovsky, telegraphed: "A majority of the troops have gone over with artillery to the revolutionists. The whole town is therefore in their hands. The burgomaster and his aide have left the city hall." *Have left* means that they fled.

All this was communicated to the tzar on the evening of March 1. Deep into the night they coaxed and argued about a responsible ministry. Finally, at two o'clock in the morning the tzar gave his consent, and those around him drew a sigh of relief. Since they took it for granted that this would settle the problem of the revolution, an order was issued at the same time that the troops which had been sent to Petrograd to put down the insurrection should return to the front. Ruszky hurried at dawn to convey the good news to Rodzianko. But the tzar's clock was way behind. Rodzianko in the Tauride Palace, already buried under a pile of democrats, socialists, soldiers, workers' deputies, replied to Ruszky: "Your proposal is not enough; it is now a question of the dynasty itself. . . . Everywhere the troops are taking the side of the Duma, and the people are demanding an abdication in favor of the Heir with Mikhail Alexandrovich as regent." Of course the troops never thought of demanding either the Heir or Mikhail Alexandrovich. Rodzianko merely attributed to the troops and the people that slogan upon which the Duma was still hoping to stop the revolution. But in either case the tzar's concession had come too late: "The anarchy has reached such proportions that I (Rodzianko) was this night compelled to appoint a Provisional Government. Unfortunately, the edict has come too late. . . ." These majestic words bear witness that the President of the Duma had succeeded in drying the tears shed over Golytsin. The tzar read the conversation between Rodzianko and Ruszky, and hesitated, read it over again, and decided to wait. But now the military chiefs had begun to sound the alarm: the matter concerned them too a little!

General Alexeiev carried out during the hours of that night a sort of plebiscite among the commanders-in-chief at the fronts. It is a good thing present-day revolutions are accomplished with the help of the telegraph, so that the very first impulses and reactions of those in power are preserved to history on the tape. The conversations of the tzarist field-marshals on the night of March 1–2 are an incomparable human document. Should the tzar abdicate or not? The commander-in-chief of the western front, General Evert, consented to give his opinion only after Generals Ruszky and Brussilov had expressed themselves. The commander-in-chief of the Roumanian front, General Sakharov, demanded that before he express himself the conclusions of all the other commanders-in-chief should be communicated to him. After long delays this valiant chieftain announced that his warm love for the monarch would not permit his soul to reconcile itself with an acceptance of the "base suggestion"; nevertheless, "with sobs" he advised the tzar to abdicate in order to avoid "still viler pretensions." Adjutant-General Evert quite reasonably explained the necessity for capitulation: "I am taking all measures to prevent information as to the present situation in the capital from penetrating the army, in order to protect it against indubitable disturbances. No means exist for putting down the revolution in the capitals." Grand Duke Nikolai Nikolaievich on the Caucasian front beseeched the tzar on bended knee to adopt the "supermeasure" and renounce the throne. A similar prayer came from Generals Alexeiev and Brussilov and Admiral Nepenin. Ruszky spoke orally to the same effect. The generals respectfully presented seven revolver barrels to the temple of the adored monarch. Fearing to let slip the moment for reconciliation with the new power, and no less fearing their own troops, these military chieftains, accustomed as they were to surrendering positions, gave the tzar and the High Commander-in-Chief a quite unanimous counsel: Retire without fighting. This was no longer distant Petrograd against which, as it seemed, one might send troops; this was the front from which the troops had to be borrowed.

Having listened to this suggestively circumstanced report,

the tzar decided to abdicate the throne which he no longer possessed. A telegram to Rodzianko suitable to the occasion was drawn up; "There is no sacrifice that I would not make in the name of the real welfare and salvation of my native mother Russia. Thus I am ready to abdicate the throne in favor of my son, and in order that he may remain with me until he is of age, under the regency of my brother, Mikhail Alexandrovich. Nicholas." This telegram too, however, was not despatched, for news came from the capital of the departure for Pskov of the deputies Guchkov and Shulgin. This offered a new pretext to postpone the decision. The tzar ordered the telegram returned to him. He obviously dreaded to sell too cheap, and still hoped for comforting news—or more accurately, hoped for a miracle. Nicholas received the two deputies at twelve o'clock midnight March 2–3. The miracle did not come, and it was impossible to evade longer. The tzar unexpectedly announced that he could not part with his son —what vague hopes were then wandering in his head?—and signed an abdication in favor of his brother. At the same time edicts to the Senate were signed, naming Prince Lvov President of the Council of Ministers, and Nikolai Nikolaievich Supreme Commander-in-Chief. The family suspicions of the tzarina seemed to have been justified: the hated "Nikolasha" came back to power along with the conspirators. Guchkov apparently seriously believed that the revolution would accept the Most August War Chief. The latter also accepted his appointment in good faith. He even tried for a few days to give some kind of orders and make appeals for the fulfillment of patriotic duty. However the revolution painlessly removed him.

In order to preserve the appearance of a free act, the abdication was dated three o'clock in the afternoon, on the pretense that the original decision of the tzar to abdicate had taken place at that hour. But as a matter of fact that afternoon's "decision," which gave the scepter to his son and not to his brother, had been taken back in anticipation of a more favorable turn of the wheel. Of that, however, nobody spoke out loud. The tzar made a last effort to save his face before the hated deputies, who upon their part permitted this falsification of a historic act—this deceiving of the people. The monarchy retired from the scene preserving its usual style; and its successors also remained true to themselves. They probably even regarded their connivance as the magnanimity of a conqueror to the conquered.

Departing a little from the phlegmatic style of his diary, Nicholas writes on March 2: "This morning Ruszky came and read me a long conversation over the wire with Rodzianko. According to his words the situation in Petrograd is such that a ministry of the members of the State Duma will be powerless to do anything, for it is being opposed by the social-democratic party in the person of a workers' committee. My abdication is necessary. Ruszky transmitted this conversation to Alexeiev at headquarters and to all the commanders-in-chief. Answers arrived at 12:30. To save Russia and keep the army at the front, I decided upon this step. I agreed, and they sent from headquarters the text of an abdication. In the evening came Guchkov and Shulgin from Petrograd, with whom I talked it over and gave them the document amended and signed. At 1 o'clock in the morning I left Pskov with heavy feelings; around me treason, cowardice, deceit."

The bitterness of Nicholas was, we must confess, not without foundation. It was only as short a time ago as February 28, that General Alexeiev had telegraphed to all the commanders-in-chief at the front: "Upon us all lies a sacred duty before the sovereign and the fatherland to preserve loyalty to oath and duty in the troops of the active army." Two days later Alexeiev appealed to these same commanders-in-chief to violate their "loyalty to oath and duty." In all the commanding staff there was not found one man to take action in behalf of his tzar. They all hastened to transfer to the ship of the revolution, firmly expecting to find comfortable cabins there. Generals and admirals one and all removed the tzarist braid and put on the red ribbon. There was news subsequently of one single righteous soul, some commander of a corps, who died of heart failure taking the new oath. But it is not established that his heart failed through injured monarchist feelings, and not through other causes. The civil officials naturally were not obliged to show more courage than the military—each one was saving himself as he could.

But the clock of the monarchy decidedly did not coincide

with the revolutionary clocks. At dawn of March 3, Ruszky was again summoned to the direct wire from the capital: Rodzianko and Prince Lvov were demanding that he hold up the tzar's abdication, which had again proved too late. The installation of Alexei—said the new authorities evasively—might perhaps be accepted—by whom?—but the installation of Mikhail was absolutely unacceptable. Ruszky with some venom expressed his regret that the deputies of the Duma who had arrived the night before had not been sufficiently informed as to the aims and purposes of their journey. But here too the deputies had their justification. "Unexpectedly to us all there broke out such a soldiers' rebellion as I never saw the like of," explained the Lord Chamberlain to Ruszky, as though he had done nothing all his life but watch soldiers' rebellions. "To proclaim Mikhail emperor would pour oil on the fire and there would begin a ruthless extermination of everything that can be exterminated." How it whirls and shakes and bends and contorts them all!

The generals silently swallowed this new "vile pretension" of the revolution. Alexeiev alone slightly relieved his spirit in a telegraphic bulletin to the commanders-in-chief: "The left parties and the workers' deputies are exercising a powerful pressure upon the President of the Duma, and there is no frankness or sincerity in the communications of Rodzianko." The only thing lacking to the generals in those hours was sincerity!

But at this point the tzar again changed his mind. Arriving in Moghilev from Pskov, he handed to his former chief-of-staff, Alexeiev, for transmission to Petrograd, a sheet of paper with his consent to the handing over of the scepter to his son. Evidently he found this combination in the long run more promising. Alexeiev, according to Denikin's story, went away with the telegram and . . . did not send it. He thought that those two manifestoes which had already been published to the army and the country were enough. The discord arose from the fact that not only the tzar and his counselors, but also the Duma liberals, were thinking more slowly than the revolution.

Before his final departure from Moghilev on March 8, the tzar, already under formal arrest, wrote an appeal to the troops ending with these words: "Whoever thinks now of peace, whoever desires it, that man is a traitor to the fatherland, its betrayer." This was in the nature of a prompted attempt to snatch out of the hands of liberalism the accusation of Germanophilism. The attempt had no result: they did not even dare publish the appeal.

Thus ended a reign which had been a continuous chain of ill luck, failure, misfortune, and evil-doing, from the Khodynka catastrophe during the coronation, through the shooting of strikers and revolting peasants, the Russo-Japanese war, the frightful putting-down of the revolution of 1905, the innumerable executions, punitive expeditions and national pogroms —and ending with the insane and contemptible participation of Russia in the insane and contemptible world war.

Upon arriving at Tzarskoe Selo, where he and his family were confined in the palace, the tzar, according to Vyrubova, softly said: "There is no justice among men." But those very words irrefutably testify that historic justice, though it comes late, does exist.

The similarity of the last Romanov couple to the French royal pair of the epoch of the Great Revolution is very obvious. It has already been remarked in literature, but only in passing and without drawing inferences. Nevertheless it is not at all accidental, as appears at the first glance, but offers valuable material for an inference.

Although separated from each other by five quarter centuries, the tzar and the king were at certain moments like two actors playing the same rôle. A passive, patient, but vindictive treachery was the distinctive trait of both—with this difference, that in Louis it was disguised with a dubious kindliness, in Nicholas with affability. They both make the impression of people who are overburdened by their job, but at the same time unwilling to give up even a part of those rights of which they are unable to make any use. The diaries of both, similar in style or lack of style, reveal the same depressing spiritual emptiness.

The Austrian woman and the Hessian German form also a striking symmetry. Both queens stand above their kings, not only in physical but also in moral growth. Marie Antoinette was less pious than Alexandra Feodorovna, and unlike the latter was passionately fond of pleasures. But both alike scorned the people, could not endure the thought of concessions, alike mistrusted the courage of their husbands, looking down upon them—Antoinette with a shade of contempt, Alexandra with pity.

When the authors of memoirs, approaching the Petersburg court of their day, assure us that Nicholas II, had he been a private individual, would have left a good memory behind him, they merely reproduce the long-ago stereotyped remarks about Louis XVI, not enriching in the least our knowledge either of history or of human nature.

We have already seen how Prince Lvov became indignant when, at the height of the tragic events of the first revolution, instead of a depressed tzar, he found before him a "*jolly, sprightly little man* in a raspberry-colored shirt." Without knowing it, the prince merely repeated the comment of Gouverneur Morris writing in Washington in 1790 about Louis: "What will you have from a creature who, situated as he is, eats and drinks and sleeps well, and laughs and is as merry a grig as lives?"

When Alexandra Feodorovna, three months before the fall of the monarchy, prophesies: "All is coming out for the best, the dreams of our Friend mean so much!", she merely repeats Marie Antoinette, who one month before the overthrow of the royal power wrote: "I feel a liveliness of spirit, and something tells me that we shall soon be happy and safe." They both see rainbow dreams as they drown.

Certain elements of similarity of course are accidental, and have the interest only of historic anecdotes. Infinitely more important are those traits of character which have been grafted, or more directly imposed, on a person by the mighty force of conditions, and which throw a sharp light on the interrelation of personality and the objective factors of history.

"He did not know how to wish: that was his chief trait of character," says a reactionary French historian of Louis. Those words might have been written of Nicholas: neither of them knew how to wish, but both knew how to not wish. But what really could be "wished" by the last representatives of a hopelessly lost historic cause? "Usually he listened, smiled, and rarely decided upon anything. His first word was usually *No.*"

Of whom is that written? Again of Capet. But if this is so, the manners of Nicholas were an absolute plagiarism. They both go toward the abyss "with the crown pushed down over their eyes." But would it after all be easier to go to an abyss, which you cannot escape anyway, with your eyes open? What difference would it have made, as a matter of fact, if they had pushed the crown way back on their heads?

Some professional psychologist ought to draw up an anthology of the parallel expressions of Nicholas and Louis, Alexandra and Antoinette, and their courtiers. There would be no lack of material, and the result would be a highly instructive historic testimony in favor of the materialist psychology. Similar (of course, far from identical) irritations in similar conditions call out similar reflexes; the more powerful the irritation, the sooner it overcomes personal peculiarities. To a tickle, people react differently, but to a red-hot iron, alike. As a steam-hammer converts a sphere and a cube alike into sheet metal, so under the blow of too great and inexorable events resistances are smashed and the boundaries of "individuality" lost.

Louis and Nicholas were the last-born of a dynasty that had lived tumultuously. The well-known equability of them both, their tranquillity and "gaiety" in difficult moments, were the well-bred expression of a meagerness of inner powers, a weakness of the nervous discharge, poverty of spiritual resources. Moral castrates, they were absolutely deprived of imagination and creative force. They had just enough brains to feel their own triviality, and they cherished an envious hostility toward everything gifted and significant. It fell to them both to rule a country in conditions of deep inner crisis and popular revolutionary awakening. Both of them fought off the intrusion of new ideas, and the tide of hostile forces. Indecisiveness, hypocrisy, and lying were in both cases the expression, not so much of personal weakness, as of the complete impossibility of holding fast to their hereditary positions.

And how was it with their wives? Alexandra, even more than Antoinette, was lifted to the very heights of the dreams of a princess, especially such a rural one as this Hessian, by her marriage with the unlimited despot of a powerful country. Both of them were filled to the brim with the consciousness of their high mission: Antoinette more frivolously, Alexandra in a spirit of Protestant bigotry translated into the Slavonic language of the Russian Church. An unlucky reign and a growing discontent of the people ruthlessly destroyed the fantastic world which these two enterprising but nevertheless chickenlike heads had built for themselves. Hence the growing bitterness, the gnawing hostility to an alien people that would not bow before them; the hatred toward ministers who wanted to give even a little consideration to that hostile world, to the country; hence their alienation even from their own court, and their continued irritation against a husband who had not fulfilled the expectations aroused by him as a bridegroom.

Historians and biographers of the psychological tendency not infrequently seek and find something purely personal and accidental where great historical forces are refracted through a personality. This is the same fault of vision as that of the courtiers who considered the last Russian tzar born "unlucky." He himself believed that he was born under an unlucky star. In reality his ill-luck flowed from the contradictions between those old aims which he inherited from his ancestors and the new historic conditions in which he was placed. When the ancients said that Jupiter first makes mad those whom he wishes to destroy, they summed up in superstitious form a profound historic observation. In the saying of Goethe about reason becoming nonsense—"*Vernunft wird Unsinn*"—this same thought is expressed about the impersonal Jupiter of the historical dialectic, which withdraws "reason" from historic institutions that have outlived themselves and condemns their defenders to failure. The scripts for the rôles of Romanov and Capet were prescribed by the general development of the historic drama; only the nuances of interpretation fell to the lot of the actors. The ill-luck of Nicholas, as of Louis, had its roots not in his personal horoscope, but in the historical horoscope of the bureaucratic-caste monarchy. They were both, chiefly and above all, the last-born offspring of absolutism. Their moral insignificance, deriving from their dynastic epigonism, gave the latter an especially malignant character.

You might object: if Alexander III had drunk less he might have lived a good deal longer, the revolution would have run into a very different make of tzar, and no parallel with Louis

XVI would have been possible. Such an objection, however, does not refute in the least what has been said above. We do not at all pretend to deny the significance of the personal in the mechanics of the historic process, nor the significance in the personal of the accidental. We only demand that a historic personality, with all its peculiarities, should not be taken as a bare list of psychological traits, but as a living reality grown out of definite social conditions and reacting upon them. As a rose does not lose its fragrance because the natural scientist points out upon what ingredients of soil and atmosphere it is nourished, so an exposure of the social roots of a personality does not remove from it either its aroma or its foul smell.

The consideration advanced above about a possible longer life of Alexander III is capable of illuming this very problem from another side. Let us assume that this Alexander III had not become mixed up in 1904 in a war with Japan. This would have delayed the first revolution. For how long? It is possible that the "revolution of 1905"—that is, the first test of strength, the first breach in the system of absolutism—would have been a mere introduction to the second, republican, and the third, proletarian revolution. Upon this question more or less interesting guesses are possible, but it is indubitable in any case that the revolution did not result from the character of Nicholas II, and that Alexander III would not have solved its problem. It is enough to remember that nowhere and never was the transition from the feudal to the bourgeois régime made without violent disturbances. We saw this only yesterday in China; today we observe it again in India. The most we can say is that this or that policy of the monarchy, this or that personality of the monarch, might have hastened or postponed the revolution, and placed a certain imprint on its external course.

With what angry and impotent stubbornness tzarism tried to defend itself in those last months, weeks and days, when its game was hopelessly lost! If Nicholas himself lacked the will, the lack was made up by the tzarina. Rasputin was an instrument of the action of a clique which rabidly fought for self-preservation. Even on this narrow scale the personality of the tzar merges in a group which represents the coagulum of the past and its last convulsion. The "policy" of the upper circles at Tzarskoe Selo, face-to-face with the revolution, were but the reflexes of a poisoned and weak beast of prey. If you chase a wolf over the steppe in an automobile, the beast gives out at last and lies down impotent. But attempt to put a collar on him, and he will try to tear you to pieces, or at least wound you. And indeed what else can he do in the circumstances?

The liberals imagined there was something else he might do. Instead of coming to an agreement with the enfranchised bourgeoisie in good season, and thus preventing the revolution—such is liberalism's act of accusation against the last tzar—Nicholas stubbornly shrank from concessions, and even in the last days when already under the knife of destiny, when every minute was to be counted, still kept on procrastinating, bargaining with fate, and letting slip the last possibilities. This all sounds convincing. But how unfortunate that liberalism, knowing so accurately how to save the monarchy, did not know how to save itself!

It would be absurd to maintain that tzarism never and in no circumstances made concessions. It made them when they were demanded by the necessity of self-preservation. After the Crimean defeat, Alexander II carried out the semi-liberation of the peasants and a series of liberal reforms in the sphere of land administration, courts, press, educational institutions, etc. The tzar himself expressed the guiding thought of this reformation: to free the peasants from *above* lest they free themselves from *below*. Under the drive of the first revolution Nicholas II granted a semi-constitution. Stolypin scrapped the peasant communes in order to broaden the arena of the capitalist forces. For tzarism, however, all these reforms had a meaning only in so far as the partial concession preserved the whole—that is, the foundations of a caste society and the monarchy itself. When the consequences of the reform began to splash over those boundaries the monarchy inevitably beat a retreat. Alexander II in the second half of his reign stole back the reforms of the first half. Alexander III went still farther on the road of counter-reform. Nicholas II in October 1905 retreated before the revolution, and then afterward dissolved the Dumas created by it, and as soon as the revolution grew weak, made his coup d'état. Throughout three-quarters of a century—if we begin with the reform of Alexander II—there developed a struggle of historic forces, now underground, now in the open, far transcending the personal qualities of the separate tzars, and accomplishing the overthrow of the monarchy. Only within the historic framework of this process can you find a place for individual tzars, their characters, their "biographies."

Even the most despotic of autocrats is but little similar to a "free" individuality laying its arbitrary imprint upon events. He is always the crowned agent of the privileged classes which are forming society in their own image. When these classes have not yet fulfilled their mission, then the monarchy is strong and self-confident. Then it has in its hands a reliable apparatus of power and an unlimited choice of executives—because the more gifted people have not yet gone over into the hostile camp. Then the monarch, either personally, or through the mediation of a powerful favorite, may become the agent of a great and progressive historic task. It is quite otherwise when the sun of the old society is finally declining to the west. The privileged classes are now changed from organizers of the national life into a parasitic growth; having lost their guiding function, they lose the consciousness of their mission and all confidence in their powers. Their dissatisfaction with themselves becomes a dissatisfaction with the monarchy; the dynasty becomes isolated; the circle of people loyal to the death narrows down; their level sinks lower; meanwhile the dangers grow; new forces are pushing up; the monarchy loses its capacity for any kind of creative initiative; it defends itself, it strikes back, it retreats; its activities acquire the automatism of mere reflexes. The semi-Asiatic despotism of the Romanovs did not escape this fate.

If you take the tzarism in its agony, in a vertical section, so to speak, Nicholas is the axis of a clique which has its roots in the hopelessly condemned past. In a horizontal section of the historic monarchy, Nicholas is the last link in a dynastic chain. His nearest ancestors, who also in their day were merged in a family, caste and bureaucratic collectivity—only a broader one—tried out various measures and methods of government in order to protect the old social régime against the fate advancing upon it. But nevertheless they passed on to Nicholas a chaotic empire already carrying the matured revolution in its womb. If he had any choice left, it was only between different roads to ruin.

Liberalism was dreaming of a monarchy on the British plan. But was parliamentarism born on the Thames by a peaceful evolution? Was it the fruit of the "free" foresight of a single monarch? No, it was deposited as the result of a struggle that lasted for ages, and in which one of the kings left his head at the crossroads.

The historic-psychological contrast mentioned above between the Romanovs and the Capets can, by the way, be aptly extended to the British royal pair of the epoch of the first revolution. Charles I revealed fundamentally the same combination of traits with which memoirists and historians have endowed Louis XVI and Nicholas II. "Charles, therefore, remained passive," writes Montague, "yielded where he could not resist, betrayed how unwillingly he did so, and reaped no popularity, no confidence." "He was not a stupid man," says another historian of Charles Stuart, "but he lacked firmness of character. . . . His evil fate was his wife, Henrietta, a Frenchwoman, sister of Louis XIII, saturated even more than Charles with the idea of absolutism." We will not detail the characteristics of this third—chronologically first—royal pair to be crushed by a national revolution. We will merely observe that in England the hatred was concentrated above all on the queen, as a Frenchwoman and a papist, whom they accused of plotting with Rome, secret connections with the Irish rebels, and intrigues at the French court.

But England had, at any rate, ages at her disposal. She was the pioneer of bourgeois civilization; she was not under the yoke of other nations, but on the contrary held them more and more under her yoke. She exploited the whole world. This softened the inner contradictions, accumulated conservatism, promoted an abundance and stability of fatty deposits in the form of a parasitic caste, in the form of a squirarchy, a monarchy, House of Lords, and the state church. Thanks to this exclusive historic privilege of development possessed by bourgeois England, conservatism combined with elasticity passed over from her institutions into her moral fiber. Various continental Philistines, like the Russian professor Miliukov, or the Austro-Marxist Otto Bauer, have not to this day ceased going into ecstasies over this fact. But exactly at the present moment, when England, hard pressed throughout the world, is squandering the last resources of her former privileged position, her conservatism is losing its elasticity, and even in the person of the Laborites is turning into stark reactionism. In the face of the Indian revolution the "socialist" MacDonald will find no other methods but those with which Nicholas II opposed the Russian revolution. Only a blind man could fail to see that Great Britain is headed for gigantic revolutionary earthquake shocks, in which the last fragments of her conservatism, her world domination, her present state machine, will go down without a trace. MacDonald is preparing these shocks no less successfully than did Nicholas II in his time, and no less blindly. So here too, as we see, is no poor illustration of the problem of the rôle of the "free" personality in history.

But how could Russia with her belated development, coming along at the tail end of the European nations, with her meager economic foundation underfoot, how could she develop an "elastic conservatism" of social forms—and develop it for the special benefit of professorial liberalism and its leftward shadow, reformist socialism? Russia was too far behind. And when world imperialism once took her in its grip, she had to pass through her political history in too brief a course. If Nicholas had gone to meet liberalism and replaced Stürmer with Miliukov, the development of events would have differed a little in form, but not in substance. Indeed it was just in this way that Louis behaved in the second stage of the revolution, summoning the Gironde to power: this did not save Louis himself from the guillotine, nor after him the Gironde. The accumulating social contradictions were bound to break through to the surface, and breaking through to carry out their work of purgation. Before the pressure of the popular masses, who had at last brought out into the open arena their misfortunes, their pains, indignations, passions, hopes, illusions and aims, the high-up combinations of the monarchy with liberalism had only an episodic significance. They could exert, to be sure, an influence on the order of events, maybe upon the number of actions, but not at all upon the development of the drama nor its momentous climax.

Chapter VII

FIVE DAYS

(FEBRUARY 23–27, 1917)

The 23rd of February was International Woman's Day. The social-democratic circles had intended to mark this day in a general manner: by meetings, speeches, leaflets. It had not occurred to anyone that it might become the first day of the revolution. Not a single organization called for strikes on that day. What is more, even a Bolshevik organization, and a most militant one—the Vyborg borough-committee, all workers—was opposing strikes. The temper of the masses, according to Kayurov, one of the leaders in the workers' district, was very tense; any strike would threaten to turn into an open fight. But since the committee thought the time unripe for militant action—the party not strong enough and the workers having too few contacts with the soldiers—they decided not to call for strikes but to prepare for revolutionary action at some indefinite time in the future. Such was the course followed by the committee on the eve of the 23rd of February, and everyone seemed to accept it. On the following morning, however, in spite of all directives, the women textile workers in several factories went on strike, and sent delegates to the metal workers with an appeal for support. "With reluctance," writes Kayurov, "the Bolsheviks agreed to this, and they were followed by the workers—Mensheviks and Social Revolutionaries. But once there is a mass strike, one must call everybody into the streets and take the lead." Such was Kayurov's decision, and the Vyborg committee had to agree to it. "The idea of going into the streets had long been ripening among the workers; only at that moment nobody imagined where it would lead." Let us keep in mind this testimony of a participant, important for understanding the mechanics of the events.

It was taken for granted that in case of a demonstration the soldiers would be brought out into the streets against the workers. What would that lead to? This was war time; the authorities were in no mood for joking. On the other hand, a "reserve" soldier in war time is nothing like an old soldier of the regular army. Is he really so formidable? In revolutionary circles they had discussed this much, but rather abstractly. For no one, positively no one—we can assert this categorically upon the basis of all the data—then thought that February 23 was to mark the beginning of a decisive drive against absolutism. The talk was of a demonstration which had indefinite, but in any case limited, perspectives.

Thus the fact is that the February revolution was begun from below, overcoming the resistance of its own revolutionary organizations, the initiative being taken of their own accord by the most oppressed and downtrodden part of the proletariat —the women textile workers, among them no doubt many soldiers' wives. The overgrown bread-lines had provided the last stimulus. About 90,000 workers, men and women, were on strike that day. The fighting mood expressed itself in demonstrations, meetings, encounters with the police. The movement began in the Vyborg district with its large industrial establishments; thence it crossed over to the Petersburg side. There were no strikes or demonstrations elsewhere, according to the testimony of the secret police. On that day detachments of troops were called in to assist the police—evidently not many of them—but there were no encounters with them. A mass of women, not all of them workers, flocked to the municipal duma demanding bread. It was like demanding milk from a he-goat. Red banners appeared in different parts of the city, and inscriptions on them showed that the workers wanted bread, but neither autocracy nor war. Woman's Day passed successfully, with enthusiasm and without victims. But what it concealed in itself, no one had guessed even by nightfall.

On the following day the movement not only fails to diminish, but doubles. About one-half of the industrial workers of Petrograd are on strike on the 24th of February. The workers come to the factories in the morning; instead of going to work they hold meetings; then begin processions toward the center. New districts and new groups of the population are drawn into the movement. The slogan "Bread!" is crowded out or obscured by louder slogans: "Down with autocracy!" "Down with the war!" Continuous demonstrations on the Nevsky[1]—first compact masses of workmen singing revolutionary songs, later a motley crowd of city folk interspersed with the blue caps of students. "The promenading crowd was sympathetically disposed toward us, and soldiers in some of the war-hospitals greeted us by waving whatever was at hand." How many clearly realized what was being ushered in by this sympathetic waving from sick soldiers to demonstrating workers? But the Cossacks constantly, though without ferocity, kept charging the crowd. Their horses were covered with foam. The mass of demonstrators would part to let them through, and close up again. There was no fear in the crowd. "The Cossacks promise not to shoot," passed from mouth to mouth. Apparently some of the workers had talks with individual Cossacks. Later, however, cursing, half-drunken dragoons appeared on the scene. They plunged into the crowd, began to strike at heads with their lances. The demonstrators summoned all their strength and stood fast, "They won't shoot." And in fact they didn't.

A liberal senator was looking at the dead street-cars—or was that on the following day and his memory failed him?—some of them with broken windows, some tipped over on the tracks, and was recalling the July days of 1914 on the eve of the war. "It seemed that the old attempt was being renewed." The senator's eyes did not deceive him; the continuity is clear. History was picking up the ends of the revolutionary threads broken by the war, and tying them in a knot.

Throughout the entire day, crowds of people poured from one part of the city to another. They were persistently dispelled by the police, stopped and crowded back by cavalry detachments and occasionally by infantry. Along with shouts of "Down with the police!" was heard oftener and oftener a "Hurrah!" addressed to the Cossacks. That was significant.

[1] Nevsky Prospect, the main avenue of the city. [Trans.]

Toward the police the crowd showed ferocious hatred. They routed the mounted police with whistles, stones, and pieces of ice. In a totally different way the workers approached the soldiers. Around the barracks, sentinels, patrols and lines of soldiers, stood groups of working men and women exchanging friendly words with the army men. This was a new stage, due to the growth of the strike and the personal meeting of the worker with the army. Such a stage is inevitable in every revolution. But it always seems new, and does in fact occur differently every time: those who have read and written about it do not recognize the thing when they see it.

In the State Duma that day they were telling how an enormous mass of people had flooded Znamensky Square and all Nevsky Prospect and the adjoining streets, and that a totally unprecedented phenomenon was observed: the Cossacks and the regiments with bands were being greeted by revolutionary and not patriotic crowds with shouts of "Hurrah!" To the question, "What does it all mean?" the first person accosted in the crowd answered the deputy: "A policeman struck a woman with a knout; the Cossacks stepped in and drove away the police." Whether it happened in this way or another, will never be verified. But the crowd believed that it was so, that this was possible. The belief had not fallen out of the sky; it arose from previous experience, and was therefore to become an earnest of victory.

The workers at the Erikson, one of the foremost mills in the Vyborg district, after a morning meeting came out on the Sampsonievsky Prospect, a whole mass, 2,500 of them, and in a narrow place ran into the Cossacks. Cutting their way with the breasts of their horses, the officers first charged through the crowd. Behind them, filling the whole width of the Prospect, galloped the Cossacks. Decisive moment! But the horsemen, cautiously, in a long ribbon, rode through the corridor just made by the officers. "Some of them smiled," Kayurov recalls, "and one of them gave the workers a good wink." This wink was not without meaning. The workers were emboldened with a friendly, not hostile, kind of assurance, and slightly infected the Cossacks with it. The one who winked found imitators. In spite of renewed efforts from the officers, the Cossacks, without openly breaking discipline, failed to force the crowd to disperse, but flowed through it in streams. This was repeated three or four times and brought the two sides even closer together. Individual Cossacks began to reply to the workers' questions and even to enter into momentary conversations with them. Of discipline there remained but a thin transparent shell that threatened to break through any second. The officers hastened to separate their patrol from the workers, and, abandoning the idea of dispersing them, lined the Cossacks out across the street as a barrier to prevent the demonstrators from getting to the center. But even this did not help: standing stock-still in perfect discipline, the Cossacks did not hinder the workers from "diving" under their horses. The revolution does not choose its paths: it made its first steps toward victory under the belly of a Cossack's horse. A remarkable incident! And remarkable the eye of its narrator—an eye which took an impression of every bend in the process. No wonder, for the narrator was a leader; he was at the head of over two thousand men. The eye of a commander watching for enemy whips and bullets looks sharp.

It seems that the break in the army first appeared among the Cossacks, those age-old subduers and punishers. This does not mean, however, that the Cossacks were more revolutionary than others. On the contrary, these solid property owners, riding their own horses, highly valuing their Cossack peculiarities, scorning the plain peasants, mistrustful of the workers, had many elements of conservatism. But just for this reason the changes caused by the war were more sharply noticeable in them. Besides, they were always being pulled around, sent everywhere, driven against the people, kept in suspense—and they were the first to be put to the test. They were sick of it, and wanted to go home. Therefore they winked: "Do it, boys, if you know how—we won't bother you!" All these things, however, were merely very significant symptoms. The army was still the army, it was bound with discipline, and the threads were in the hands of the monarchy. The worker mass was unarmed. The leaders had not yet thought of the decisive crisis.

On the calendar of the Council of Ministers that day there stood, among other questions, the question of disorders in the capital. Strikes? Demonstrations? This isn't the first time.

Everything is provided for. Directions have been issued. Return to the order of business.

And what were the directions? In spite of the fact that on the 23rd and 24th twenty-eight policemen were beaten up—persuasive exactness about the number!—the military commander of the district, General Khabalov, almost a dictator, did not resort to shooting. Not from kind-heartedness: everything was provided for and marked down in advance, even the time for the shooting.

The revolution caught them unawares only with regard to the exact moment. Generally speaking, both sides, the revolutionary and the governmental, were carefully preparing for it, had been preparing for years, had always been preparing. As for the Bolsheviks, all their activity since 1905 was nothing but preparation for a second revolution. And the activities of the government, an enormous share of them, were preparations to put down the new revolution. In the fall of 1916 this part of the government's work had assumed an aspect of particularly careful planning. A commission under Khabalov's chairmanship had completed by the middle of January 1917 a very exact plan for crushing a new insurrection. The city was divided into six police districts, which in turn were subdivided into rayons. The commander of the reserve guard units, General Chebykin, was placed at the head of all the armed forces. Regiments were assigned to different rayons. In each of the six police districts, the police, the gendarmes and the troops were united under the command of special staff officers. The Cossack cavalry was at the disposal of Chebykin himself for larger-scale operations. The order of action was planned as follows: first the police act alone, then the Cossacks appear on the scene with whips, and only in case of real necessity the troops go into action with rifles and machine guns. It was this very plan, developed out of the experience of 1905, that was put into operation in the February days. The difficulty lay not in lack of foresight, nor defects of the plan itself, but in the human material. Here the whole thing threatened to hang fire.

Formally the plan was based on the entire garrison, which comprised one hundred and fifty thousand soldiers, but in reality only some ten thousand came into the count. Besides the policemen, numbering three and a half thousand, a firm hope was placed in the military training schools. This is explained by the makeup of the Petrograd garrison which at that time, consisted almost exclusively of reserve units, primarily of the fourteen reserve battalions attached to the regiments of the Guard which were then at the front. In addition to that, the garrison comprised one reserve infantry regiment, a reserve bicycle battalion, a reserve armored car division, small units of sappers and artillerymen and two regiments of Don Cossacks. That was a great many—it was too many. The swollen reserve units were made up of a human mass which had either escaped training almost entirely, or succeeded in getting free of it. But for that matter, substantially the same thing was true of the entire army.

Khabalov meticulously adhered to the plan he had worked out. On the first day, the 23rd, the police operated alone. On the 24th, for the most part the cavalry was led into the streets, but only to work with whip and lance. The use of infantry and firearms was to depend on the further development of events. But events came thick and fast.

On the 25th, the strike spread wider. According to the government's figures, 240,000 workers participated that day. The most backward layers are following up the vanguard. Already a good number of small establishments are on strike. The street-cars are at a stand. Business concerns are closed. In the course of the day students of the higher schools join the strike. By noon tens of thousands of people pour to the Kazan cathedral and the surrounding streets. Attempts are made to organize street meetings; a series of armed encounters with the police occurs. Orators address the crowds around the Alexander III monument. The mounted police open fire. A speaker falls wounded. Shots from the crowd kill a police inspector, wound the chief of police and several other policemen. Bottles, petards and hand grenades are thrown at the gendarmes. The war has taught this art. The soldiers show indifference, at times hostility, to the police. It spreads excitedly through the crowd that when the police opened fire by the Alexander III monument, the Cossacks let go a volley at the horse "Pharaohs" (such was the nickname of the police) and the latter had to gallop off. This apparently was not a legend circulated for self-encouragement, since the incident, although in different versions, is confirmed from several sources.

A worker-Bolshevik, Kayurov, one of the authentic leaders in those days, relates how at one place, within sight of a detachment of Cossacks, the demonstrators scattered under the whips of the mounted police, and how he, Kayurov, and several workers with him, instead of following the fugitives, took off their caps and approached the Cossacks with the words: "Brothers—Cossacks, help the workers in a struggle for their peaceable demands; you see how the Pharaohs treat us, hungry workers. Help us!" This consciously humble manner, those caps in their hands—what an accurate psychological calculation! Inimitable gesture! The whole history of street fights and revolutionary victories swarms with such improvisations. But they are drowned without a trace in the abyss of great events—the shell remains to the historian, the generalization. "The Cossacks glanced at each other in some special way," Kayurov continues, "and we were hardly out of the way before they rushed into the fight." And a few minutes later, near the station gate, the crowd were tossing in their arms a Cossack who before their eyes had slaughtered a police inspector with his saber.

Soon the police disappear altogether—that is, begin to act secretly. Then the soldiers appear—bayonets lowered. Anxiously the workers ask them: "Comrades, you haven't come to help the police?" A rude "Move along!" for answer. Another attempt ends the same way. The soldiers are sullen. A worm is gnawing them, and they cannot stand it when a question hits the very center of the pain.

Meanwhile disarmament of the Pharaohs becomes a universal slogan. The police are fierce, implacable, hated and hating foes. To win them over is out of the question. Beat them up and kill them. It is different with the soldiers: the crowd makes every effort to avoid hostile encounters with them; on the contrary, seeks ways to dispose them in its favor, convince, attract, fraternize, merge them in itself. In spite of the auspicious rumors about the Cossacks, perhaps slightly exaggerated, the crowd's attitude toward the mounted men remains cautious. A horseman sits high above the crowd; his soul is separated from the soul of the demonstrator by the four legs of his beast. A figure at which one must gaze from below always seems more significant, more threatening. The infantry are beside one on the pavement—closer, more accessible. The masses try to get near them, look into their eyes, surround them with their hot breath. A great rôle is played by women workers in the relation between workers and soldiers. They go up to the cordons more boldly than men, take hold of the rifles, beseech, almost command: "Put down your bayonets—join us." The soldiers are excited, ashamed, exchange anxious glances, waver; someone makes up his mind first, and the bayonets rise guiltily above the shoulders of the advancing crowd. The barrier is opened, a joyous and grateful "Hurrah!" shakes the air. The soldiers are surrounded. Everywhere arguments, reproaches, appeals—the revolution makes another forward step.

Nicholas from headquarters sent Khabalov a telegraphic command to put an end to the disorders "tomorrow." The tzar's will fell in with the next step in Khabalov's "plan," and the telegram served merely as an extra stimulus. Tomorrow the troops will say their say. Isn't it too late? You can't tell yet. The question is posed, but far from answered. The indulgence of the Cossacks, the wavering of certain infantry lines—these are but much-promising episodes repeated by the thousand-voiced echo of the sensitive street. Enough to inspire the revolutionary crowd, but too little for victory. Especially since there are episodes of an opposite kind. In the afternoon a detachment of dragoons, supposedly in response to revolver shots from the crowd, first opened fire on the demonstrators near Gostinny Dvor. According to Khabalov's report to headquarters three were killed and ten wounded. A serious warning! At the same time Khabalov issued a threat that all workers registered in the draft would be sent to the front if they did not go to work before the 28th. The general issued a three-day ultimatum—that is, he gave the revolution more time than it needed to overthrow Khabalov and the monarchy into the bargain. But that will become known only after the victory. On the evening of the 25th nobody guessed what the next day had in its womb.

Let us try to get a clearer idea of the inner logic of the movement. On February 23, under the flag of "Woman's

Day," began the long-ripe and long-withheld uprising of the Petrograd working masses. The first step of the insurrection was the strike. In the course of three days it broadened and became practically general. This alone gave assurance to the masses and carried them forward. Becoming more and more aggressive, the strike merged with the demonstrations, which were bringing the revolutionary mass face to face with the troops. This raised the problem as a whole to the higher level where things are solved by force of arms. The first days brought a number of individual successes, but these were more symptomatic than substantial.

A revolutionary uprising that spreads over a number of days can develop victoriously only in case it ascends step by step, and scores one success after another. A pause in its growth is dangerous; a prolonged marking of time, fatal. But even successes by themselves are not enough; the masses must know about them in time, and have time to understand their value. It is possible to let slip a victory at the very moment when it is within arm's reach. This has happened in history.

The first three days were days of uninterrupted increase in the extent and acuteness of the strife. But for this very reason the movement had arrived at a level where mere symptomatic successes were not enough. The entire active mass of the people had come out on the streets. It was settling accounts with the police successfully and easily. In the last two days the troops had been drawn into the events—on the second day, cavalry, on the third, the infantry too. They barred the way, pushed and crowded back the masses, sometimes connived with them, but almost never resorted to firearms. Those in command were slow to change their plan, partly because they underestimated what was happening—the faulty vision of the reaction supplemented that of the leaders of the revolution—partly because they lacked confidence in the troops. But exactly on the third day, the force of the developing struggle, as well as the tzar's command, made it necessary for the government to send the troops into action in dead earnest. The workers understood this, especially their advance ranks; the dragoons had already done some shooting the day before. Both sides now faced the issue unequivocally.

On the night of the 26th about a hundred people were

arrested in different parts of the city—people belonging to various revolutionary organizations, and among them five members of the Petrograd Committee of the Bolsheviks. This also meant that the government was taking the offensive. What will happen today? In what mood will the workers wake up after yesterday's shooting? And most important: what will the troops say? The sun of February 26 came up in a fog of uncertainty and acute anxiety.

In view of the arrest of the Petrograd Committee, the guidance of the entire work in the city fell into the hands of the Vyborg rayon. Maybe this was just as well. The upper leadership in the party was hopelessly slow. Only on the morning of the 25th, the Bureau of the Bolshevik Central Committee at last decided to issue a handbill calling for an all-Russian general strike. At the moment of issue, if indeed it ever did issue, the general strike in Petrograd was facing an armed uprising. The leaders were watching the movement from above; they hesitated, they lagged—in other words, they did not lead. They dragged after the movement.

The nearer one comes to the factories, the greater the decisiveness. Today however, the 26th, there is anxiety even in the rayons. Hungry, tired, chilled, with a mighty historic responsibility upon their shoulders, the Vyborg leaders gather outside the city limits, amid vegetable gardens, to exchange impressions of the day and plan the course . . . of what? Of a new demonstration? But where will an unarmed demonstration lead, now the government has decided to go the limit? This question bores into their minds. "One thing seems evident: the insurrection is dissolving." Here we recognize the voice of Kayurov, already familiar to us, and at first it seems hardly his voice. The barometer falls so low before the storm.

In the hours when hesitation seized even those revolutionists closest to the mass, the movement itself had gone much farther than its participants realized. Even the day before, towards evening of the 25th, the Vyborg side was wholly in the hands of the insurrection. The police stations were wrecked, individual officers had been killed, and the majority had fled. The city headquarters had completely lost contact with the greater part of the capital. On the morning of the 26th it became evident that not only the Vyborg side, but also

Peski almost up to Liteiny Prospect, was in control of the insurrection. At least so the police reports defined the situation. And it was true in a sense, although the revolutionists could hardly realize it: the police in so many cases abandoned their lairs before there was any threat from the workers. But even aside from that, ridding the factory districts of the police could not have decisive significance in the eyes of the workers: the troops had not yet said their final word. The uprising is "dissolving," thought the boldest of the bold. Meanwhile it was only beginning to develop.

The 26th of February fell on a Sunday; the factories were closed, and this prevented measuring the strength of the mass pressure in terms of the extent of the strike. Moreover the workers could not assemble in the factories, as they had done on the preceding days, and that hindered the demonstrations. In the morning the Nevsky was quiet. In those hours the tzarina telegraphed the tzar: "The city is calm."

But this calmness does not last long. The workers gradually concentrate, and move from all suburbs to the center. They are stopped at the bridges. They flock across the ice: it is only February and the Neva is one solid bridge of ice. The firing at their crowds on the ice is not enough to stop them. They find the city transformed. Posses, cordons, horse-patrols everywhere. The approaches to the Nevsky are especially well guarded. Every now and then shots ring out from ambush. The number of killed and wounded grows. Ambulances dart here and there. You cannot always tell who is shooting and where the shots come from. One thing is certain: after their cruel lesson, the police have decided not to expose themselves again. They shoot from windows, through balcony doors, from behind columns, from attics. Hypotheses are formed, which easily become legends. They say that in order to intimidate the demonstrators, many soldiers are disguised in police uniforms. They say that Protopopov has placed numerous machine-gun nests in the garrets of houses. A commission created after the revolution did not discover such nests, but this does not mean that there were none. However, the police on this day occupy a subordinate place. The troops come decisively into action. They are given strict orders to shoot, and the soldiers, mostly training squads—that is, non-commissioned officers' regimental schools—do shoot. According to the official figures, on this day about forty are killed and as many wounded, not counting those led or carried away by the crowd. The struggle arrives at a decisive stage. Will the mass ebb before the lead and flow back to its suburbs? No, it does not ebb. It is bound to have its own.

Bureaucratic, bourgeois, liberal Petersburg was in a fright. On that day Rodzianko, the President of the State Duma, demanded that reliable troops be sent from the front; later he "reconsidered" and recommended to the War Minister Belyaev that the crowds be dispersed, not with lead, but with cold water out of a fire-hose. Belyaev, having consulted General Khabalov, answered that a dowse of water would produce precisely the opposite effect "because it excites." Thus in the liberal and bureaucratic upper circles they discussed the relative advantages of hot and cold douches for the people in revolt. Police reports for that day testify that the fire-hose was inadequate: "In the course of the disorders it was observed as a general phenomenon, that the rioting mobs showed extreme defiance towards the military patrols, at whom, when asked to disperse, they threw stones and lumps of ice dug up from the street. When preliminary shots were fired into the air, the crowd not only did not disperse but answered these volleys with laughter. Only when loaded cartridges were fired into the very midst of the crowd, was it found possible to disperse the mob, the participants in which, however, would most of them hide in the yards of near-by houses, and as soon as the shooting stopped come out again into the street." This police report shows that the temperature of the masses had risen very high. To be sure, it is hardly probable that the crowd would have begun of itself to bombard the troops—even the training squads—with stones and ice: that would too much contradict the psychology of the insurrectionary masses, and the wise strategy they had shown with regard to the army. For the sake of supplementary justification for mass murders, the colors in the report are not exactly what they were, and are not laid on the way they were, in actual fact. But the essentials are reported truly and with remarkable vividness: the masses will no longer retreat, they resist with optimistic brilliance, they stay on the street even after murderous volleys, they cling, not to their lives, but to the pavement, to stones, to pieces of ice. The crowd is not only bitter, but audacious. This is because, in spite of the shooting, it keeps its faith in the army. It counts on victory and intends to have it at any cost.

The pressure of the workers upon the army is increasing—countering the pressure from the side of the authorities. The Petrograd garrison comes into the focus of events. The expectant period, which has lasted almost three days, during which it was possible for the main mass of the garrison to keep up friendly neutrality toward the insurrection, has come to an end. "Shoot the enemy!" the monarchy commands. "Don't shoot your brothers and sisters!" cry the workers. And not only that: "Come with us!" Thus in the streets and squares, by the bridges, at the barrack-gates, is waged a ceaseless struggle—now dramatic, now unnoticeable—but always a desperate struggle, for the heart of the soldier. In this struggle, in these sharp contacts between working men and women and the soldiers, under the steady crackling of rifles and machine guns, the fate of the government, of the war, of the country, is being decided.

The shooting of demonstrators increased the uncertainty among the leaders. The very scale of the movement began to seem dangerous. Even at the meeting of the Vyborg committee the evening of the 26th—that is, twelve hours before the victory—arose discussions as to whether it was not time to end the strike. This may seem astonishing. But remember, it is far easier to recognize victory the day after, than the day before. Besides, moods change frequently under the impact of events and the news of them. Discouragement quickly gives way to a flow of enthusiasm. Kayurovs and Chugurins have plenty of personal courage, but at moments a feeling of responsibility for the masses clutches them. Among the rank-and-file workers there were fewer oscillations. Reports about their moods were made to the authorities by a well-informed agent in the Bolshevik organization, Shurkanov. "Since the army units have not opposed the crowd," wrote this provocateur, "and in individual cases have even taken measures paralyzing the initiative of the police officers, the masses have got a sense of impunity, and now, after two days of unobstructed walking the streets, when the revolutionary circles have advanced the slogans 'Down with war' and 'Down with the autocracy!', the people have become convinced that the revolution has begun, that success is with the masses, that the authorities are powerless to suppress the movement because the troops are with it, that a decisive victory is near, since the troops will soon openly join the side of the revolutionary forces, that the movement begun will not subside, but will ceaselessly grow to a complete victory and a state revolution." A characterization remarkable for compactness and clarity! The report is a most valuable historic document. This did not, of course, prevent the victorious workers from executing its author.

These provocateurs, whose number was enormous, especially in Petrograd, feared, more than anyone else did, the victory of the revolution. They followed a policy of their own: in the Bolshevik conferences Shurkanov defended the most extreme actions; in his reports to the secret police he suggested the necessity of a decisive resort to firearms. It is possible that with this aim, Shurkanov tried even to exaggerate the aggressive confidence of the workers. But in the main he was right: events would soon confirm his judgment.

The leaders in both camps guessed and vacillated, for not one of them could estimate *a priori* the relation of forces. External indications ceased absolutely to serve as a measure. Indeed one of the chief features of a revolutionary crisis consists in this sharp contradiction between the present consciousness and the old forms of social relationship. A new relation of forces was mysteriously implanting itself in the consciousness of the workers and soldiers. It was precisely the government's offensive, called forth by the previous offensive of the revolutionary masses, which transformed the new relation of forces from a potential to an active state. The worker looked thirstily and commandingly into the eyes of the soldier, and the soldier anxiously and diffidently looked away. This meant that, in a way, the soldier could no longer answer for himself. The worker approached the soldier more boldly. The soldier sullenly, but without hostility—guiltily rather—refused to answer. Or sometimes—now more and more often—he answered with pretended severity in order to conceal how anxiously his heart was beating in his breast. Thus the change was accomplished. The soldier was clearly shaking off his soldiery. In doing so he could not immediately recognize himself. The authorities said that the revolution intoxicated the soldier. To the soldier it seemed, on the contrary, that he was sobering up from the opium of the barracks. Thus the decisive day was prepared—the 27th of February.

However, on the eve of that day an incident occurred which in spite of its episodic nature paints with a new color all the events of the 26th. Towards evening the fourth company of the Pavlovsky regiment of the Imperial Guard mutinied. In the written report of a police inspector the cause of the mutiny is categorically stated: "Indignation against the training squad of the same regiment which, while on duty in the Nevsky, fired on the crowd." Who informed the fourth company of this? A record has been accidentally preserved. About two o'clock in the afternoon, a handful of workers ran up to the barracks of the Pavlovsky regiment. Interrupting each other, they told about a shooting on the Nevsky. "Tell your comrades that the Pavlovtsi, too, are shooting at us—we saw soldiers in your uniform on the Nevsky." That was a burning reproach, a flaming appeal. "All looked distressed and pale." The seed fell not upon the rock. By six o'clock the fourth company had left the barracks without permission under the command of a non-commissioned officer—Who was he? His name is drowned forever among hundreds and thousands of equally heroic names—and marched to the Nevsky to recall its training squad. This was not a mere soldiers' mutiny over wormy meat; it was an act of high revolutionary initiative. On their way down, the company had an encounter with a detachment of mounted police. The soldiers opened fire. One policeman and one horse were killed; another policeman and another horse were wounded. The further path of the mutineers in the hurricane of the streets is unknown. The company returned to the barracks and aroused the entire regiment. But their arms had been hidden. According to some sources, they nevertheless got hold of thirty rifles. They were soon surrounded by the Preobrazhentsi. Nineteen Pavlovtsi were arrested and imprisoned in the fortress; the rest surrendered. According to other information, the officers on that evening found twenty-one soldiers with rifles missing. A dangerous leak! These twenty-one soldiers would be seeking allies and defenders all night long. Only the victory of the revolution could save them. The workers would surely learn from them what had happened. This was not a bad omen for tomorrow's battles.

Nabokov, one of the most prominent liberal leaders, whose truthful memoirs seem at times to be the very diary of his party and of his class, was returning home from a visit at one o'clock in the morning along the dark and watchful streets. He was "perturbed and filled with dark forebodings." It is possible that at one of the crossings he met a fugitive Pavlovetz. Both hurried past: they had nothing to say to each other. In the workers' quarters and the barracks some kept watch or conferred, others slept the half-sleep of the bivouac, or dreamed feverishly about tomorrow. Here the fugitive Pavlovetz found shelter.

How scant are the records of the mass fighting in the February days—scant even in comparison with the slim records of the October fights. In October the party directed the insurrection from day to day; in its articles, proclamations, and reports, at least the external continuity of the struggle is recorded. Not so in February. The masses had almost no leadership from above. The newspapers were silenced by the strike. Without a look back, the masses made their own history. To reconstruct a living picture of the things that happened in the streets, is almost unthinkable. It would be well if we could re-create at least the general continuity and inner order of events.

The government, which had not yet lost hold of the machinery of power, observed the events on the whole even less ably than the left parties, which, as we know, were far from brilliant in this direction. After the "successful" shootings of the 26th, the ministers took heart for an instant. At dawn of the 27th Protopopov reassuringly reported that, according to information received, "part of the workers intend to return to work." But the workers never thought of going back to the shops. Yesterday's shootings and failures had not discouraged the masses. How explain this? Apparently the losses were out-balanced by certain gains. Pouring through the streets, colliding with the enemy, pulling at the arms of soldiers, crawling under horses' bellies, attacking, scattering, leaving their corpses on the crossings, grabbing a few firearms, spreading the news, catching at rumors, the insurrectionary mass becomes a collective entity with numberless eyes, ears and antennæ. At night, returning home from the arena of struggle to the workers' quarter, it goes over the impressions of the day, and sifting away what is petty and accidental, casts its own thoughtful balance. On the night of the 27th, this balance was practically identical with the report made to the authorities by the provocateur, Shurkanov.

In the morning the workers streamed again to the factories, and in open meetings resolved to continue the struggle. Especially resolute, as always, were the Vyborgtsi. But in other districts too these morning meetings were enthusiastic. To continue the struggle! But what would that mean today? The general strike had issued in revolutionary demonstrations by immense crowds, and the demonstrations had led to a collision with the troops. To continue the struggle today would mean to summon an armed insurrection. But nobody had formulated this summons. It had grown irresistibly out of the events, but it was never placed on the order of the day by a revolutionary party.

The art of revolutionary leadership in its most critical moments consists nine-tenths in knowing how to sense the mood of the masses—just as Kayurov detected the movement of the Cossack's eyebrow, though on a larger scale. An unexcelled ability to detect the mood of the masses was Lenin's great power. But Lenin was not in Petrograd. The legal and semi-legal "socialistic" staffs, Kerensky, Cheidze, Skobelev, and all those who circled around them, pronounced warnings and opposed the movement. But even the central Bolshevik staff, composed of Shliapnikov, Zalutsky and Molotov was amazing in its helplessness and lack of initiative. In fact, the districts and barracks were left to themselves. The first proclamation to the army was released only on the 26th by one of the Social Democratic organizations close to the Bolsheviks. This proclamation, rather hesitant in character—not even containing an appeal to come over to the people—was distributed throughout all the city districts on the morning of the 27th. "However," testifies Yurenev, the leader of this organization, "the tempo of the revolutionary events was such that our slogans were already lagging behind it. By the time the leaflets had penetrated into the thick of the troops, the latter had already come over." As for the Bolshevik center—Shliapnikov, at the demand of Chugurin, one of the best worker-leaders of the February days, finally wrote an appeal to the soldiers on the morning of the 27th. Was it ever published? At best it might have come in at the finish. It could not possibly have influenced the events of February 27. We must lay it down as a general rule for those days that the higher the leaders, the further they lagged behind.

But the insurrection, not yet so named by anyone, took its own place on the order of the day. All the thoughts of the workers were concentrated on the army. "Don't you think we can get them started?" Today haphazard agitation would no longer do. The Vyborg section staged a meeting near the barracks of the Moscow regiment. The enterprise proved a failure. Is it difficult for some officer or sergeant-major to work the handle of a machine gun? The workers were scattered by a cruel fire. A similar attempt was made at the barracks of a Reserve regiment. And there too: officers with machine guns interfered between the workers and soldiers. The leaders of the workers fumed, looked for firearms, demanded them from the party. And the answer was: "The soldiers have the firearms, go get them." That they knew themselves. But how to get them? Isn't everything going to collapse all at once today? Thus came on the critical point of the struggle. Either the machine gun will wipe out the insurrection, or the insurrection will capture the machine gun.

In his recollections, Shliapnikov, the chief figure in the Petrograd center of the Bolsheviks, tells how he refused the demands of the workers for firearms—or even revolvers—sending them to the barracks to get them. He wished in this way to avoid bloody clashes between workers and soldiers, staking everything on agitation—that is, on the conquest of the soldiers by work and example. We know of no other testimony which confirms or refutes this statement of a prominent leader of those days—a statement which testifies to sidestepping rather than foresight. It would be simpler to confess that the leaders had no firearms.

There is no doubt that the fate of every revolution at a certain point is decided by a break in the disposition of the army. Against a numerous, disciplined, well-armed and ably led military force, unarmed or almost unarmed masses of the people cannot possibly gain a victory. But no deep national crisis can fail to affect the army to some extent. Thus along with the conditions of a truly popular revolution there develops a possibility—not, of course, a guarantee—of its victory. However, the going over of the army to the insurrection does not happen of itself, nor as a result of mere agitation. The army is heterogeneous, and its antagonistic elements are held together by the terror of discipline. On the very eve of the decisive hour, the revolutionary soldiers do not know how much power they have, or what influence they can exert. The working masses, of course, are also heterogeneous. But they have immeasurably more opportunity for testing their ranks in the process of preparation for the decisive encounter. Strikes, meetings, demonstrations, are not only acts in the struggle, but also measures of its force. The whole mass does not participate in the strike. Not all the strikers are ready to fight. In the sharpest moments the most daring appear in the streets. The hesitant, the tired, the conservative, sit at home. Here a revolutionary selection takes place of itself; people are sifted through the sieve of events. It is otherwise with the army. The revolutionary soldiers—sympathetic, wavering or antagonistic—are all tied together by a compulsory discipline whose threads are held, up to the last moment, in the officer's fist. The soldiers are told off daily into first and second files, but how are they to be divided into rebellious and obedient?

The psychological moment when the soldiers go over to the revolution is prepared by a long molecular process, which, like other processes of nature, has its point of climax. But how determine this point? A military unit may be wholly prepared to join the people, but may not receive the needed stimulus. The revolutionary leadership does not yet believe in the possibility of having the army on its side, and lets slip the victory. After this ripened but unrealized mutiny, a reaction may seize the army. The soldiers lose the hope which flared in their breasts; they bend their necks again to the yoke of discipline, and in a new encounter with the workers, especially at a distance, will stand opposed to the insurrection. In this process there are many elements imponderable or difficult to weigh, many crosscurrents, collective suggestions and autosuggestions. But out of this complicated web of material and psychic forces one conclusion emerges with irrefutable clarity: the more the soldiers in their mass are convinced that the rebels are really rebelling—that this is not a demonstration after which they will have to go back to the barracks and report, that this is a struggle to the death, that the people may win if they join them, and that this winning will not only guarantee impunity, but alleviate the lot of all—the more they realize this, the more willing they are to turn aside their bayonets, or go over with them to the people. In other words, the revolutionists can create a break in the soldiers' mood only if they themselves are actually ready to seize the victory at any price whatever, even the price of blood. And this highest determination never can, or will, remain unarmed.

The critical hour of contact between the pushing crowd and the soldiers who bar their way has its critical minute. That is when the gray barrier has not yet given way, still holds together shoulder to shoulder, but already wavers, and the officer, gathering his last strength of will, gives the command: "Fire!" The cry of the crowd, the yell of terror and threat, drowns the command, but not wholly. The rifles waver. The crowd pushes. Then the officer points the barrel of his revolver at the most suspicious soldier. From the decisive minute now stands out the decisive second. The death of the boldest soldier, to whom the others have involuntarily looked for guidance, a shot into the crowd by a corporal from the dead man's rifle, and the barrier closes, the guns go off of themselves, scattering the crowd into the alleys and backyards. But how many times since 1905 it has happened otherwise! At the critical moment, when the officer is ready to pull the trigger, a shot from the crowd—which has its Kayurovs and Chugurins—forestalls him. This decides not only the fate of the street skirmish, but perhaps the whole day, or the whole insurrection.

The task which Shliapnikov set himself of protecting the

workers from hostile clashes with the troops by not giving firearms to the insurrectionists, could not in any case be carried out. Before it came to these clashes with the troops, innumerable clashes had occurred with the police. The street fighting began with the disarming of the hated Pharaohs, their revolvers passing into the hands of the rebels. The revolver by itself is a weak, almost toy-like weapon against the muskets, rifles, machine guns and cannon of the enemy. But are these weapons genuinely in the hands of the enemy? To settle this question the workers demanded arms. It was a psychological question. But even in an insurrection psychic processes are inseparable from material ones. The way to the soldier's rifle leads through the revolver taken from the Pharaoh.

The feelings of the soldiers in those hours were less active than those of the workers, but not less deep. Let us recall again that the garrison consisted mainly of reserve battalions many thousand strong, destined to fill up the ranks of those at the front. These men, most of them fathers of families, had the prospect of going to the trenches when the war was lost and the country ruined. They did not want war, they wanted to go home to their farms. They knew well enough what was going on at court, and had not the slightest feeling of attachment to the monarchy. They did not want to fight with the Germans, and still less with the Petrograd workers. They hated the ruling class of the capital, who had been having a good time during the war. Among them were workers with a revolutionary past, who knew how to give a generalized expression to all these moods.

To bring the soldiers from a deep but as yet hidden revolutionary discontent to overt mutinous action—or, at least, first to a mutinous refusal to act—that was the task. On the third day of the struggle the soldiers totally ceased to be able to maintain a benevolent neutrality toward the insurrection. Only accidental fragments of what happened in those hours along the line of contact between workers and soldiers have come down to us. We heard how yesterday the workers complained passionately to the Pavlovsky regiment about the behavior of its training squad. Such scenes, conversations, reproaches, appeals, were occurring in every corner of the city. The soldiers had no more time for hesitation. They were compelled to shoot yesterday, and they would be again today. The workers will not surrender or retreat; under fire they are still holding their own. And with them their women—wives, mothers, sisters, sweethearts. Yes, and this is the very hour they had so often whispered about: "If only we could all get together. . . ." And in the moment of supreme agony, in the unbearable fear of the coming day, the choking hatred of those who are imposing upon them the executioner's rôle, there ring out in the barrack room the first voices of open indignation, and in those voices—to be forever nameless—the whole army with relief and rapture recognizes itself. Thus dawned upon the earth the day of destruction of the Romanov monarchy.

At a morning conference in the home of the indefatigable Kayurov, where over forty shop and factory representatives had assembled, a majority spoke for continuing the movement. A majority, but not all. Too bad we cannot establish what majority, but in those hours there was no time for records. Anyway, the decision was belated. The meeting was interrupted by the intoxicating news of the soldiers' insurrection and the opening of the jails. Shurkanov kissed all those present. A kiss of Judas, but not, fortunately, to be followed by a crucifixion.

One after another, from early morning, the Reserve Guard battalions mutinied before they were led out of the barracks, continuing what the 4th Company of the Pavlovsky regiment had begun the day before. In the documents, records, memoirs, this grandiose event of human history has left but a pale, dim imprint. The oppressed masses, even when they rise to the very heights of creative action, tell little of themselves and write less. And the overpowering rapture of the victory later erases memory's work. Let us take up what records there are.

The soldiers of the Volynsky regiment were the first to revolt. As early as seven o'clock in the morning a battalion commander disturbed Khabalov with a telephone call and this threatening news: the training squad—that is, the unit especially relied on to put down the insurrection—had refused to march out, its commander was killed, or had shot himself in front of the troops. The latter version, by the way, was soon rejected. Having burned their bridges behind them, the Volintzi hastened to broaden the base of the insurrection. In that lay their only salvation. They rushed into the neighboring barracks of the Litovsky and Preobrazhensky regiments "calling out" the soldiers, as strikers go from factory to factory calling out the workers. Some time after, Khabalov received a report that the Volynsky regiment had not only refused to surrender their rifles when ordered by the general, but together with the Litovsky and Preobrazhensky regiments—and what is even more alarming, "having joined the workers"—had wrecked the barracks of the political police. This meant that yesterday's experiment of the Pavlovtsi had not been in vain: the insurrection had found leaders, and at the same time a plan of action.

In the early hours of the 27th, the workers thought the solution of the problem of the insurrection infinitely more distant than it really was. It would be truer to say that they saw the problem as almost entirely ahead of them, when it was really nine-tenths behind. The revolutionary pressure of the workers on the barracks fell in with the existing revolutionary movement of the soldiers to the streets. During the day these two mighty currents united to wash out clean and carry away the walls, the roof, and later the whole groundwork of the old structure.

Chugurin was among the first to appear at the Bolshevik headquarters, a rifle in his hands, a cartridge belt over his shoulder, "all spattered up, but beaming and triumphant." Why shouldn't he beam? Soldiers with rifles in their hands are coming over to us! In some places the workers had succeeded in uniting with the soldiers, penetrating the barracks and receiving rifles and cartridges. The Vyborgtsi,[2] together with the most daring of the soldiers, outlined a plan of action: seize the police stations where the armed police have entrenched themselves; disarm all policemen; free the workers held in the police stations, and the political prisoners in the jails; rout the government troops in the city proper; unite with the still inactive troops and with the workers of other districts.

The Moscow regiment joined the uprising not without inner

[2] *Vyborgtsi* means the men of the Vyborg district—the workers—just as *Pavlovtsi* means men of the Pavlovsky regiment. In the singular, *Pavlovetz.* [Trans.]

struggle. Amazing that there was so little struggle among the regiments. The monarchist command impotently fell away from the soldier mass, and either hid in the cracks or hastened to change its colors. "At two o'clock," remembers Korolev, a worker from the "Arsenal" factory, "when the Moscow regiment marched out, we armed ourselves. . . . We took a revolver and rifle apiece, picked out a group of soldiers who came up (some of them asked us to take command and tell them what to do), and set out for Tikhvinskaia street to shoot up the police station." The workers, it seems, did not have a moment's trouble telling the soldiers "what to do."

One after another came the joyful reports of victories. Our own armored cars have appeared! With red flags flying, they are spreading terror through the districts to all who have not yet submitted. Now it will no longer be necessary to crawl under the belly of a Cossack's horse. The revolution is standing up to its full height.

Toward noon Petrograd again became the field of military action; rifles and machine guns rang out everywhere. It was not easy to tell who was shooting or where. One thing was clear: the past and the future were exchanging shots. There was much casual firing; young boys were shooting off revolvers unexpectedly acquired. The arsenal was wrecked. "They say that several tens of thousands of Brownings alone were carried off." From the burning buildings of the District Court and the police stations pillars of smoke rolled to the sky. At some points clashes and skirmishes thickened into real battles. On Sampsonievsky boulevard the workers came up to a barrack occupied by the bicycle men, some of whom crowded into the gate. "Why don't you get on the move, comrades?" The soldiers smiled—"not a good smile," one of the participants testifies—and remained silent, while the officers rudely commanded the workers to move on. The bicyclists, along with the cavalry, proved to be the most conservative part of the army in the February, as in the October revolution. A crowd of workers and revolutionary soldiers soon gathered round the fence. "We must pull out the suspicious battalion!" Someone reported that the armored cars had been sent for; perhaps there was no other way of getting these bicyclists, who had set up the machine guns. But it is hard for a crowd to wait;

it is anxiously impatient, and quite right in its impatience. Shots rang out from both sides. But the board fence stood in the way, dividing the soldiers from the revolution. The attackers decided to break down the fence. They broke down part of it and set fire to the rest. About twenty barracks came into view. The bicyclists were concentrated in two or three of them. The empty barracks were set fire to at once. Six years later Kayurov would recall: "The flaming barracks and the wreckage of the fence around them, the fire of machine guns and rifles, the excited faces of the besiegers, a truckload of armed revolutionists dashing up, and finally an armored car arriving with its gleaming gun-mouths, made a memorable and magnificent picture." This was the old tzarist, feudal, priestly, police Russia burning down, barracks and fences and all, expiring in fire and smoke, spewing out its soul with the hiccough of machine-gun shots. No wonder Kayurov, and tens, hundreds, thousands of Kayurovs, rejoiced! The arriving armored car fired several shells at the barrack where the bicyclists and officers were barricaded. The commander was killed. The officers, tearing off their epaulets and other insignia, fled through the vegetable gardens adjoining the barracks; the rest gave themselves up. This was probably the biggest encounter of the day.

The military revolt had meanwhile become epidemic. Only those did not mutiny that day who did not get around to it. Toward evening the Semenovsky regiment joined in, a regiment notorious for its brutal putting down of the Moscow uprising of 1905. Eleven years had not passed in vain. Together with the chasseurs, the Semenovtsi late at night "called out" the Izmailovtsi, whom the command were holding locked up in their barracks. This regiment, which on December 3, 1905 had surrounded and arrested the first Petrograd soviet, was even now considered one of the most backward.

The tzarist garrison of the capital, numbering 150,000 soldiers, was dwindling, melting, disappearing. By night it no longer existed.

After the morning's news of the revolt of the regiments, Khabalov still tried to offer resistance, sending against the revolution a composite regiment of about a thousand men with the most drastic orders. But the fate of that regiment has become quite a mystery. "Something impossible begins to happen on that day," the incomparable Khabalov relates after the revolution, ". . . the regiment starts, starts under a brave, a resolute officer (meaning Colonel Kutyepov), but . . . there are no results." Companies sent after that regiment also vanished, leaving no trace. The general began to draw up reserves on Palace Square, "but there were no cartridges and nowhere to get them." This is taken from Khabalov's authentic testimony before the Commission of Inquiry of the Provisional Government. What became of the punitive regiments? It is not hard to guess that as soon as they marched out they were drowned in the insurrection. Workers, women, youths, rebel soldiers, swarmed around Khabalov's troops on all sides, either considering the regiment their own or striving to make it so, and did not let them move any way but with the multitude. To fight with this thick-swarming, inexhaustible, all-penetrating mass, which now feared nothing, was as easy as to fence in dough.

Together with reports of more and more military revolts, came demands for reliable troops to put down the rebels, to defend the telephone building, the Litovsky Castle, the Marinsky Palace, and other even more sacred places. Khabalov demanded by telephone that loyal troops be sent from Kronstadt, but the commandant replied that he himself feared for the fortress. Khabalov did not yet know that the insurrection had spread to the neighboring garrisons. The general attempted, or pretended to attempt, to convert the Winter Palace into a redoubt, but the plan was immediately abandoned as unrealizable, and the last handful of "loyal" troops was transferred to the Admiralty. Here at last the dictator occupied himself with a most important and urgent business: he printed for publication the last two governmental decrees: on the retirement of Protopopov "owing to illness," and on the state of siege in Petrograd. With the latter he really had to hurry, for several hours later Khabalov's army lifted the "siege" and departed from the Admiralty for their homes. It was due only to ignorance that the revolution had not already on the evening of the 27th arrested this formidably empowered but not at all formidable general. This was done without any complications the next day.

Can it be that that was the whole resistance put up by the redoubtable Russian Empire in the face of mortal danger? Yes, that was about all—in spite of its great experience in crushing the people and its meticulously elaborated plans. When they came to themselves later, the monarchists explained the ease of the February victory of the people by the peculiar character of the Petrograd garrison. But the whole further course of the revolution refutes this explanation. True, at the beginning of the fatal year, the camarilla had already suggested to the tzar the advisability of renovating the garrison. The tzar had easily allowed himself to be persuaded that the cavalry of the Guard, considered especially loyal, "had been under fire long enough" and had earned a rest in its Petrograd barracks. However, after respectful representations from the front, the tzar agreed that four regiments of the cavalry Guard should be replaced by three crews of the naval Guard. According to Protopopov's version, this replacement was made by the command without the tzar's consent, and with treacherous design: ". . . The sailors are recruited from among the workers and constitute the most revolutionary element of the forces." But this is sheer nonsense. The highest officers of the Guard, and particularly the cavalry, were simply cutting out too good a career for themselves at the front to want to come back. Besides that, they must have thought with some dread of the punitive functions to be allotted to them. In these they would be at the head of troops totally different after their experience at the front from what they used to be on the parade grounds of the capital. As events at the front soon proved, the horse Guard at this time no longer differed from the rest of the cavalry, and the naval Guard, which was transferred to the capital, did not play an active part in the February revolution. The whole truth is that the fabric of the régime had completely decayed; there was not a live thread left.

During the 27th of February the crowd liberated without bloodshed from the many jails of the capital, all political prisoners—among them the patriotic group of the Military and Industrial Committee, which had been arrested on the 26th of January, and the members of the Petrograd Committee of the Bolsheviks, seized by Khabalov forty hours earlier. A political division occurred immediately outside the prison gates. The Menshevik-patriots set out for the Duma, where functions and places were to be assigned; the Bolsheviks marched to the districts, to the workers and soldiers, to finish with them the conquest of the capital. The enemy must have no time to breathe. A revolution, more than any other enterprise, has to be carried through to the end.

It is impossible to say who thought of leading the mutinous troops to the Tauride Palace. This political line of march was dictated by the whole situation. Naturally all the elements of radicalism not bound up with the masses gravitated toward the Tauride Palace as the center of oppositional information. Quite probably these elements, having experienced on the 27th a sudden injection of vital force, became the guides of the mutinous soldiers. This was an honorable rôle and now hardly a dangerous one. In view of its location, Potemkin's palace was well fitted to be the center of the revolution. The Tauride park is separated by just one street from the whole military community, containing the barracks of the Guard and a series of military institutions. It is true that for many years this part of the city was considered both by the government and the revolutionists to be the military stronghold of the monarchy. And so it was. But now everything had changed. The soldiers' rebellion had begun in the Guard sector. The mutinous troops had only to cross the street in order to reach the park of the Tauride Palace, which in turn was only one block from the Neva River. And beyond the Neva lies the Vyborg district, the very cauldron of the revolution. The workers need only cross Alexander's Bridge, or if that is up, walk over the ice of the river, to reach the Guards' barracks or the Tauride Palace. Thus the heterogeneous, and in its origins contradictory, northeast triangle of Petrograd—the Guards, Potemkin's palace, and the giant factories—closely interlocked—became the field of action of the revolution.

In the Tauride Palace various centers are already created, or at least sketched out—among them the field staff of the insurrection. It has no very serious character. The revolutionary officers—that is, those officers who had somehow or other, even though by mistake, got connected with the revolution in the past, but who have safely slept through the insurrection—hasten after the victory to call attention to themselves, or upon summons from others arrive "to serve the revolution." They survey the situation with profound thought and pessimistically shake their heads. These tumultuous crowds of soldiers, often unarmed, are totally unfit for battle. No artillery, no machine guns, no communications, no commanders. One strong regiment is all the enemy needs! To be sure, just now the revolutionary crowds prevent any planned maneuvers in the streets. But the workers will go home for the night, the residents will quiet down, the town will be emptied. If Khabalov were to strike with a strong regiment at the barracks, he might become master of the situation. This idea, by the way, will meet us in different versions throughout all the stages of the revolution. "Give me a strong regiment," gallant colonels will more than once exclaim to their friends, "and in two seconds I will clean up all this mess!" And some of them, as we shall see, will make the attempt. But they will all have to repeat Khabalov's words: "The regiment starts, starts under a brave officer, but . . . there are no results."

Yes, and how could there be results? The most reliable of all possible forces had been the police and the gendarmes, and the training squads of certain regiments. But these proved as pitiful before the assault of the real masses as the Battalion of St. George and the officers' training schools were to prove eight months later in October. Where could the monarchy get that salvation regiment, ready and able to enter a prolonged and desperate duel with a city of two million? The revolution seems defenseless to these verbally so enterprising colonels, because it is still terrifically chaotic. Everywhere aimless movements, conflicting currents, whirlpools of people, individuals astounded as though suddenly gone deaf, unfastened trench coats, gesticulating students, soldiers without rifles, rifles without soldiers, boys firing into the air, a thousand-voiced tumult, hurricanes of wild rumor, false alarms, false rejoicings. Enough, you would think, to lift a sword over all that chaos, and it would scatter apart and leave never a trace. But that is a crude error of vision. It is only a seeming chaos. Beneath it is proceeding an irresistible crystallization of the masses around new axes. These innumerable crowds have not yet clearly defined what they want, but they are saturated with an acid hatred of what they do not want. Behind them is an irreparable historic avalanche. There is no way back. Even if there were someone to scatter them, they would be gathering again in an hour, and the second flood would be more furious and bloodier than the first. After the February days the atmosphere of Petrograd becomes so red hot that every hostile military detachment arriving in that mighty forge, or even coming near to it, scorched by its breath, is transformed, loses confidence, becomes paralyzed, and throws itself upon the mercy of the victor without a struggle. Tomorrow General Ivanov, sent from the front by the tzar with a battalion of the Knights of St. George, will find this out. In five months the same fate will befall General Kornilov, and in eight months it will happen to Kerensky.

On the streets in the preceding days the Cossacks had seemed the most open to persuasion; it was because they were the most abused. But when it came to the actual insurrection, the cavalry once more justified its conservative reputation and lagged behind the infantry. On the 27th, it was still preserving the appearance of watchful neutrality. Though Khabalov no longer relied upon it, the revolution still feared it.

The fortress of Peter and Paul, which stands on an island in the Neva opposite the Winter Palace and the palaces of the grand dukes, remained a puzzle. Behind its walls the garrison of the fortress was, or seemed to be, a little world completely shielded from outside influences. The fortress had no permanent artillery—except for that antiquated cannon which daily announced the noon hour to Petrograd. But today field guns are set up on the walls and aimed at the bridge. What are they getting ready for? The Tauride staff has worried all night what to do about the fortress, and in the fortress they were worrying—what will the revolution do with us? By morning the puzzle is solved: "On condition that officers remain inviolable," the fortress will surrender to the Tauride Palace. Having analyzed the situation—not so difficult a thing to do—the officers of the fort hastened to forestall the inevitable march of events.

Towards evening of the 27th, a stream of soldiers, workers, students and miscellaneous people flows toward the Tauride Palace. Here they hope to find those who know everything—

to get information and instructions. From all sides ammunition is being carried by armfuls into the palace, and deposited in a room that has been converted into an arsenal. At nightfall, the revolutionary staff settles down to work. It sends out detachments to guard the railway stations, and despatches reconnoitering squads wherever danger lurks. The soldiers carry out eagerly and without a murmur, although very unsystematically, the orders of the new authorities. But they always demand a written order. The initiative in this probably came from the fragments of the military staff which had remained with the troops, or from the military clerks. But they were right; it is necessary to bring order immediately into the chaos. The staff, as well as the newborn Soviet, had as yet no seals. The revolution has still to fit itself out with the implements of bureaucratic management. In time this will be done—alas, too well.

The revolution begins a search for enemies. Arrests are made all over the city—"arbitrarily," as the Liberals will say reproachfully later. But the whole revolution is arbitrary. Streams of people are brought into the Tauride under arrest—such people as the Chairman of the State Council, ministers, policemen, secret service men, the "pro-German" countess, whole broods of gendarme officers. Several statesmen, such as Protopopov, will come of their own volition to be arrested: it is safer so. "The walls of the chamber, which had resounded to hymns in praise of absolutism, now heard but sobbing and sighs," the countess will subsequently relate. "An arrested general sank down exhausted on a near-by chair. Several members of the Duma kindly offered me a cup of tea. Shaken to the depths of his soul, the general was saying excitedly: 'Countess, we are witnessing the death of a great country.'"

Meanwhile, the great country, which had no intention of dying, marched by these people of the past, stamping its boots, clanging the butts of its rifles, rending the air with its shouts and stepping all over their feet. A revolution is always distinguished by impoliteness, probably because the ruling classes did not take the trouble in good season to teach the people fine manners.

The Tauride became the temporary field headquarters, governmental center, arsenal, and prison-fortress of the revolution, which had not yet wiped the blood and sweat from its face. Into this whirlpool some enterprising enemies also made their way. A disguised captain of gendarmes was accidentally discovered taking down notes in a corner—not for history, but for the courts-martial. The soldiers and workers wanted to end him right there. But people from the "staff" interfered, and easily led the gendarme out of the crowd. The revolution was then still good-natured—trustful and kind-hearted. It will become ruthless only after a long series of treasons, deceits and bloody trials.

The first night of the triumphant revolution was full of alarms. The improvised commissars of the railway terminals and other points, most of them chosen haphazard from the intelligentsia through personal connection, upstarts and chance acquaintances of the revolution—non-commissioned officers, especially of worker origin, would have been more useful—got nervous, saw danger on all sides, nagged the soldiers and ceaselessly telephoned to the Tauride asking for reënforcements. But in the Tauride too they were nervous. They were telephoning. They were sending out reënforcements which for the most part did not arrive. "Those who receive orders," said a member of the Tauride night staff, "do not execute them; those who act, act without orders."

The workers' districts act without orders. The revolutionary chiefs who have led out their factories, seized the police stations, "called out" the soldiers and wrecked the strongholds of the counter-revolution, do not hurry to the Tauride Palace, to the staffs, to the administrative centers. On the contrary, they jerk their heads in that direction with irony and distrust: "Those brave boys are getting in early to divide the game they didn't kill—before it's even killed." Worker-Bolsheviks, as well as the best workers of the other Left parties, spend their days on the streets, their nights in the district headquarters, keeping in touch with the barracks and preparing tomorrow's work. On the first night of victory they continue, and they enlarge, the same work they have been at for the whole five days and nights. They are the young bones of the revolution, still soft, as all revolutions are in the first days.

On the 27th, Nabokov, already known to us as a member of the Kadet center, and at that time working—a legalized deserter—at General Headquarters, went to his office as usual and stayed until three o'clock, knowing nothing of the events. Toward evening shots were heard on the Morskaia. Nabokov listened to them from his apartment. Armored cars dashed along, individual soldiers and sailors ran past, sidling along the wall. The respected liberal observed them from the side windows of his vestibule. "The telephone continued to function, and my friends, I remember, kept me in touch with what was going on during the day. At the usual time we went to bed." This man will soon become one of the inspirators of the revolutionary (!) Provisional Government, occupying the position of General Administrator. Tomorrow an unknown old man will approach him on the street—a bookkeeper, perhaps, or a teacher—bow low and remove his hat, and say to him: "Thank you for all that you have done for the people." Nabokov, with modest pride, will relate the incident himself.

Chapter VIII

WHO LED THE FEBRUARY INSURRECTION?

Lawyers and journalists belonging to the classes damaged by the revolution wasted a good deal of ink subsequently trying to prove that what happened in February was essentially a petticoat rebellion, backed up afterwards by a soldiers' mutiny and given out for a revolution. Louis XVI in his day also tried to think that the capture of the Bastille was a rebellion, but they respectfully explained to him that it was a revolution. Those who lose by a revolution are rarely inclined to call it by its real name. For that name, in spite of the efforts of spiteful reactionaries, is surrounded in the historic memory of mankind with a halo of liberation from all shackles and all prejudices. The privileged classes of every age, as also their lackeys, have always tried to declare the revolution which overthrew them, in contrast to past revolutions, a mutiny, a riot, a revolt of the rabble. Classes which have outlived themselves are not distinguished by originality.

Soon after the 27th of February attempts were also made to liken the revolution to the military coup d'état of the Young Turks, of which, as we know, they had been dreaming not a little in the upper circles of the Russian bourgeoisie. This comparison was so hopeless, however, that it was seriously opposed even in one of the bourgeois papers. Tugan-Baranovsky, an economist who had studied Marx in his youth, a Russian variety of Sombart, wrote on March 10 in the *Birzhevoe Vedomosti:*

"The Turkish revolution consisted in a victorious uprising of the army, prepared and carried out by the leaders of the army; the soldiers were merely obedient executives of the plans of their officers. But the regiments of the Guard which on February 27 overthrew the Russian throne, came without their officers . . . Not the army but the workers began the insurrection; not the generals but the soldiers came to the State Duma. The soldiers supported the workers not because they were obediently fulfilling the commands of their officers, but because . . . they felt themselves blood brothers of the workers as a class composed of toilers like themselves. The peasants and the workers—those are the two social classes which made the Russian revolution."

These words require neither correction, nor supplement. The further development of the revolution sufficiently confirmed and reënforced their meaning. In Petrograd the last day of February was the first day after the victory: a day of raptures, embraces, joyful tears, voluble outpourings; but at the same time a day of final blows at the enemy. Shots were still crackling in the streets. It was said that Protopopov's Pharaohs, not informed of the people's victory, were still shooting from the roofs. From below they were firing into attics, false windows and belfries where the armed phantoms of tzarism might still be lurking. About four o'clock they occupied the Admiralty where the last remnants of what was formerly the state power had taken refuge. Revolutionary organizations and improvised groups were making arrests throughout the town. The Schlüsselburg hard-labor prison was taken without a shot. More and more regiments were joining the revolution, both in the capital and in the environs.

The overturn in Moscow was only an echo of the insurrection in Petrograd. The same moods among the workers and soldiers, but less clearly expressed. A slightly more leftward tendency among the bourgeoisie. A still greater weakness among the revolutionary organizations than in Petrograd. When the events began on the Neva, the Moscow radical intelligentsia called a conference on the question what to do, and came to no conclusion. Only on the 27th of February strikes began in the shops and factories of Moscow, and then demonstrations. The officers told the soldiers in the barracks that a rabble was rioting in the streets and they must be put down. "But by this time," relates the soldier Shishilin, "the soldiers understood the word rabble in the opposite sense." Towards two o'clock there arrived at the building of the city duma many soldiers of various regiments inquiring how to join the revolution. On the next day the strikes increased. Crowds flowed toward the duma with flags. A soldier of an automobile company, Muralov, an old Bolshevik, an agriculturist, a good-natured and courageous giant, brought to the duma the first complete and disciplined military detachment, which occupied the wireless station and other points. Eight months later Muralov will be in command of the troops of the Moscow military district.

The prisons were opened. The same Muralov was driving an automobile truck filled with freed political prisoners: a police officer with his hand at his vizor asked the revolutionist whether it was advisable to let out the Jews also. Dzerzhinsky, just liberated from a hard labor prison and without changing his prison dress, spoke in the duma building where a soviet of deputies was already formed. The artillerist Dorofeev relates how on March 1 workers from the Siou candy factory came with banners to the barracks of an artillery brigade to fraternize with the soldiers, and how many could not contain their joy, and wept. There were cases of sniping in the town, but in general neither armed encounters nor casualties: Petrograd answered for Moscow.

In a series of provincial cities the movement began only on March 1, after the revolution was already achieved even in Moscow. In Tver the workers went from their work to the barracks in a procession and having mixed with the soldiers marched through the streets of the city. At that time they were still singing the "Marseillaise," not the "International." In Nizhni-Novgorod thousands of workers gathered round the city duma building, which in a majority of the cities played the rôle of the Tauride Palace. After a speech from the mayor the workers marched off with red banners to free the politicals from the jails. By evening, eighteen out of the twenty-one military divisions of the garrison had voluntarily come over to the revolution. In Samara and Saratov meetings were held, soviets of workers' deputies organized. In Kharkov the chief of police, having gone to the railroad station and got news of the revolution, stood up in his carriage before an excited crowd and, lifting his hat, shouted at the top of his lungs: "Long live the revolution. Hurrah!" The news came to Ekaterinoslav from Kharkov. At the head of the demonstration strode the assistant chief of police carrying in his hand a long saber as in the grand parades on saints' days. When it became finally clear that the monarchy could not rise, they began cautiously to remove the tzar's portraits from the government institutions and hide them in the attics. Anecdotes about this, both authentic and imaginary, were much passed around in liberal circles, where they had not yet lost a taste for the jocular tone when speaking of the revolution. The workers, and the soldier barracks as well, took the events in a very different way. As to a series of other provincial cities (Pskov, Orel, Rybinsk, Penza, Kazan, Tzaritsyn, and others), the *Chronicle* remarks under date of March 2: "News came of the uprising and the population joined the revolution." This description, notwithstanding its summary character, tells with fundamental truth what happened.

News of the revolution trickled into the villages from the near-by cities, partly through the authorities, but chiefly through the markets, the workers, the soldiers on furlough. The villages accepted the revolution more slowly and less enthusiastically than the cities, but felt it no less deeply. For them it was bound up with the question of war and land.

It would be no exaggeration to say that Petrograd achieved the February revolution. The rest of the country adhered to it. There was no struggle anywhere except in Petrograd. There were not to be found anywhere in the country any groups of the population, any parties, institutions, or military units which were ready to put up a fight for the old régime. This shows how ill-founded was the belated talk of the reactionaries to the effect that if there had been cavalry of the Guard in the Petersburg garrison, or if Ivanov had brought a reliable brigade from the front, the fate of the monarchy would have been different. Neither at the front nor at the rear was there a brigade or regiment to be found which was prepared to do battle for Nicholas II.

The revolution was carried out upon the initiative and by the strength of one city, constituting approximately about 1/75 of the population of the country. You may say, if you will, that this most gigantic democratic act was achieved in a most undemocratic manner. The whole country was placed before a *fait accompli.* The fact that a Constituent Assembly was in prospect does not alter the matter, for the dates and methods of convoking this national representation were determined by institutions which issued from the victorious insurrection of Petrograd. This casts a sharp light on the question of the function of democratic forms in general, and in a revolutionary epoch in particular. Revolutions have always struck such blows at the judicial fetichism of the popular will, and the blows have been more ruthless the deeper, bolder and more democratic the revolutions.

It is often said, especially in regard to the great French revolution, that the extreme centralization of a monarchy subsequently permits the revolutionary capital to think and act for the whole country. That explanation is superficial. If revolutions reveal a centralizing tendency, this is not in imitation of overthrown monarchies, but in consequence of irresistible demands of the new society, which cannot reconcile itself to particularism. If the capital plays as dominating a rôle in a revolution as though it concentrated in itself the will of the nation, that is simply because the capital expresses most clearly and thoroughly the fundamental tendencies of the new society. The provinces accept the steps taken by the capital as their own intentions already materialized. In the initiatory rôle of the centers there is no violation of democracy, but rather its dynamic realization. However, the rhythm of this dynamic has never in great revolutions coincided with the rhythm of formal representative democracy. The provinces adhere to the activity of the center, but belatedly. With the swift development of events characteristic of a revolution this produces sharp crises in revolutionary parliamentarism, which cannot be resolved by the methods of democracy. In all genuine revolutions the national representation has invariably come into conflict with the dynamic force of the revolution, whose principal seat has been the capital. It was so in the seventeenth century in England, in the eighteenth in France, in the twentieth in Russia. The rôle of the capital is determined not by the tradition of a bureaucratic centralism, but by the situation of the leading revolutionary class, whose vanguard is naturally concentrated in the chief city: this is equally true for the bourgeoisie and the proletariat.

When the February victory was fully confirmed, they began to count up the victims. In Petrograd they counted 1443 killed and wounded, 869 of them soldiers, and 60 of these officers. By comparison with the victims of any battle in the Great Slaughter these figures are suggestively tiny. The liberal press declared the February revolution bloodless. In the days of general salubrity and mutual amnesty of the patriotic parties, nobody took the trouble to establish the truth. Albert Thomas, a friend of everything victorious, even a victorious insurrection, wrote at that time about the "sunniest, most holiday-like, most bloodless Russian revolution." To be sure, he was hopeful that this revolution would remain at the disposal of the French Bourse. But after all Thomas did not invent this habit. On the 27th of June 1789, Mirabeau exclaimed: "How fortunate that this great revolution will succeed without evil-doing and without tears! . . . History has too long been telling us only of the actions of beasts of prey. . . . We may well hope that we are beginning the history of human beings." When all the three estates were united in the National Assembly the ancestors of Albert Thomas wrote: "The revolution is ended. It has not cost a drop of blood." We must acknowledge, however, that at that period blood had really not yet flowed. Not so in the February days. Nevertheless the legend of a bloodless revolution stubbornly persisted, answering the need of the liberal bourgeois to make things look as though the power had come to him of its own accord.

Although the February revolution was far from bloodless, still one cannot but be amazed at the insignificant number of victims, not only at the moment of revolution but still more in the first period after it. This revolution, we must remember, was a paying-back for oppression, persecution, taunts, vile blows, suffered by the masses of the Russian people throughout the ages! The sailors and soldiers did in some places, to be sure, take summary revenge upon the most contemptible torturers in the person of their officers, but the number of these acts of settlement was at first insignificant in comparison with the number of the old bloody insults. The masses shook off their good-naturedness only a good while later, when they were convinced that the ruling classes wanted to drag everything back and appropriate to themselves a revolution not achieved by them, just as they had always appropriated the good things of life not produced by themselves.

Tugan-Baranovsky is right when he says that the February revolution was accomplished by workers and peasants—the latter in the person of the soldiers. But there still remains the great question: Who led the revolution? Who raised the workers to their feet? Who brought the soldiers into the streets? After the victory these questions became a subject of party conflict. They were solved most simply by the universal formula: Nobody led the revolution, it happened of itself. The theory of "spontaneousness" fell in most opportunely with the minds not only of all those gentlemen who had yesterday been peacefully governing, judging, convicting, defending, trading, or commanding, and today were hastening to make up to the revolution, but also of many professional politicians and former revolutionists, who having slept through the revolution wished to think that in this they were not different from all the rest.

In his curious *History of the Russian Disorders,* General Denikin, former commander of the White Army, says of the 27th of February: "On that decisive day there were no leaders, there were only the elements. In their threatening current there were then visible neither aims, nor plans, nor slogans." The learned historian Miliukov delves no deeper than this general with a passion for letters. Before the revolution the liberal leader had declared every thought of revolution a suggestion of the German Staff. But the situation was more complicated after a revolution which had brought the liberals to power. Miliukov's task was now not to dishonor the revolution with a Hohenzollern origin, but on the contrary to withhold the honor of its initiation from revolutionists. Liberalism therefore has whole-heartedly fathered the theory of a spontaneous and impersonal revolution. Miliukov sympathetically cites the semi-liberal, semi-socialist Stankevich, a university instructor who became Political Commissar at the headquarters of the Supreme Command: "The masses moved of themselves, obeying some unaccountable inner summons . . ." writes Stankevich of the February days. "With what slogans did the soldiers come out? Who led them when they conquered Petrograd, when they burned the District Court? Not a political idea, not a revolutionary slogan, not a conspiracy, and not a revolt, but a spontaneous movement suddenly consuming the entire old power to the last remnant." Spontaneousness here acquires an almost mystic character.

This same Stankevich offers a piece of testimony in the highest degree valuable: "At the end of January, I happened in a very intimate circle to meet with Kerensky. . . . To the possibility of a popular uprising they all took a definitely negative position, fearing lest a popular mass movement once aroused might get into an extreme leftward channel and this would create vast difficulties in the conduct of the war." The views of Kerensky's circle in nowise essentially differed from those of the Kadets. The initiative certainly did not come from there.

"The revolution fell like thunder out of the sky," says the president of the Social Revolutionary party, Zenzinov. "Let us be frank: it arrived joyfully unexpected for us too, revolutionists who had worked for it through long years and waited for it always."

It was not much better with the Mensheviks. One of the journalists of the bourgeois emigration tells about his meeting in a tramcar on February 21 with Skobelev, a future minister of the revolutionary government: "This Social Democrat, one of the leaders of the movement, told me that the disorders had the character of plundering which it was necessary to put down. This did not prevent Skobelev from asserting a month later that he and his friends had made the revolution." The colors here are probably laid on a little thick, but fundamentally the position of the legal Social Democrats, the Mensheviks, is conveyed accurately enough.

Finally, one of the most recent leaders of the left wing of the Social Revolutionaries, Mstislavsky, who subsequently went over to the Bolsheviks, says of the February uprising: "The revolution caught us, the party people of those days, like the foolish virgins of the Bible, napping." It does not matter how much they resembled virgins, but it is true they were all fast asleep.

How was it with the Bolsheviks? This we have in part already seen. The principal leaders of the underground Bolshevik organization were at that time three men: the former workers Shliapnikov and Zalutsky, and the former student Molotov. Shliapnikov, having lived for some time abroad and in close association with Lenin, was in a political sense the most mature and active of these three who constituted the Bureau of the Central Committee. However, Shliapnikov's own memoirs best of all confirm the fact that the events were too much for the trio. Up to the very last hour these leaders thought that it was a question of a revolutionary manifestation, one among many, and not at all of an armed insurrection. Our friend Kayurov, one of the leaders of the Vyborg section, asserts categorically: "Absolutely no guiding initiative from the party centers was felt . . . the Petrograd Committee had been arrested and the representative of the Central Committee, Comrade Shliapnikov, was unable to give any directives for the coming day."

The weakness of the underground organizations was a direct result of police raids, which had given exceptional results amid the patriotic moods at the beginning of the war. Every organization, the revolutionary included, has a tendency to fall behind its social basis. The underground organization of the Bolsheviks at the beginning of 1917 had not yet recovered from its oppressed and scattered condition, whereas in the masses the patriotic hysteria had been abruptly replaced by revolutionary indignation.

In order to get a clear conception of the situation in the sphere of revolutionary leadership it is necessary to remember that the most authoritative revolutionists, the leaders of the left parties, were abroad and, some of them, in prison and exile. The more dangerous a party was to the old régime, the more cruelly beheaded it appeared at the moment of revolution. The Narodniks had a Duma faction headed by the nonparty radical Kerensky. The official leader of the Social Revolutionaries, Chernov, was abroad. The Mensheviks had a party faction in the Duma headed by Cheidze and Skobelev; Martov was abroad; Dan and Tseretelli, in exile. A considerable number of socialistic intellectuals with a revolutionary past were grouped around these left factions—Narodnik and

Menshevik. This constituted a kind of political staff, but one which was capable of coming to the front only after the victory. The Bolsheviks had no Duma faction: their five worker-deputies, in whom the tzarist government had seen the organizing center of the revolution, had been arrested during the first few months of the war. Lenin was abroad, Zinoviev with him; Kamenev was in exile; in exile also, the then little known practical leaders: Sverdlov, Rykov, Stalin. The Polish social democrat, Dzerzhinsky, who did not yet belong to the Bolsheviks, was at hard labor. The leaders accidentally present, for the very reason that they had been accustomed to act under unconditionally authoritative supervisors, did not consider themselves and were not considered by others capable of playing a guiding rôle in revolutionary events.

But if the Bolshevik Party could not guarantee the insurrection an authoritative leadership, there is no use talking of other organizations. This fact has strengthened the current conviction as to the spontaneous character of the February revolution. Nevertheless the conviction is deeply mistaken, or at least meaningless.

The struggle in the capital lasted not an hour, or two hours, but five days. The leaders tried to hold it back; the masses answered with increased pressure and marched forward. They had against them the old state, behind whose traditional façade a mighty power was still assumed to exist, the liberal bourgeoisie with the State Duma, the Land and City Unions, the military-industrial organizations, academies, universities, a highly developed press, and finally the two strong socialist parties who put up a patriotic resistance to the assault from below. In the party of the Bolsheviks the insurrection had its nearest organization, but a headless organization with a scattered staff and with weak illegal nuclei. And nevertheless the revolution, which nobody in those days was expecting, unfolded, and just when it seemed from above as though the movement was already dying down, with an abrupt revival, a mighty convulsion, it seized the victory.

Whence came this unexampled force of aggression and self-restraint? It is not enough to refer to bitter feelings. Bitterness alone is little. The Petersburg workers, no matter how diluted during the war years with human raw material, had in their past a great revolutionary experience. In their aggression and self-restraint, in the absence of leadership and in the face of opposition from above, was revealed a vitally well-founded, although not always expressed, estimate of forces and a strategic calculation of their own.

On the eve of the war the revolutionary layers of the workers had been following the Bolsheviks, and leading the masses after them. With the beginning of the war the situation had sharply changed: conservative groups lifted their heads, dragging after them a considerable part of the class. The revolutionary elements found themselves isolated, and quieted down. In the course of the war the situation began to change, at first slowly, but after the defeats faster and more radically. An active discontent seized the whole working class. To be sure, it was to an extent patriotically colored, but it had nothing in common with the calculating and cowardly patriotism of the possessing classes, who were postponing all domestic questions until after the victory. The war itself, its victims, its horror, its shame, brought not only the old, but also the new layers of workers into conflict with the tzarist régime. It did this with a new incisiveness and led them to the conclusion: we can no longer endure it. The conclusion was universal; it welded the masses together and gave them a mighty dynamic force.

The army had swollen, drawing into itself millions of workers and peasants. Every individual had his own people among the troops: a son, a husband, a brother, a relative. The army was no longer insulated, as before the war, from the people. One met with soldiers now far oftener; saw them off to the front, lived with them when they came home on leave, chatted with them on the streets and in the tramways about the front, visited them in the hospitals. The workers' districts, the barracks, the front, and to an extent the villages too, became communicating vessels. The workers would know what the soldiers were thinking and feeling. They had innumerable conversations about the war, about the people who were getting rich out of the war, about the generals, government, tzar and tzarina. The soldier would say about the war: To hell with it! And the worker would answer about the government: To hell with it! The soldier would say: Why then do you sit still here in the center? The worker would answer: We can't do anything with bare hands; we stubbed our toe against the army in 1905. The soldier would reflect: What if we should all start at once! The worker: That's it, all at once! Conversations of this kind before the war were conspirative and carried on by twos; now they were going on everywhere, on every occasion, and almost openly, at least in the workers' districts.

The tzar's intelligence service every once in a while took its soundings very successfully. Two weeks before the revolution a spy, who signed himself with the name Krestianinov, reported a conversation in a tramcar traversing the workers' suburb. The soldier was telling how in his regiment eight men were under hard labor because last autumn they refused to shoot at the workers of the Nobel factory, but shot at the police instead. The conversation went on quite openly, since in the workers' districts the police and the spies preferred to remain unnoticed. "'We'll get even with them,' the soldier concluded." The report reads further: "A skilled worker answered him: 'For that it is necessary to organize so that all will be like one.' The soldier answered: 'Don't you worry, we've been organized a long time. . . . They've drunk enough blood. Men are suffering in the trenches and here they are fattening their bellies!' . . . No special disturbance occurred. February 10, 1917. Krestianinov." Incomparable spy's epic. "No special disturbance occurred." They will occur, and that soon: this tramway conversation signalizes their inexorable approach.

The spontaneousness of the insurrection Mstislavsky illustrates with a curious example: When the "Union of Officers of February 27," formed just after the revolution, tried to determine with a questionnaire who first led out the Volynsky regiment, they received seven answers naming seven initiators of this decisive action. It is very likely, we may add, that a part of the initiative really did belong to several soldiers, nor is it impossible that the chief initiator fell in the street fighting, carrying his name with him into oblivion. But that does not diminish the historic importance of his nameless initiative. Still more important is another side of the matter which will carry us beyond the walls of the barrack room. The insurrection of the battalions of the Guard, flaring up a complete surprise to the liberal and legal socialist circles, was no surprise at all to the workers. Without the insurrection of the workers the Volynsky regiment would not have gone into the street. That street encounter of the workers with the Cossacks, which a lawyer observed from his window and which he communicated by telephone to the deputy, was to them both an episode in an impersonal process: a factory locust stumbled against a locust from the barracks. But it did not seem that way to the Cossack who had dared wink to the worker, nor to the worker who instantly decided that the Cossack had "winked in a friendly manner." The molecular interpenetration of the army with the people was going on continuously. The workers watched the temperature of the army and instantly sensed its approach to the critical mark. Exactly this was what gave such inconquerable force to the assault of the masses, confident of victory.

Here we must introduce the pointed remark of a liberal official trying to summarize his February observations: "It is customary to say that the movement began spontaneously, the soldiers themselves went into the street. I cannot at all agree with this. After all, what does the word 'spontaneously' mean? . . . Spontaneous conception is still more out of place in sociology than in natural science. Owing to the fact that none of the revolutionary leaders with a name was able to hang his label on the movement, it becomes not impersonal but merely nameless." This formulation of the question, incomparably more serious than Miliukov's references to German agents and Russian spontaneousness, belongs to a former Procuror who met the revolution in the position of a tzarist senator. It is quite possible that his experience in the courts permitted Zavadsky to realize that a revolutionary insurrection cannot arise either at the command of foreign agents, or in the manner of an impersonal process of nature.

The same author relates two incidents which permitted him to look as through a keyhole into the laboratory of the revolutionary process. On Friday, February 24, when nobody in the upper circles as yet expected a revolution in the near future, a tramcar in which the senator was riding turned off quite unexpectedly, with such a jar that the windows rattled and one was broken, from the Liteiny into a side street, and there stopped. The conductor told everybody to get off: "The car isn't going any farther." The passengers objected, scolded, but got off. "I can still see the face of that unanswering conductor: angrily resolute, a sort of wolf look." The movement of the tramways stopped everywhere as far as the eye could see. That resolute conductor, in whom the liberal official could already catch a glimpse of the "wolf look," must have been dominated by a high sense of duty in order all by himself to stop a car containing officials on the streets of imperial Petersburg in time of war. It was just such conductors who stopped the car of the monarchy and with practically the same words —this car does not go any farther!—and who ushered out the bureaucracy, making no distinction in the rush of business between a general of gendarmes and a liberal senator. The conductor on the Liteiny boulevard was a conscious factor of history. It had been necessary to educate him in advance.

During the burning of the District Court a liberal jurist from the circle of that same senator started to express in the street his regret that a roomful of judicial decisions and notarial archives was perishing. An elderly man of somber aspect dressed as a worker angrily objected: "We will be able to divide the houses and the lands ourselves, and without your archives." Probably the episode is rounded out in a literary manner. But there were plenty of elderly workers like that in the crowd, capable of making the necessary retort. They themselves had nothing to do with burning the District Court: why burn it? But at least you could not frighten them with "excesses" of this kind. They were arming the masses with the necessary ideas not only against the tzarist police, but against liberal jurists who feared most of all lest there should burn up in the fire of the revolution the notarial deeds of property. Those nameless, austere statesmen of the factory and street did not fall out of the sky: they had to be educated.

In registering the events of the last days of February the Secret Service also remarked that the movement was "spontaneous," that is, had no planned leadership from above; but they immediately added: "with the generally propagandized condition of the proletariat." This appraisal hits the bull's-eye: the professionals of the struggle with the revolution, before entering the cells vacated by the revolutionists, took a much closer view of what was happening than the leaders of liberalism.

The mystic doctrine of spontaneousness explains nothing. In order correctly to appraise the situation and determine the moment for a blow at the enemy, it was necessary that the masses or their guiding layers should make their examination of historical events and have their criteria for estimating them. In other words, it was necessary that there should be not masses in the abstract, but masses of Petrograd workers and Russian workers in general, who had passed through the revolution of 1905, through the Moscow insurrection of December 1905, shattered against the Semenovsky Regiment of the Guard. It was necessary that throughout this mass should be scattered workers who had thought over the experience of 1905, criticized the constitutional illusions of the liberals and Mensheviks, assimilated the perspectives of the revolution, meditated hundreds of times about the question of the army, watched attentively what was going on in its midst—workers capable of making revolutionary inferences from what they observed and communicating them to others. And finally, it was necessary that there should be in the troops of the garrison itself progressive soldiers, seized, or at least touched, in the past by revolutionary propaganda.

In every factory, in each guild, in each company, in each tavern, in the military hospital, at the transfer stations, even in the depopulated villages, the molecular work of revolutionary thought was in progress. Everywhere were to be found the interpreters of events, chiefly from among the workers, from whom one inquired, "What's the news?" and from whom one awaited the needed words. These leaders had often been left to themselves, had nourished themselves upon fragments of revolutionary generalizations arriving in their hands by various routes, had studied out by themselves between the lines of the liberal papers what they needed. Their class instinct was refined by a political criterion, and though they did not think all their ideas through to the end, nevertheless their thought ceaselessly and stubbornly worked its way in a single direction. Elements of experience, criticism, initiative, self-sacrifice, seeped down through the mass and created, invisibly to a superficial glance but no less decisively, an inner mechanics of the revolutionary movement as a conscious process. To the smug politicians of liberalism and tamed socialism everything that happens among masses is customarily represented as an instinctive process, no matter whether they are dealing with an anthill or a beehive. In reality the thought which was drilling through the thick of the working class was far bolder, more penetrating, more conscious, than those little ideas by which the educated classes live. Moreover, this thought was more scientific: not only because it was to a considerable degree fertilized with the methods of Marxism, but still more because it was ever nourishing itself on the living experience of the masses which were soon to take their place on the revolutionary arena. Thoughts are scientific if they correspond to an objective process and make it possible to influence that process and guide it. Were these qualities possessed in the slightest degree by the ideas of those government circles who were inspired by the Apocalypse and believed in the dreams of Rasputin? Or maybe the ideas of the liberals were scientifically grounded, who hoped that a backward Russia, having joined the scrimmage of the capitalist giants, might win at one and the same time victory and parliamentarism? Or maybe the intellectual life of those circles of the intelligentsia was scientific, who slavishly adapted themselves to this liberalism, senile since childhood, protecting their imaginary independence the while with long-dead metaphors? In truth here was a kingdom of spiritual inertness, specters, superstition and fictions, a kingdom, if you will, of "spontaneousness." But have we not in that case a right to turn this liberal philosophy of the February revolution exactly upside down? Yes, we have a right to say: At the same time that the official society, all that many-storied superstructure of ruling classes, layers, groups, parties and cliques, lived from day to day by inertia and automatism, nourishing themselves with the relics of worn-out ideas, deaf to the inexorable demands of evolution, flattering themselves with phantoms and foreseeing nothing—at the same time, in the working masses there was taking place an independent and deep process of growth, not only of hatred for the rulers, but of critical understanding of their impotence, an accumulation of experience and creative consciousness which the revolutionary insurrection and its victory only completed.

To the question, Who led the February revolution? we can then answer definitely enough: Conscious and tempered workers educated for the most part by the party of Lenin. But we must here immediately add: This leadership proved sufficient to guarantee the victory of the insurrection, but it was not adequate to transfer immediately into the hands of the proletarian vanguard the leadership of the revolution.

Chapter IX

THE PARADOX OF THE FEBRUARY REVOLUTION

The insurrection triumphed. But to whom did it hand over the power snatched from the monarchy? We come here to the central problem of the February revolution: Why and how did the power turn up in the hands of the liberal bourgeoisie?

In Duma circles and in bourgeois "society" no significance was attributed to the agitation beginning the 23rd of February. The liberal deputies and patriotic journalists were assembling in drawing rooms as before, talking over the questions of Trieste and Fiume, and again confirming Russia's need of the Dardanelles. When the decree dissolving the Duma was already signed, a Duma commission was still hastily considering the question of turning over the food problem to the city administration. Less than twelve hours before the insurrection of the battalions of the Guard, the Society for Slavic Reciprocity was peacefully listening to its annual report. "Only when I had returned home on foot from that meeting," remembers one of the deputies, "I was struck by some sort of awesome silence and emptiness in the usually lively streets." That awesome emptiness was forming around the old ruling classes and already oppressing the hearts of their future inheritors.

By the 26th the seriousness of the movement had become clear both to the government and to the liberals. On that day negotiations about a compromise were going on between the tzar's ministers and members of the Duma, negotiations from which even subsequently the liberals never lifted the curtain.

Protopopov states in his testimony that the leaders of the Duma bloc demanded as formerly the naming of new ministers from among people enjoying social confidence: "This measure perhaps will pacify the people." But the 26th created, as we know, a certain stoppage in the development of the revolution, and for a brief moment the government felt firmer. When Rodzianko called on Golytsin to persuade him to resign, the Premier pointed in answer to a portfolio on his desk in which lay the completed edict dissolving the Duma, with the signature of Nicholas but without a date. Golytsin put in the date. How could the government decide upon such a step at the moment of growing pressure from the revolution? Upon this question the ruling bureaucrats long ago arrived at a firm conviction. "Whether we have a bloc or not, it is all the same to the workers' movement. We can handle that movement by other means, and up till now the Ministry of the Interior has managed to deal with it." Thus Goremykin had spoken in August 1915. On the other hand, the bureaucracy believed that the Duma, in case of its dissolution, would not venture upon any bold step. Again in August 1915, in discussing the question of dissolving a discontented Duma, the Minister of the Interior, Prince Sherbatov, had said: "The Duma will hardly venture upon direct disobedience. The vast majority are after all cowards and are trembling for their hides." The prince expressed himself none too nicely, but in the long run correctly. In its struggle with the liberal opposition, then, the bureaucracy felt plenty of firm ground under its feet.

On the morning of the 27th, the Deputies, alarmed at the mounting events, assembled at a regular session. The majority learned only here that the Duma had been dissolved. The news seemed the more surprising as on the very day before they had been carrying on peace negotiations with the ministers. "And nevertheless," writes Rodzianko with pride, "the Duma submitted to the law, still hoping to find a way out of the tangled situation, and passed no resolution that it would not disperse, or that it would illegally continue its sessions." The deputies gathered at a private conference in which they made confessions of impotence to each other. The moderate liberal Shidlovsky subsequently remembered, not without a malicious pleasure, a proposal made by an extreme left Kadet,

Nekrasov, a future colleague of Kerensky, "to establish a military dictatorship, handing over the whole power to a popular general." At that time a practical attempt at salvation was undertaken by the leaders of the Progressive Bloc, not present at this private conference of the Duma. Having summoned the Grand Duke Mikhail to Petrograd, they proposed to him to take upon himself the dictatorship, to "impel" the personal staff of the government to resign, and to demand of the tzar by direct wire that he "grant" a responsible ministry. In those hours, when the uprising of the first Guard regiments was beginning, the liberal bourgeoisie were making a last effort to put down the insurrection with the help of a dynastic dictator, and at the same time at the expense of the revolution to enter into an agreement with the monarchy. "The hesitation of the grand duke," complains Rodzianko, "contributed to the letting slip of the favorable moment."

How easily a radical intelligentsia believes whatever it wants to, is testified by a non-party socialist, Sukhanov, who begins in this period to play a certain political rôle in the Tauride Palace. "They told me the fundamental political news of those morning hours of that unforgettable day," he relates in his extensive memoirs: "The decree dissolving the State Duma had been promulgated, and the Duma had answered with a refusal to disperse, electing a Provisional Committee." This is written by a man who hardly ever left the Tauride Palace, and was there continually buttonholing his deputy friends. Miliukov in his history of the revolution, following Rodzianko, categorically declares: "There was adopted after a series of hot speeches a resolution not to leave Petrograd, but no resolution that the State Duma should as an institution 'not disperse,' as the legend runs." "Not to disperse" would have meant to take upon themselves, however belatedly, a certain initiative. "Not to leave Petrograd" meant to wash their hands of the matter and wait to see which way the course of events would turn. The credulousness of Sukhanov has, by the way, mitigating circumstances. The rumor that the Duma had adopted a revolutionary resolution not to submit to the tzar's decree was slipped in hurriedly by the Duma journalists in their information bulletin, the only paper published at that time owing to the general strike. Since the insurrection triumphed during that day the deputies were in no hurry to correct this mistake, being quite willing to sustain the illusions of their "left" friends. They did not in fact undertake to establish the facts of the matter until they were out of the country. The episode seems secondary, but it is full of meaning. The revolutionary rôle of the Duma on the 27th of February was a complete myth, born of the political credulity of the radical intelligentsia delighted and frightened by the revolution, distrusting the ability of the masses to carry the business through, and eager to lean as quickly as possible toward the enfranchised bourgeoisie.

In the memoirs of the deputies belonging to the Duma majority, there is preserved by good luck a story of how the Duma did meet the revolution. According to the account of Prince Mansyrev, one of the right Kadets, among the deputies who assembled in great numbers on the morning of the 27th there were no members of the praesidium, no leaders of parties, nor heads of the Progressive Bloc: they already knew of the dissolution and the insurrection and had preferred as long as possible to refrain from showing their heads. Moreover, at just that time they were, it seems, negotiating with Mikhail about the dictatorship. "A general consternation and bewilderment prevailed in the Duma," says Mansyrev. "Even lively conversations ceased, and in their place were heard sighs and brief ejaculations like 'It's come,' or indeed frank expressions of fear for life." Thus speaks a very moderate deputy who sighed the loudest of all. At two o'clock in the afternoon, when the leaders had found themselves obliged to appear in the Duma, the secretary of the praesidium brought in the joyful but ill-founded news: "The disorders will soon be put down, because measures have been taken." It is possible that by "measures" was meant the negotiations for a dictatorship, but the Duma was downcast and awaited a decisive word from the leader of the Progressive Bloc. "We cannot adopt any decision at the present moment," Miliukov announced, "because the extent of the disorders is unknown to us; likewise it is unknown upon which side a majority of the local troops, workers and social organizations will take their stand. It is necessary to gather accurate information about this, and then will be time enough to judge the situation. At present it is too soon." At two o'clock in the afternoon of February 27 it is still for liberalism "too soon"! "Gather information" means wash your own hands and await the outcome of the struggle. But Miliukov had not ended his speech—which, by the way, he began with a view to ending in nothing—when Kerensky came running into the hall in high excitement: An enormous crowd of people and soldiers is coming to the Tauride Palace, he announces, and intends to demand of the Duma that it seize the power in its hands! The radical deputy knows accurately just what the enormous crowd of people is going to demand. In reality it is Kerensky himself who first demands that the power shall be seized by a Duma which is still hoping in its soul that the insurrection may yet be put down. Kerensky's announcement is met with "general bewilderment and dismayed looks." He has however not finished speaking when a frightened Duma attendant, rushing in, interrupts him: the advanced detachment of the soldiers has already reached the Palace, a detachment of sentries stopped them at the entrance, the chief of the sentries, it seems, was heavily wounded. A minute later it transpires that the soldiers have entered the Palace. It will be declared later in speeches and articles that the soldiers came to greet the Duma and swear loyalty to it, but right now everything is in mortal panic. The water is up to their necks. The leaders whisper together. We must get a breathing space. Rodzianko hastily introduces a proposal, suggested to him by somebody, that they form a Provisional Committee. Affirmative cries. But they all want to get out of there as quickly as possible. No time for voting. The president, no less frightened than the others, proposes that they turn over the formation of the committee to the council of elders. Again affirmative cries from the few still remaining in the hall. The majority have already vanished. Such was the first reaction of the Duma, dissolved by the tzar, to the victory of the insurrection.

At that time the revolution was creating in the same building, only in a less showy part of it, another institution. The revolutionary leaders did not have to invent it; the experience of the *Soviets* of 1905 was forever chiseled into the consciousness of the workers. At every lift of the movement, even in war time, the idea of soviets was almost automatically reborn. And although the appraisal of the rôle of the soviets was different among Bolsheviks and Mensheviks—the Social Revolutionaries had in general no stable appraisals—the form of organization itself stood clear of all debate. The Mensheviks liberated from prison, members of the Military-Industrial Committee, meeting in the Tauride Palace with leaders of the Trade Union and Coöperative movements, likewise of the right wing, and with the Menshevik deputies of the Duma, Cheidze and Skobelev, straightway formed a "Provisional Executive Committee of the Soviet of Workers' Deputies," which in the course of the day was filled out principally with former revolutionists who had lost connection with the masses but still preserved their "names." This Executive Committee, including also Bolsheviks in its staff, summoned the workers to elect deputies at once. The first session was appointed for the same evening in the Tauride Palace. It actually met at nine o'clock and ratified the staff of the Executive Committee, supplementing it with official representatives from all the socialist parties. But not here lay the significance of this first meeting of representatives of the victorious proletariat of the capital. Delegates from the mutinied regiments made speeches of greeting at this meeting. Among their number were completely gray soldiers, shell-shocked as it were by the insurrection, and still hardly in control of their tongues. But they were just the ones who found the words which no orator could find. That was one of the most moving scenes of the revolution, now first feeling its power, feeling the unnumbered masses it has aroused, the colossal tasks, the pride in success, the joyful failing of the heart at the thought of the morrow which is to be still more beautiful than today. The revolution still has no ritual, the streets are in smoke, the masses have not yet learned the new songs. The meeting flows on without order, without shores, like a river at flood. The Soviet chokes in its own enthusiasm. The revolution is mighty but still naïve, with a childish naïveness.

At this first session it was decided to unite the garrison with the workers in a general Soviet of Workers' and Soldiers' Deputies. Who first proposed this resolution? It probably arose from various, or rather from all sides, as an echo of that fraternization of workers and soldiers which had this day decided the fate of the revolution. From the moment of its formation the

Soviet, in the person of its Executive Committee, begins to function as a sovereign. It elects a temporary food commission and places it in charge of the mutineers and of the garrison in general. It organizes parallel with itself a Provisional revolutionary staff—everything was called provisional in those days—of which we have already spoken above. In order to remove financial resources from the hands of the officials of the old power, the Soviet decides to occupy the State Bank, the Treasury, the Mint and the Printing Office with a revolutionary guard. The tasks and functions of the Soviet grow unceasingly under pressure from the masses. The revolution finds here its indubitable center. The workers, the soldiers, and soon also the peasants, will from now on turn only to the Soviet. In their eyes the Soviet becomes the focus of all hopes and all authority, an incarnation of the revolution itself. But representatives of the possessing classes will also seek in the Soviet, with whatever grindings of teeth, protection and counsel in the resolving of conflicts.

However, even in those very first days of victory, when the new power of the revolution was forming itself with fabulous speed and inconquerable strength, those socialists who stood at the head of the Soviet were already looking around with alarm to see if they could find a real "boss." They took it for granted that the power ought to pass to the bourgeoisie. Here the chief political knot of the new régime is tied: one of its threads leads into the chamber of the Executive Committee of workers and soldiers, the other into the central headquarters of the bourgeois parties.

The Council of the Elders at three o'clock in the afternoon, when the victory was already fully assured in the capital, elected a "Provisional Committee of Members of the Duma" made up from the parties of the Progressive Bloc with the addition of Cheidze and Kerensky. Cheidze declined, Kerensky wiggle-waggled. The designation prudently indicated that it was not a question of an official committee of the State Duma, but a private committee of a conference of members of the Duma. The leaders of the Progressive Bloc thought to the very end of but one thing: how to avoid responsibility and not tie their own hands. The task of the committee was defined with meticulous equivocation: "The restoration of order and conducting of negotiations with institutions and persons." Not a word as to the kind of order which those gentlemen intended to restore, nor with what institutions they intended to negotiate. They were not yet openly reaching out their hands toward the bear's hide: what if he is not killed but only badly wounded? Only at eleven o'clock in the evening of the 27th, when, as Miliukov acknowledged, "the whole scope of the revolutionary movement had become clear, did the Provisional Committee decide upon a further step, and take in its hands the power which had fallen from the hands of the government." Imperceptibly the new institution changed from a committee of the members of the Duma to a committee of the Duma itself. There is no better means of preserving the state juridical succession than forgery. But Miliukov remains silent about the chief thing: the leaders of the Executive Committee of the Soviet, created during that day, had already appeared before the Provisional Committee and insistently demanded that it take the power into its hands. This friendly push had its effect. Miliukov subsequently explained the decision of the Duma Committee by saying that the government was supposed to be sending loyal troops against the insurrectionists, "and on the streets of the capital it threatened to come to actual battle." In reality the government was already without troops, the revolution was wholly in the past. Rodzianko subsequently wrote that in case they had declined the power, "the Duma would have been arrested and killed off to the last man by the mutinied troops, and the power would have gone immediately to the Bolsheviks." That is, of course, an inept exaggeration, wholly in the character of the respected Lord Chamberlain; but it unmistakably reflects the feelings of the Duma, which regarded the transfer of power to itself as an act of political rape.

With such feelings the decision was not easily arrived at. Rodzianko especially stormed and vacillated, putting a question to the others: "What will this be? Is it a rebellion or not a rebellion?" The monarchist deputy Shulgin answered him, according to his own report: "There is no rebellion in this at all; take the power as a loyal subject . . . If the ministers have run away somebody has got to take their place . . . There may be two results: Everything quiets down—the sovereign names a new government, we turn over the power to him. Or it doesn't quiet down. In that case if we don't take the power, others will take it, those who have already elected some sort of scoundrels in the factories. . . ." We need not take offense at the low-class abuse directed by the reactionary gentleman toward the workers: the revolution had just firmly stepped on the tails of all these gentlemen. The moral is clear: if the monarchy wins, we are with it; if the revolution wins, we will try to plunder it.

The conference lasted long. The democratic leaders were anxiously waiting for a decision. Finally, Miliukov came out of the office of Rodzianko. He wore a solemn expression. Approaching the Soviet delegation Miliukov announced: "The decision is reached, we will take the power. . . ." "I did not inquire whom he meant by *we*," relates Sukhanov with rapture, "I asked nothing further, but I felt with all my being, as they say, a new situation. I felt that the ship of the revolution, tossed in the squall of those hours by the complete caprice of the elements, had put up a sail, acquired stability and regularity in its movements amid the terrible storm and the rocking." What a high-flying formula for a prosaic recognition of the slavish dependence of the petty bourgeois democracy upon capitalistic liberalism! And what a deadly mistake in political perspective. The handing over of power to the liberals not only will not give stability to the ship of state, but, on the contrary, will become from that moment a source of headlessness of the revolution, enormous chaos, embitterment of the masses, collapse of the front, and in the future extreme bitterness of the civil war.

If you look only backward, to past ages, the transfer of power to the bourgeoisie seems sufficiently regular: in all past revolutions those who fought on the barricades were workers, apprentices, in part students, and the soldiers came over to their side. But afterwards the solid bourgeoisie, having cautiously watched the barricades through their windows, gathered up the power. But the February revolution of 1917 was distinguished from former revolutions by the incomparably higher social character and political level of the revolutionary class, by the hostile distrust of the insurrectionists toward the liberal bourgeoisie, and the consequent formation at the very moment of victory of a new organ of revolutionary power, the Soviet, based upon the armed strength of the masses. In these circumstances the transfer of power to a politically isolated and unarmed bourgeoisie demands explanation.

First of all, we must examine more closely the correlation of forces which resulted from the revolution. Was not the Soviet democracy compelled by the objective situation to renounce the power in favor of the big bourgeoisie? The bourgeoisie itself did not think so. We have already seen that it not only did not expect power from the revolution, but on the contrary foresaw in it a mortal danger to its whole social situation. "The moderate parties not only did not desire a revolution," writes Rodzianko, "but were simply afraid of it. In particular the Party of the People's Freedom, 'the Kadets,' as a party standing at the left wing of the moderate group, and therefore having more than the rest a point of contact with the revolutionary parties of the country, was more worried by the advancing catastrophe than all the rest." The experience of 1905 had too significantly hinted to the liberals that a victory of the workers and peasants might prove no less dangerous to the bourgeoisie than to the monarchy. It would seem that the course of the February insurrection had only confirmed this foresight. However formless in many respects may have been the political ideas of the revolutionary masses in those days, the dividing line between the toilers and the bourgeoisie was at any rate implacably drawn.

Instructor Stankevich who was close to liberal circles—a friend, not an enemy of the Progressive Bloc—characterizes in the following way the mood of those circles on the second day after the overturn which they had not succeeded in preventing: "Officially they celebrated, eulogized the revolution, cried 'Hurrah!' to the fighters for freedom, decorated themselves with red ribbons and marched under red banners . . . But in their souls, in their conversations tête-à-tête, they were horrified, they shuddered, they felt themselves captives in the hands of hostile elements traveling an unknown road. Unforgettable is the figure of Rodzianko, that portly lord and imposing personage, when, preserving a majestic dignity but with an expression of deep suffering despair frozen on his pale face, he made his way through a crowd of dishevelled soldiers in the corridor of the Tauride Palace. Officially it was recorded: The soldiers have come to support the Duma in its struggle with the government. But actually the Duma had been abolished from the very first day. And the same expression was on the faces of all the members of the Provisional Committee of the Duma and those circles which surrounded it. They say that the representatives of the Progressive Bloc in their own homes wept with impotent despair."

This living testimony is more precious than any sociological research into the correlation of forces. According to his own tale, Rodzianko trembled with impotent indignation when he saw unknown soldiers, "at whose orders is not recorded" arresting the officials of the old régime and bringing them to the Duma. The Lord Chamberlain turned out to be something in the nature of a jailer in relation to people, with whom he had, to be sure, his differences, but who nevertheless remained people of his own circle. Shocked by this "arbitrary" action, Rodzianko invited the arrested Minister Sheglovitov into his office, but the soldiers brusquely refused to turn over to him the hated official. "When I tried to show my authority," relates Rodzianko, "the soldiers surrounded their captive and with the most challenging and insolent expression pointed to their rifles, after which without more ado they led Sheglovitov away I know not where." Would it be possible to confirm more absolutely Stankevich's assertion that the regiments supposedly coming to support the Duma, in reality abolished it?

That the power was from the very first moment in the hands of the Soviet—upon that question the Duma members less than anybody else could cherish any illusion. The Octobrist deputy Shidlovsky, one of the leaders of the Progressive Bloc, relates how, "The Soviet seized all the Post and Telegraph bureaus, the wireless, all the Petrograd railroad stations, all the printing establishments, so that without its permission it was impossible to send a telegram, to leave Petrograd, or to print an appeal." In this unequivocal characterization of the correlation of forces, it is necessary to introduce one slight correction: the "seizure" by the Soviet of the telegraph, railroad stations, printing establishments, etc., meant merely that the workers and clerks in those enterprises refused to submit to anybody but the Soviet.

The plaint of Shidlovsky is admirably illustrated by an incident which occurred at the very height of the negotiations about the power between the leaders of the Soviet and the Duma. Their joint session was interrupted by an urgent communication from Pskov, where after his railroad wanderings the tzar had now come to a stand, stating that they wanted Rodzianko on the direct wire. The all-powerful President of the Duma declared that he would not go to the telegraph office alone. "Let some of these messieurs soldiers' and workers' deputies give me a bodyguard or go with me, otherwise I will be arrested there in the telegraph office. Look here, you've got the power and the sovereignty," he continued excitedly, "you can, of course, arrest me . . . maybe you are going to arrest us all, how do we know?" This happened on the 1st of March, less than twenty-four hours after the power was "taken over" by the Provisional Committee with Rodzianko at its head.

How did it happen then that in such a situation the liberals turned out to be in power? How and by whom were they authorized to form a government as the result of a revolution which they had dreaded, which they resisted, which they tried to put down, which was accomplished by masses completely hostile to them, and accomplished with such audacity and decisiveness that the Soviet of Workers and Soldiers arising from the insurrection became the natural, and by all unequivocally recognized, master of the situation?

Let us listen now to the other side, to those who surrendered the power. "The people did not gravitate toward the State Duma," writes Sukhanov of the February days, "they were not interested in it, and never thought of making it either politically or technically the center of the movement." This acknowledgment is the more remarkable in that its author will soon devote all his force to getting the power handed over to a committee of the State Duma. "Miliukov perfectly understood," says Sukhanov further, speaking of the negotiations of March 1, "that the Executive Committee was in a perfect position either to give the power to the bourgeois government, or not give it." Could it be more categorically expressed? Could a political situation be clearer? And nevertheless Sukhanov, in direct contradiction to the situation and to himself, immediately adds: "The power destined to replace tzarism must be only a bourgeois power . . . we must steer our course by this principle. Otherwise the uprising will not succeed and the revolution will collapse." The revolution will collapse without Rodzianko!

The problem of the living relations of social forces is here replaced by an *a priori* scheme and a conventional terminology: and this is the very essence of the doctrinairism of the intelligentsia. But we shall see later that this doctrinairism was by no means Platonic: it fulfilled a very real political function, although with blindfolded eyes.

We have quoted Sukhanov for a reason. In that first period the inspirer of the Executive Committee was not its president, Cheidze, an honest and limited provincial, but this very Sukhanov, a man, generally speaking, totally unsuited for revolutionary leadership. Semi-Narodnik, semi-Marxist, a conscientious observer rather than a statesman, a journalist rather than a revolutionist, a rationalizer rather than a journalist—he was capable of standing by a revolutionary conception only up to the time when it was necessary to carry it into action. A passive internationalist during the war, he decided on the very first day of the revolution that it was necessary just as quickly as possible to toss the power and the war over to the bourgeoisie. As a theorist—that is, at least in his feeling of the need that things should be reasoned out, if not in his ability to fulfill it—he stood above all the then members of the Executive Committee. But his chief strength lay in his ability to translate into a language of doctrinairism the organic traits of all that many-colored and yet nevertheless homogeneous brotherhood: distrust of their own powers, fear of the masses, and a heartily respectful attitude toward the bourgeoisie. Lenin described Sukhanov as one of the best representatives of the petty bourgeoisie, and that is the most flattering thing that can be said of him.

Only in this connection it must not be forgotten that the question is here of a new capitalist type of petty bourgeoisie, of industrial, commercial and bank clerks, the functionaries of capital on one side, and the workers' bureaucracy on the other—that is of that *new middle caste,* in whose name the well-known German social democrat Edward Bernstein undertook at the end of the last century a revision of the revolutionary conceptions of Marx. In order to answer the question how a revolution of workers and peasants came to surrender the power to the bourgeoisie, it is necessary to introduce into the political chain an intermediate link: the petty bourgeois democrats and socialists of the Sukhanov type, journalists and politicians of the new middle caste, who had taught the masses that the bourgeoisie is an enemy, but themselves feared more than anything else to release the masses from the control of that enemy. The contradiction between the character of the revolution and the character of the power that issued from it, is explained by the contradictory character of this new petty bourgeois partition-wall between the revolutionary masses and the capitalist bourgeoisie. In the course of further events the political rôle of this petty bourgeois democracy of the new type will fully open before us. For the time being we will limit ourselves to a few words.

A minority of the revolutionary class actually participates in the insurrection, but the strength of that minority lies in the support, or at least sympathy, of the majority. The active and militant minority inevitably puts forward under fire from the enemy its more revolutionary and self-sacrificing element. It is thus natural that in the February fights the worker-Bolsheviks occupied the leading place. But the situation changes the moment the victory is won and its political fortification begins. The elections to the organs and institutions of the victorious revolution attract and challenge infinitely broader masses than those who battled with arms in their hands. This is true not only of general democratic institutions like the city dumas and zemstvos, or later on, the Constituent Assembly, but also of class institutions, like the Soviet of Workers' Deputies. An overwhelming majority of the workers, Menshevik, Social Revolutionary and non-party, supported the Bolsheviks at the moment of direct grapple with tzarism. But only a small minority of the workers understood that the Bolsheviks were different from other socialist parties. At the same time, however, all the workers drew a sharp line between themselves and the bourgeoisie. This fact determined the political situation after the victory. The workers elected socialists, that is, those who were not only against the monarchy, but against the bourgeoisie. In doing this they made almost no distinction between the three socialist parties. And since the Mensheviks and Social Revolutionaries comprised infinitely larger ranks of the intelligentsia—who came pouring in from all sides—and thus got into their hands immediately an immense staff of agitators, the elections, even in shops and factories, gave them an enormous majority. An impulse in the same direction, but an incomparably stronger one, came from the awakening army. On the fifth day of the insurrection the Petrograd garrison followed the workers. After the victory it found itself summoned to hold elections for the Soviet. The soldiers trustfully elected those who had been for the revolution against monarchist officers, and who knew how to say this out loud: these were volunteers, clerks, assistant-surgeons, young war time officers from the intelligentsia, petty military officials—that is, the lowest layers of that *new middle caste.* All of them almost to the last man inscribed themselves, beginning in March, in the party of the Social Revolutionaries, which with its intellectual formlessness perfectly expressed their intermediate social situation and their limited political outlook. The representation of the garrison thus turned out to be incomparably more moderate and bourgeois than the soldier masses. But the latter were not conscious of this difference: it would reveal itself to them only during the experience of the coming months. The workers, on their part, were trying to cling as closely as possible to the soldiers, in order to strengthen their blood-bought union and more permanently arm the revolution. And since the spokesmen of the army were predominantly half-baked Social Revolutionaries, this fact could not help raising the authority of that party along with its ally, the Mensheviks, in the eyes of the workers themselves. Thus resulted the predominance in the soviets of the two Compromise parties. It is sufficient to remark that even in the soviet of the Vyborg district the leading rôle in those first times belonged to the worker-Mensheviks. Bolshevism in that period was still only simmering in the depths of the revolution. Thus the official Bolsheviks, even in the Petrograd Soviet, represented an insignificant minority, who had moreover none too clearly defined its tasks.

Thus arose the paradox of the February revolution. The power was in the hands of the democratic socialists. It had not been seized by them accidentally by way of a Blanquist coup; no, it was openly delivered to them by the victorious masses of the people. Those masses not only did not trust or support the bourgeoisie, but they did not even distinguish them from the nobility and the bureaucracy. They put their weapons at the disposal only of the soviets. Meanwhile the socialists, having so easily arrived at the head of the soviets, were worrying about only one question: Will the bourgeoisie, politically isolated, hated by the masses and hostile through and through to the revolution, consent to accept the power from our hands? Its consent must be won at any cost. And since obviously a bourgeoisie cannot renounce its bourgeois program, we, the "socialists," will have to renounce ours: we will have to keep still about the monarchy, the war, the land, if only the bourgeoisie will accept the gift of power. In carrying out this operation, the "socialists," as though to ridicule themselves, continued to designate the bourgeoisie no otherwise than as their class enemy. In the ceremonial forms of their worship was thus introduced an act of arrant blasphemy. A class struggle carried to its conclusion is a struggle for state power. The fundamental character of a revolution lies in its carrying the class struggle to its conclusion. A revolution is a direct struggle for power. Nevertheless, our "socialists" are not worried about getting the power away from the class enemy who does not possess it, and could not with his own forces seize it, but, just the opposite, with forcing this power upon him at any cost. Is not this indeed a paradox? It seems all the more striking, because the experience of the German revolution of 1918 did not then exist, and humanity had not yet witnessed a colossal and still more successful operation of this same type carried out by the "new middle caste" led by the German social democracy.

How did the Compromisers explain their conduct? One explanation had a doctrinaire character: Since the revolution is bourgeois, the socialists must not compromise themselves with the power—let the bourgeoisie answer for itself. This sounded very implacable. In reality, however, the petty bourgeoisie disguised with this false implacability its obsequiousness before the power of wealth, education, enfranchised citizenship. The right of the big bourgeoisie to power, the petty bourgeois acknowledged as a right of primogeniture, independent of the correlation of forces. Fundamentally we had here the same almost instinctive movement which has compelled the small merchant or teacher to step aside respectfully in the stations or theaters to let a Rothschild pass. Doctrinaire arguments served as a compensation for the consciousness of a personal insignificance. In only two months, when it became evident that the bourgeoisie was totally unable with its own force to keep the power thus delivered to it, the Compromisers had no difficulty in tossing away their "socialistic" prejudices and entering a coalition ministry—not in order to crowd out the bourgeoisie but, on the contrary, in order to save it—not against its will but, on the contrary, at its invitation, which sounded almost like a command. Indeed, the bourgeoisie threatened the democrats, if they refused, to let the power drop on their heads.

The second argument for refusing the power, although no more serious in essence, had a more practical appearance. Our friend Sukhanov made the most of the "scatteredness" of democratic Russia: "The democrats had at that time no stable or influential organizations, party, professional or municipal." That sounds almost like a joke! Not a word about the soviets of workers' and soldiers' deputies from this socialist who is acting in the name of the soviets. As a matter of fact, thanks to the tradition of 1905, the soviets sprang up as though from under the earth, and immediately became incomparably more powerful than all the other organizations which later tried to compete with them (the municipalities, the coöperatives, and in part the trade unions). As for the peasantry, a class by its very nature scattered, thanks to the war and revolution it was exactly at that moment organized as never before. The war had assembled the peasants into an army, and the revolution had given the army a political character! No fewer than eight million peasants were united in companies and squadrons, which had immediately created their revolutionary representation and could through it at any moment be brought to their feet by a telephone call. Is this at all similar to "scatteredness"?

You may say, to be sure, that at the moment of deciding the question of power, the democracy did not know what would be the attitude of the army at the front. We will not raise the question whether there was the slightest basis for fearing or hoping that the soldiers at the front, worn out with the war, would want to support the imperialist bourgeoisie. It is sufficient to remark that this question was fully decided during the next two or three days, which the Compromisers passed in the backstage preparation of a bourgeois government. "The revolution was successfully achieved by the 3rd of March," concedes Sukhanov. In spite of the adherence of the whole army to the soviets, the leaders of the latter continued with all their strength to push away the power: they feared it the more, the more completely it became concentrated in their hands.

But why? How could those democrats, "socialists," directly supported by such human masses as no democracy in history ever had behind it—masses, moreover, with a considerable experience, disciplined and armed, and organized in soviets—how could that all-powerful and apparently inconquerable democracy fear the power? This apparently intricate enigma is explained by the fact that the democracy did not trust its own support, feared those very masses, did not believe in the stability of their confidence in itself, and worst of all dreaded what they called "anarchy," that is, that having seized the power, they might along with the power prove a mere plaything of the so-called unbridled elements. In other words, the democracy felt that it was not called to be the leader of the people at the moment of its revolutionary uprising, but the left wing of a bourgeois order, its feeler stretched out toward the masses. It called itself, and even deemed itself "socialistic," in order to disguise not only from the masses, but from itself too, its actual rôle: without this self-inebriation it could not have fulfilled this rôle. This is the solution of the fundamental paradox of the February revolution.

On the evening of March 1, representatives of the Executive Committee, Cheidze, Steklov, Sukhanov and others, appeared at a meeting of the Duma Committee, in order to discuss the conditions upon which the soviets would support the new government. The program of the democrats flatly ignored the question of war, republic, land, eight-hour day, and confined itself to one single demand: to give the left parties freedom of agitation. An example of disinterestedness for all peoples and ages! Socialists, having all the power in their hands, and upon whom alone it depended whether freedom of agitation should be given to others or not, handed over the power to their "class enemy" upon the condition that the latter should promise them . . . freedom of agitation! Rodzianko was afraid to go to the telegraph office and said to Cheidze and Sukhanov: "You have the power, you can arrest us all." Cheidze and Sukhanov answered him: "Take the power, but don't arrest us for propaganda." When you study the negotiations of the Compromisers with the liberals, and in general all the incidents of the interrelation of the left and right wings at the Tauride Palace in those days, it seems as though upon that gigantic stage upon which the historic drama of a people is developing, a group of provincial actors, availing themselves of a vacant corner and a pause, were playing out a cheap quick-change vaudeville act.

The leaders of the bourgeoisie, we must do them justice, never expected anything of the kind. They would surely have less dreaded the revolution if they had counted upon this kind of politics from its leaders. To be sure, they would have miscalculated even in that case, but at least together with the latter. Fearing, nevertheless, that the bourgeoisie might not agree to take the power on the proposed conditions, Sukhanov delivered a threatening ultimatum: "Either we or nobody can control the elements . . . there is but one way out—agree to our terms." In other words: accept the program, which is your program; for this we promise to subdue for you the masses who gave us the power. Poor subduers of the elements!

Miliukov was astonished. "He did not try to conceal," remembers Sukhanov, "his satisfaction and his agreeable astonishment." When the Soviet delegates, to make it sound more important, added that their conditions were "final," Miliukov even became expansive and patted them on the head with the remark: "Yes, I was listening and I was thinking how far forward our workers' movement has progressed since the days of

1905 . . ." In the same tone of the good-natured crocodile the Hohenzollern diplomat at Brest-Litovsk conversed with the delegates of the Ukranian Rada, complimenting them upon their statesman-like maturity just before swallowing them up. If the Soviet democracy was not swallowed up by the bourgeoisie, it was not Miliukov's fault, and no thanks to Sukhanov. The bourgeoisie received the power behind the backs of the people. It had no support in the toiling classes. But along with the power it received a simulacrum of support second hand. The Mensheviks and Social Revolutionaries, lifted aloft by the masses, delivered as if from themselves a testimonial of confidence to the bourgeoisie. If you look at this operation of formal democracy in cross-section you have a picture of a twofold election, in which the Mensheviks and Social Revolutionaries play the technical rôle of a middle link, that is, Kadet electors. If you take the question politically, it must be conceded that the Compromisers betrayed the confidence of the masses by calling to power those against whom they themselves were elected. And finally from a deeper, more social point of view, the question presents itself thus: the petty bourgeois parties, having in everyday circumstances shown an extraordinary pretentiousness and satisfaction with themselves, as soon as they were raised by a revolution to the heights of power, were frightened by their own inadequacy and hastened to surrender the helm to representatives of capital. In this act of prostration is immediately revealed the terrible shakiness of the new middle caste and its humiliating dependence upon the big bourgeoisie. Realizing or only feeling that the power in their hands would not last long anyway, that they would soon have to surrender it either to the right or the left, the democrats decided that it was better to give it today to the solid liberals than tomorrow to the extreme representatives of the proletariat. But in this view also, the rôle of the Compromisers, in spite of its social conditioning, does not cease to be a treachery to the masses.

In giving their confidence to the socialists the workers and soldiers found themselves, quite unexpectedly, expropriated politically. They were bewildered, alarmed, but did not immediately find a way out. Their own betrayers deafened them from above with arguments to which they had no ready answer, but which conflicted with all their feelings and intentions. The revolutionary tendencies of the masses, even at the moment of the February revolution, did not at all coincide with the Compromise tendencies of the petty bourgeois parties. The proletariat and the peasantry voted for the Mensheviks and the Social Revolutionaries not as compromisers, but as opponents of the tzar, the capitalists and the landowners. But in voting for them they created a partition-wall between themselves and their own aims. They could not now move forward at all without bumping into this wall erected by themselves, and knocking it over. Such was the striking *quid pro quo* comprised in the class relations as they were uncovered by the February revolution.

To this fundamental paradox a supplementary one was immediately added. The liberals agreed to take the power from the hands of the socialists only on condition that the monarchy should agree to take it from their hands. During the time when Guchkov, with the monarchist Shulgin, already known to us, was traveling out to Pskov to save the dynasty, the problem of a constitutional monarchy was at the center of negotiation between the two committees in the Tauride Palace. Miliukov was trying to convince the democrats who had come to him with the power in the palms of their hands, that the Romanovs could now no longer be dangerous, that Nicholas, to be sure, would have to be removed, but that the tzarevich Alexei, with Mikhail as regent, could fully guarantee the welfare of the country: "The one is a sick child, the other an utterly stupid man." We will add also a characterization which the liberal monarchist Shidlovsky gave of the candidate for tzar: "Mikhail Alexandrovich has tried every way possible to avoid interfering in any affairs of state, devoting himself whole-heartedly to horse-racing." A striking recommendation, especially if it were repeated before the masses. After the flight of Louis XVI to Varennes, Danton proclaimed in the Jacobin Club that once a man is weak-minded he can no longer be king. The Russian liberals thought on the contrary that the weak-mindedness of a monarch would serve as the best possible decoration for a constitutional régime. However, this was a random argument calculated to impress the mentality of the "left" simpletons—a little too crude, however, even for them. It was suggested to broad circles of the liberal Philistines that Mikhail was an "Anglomaniac"—without making clear whether in the matter of horse-racing or parliamentarism. But the main argument was that they needed a "customary symbol of power." Otherwise the people would imagine that anarchy had come.

The democrats listened, were politely surprised and tried to persuade them . . . to declare a republic? No. Only not to decide the question in advance. The third point of the Executive Committee's conditions read: "The Provisional Government shall not undertake any steps which would define in advance the future form of government." Miliukov made of the question of the monarchy an ultimatum. The democrats were in despair. But here the masses came to their help. At the meetings in the Tauride Palace absolutely nobody, not only among the workers, but among the soldiers, wanted a tzar, and there was no means of imposing one upon them. Nevertheless, Miliukov tried to swim against the current, and to save the throne and dynasty over the heads of his left allies. In his history of the revolution he himself cautiously remarks that towards the end of the 2nd of March the excitement produced by his announcement of the Regency of Mikhail "had considerably increased." Rodzianko far more colorfully paints the effect upon the masses produced by this monarchist maneuver of the liberals. The moment he arrived from Pskov with the tzar's abdication in favor of Mikhail, Guchkov upon the demand of the workers went from the station to the railroad shops to tell what had happened, and having read the act of abdication he concluded: "Long live the Emperor Mikhail!" The result was unexpected. The orator was, according to Rodzianko, immediately arrested by the workers, and even apparently threatened with execution. "He was liberated with great difficulty, with the help of a sentry company of the nearest regiment." Rodzianko, as always, exaggerates a little, but the essence of the matter is correctly stated. The country had so radically vomited up the monarchy that it could not ever crawl down the people's throat again. The revolutionary masses did not permit even the thought of a new tzar.

Facing such a situation the members of the Provisional

Committee sidled away from Mikhail one after another—not decisively, but "until the Constituent Assembly" and then we shall see. Only Miliukov and Guchkov stood out for monarchy to the end, continuing to make it a condition of their entering the cabinet. What to do? The democrats thought that without Miliukov it was impossible to create a bourgeois government, and without a bourgeois government to save the revolution. Bickerings and persuasions went on without end. At a morning conference on March 3, a conviction of the necessity of "persuading the grand duke to abdicate"—they considered him tzar then, after all!—seemed to gain the upper hand completely in the Provisional Committee. The left Kadet Nekrasov even drew up a text of the abdication. But since Miliukov stubbornly refused to yield, a decision was finally reached after further passionate quarrels: "Both sides shall present before the grand duke their opinions and without further argument leave the decision to the grand duke himself." Thus an "utterly stupid man," to whom his older brother overthrown by the insurrection had tried, in conflict even with the dynastic statute, to slip the throne, unexpectedly became the super-umpire on the question of the state structure of the revolutionary country. However improbable it may seem, a betting competition had arisen over the fate of the state. In order to induce the duke to tear himself away from the stables for the throne, Miliukov assured him that there was an excellent possibility of collecting outside of Petrograd a military force to defend his rights. In other words, having barely received the power from the hands of the socialists, Miliukov advanced a plan for a monarchist coup d'état. At the end of the speeches for and against, of which there were not a few, the grand duke requested time for reflection. Inviting Rodzianko into another room Mikhail flatly asked him: Would the new authorities guarantee him only the crown, or also his head? The incomparable Lord Chamberlain answered that he could only promise the monarch in case of need to die with him. This did not at all satisfy the candidate. Coming out to the deputies after an embrace with Rodzianko, Mikhail Romanov "pretty firmly" declared that he would decline the lofty but risky position offered to him. Here Kerensky, who personified in these negotiations the conscience of the democracy, ecstatically jumped up from his chair with the words: "Your Highness, you are a noble man!"—and swore that from that time on he would proclaim this everywhere. "Kerensky's grandiloquence," comments Miliukov drily, "harmonized badly with the prose of the decision just taken." It is impossible to disagree. The text of this interlude truly left no place for pathos. To our comparison with a vaudeville played in the corner of an ancient amphitheater, it is necessary to add that the stage was divided by screens into two halves: in one the revolutionists were begging the liberals to save the revolution, in the other the liberals were begging the monarchy to save liberalism.

The representatives of the Executive Committee were sincerely perplexed as to why such a cultured and farsighted man as Miliukov should be obstinate about some old monarchy, and even be ready to renounce the power if he could not get a Romanov thrown in. Miliukov's monarchism, however, was neither doctrinaire, nor romantic; on the contrary, it was a result of the naked calculation of the frightened property owners. In its nakedness indeed lay its hopeless weakness. Miliukov the historian, might, it is true, cite the example of the leader of the French revolutionary bourgeoisie, Mirabeau, who also in his day strove to reconcile the revolution with the king. There too at the bottom it was the fear of the property owners for their property: the more prudent policy was to disguise it with the monarchy, just as the monarchy had disguised itself with the church. But in 1789 the tradition of kingly power in France had still a universal popular recognition, to say nothing of the fact that all surrounding Europe was monarchist. In clinging to the king the French bourgeoisie was still on common ground with the people—at least in the sense that it was using against the people their own prejudices. The situation was wholly different in Russia in 1917. Aside from the shipwreck of the monarchist régime in various other countries of the world, the Russian monarchy itself had been irremediably damaged already in 1905. After the 9th of January, Father Gapon had cursed the tzar and his "serpent offspring." The Soviet of Workers' Deputies of 1905 had stood openly for a republic. The monarchist feelings of the peasantry, upon which the monarchy itself had long counted, and with references to which the bourgeoisie camouflaged its own monarchism, simply did not exist. The militant counter-revolution which arose later, beginning with Kornilov, although hypocritically, nevertheless all the more demonstratively, disavowed the tzarist power—so little was left of the monarchist roots in the people. But that same revolution of 1905, which mortally wounded the monarchy, had undermined forever the unstable republican tendencies of the "advanced" bourgeoisie. In contradicting each other, these two processes supplemented each other. Feeling in the first hours of the February revolution that it was drowning, the bourgeoisie grabbed at a straw. It needed the monarchy, not because that was a faith common to it and the people; on the contrary, the bourgeoisie had nothing left to set against the faith of the people but a crowned phantom. The "educated" classes of Russia entered the arena of the revolution not as the announcers of a rational state, but as defenders of medieval institutions. Having no support either in the people or in themselves, they sought it above themselves. Archimedes undertook to move the earth if they would give him a point of support. Miliukov was looking for a point of support in order to prevent the overthrow of the landlord's earth.[1] He felt in this operation much nearer to the calloused Russian generals and the hierarchs of the orthodox church, than to these tame democrats who were worried about nothing but the approval of the liberals. Not being in a position to break the revolution, Miliukov firmly decided to outwit it. He was ready to swallow a great deal: civil liberty for soldiers, democratic municipalities, Constituent Assembly, but on one condition: that they should give him an Archimedian point of support in the form of monarchy. He intended gradually and step by step to make the monarchy the axis of a group of generals, a patched-up bureaucracy, princes of the church, property owners, all those who were dissatisfied with the revolution, and starting with a "symbol," to create gradually a real monarchist bridle for the masses as soon as the latter should get tired of the revolution. If only he could gain time. Another leader of the Kadet Party, Nabokov, explained later what a capital advantage would have been gained if Mikhail had consented to take the throne:

[1] In Russian, the words *earth* and *land* are the same. [Trans.]

"The fatal question of convoking a Constituent Assembly in war time would have been removed." We must bear those words in mind. The conflict about the date of the Constituent Assembly occupied a great place between February and October, during which time the Kadets categorically denied their intention to delay the summoning of the people's representatives, while insistently and stubbornly carrying out a policy of postponement in fact. Alas, they had only themselves to rely on in this effort: the monarchist camouflage they never got. After the desertion of Mikhail, Miliukov had not even a straw to grab.

Chapter X

THE NEW POWER

The belated Russian bourgeoisie, separated from the people, bound up much more closely with foreign finance capital than with its own toiling masses, hostile to the revolution which had triumphed, could not in its own name find a single justification for its pretense to power. And yet some justification was necessary, for the revolution was subjecting to a ruthless examination not only inherited rights but new claims. Least of all capable of presenting convincing arguments to the masses was the President of the Provisional Committee, Rodzianko, who arrived at the head of the revolutionary nation during the first days of the uprising.

A page in the court of Alexander II, an officer of the Cavalier Guard, head of the nobles of his province, Lord Chamberlain under Nicholas II, a monarchist through and through, a rich landlord and agrarian administrator, a member of the Octobrist Party, a deputy in the State Duma, Rodzianko was finally elected its president. This happened after the resignation of Guchkov, who was hated by the court as a "Young Turk." The Duma hoped that through the mediation of the Lord Chamberlain it would find easier access to the heart of the monarch. Rodzianko did what he could: sincerely enough assured the tzar of his loyalty to the dynasty, begged the honor of being presented to the Heir Apparent, and introduced himself to the latter as "the biggest and fattest man in Russia." In spite of all his Byzantine clowning, the Lord Chamberlain did not win over the tzar to the constitution, and the tzarina briefly referred to Rodzianko in her letters as a scoundrel. During the war the President of the Duma undoubtedly gave the tzar not a few unpleasant moments, cornering him when making personal reports and filling his ears with prolix exhortations, patriotic criticisms and gloomy forebodings. Rasputin considered Rodzianko a personal enemy. Kurlov, who was close to the court gang, speaks of Rodzianko's "insolence combined with obvious limitations." Witte spoke in better terms, although condescendingly, of the President of the Duma: "Not a stupid man, rather sensible; but still Rodzianko's chief talent lies not in his mind but his voice—he has an excellent bass." At first Rodzianko tried to put down the revolution with the help of the fire-hose; he wept when he found out that the government of Count Golytsin had abandoned its post; declined with terror the power which the socialists offered him; afterwards decided to take it, but only in order as a loyal subject to restore the lost property as soon as possible to the monarch. It wasn't Rodzianko's fault if that opportunity never arrived. However the revolution—with the help of the socialists—did offer the Lord Chamberlain a grand opportunity to exercise his thunderous bass before the revolting troops. As early as the 27th of February this retired Captain of the Guard said to a cavalier regiment which had come to the Tauride Palace: "Christian warriors, hearken to my counsel. I am an old man; I will not deceive you—obey your officers—they will not teach you evil, and will act in full agreement with the State Duma. Long live holy Russia!" Such a revolution as that would have been agreeable to all the Guard officers, but the soldiers couldn't help wondering what was the use making such a revolution. Rodzianko feared the soldiers, feared the workers, considered Cheidze and other left deputies German agents, and while he stood at the head of the revolution kept looking around every few minutes to see whether the Soviet was going to arrest him.

The figure of Rodzianko was a little funny, but by no means accidental. This Lord Chamberlain with an excellent bass personified the union of the two ruling classes of Russia, the landlords and the bourgeoisie, with the progressive priesthood adhering to them. Rodzianko himself was very pious and expert in hymn singing—and the liberal bourgeoisie, whatever its attitude towards Greek orthodoxy, considered a union with the church just as necessary to law and order as a union with the monarchy. The venerable monarchist, having received the power from the hands of conspirators, rebels and tyrannicides, wore a haunted expression in those days. And the other members of the Provisional committee felt but little better. Some of them never appeared at the Tauride Palace at all, considering that the situation had not yet sufficiently defined itself. The wisest of them sneaked on tiptoe round the blaze of the revolution, choking from the smoke, and saying to themselves: let it burn down to the coals, then we'll try to cook up something. Although it agreed to accept the power, the Committee did not immediately decide to form a ministry. "Awaiting the proper moment for the formation of a government"—as Miliukov expresses it—the Committee confined itself to the naming of commissars from the membership of the Duma to the principal governmental departments. That left them a chance to retreat.

To the Ministry of the Interior they delegated the deputy Karaulov, insignificant but rather less cowardly than the others, and he issued on March 1 an order for the arrest of all police officials, public, secret and political. This ferocious revolutionary gesture was purely platonic in character, for the police were already being arrested and the jails were their only refuge from massacre. It was some time later that the reaction began to regard this demonstrative act of Karaulov as the beginning of all their troubles.

As commander of Petrograd, they appointed Colonel Engelhardt, an officer of the Cavalier Guard, owner of a racing stud and vast landed properties. Instead of arresting the "dictator" Ivanov, sent from the front to pacify the capital, Engelhardt put at his disposition a reactionary officer in the capacity of chief of staff. It was all a matter between friends.

To the Ministry of Justice they delegated a bright light of the Moscow liberal bar, the eloquent and empty Maklakov, who began by giving the reactionary bureaucrats to understand that he did not want to accept the ministry as a favor from the revolution, and "glancing around at a messenger boy who had just come in," said in French: "*Le danger est à gauche.*" The workers and soldiers did not have to understand French in order to recognize in all these gentlemen their mortal enemies.

Rodzianko's reverberations at the head of the Committee did not last very long. His candidacy for president of the revolution faded away of itself. The mediator between the monarchy and the property owners was too obviously useless as a mediator between the property owners and the revolution. But he did not disappear from the scene. He stubbornly attempted to revive the Duma as a counter-weight to the Soviet, and invariably appears in the center of all attempts to solidify the capitalist-landlord counter-revolution. We shall hear of him again.

On the 1st of March the Provisional Committee undertook the formation of a ministry, appointing to it those men whom the Duma had been recommending to the tzar since 1915 as enjoying the confidence of the country. They were big landlords and industrialists, opposition deputies in the Duma, leaders of the Progressive Bloc. The fact is that, with one single exception, the revolution accomplished by workers and soldiers found no reflection whatever in the staff of the revolutionary government. The exception was Kerensky. The distance from Rodzianko to Kerensky appeared officially to represent the whole gamut of the February revolution.

Kerensky entered the government somewhat in the character of a plenipotentiary ambassador. His connection with the revolution, however, was that of a provincial lawyer who had defended political cases. Kerensky was not a revolutionist; he merely hung around the revolution. Arriving in the fourth Duma thanks to his legal position, Kerensky became the president of a gray and characterless faction, the Trudoviks, anemic fruit of a cross-breeding between liberalism and Narodnikism. He had no theoretical preparation, no political schooling, no ability to think, no political will. The place of these qualities was occupied by a nimble susceptibility, an inflammable temperament, and that kind of eloquence which operates neither upon mind nor will, but upon the nerves. His speeches in the Duma, couched in a spirit of declamatory radicalism which had no lack of occasions, gave Kerensky, if not popularity, at least a certain notoriety. During the war Kerensky, a patriot, had looked with the liberals upon the very idea of revolution as ruinous. He acknowledged the revolution only after it had come and catching him up by his pseudo-popularity lifted him aloft. The revolution naturally identified itself for him with the new power. The Executive Committee decided, however, that it was a bourgeois revolution and the power should belong to the bourgeoisie. This formula seemed false to Kerensky, if only because it slammed the doors of the ministry in his face. Kerensky was quite rightly convinced that his socialism would not trouble the bourgeois revolution, nor would the bourgeois revolution do any damage to his socialism. The Provisional Committee of the Duma decided to try to draw this radical deputy away from the Soviet, and achieved it with no difficulty by offering him the portfolio of Justice, which had already been refused by Maklakov. Kerensky buttonholed his friends in the *couloirs,* and asked: Shall I take it or not? His friends had no doubt whatever that he would take it. Sukhanov, who was very friendly toward Kerensky at that period, attributes to him in his subsequent memoirs, "a confidence in some mission of his own . . . and an enormous vexation with those who had not yet found out about that mission." In the long run his friends, and Sukhanov among them, advised Kerensky to take the portfolio: We will be safer this way—we will have our own man to tell us what is going on among those foxy liberals. But while pushing Kerensky *sub rosa* toward that sin to which he himself aspired with all his heart, the leaders of the Executive Committee refused him their official sanction. As Sukhanov reminded Kerensky, the Executive Committee had already expressed itself against its members' entering the government, and to raise the question again in the Soviet would be "not without danger," for the Soviet might simply answer: "The power ought to belong to the soviet democracy." Those are the very words of Sukhanov himself, an unbelievable mixture of naïveté and cynicism. The inspirer of this whole governmental mystification thus openly acknowledges that, as early as the 2nd of March, the Petrograd Soviet was in a mood for the *formal* seizure of that power which had belonged to it *in fact* since the evening of February 27—that only behind the backs of the workers and soldiers, without their knowledge, and against their actual will, had the socialist leaders been able to expropriate this power for the benefit of the bourgeoisie. In Sukhanov's account this deal between the democrats and the liberals acquires all the necessary juridical marks of a crime against the revolution, a veritable secret conspiracy against the sovereignty and rights of the people.

Discussing Kerensky's impatience, the leaders of the Executive Committee whispered that it would be embarrassing for the socialists to take back from the members of the Duma a small piece of the power when they had only just handed the whole thing over to them. Better let Kerensky do it on his own responsibility. Truly those gentlemen had an infallible instinct for finding in every situation the most false and tangled-up solution possible. But Kerensky did not want to enter the government in the business suit of a radical deputy; he wanted to wear the cloak of a plenipotentiary of the triumphant revolution. In order to avoid obstacles, he did not appeal for sanction either to that party of which he professed himself a member, nor to the Executive Committee of which he was one of the vice presidents. Without warning the leaders, he appeared at a plenary session of the Soviet—chaotic meetings in those days—requested the floor for a special announcement, and in a speech which some describe as incoherent, others as hysterical—in which, to be sure, there is no contradiction—demanded the personal confidence of the deputies, and spoke of his general readiness to die for the revolution, and his more immediate readiness to take the portfolio of Minister of Justice. He had only to mention the necessity of complete political amnesty and a prosecution of the tzar's officials, in order to win tumultuous applause from that inexperienced and leaderless assembly. "This farce," Shliapnikov remembers, "produced in many a deep indignation and disgust for Kerensky." But nobody opposed him. Having turned over the power to the bourgeoisie, the socialists, as we have heard, wanted to avoid raising that question before the masses. There was no vote. Kerensky decided to interpret the applause as a vote of confidence. In a way he was right. The Soviet was undoubtedly in favor of socialists entering the ministry, seeing in that a step toward the liquidation of the bourgeois government with which it had not for a moment reconciled itself. At any rate, Kerensky, flouting the official doctrine of the sovereignty, accepted on March 2 the post of Minister of Justice. "He was highly pleased with his appointment," the Octobrist

Shidlovsky relates, "and I distinctly remember him in the chambers of the Provisional Committee, lying in an armchair, telling us heatedly upon what an unattainably high pedestal he was going to place justice in Russia." He demonstrated this some months later in his prosecution of the Bolsheviks.

The Menshevik Cheidze, upon whom the liberals—guided by a too simple calculation and an international tradition—wanted in a hard moment to unload the Ministry of Labor, categorically refused, and remained President of the Soviet. Although less brilliant than Kerensky, Cheidze was made of more serious material.

The axis of the Provisional Government, although not formally its head, was Miliukov, the indubitable leader of the Kadet Party. "Miliukov was incomparably above his colleagues in the cabinet," wrote the Kadet Nabokov, after he had broken with Miliukov, "as an intellectual force, as a man of enormous, almost inexhaustible knowledge and wide intelligence." Sukhanov, while blaming Miliukov personally for the wreck of Russian liberalism, nevertheless wrote: "Miliukov was then the central figure, the soul and brain of all the bourgeois political circles. . . . Without him there would have been no bourgeois policy in the first period of the revolution." In spite of their slightly exalted tone, these reports truly indicate the superiority of Miliukov to the other political men of the Russian bourgeoisie. His strength lay, and his weakness too, in this: he expressed more fully and elegantly than others in the language of politics the fate of the Russian bourgeoisie—the fact that it was caught historically in a blind alley. The Mensheviks wept because Miliukov ruined liberalism, but it would be truer to say that liberalism ruined Miliukov.

In spite of his Neo-Slavism warmed over for imperialistic purposes, Miliukov always remained a bourgeois "Westerner." The goal of his party was always the triumph in Russia of European civilization. But the farther he went, the more he feared those revolutionary paths upon which the Western peoples were traveling. His "Westernism" therefore reduced itself to an impotent envy of the West.

The English and French bourgeoisie created a new society in their own image. The Germans came later, and they were compelled to live for a long time on the pale gruel of philosophy. The Germans invented the phrase "speculative world," which does not exist in English or French. While these nations were creating a new world the Germans were thinking one up. But the German bourgeoisie, although poor in political activity, created the classical philosophy, and that is no small achievement. Russia came much later. To be sure, she translated the German phrase "speculative world" into Russian, and that with several variations, but this only the more clearly exposed both her political impotence and her deadly philosophical poverty. She imported ideas as well as machines, establishing high tariffs for the latter, and for the former a quarantine of fear. To these characteristics of his class Miliukov was called to give a political expression.

A former Moscow professor of history, author of significant scholarly works, founder of the Kadet Party—a union of the liberal landlords and the left intelligentsia—Miliukov was completely free from that insufferable, half-aristocratic and half-intellectual political dilettantism which is proper to the majority of Russian liberal men of politics. Miliukov took his profession very seriously and that alone distinguished him.

Before 1905, the Russian liberals were customarily embarrassed about being liberal. A tinge of Narodnikism, and later of Marxism, long served them as a defensive coloration. This rather shallow, shamefaced capitulation to socialism on the part of wide bourgeois circles, among them a number of young industrialists, expressed the lack of self-confidence of a class which appeared soon enough to concentrate millions in its hands, but too late to stand at the head of the nation. The bearded fathers, wealthy peasants and shopkeepers, had piled up their money, thinking nothing of their social rôle. Their sons graduated from the university in the period of prerevolutionary intellectual ferment, and when they tried to find their place in society, they were in no hurry to adopt the banner of liberalism, already worn out in advanced countries, patched and half faded. For a period of time they gave a part of their souls, and even a part of their incomes, to the revolutionists. This is especially true of the representatives of the liberal professions. A very considerable number of them passed through a stage of socialistic sympathy in their youth.

Professor Miliukov never had these measles. He was organically bourgeois and not ashamed of it.

It is true that at the time of the first revolution, Miliukov did not wholly renounce the idea of utilizing the revolutionary masses—with the help of tame and well-trained socialist parties. Witte relates that when he was forming his constitutional cabinet in October 1905, and appealed to the Kadets to "cut off their revolutionary tail," the answer was that they could no more get along without the armed forces of the revolution than Witte could without the army. In the essence of the matter, this was a bluff even then: in order to raise their own price, the Kadets tried to frighten Witte with the masses whom they themselves feared. It was precisely the experience of 1905 which convinced Miliukov that, no matter how strong the liberal sympathies of the socialist groups of the intelligentsia might be, the genuine forces of the revolution, the masses, would never give up their weapons to the bourgeoisie, and would be the more dangerous the better armed they were. When he declared openly that the red flag is a red rag, Miliukov ended to everybody's relief a romance which in reality nobody had seriously begun. The isolation of the so-called intelligentsia from the people has been one of the traditional themes of Russian journalism—and by "intelligentsia" the liberals, in contrast with the socialists, mean all the "educated," that is, possessing, classes. Ever since that isolation proved such a calamity to the liberals in the first revolution, the ideologues of the "educated" classes have lived in a kind of perpetual expectation of the judgment day. One of the liberal writers, a philosopher not restrained by the exigencies of politics, has expressed this fear of the masses with an ecstatic force which reminds us of the epileptic reactionism of Dostoyevsky: "Whatever we stand for, we must not dream of uniting with the people—we must fear them more than all the persecutions of the government, and we must give thanks to the government which alone protects us with its prisons and bayonets from the ferocity of the people." With such political feelings, could the liberals possibly dream of leading a revolutionary nation? Miliukov's whole policy is marked with a stamp of hopelessness. At the moment of national crisis his party thinks about dodging the blow, not dealing it.

As a writer, Miliukov is heavy, prolix and wearisome. He has the same quality as an orator. Decorativeness is unnatural to him. That might have been an advantage, if the niggardly policies of Miliukov had not so obviously needed a disguise—or if they had had, at least, an objective disguise in the shape of a great tradition. There was not even a little tradition. The official policy in France—quintessence of bourgeois perfidy and egotism—has two mighty allies: tradition and rhetoric. Each promoting the other, they surround with a defensive covering any bourgeois politician, even such a prosaic clerk of the big proprietors as Poincaré. It is not Miliukov's fault if he had no glorious ancestors, and if he was compelled to conduct a policy of bourgeois egotism on the borders of Europe and Asia.

"Along with a sympathy for Kerensky," we read in the memoirs of the Social Revolutionary, Sokolov, "one felt from the beginning an immense and unconcealed, and yet rather strange, antipathy for Miliukov. I did not understand, and do not now, why that respectable social reformer was so unpopular." If the Philistines had understood the cause of their admiration for Kerensky and their distaste for Miliukov, they would have ceased to be Philistines. The everyday bourgeois did not like Miliukov, because Miliukov too prosaically and soberly, without adornment, expressed the political essence of the Russian bourgeoisie. Beholding himself in the Miliukov mirror, the bourgeois saw that he was gray, self-interested and cowardly; and, as so often happens, he took offense at the mirror.

On his side, observing the displeased grimaces of the liberal bourgeois, Miliukov quietly and confidently remarked: "The everyday man is a fool." He pronounced these words without irritation, almost caressingly, as though to say: He does not understand me today, but never mind, he will understand later. Miliukov was deeply confident that the bourgeoisie would not betray him, that it would obey the logic of the situation and follow, for it had no other way to go. And in reality, after the February revolution all the bourgeois parties, even those to the right, followed the Kadet leader, abusing and even cursing him.

It was very different with the democratic politicians of a socialist coloring, men of the type of Sukhanov. This was no ordinary Philistine, but on the contrary a professional man-of-politics, sufficiently expert in his small trade. He could never look intelligent, because one saw too plainly the continual contrast between what he wanted, and what he arrived at. But he intellectualized and blundered and bored. In order to lead him after you, it was necessary to deceive him by acknowledging his genuine independence, even accusing him of being self-willed, excessively given to command. That flattered him and reconciled him to the rôle of helper. It was in conversation with just these socialistic highbrows that Miliukov tossed out that phrase: "The everyday man is a fool." This was delicate flattery: "Only you and I are intelligent." As a matter of fact, at that very moment Miliukov was hooking a ring in the noses of his democratic friends. By that ring they were subsequently led out of the way.

His personal unpopularity prevented Miliukov from standing at the head of the government. He took the Ministry of Foreign Affairs, which had been his specialty in the Duma.

The War Minister of the revolution was the big Moscow industrialist, Guchkov, already known to us—in his youth a liberal with an adventurous temperament, but afterward, in the period of the defeat of the first revolution, the trusted man of the big bourgeoisie under Stolypin. The dissolution of the first two Dumas, dominated by the Kadets, led to the governmental overturn of the 3rd of June 1907, which changed the election law to the benefit of the party of Guchkov. It became the leader of the two subsequent Dumas and continued so right up to the day of the revolution. In Kiev in 1911, at the unveiling of a monument to Stolypin who was killed by a terrorist, Guchkov, in placing a wreath, bowed silently down to the ground: a gesture in the name of his class. In the Duma, Guchkov dedicated himself chiefly to the question of "military might," and in preparing for war walked hand-in-hand with Miliukov. In the position of President of the Central Military-Industrial Committee, Guchkov united the industrialists under the banner of a patriotic opposition—not however preventing the leaders of the Progressive Bloc, including Rodzianko, from getting a rake-off on military contracts. For revolutionary recommendation there was attached to Guchkov's name that semi-legend about the plot of a palace revolution. A former chief of police asserted, moreover, that Guchkov "had permitted himself in private conversations about the monarch to employ an epithet insulting in the highest degree." That was very likely true, but in that Guchkov was no exception. The pious tzarina hated Guchkov, lavished crude abuse upon him in her letters, and expressed the hope that he would hang "on a high tree." But the tzarina had many others in view for this same high position. Somehow, at any rate, this man who bowed to the earth in honor of the hangman of the first revolution became the War Minister of the second.

The Minister of Agriculture was the Kadet Shingarev, a provincial doctor who had subsequently become a deputy in the Duma. His close associates in the party considered him an honest mediocrity or, as Nabokov expressed it, "a Russian provincial intellectual, designed on a small-town or county, rather than a national, scale." The indefinite radicalism of his early years had long washed away, and the chief anxiety of Shingarev was to demonstrate his statesmanlike maturity to the possessing classes. Although the old Kadet program spoke of the "confiscation with just indemnity of the landed estates," none of the property owners took this program seriously—especially now in the years of the war inflation. And Shingarev made it his chief task to delay the decision of the agrarian problem, deluding the peasants with the mirage of a Constituent Assembly which the Kadets did not want to summon. On the land question and the question of war, the February revolution was destined to break its neck. Shingarev helped all he could.

The portfolio of Finance was given to a young man named Tereshchenko. "Where did they get him?" everybody was inquiring with bewilderment in the Tauride Palace. The well-informed explained that this was an owner of sugar factories, estates, forests, and other innumerable properties, worth some eighty million roubles in gold, president of the Military-Industrial Committee of Kiev, possessed of a good French pronunciation, and on top of it all a connoisseur of the ballet. And they added—more importantly—that as the favorite of Guchkov, Tereshchenko had almost taken part in the great conspiracy which was to have overthrown Nicholas II. The revolution which prevented that conspiracy was of great help to Tereshchenko.

In the course of those five February days when the revolutionary fight was being waged in the cold streets of the capital, there flitted before us several times like a shadow the figure of a liberal of noble family, the son of a former tzarist minister, Nabokov—almost symbolic in his self-satisfied correctness and dry egotism. Nabokov passed the decisive days of the insurrection within the four walls of the chancellery, or his home, "in dull and anxious expectancy." He now became General Administrator of the Provisional Government, actually a minister without portfolio. In his Berlin exile where he was finally killed by the stray bullet of a White Guard, he left memoirs of the Provisional Government which are not without interest. Let us place that to his credit.

But we have forgotten to mention the Prime Minister—whom, by the way, in the most serious moments of his brief term everybody forgot. On March 2, in recommending the new government to a meeting at the Tauride Palace, Miliukov described Prince Lvov as "the incarnation of the Russian social consciousness so persecuted by the tzarist régime." Later, in his history of the revolution, Miliukov prudently remarks that at the head of the government was placed Prince Lvov, "personally little known to the majority of the Provisional Committee." The historian here tries to relieve the politician of responsibility for this choice. As a matter of fact, the prince had long been a member of the Kadet Party, belonging to its right wing. After the dissolution of the first Duma, at that famous meeting of the deputies at Vyborg which addressed the population with the ritual of offended liberalism: "Refuse to pay the taxes!" Prince Lvov attended but did not sign the appeal. Nabokov relates that immediately upon his arrival at Vyborg the prince fell sick, and his sickness was "attributed to the emotional condition in which he found himself." The prince was evidently not built for revolutionary excitement. This moderate prince, owing to a political indifference that looked like broadmindedness, tolerated in the organizations which he administered a large number of left intellectuals, former revolutionists, socialistic patriots, and draft-dodgers. They worked just as well as the bureaucrats, did not graft, and moreover created for the prince a simulacrum of popularity. A prince, a rich man, and a liberal—that was very impressive to the average bourgeois. For that reason Prince Lvov was marked for the premiership even under the tzar. To sum it all up in a word, the head of the government of the February revolution was an illustrious but notoriously empty spot. Rodzianko would at least have been more colorful.

The legendary history of the Russian state begins with a tale in the *Chronicle* to the effect that delegates of the Slavic tribes went to the Scandinavian princes with the request: "Come and rule and be princes over us." The pitiable representatives of the social democracy transformed this historic legend into a fact—not in the ninth but in the twentieth century, and with this difference, that they did not address themselves to princes over the sea, but to their own home princes. Thus as a result of a victorious insurrection of workers and soldiers, there appeared at the helm of government a handful of the very richest landlords and industrialists, remarkable for less than nothing, political dilettantes without a program—and at the head of them a prince with a strong dislike for excitement.

The composition of the new government was greeted with satisfaction in the Allied embassies, in the bourgeois and bureaucratic salons, and in the broader circles of the middle, and part of the petty, bourgeoisie. Prince Lvov, Octobrist Guchkov, Kadet Miliukov—those names sounded reassuring. The name of Kerensky perhaps caused some eyebrows to rise among the Allies, but they were not badly frightened. The more far-seeing understood: after all, there is a revolution in the country; with such a steady wheel-horse as Miliukov, a mettlesome teammate can only be helpful. Thus the French ambassador Paléologue, a great lover of Russian metaphors, must have expressed it.

Among the workers and soldiers the composition of the government created an immediate feeling of hostility, or at the best a dumb bewilderment. The name of Miliukov or Guchkov did not evoke one voice of greeting in either factory or barrack. There exists no little testimony to this. Officer Mstislavisky reports the sullen alarm of his soldiers at the news that the power had passed from tzar to prince: Is that worth shedding blood for? Stankevich, one of Kerensky's intimate circle, made the rounds of his sapper battalion, company by company, recommending the new government, which he himself considered the best possible and of which he spoke with great enthusiasm. "But I felt a coolness in the audience." Only when the officer mentioned Kerensky did the soldiers "kindle with sincere satisfaction." By that time the bourgeois social opinion of the capital had already converted Kerensky into the central hero of the revolution. The soldiers even more than the workers desired to see in Kerensky a counterpoise to the bourgeois government, and only wondered why he was there alone. Kerensky was not a counterpoise, however, but a finishing touch, a screen, a decoration. He was defending the same interests as Miliukov, but with magnesium flashlights.

What was the real constitution of the country after the inauguration of the new power?

The monarchist reaction was hiding in the cracks. With the very first ebb of the wave, property owners of all kinds and tendencies gathered around the banner of the Kadet Party, which had suddenly become the only non-socialist party—and at the same time the extreme right party—in the open arena.

The masses went over in droves to the socialists, whom they identified with the Soviet. Not only the workers and soldiers of the enormous garrisons in the rear, but all the many-colored small people of the towns—mechanics, street peddlers, petty officials, cab-drivers, janitors, servants of all kinds—feeling alien to the Provisional Government and its bureaus, were seeking a closer and more accessible authority. In continually increasing numbers, peasant delegates were appearing at the Tauride Palace. The masses poured into the Soviet as though into the triumphal gates of the revolution. All that remained outside the boundaries of the Soviet seemed to fall away from the revolution, seemed somehow to belong to a different world. And so it was in reality. Beyond the boundaries of the Soviet remained the world of the property owner, in which all colors mingled now in one grayish-pink defensive tint.

Not all the toiling masses chose the Soviet; not all awakened at once; not every layer of the oppressed dared instantly believe that the revolution concerned them. In the consciousness of many only an undiscriminating hope was stirring. But all the active elements of the masses poured into the Soviet, and activity prevails in times of revolution. Moreover, since mass activity was growing from day to day, the basis of the Soviet was continually broadening. It was the sole genuine basis of the revolution.

In the Tauride Palace there were two halves: the Duma and the Soviet. The Executive Committee was at first crowded into some narrow secretarial chambers, through which flowed an uninterrupted human flood. The deputies of the Duma tried to feel like proprietors in their sumptuous chambers. But the barriers were soon swept away by the overflow of the revolution. In spite of all the indecisiveness of its leaders, the Soviet spread out irresistibly, and the Duma was crowded away into the backyard. The new correlation of forces broke its path everywhere.

Deputies in the Tauride Palace, officers in their regiments, commanders in the staffs, directors and managers in factories, on the railroads, in the telegraph offices, landlords or managers of estates—all felt themselves during those first days of the revolution to be under the suspicious and tireless scrutiny of the masses. In the eyes of those masses the Soviet was an organized expression of their distrust of all who had oppressed them. Typesetters would jealously follow the text of the articles which they had set up, railroad workers would anxiously and vigilantly watch over the military trains, telegraphers would become absorbed in rereading the texts of telegrams, soldiers would glance around suspiciously every time their officer made a move, workers would dismiss from the factory an overseer belonging to the Black Hundreds and take in under observation a liberal manager. The Duma from the first hours of the revolution, and the Provisional Government from its first days, became reservoirs into which flowed a continuous stream of complaints and objections from the upper layers of society, their protests against "excesses," their woeful comments and dark forebodings.

"Without the bourgeoisie we cannot manage the state apparatus," reasoned the socialistic petty bourgeois, timidly looking up at the official buildings where the skeleton of the old government looked out with empty eyes. The problem was solved by setting some sort of a liberal head on the institution which the revolution had beheaded. The new ministers entered into the tzarist bureaus, took possession of the apparatus of typewriters, telephones, couriers, stenographers and clerks, and found out from day to day that the machine was running empty.

Kerensky subsequently related how the Provisional Government "took the power in its hands on the third day of all-Russian anarchy, when throughout the whole extent of the Russian land there existed not only no governmental power, but literally not one policeman." The soviets of workers' and soldiers' deputies standing at the head of millions of people, counted for nothing: that of course was merely one element of the anarchy. The orphaned condition of the country is summed up for Kerensky in the disappearance of policemen. In that confession of faith of the most leftward of the ministers, you have the key to the whole policy of the government.

The place of the governors of provinces was occupied, on the order of Prince Lvov, by the presidents of the provincial zemstvos, who differed but little from their predecessors. Often enough they were feudal landlords who regarded even the governors as Jacobins. At the head of the counties stood the presidents of the county zemstvos. Under the new name of "commissars" the population recognized their old enemies. "New Presbyter is but Old Priest writ large," as Milton once said of the cowardly Presbyterian reformation. The provincial and district commissars took possession of the typewriters, correspondence, and clerks of the governors and chiefs of police, only to find out that they had inherited no real power. Real life both in the provinces and in the counties concentrated around the Soviet. A two-power system thus reigned from top to bottom. But in the provinces the Soviet leaders, those same Social Revolutionaries and Mensheviks, were a little simpler and by no means everywhere renounced that power which the whole situation was imposing upon them. As a result of this, the activity of the provincial commissars consisted mainly of submitting complaints as to the complete impossibility of fulfilling the duties of their office.

Two days after the formation of the liberal ministry the bourgeoisie were feeling that they had not acquired the power, but lost it. In spite of all the fantastic caprices of the

Rasputin clique before the revolution, its real power had been limited. The influence of the bourgeoisie upon the government had been enormous. The very participation of Russia in the war was more the work of the bourgeoisie than the monarchy. But the main thing was that the tzarist government had guaranteed to the property owners their factories, land, banks, houses, newspapers; it was consequently upon the most vital questions *their* government. The February revolution changed the situation in two contrary directions: it solemnly handed over to the bourgeoisie the external attributes of power, but at the same time it took from them that share in the actual rulership which they had enjoyed before the revolution. The former employees of the zemstvos where Prince Lvov was the boss, and of the Military-Industrial Committee where Guchkov was in command, became today, under the name of Social Revolutionaries and Mensheviks, lords of the situation in the country and on the front, in the city and in the village. They appointed Lvov and Guchkov to the ministry, and laid down the conditions of their work as though they were hiring stewards.

On the other hand, the Executive Committee, having created a bourgeois government, could not make up its mind like the Bible God to call the creation good. On the contrary, it made great haste to increase the distance between itself and the work of its hands, and announced that it intended to support the new power only in so far as it should truly serve the democratic revolution. The Provisional Government very well knew that it could not survive an hour without the support of the official democracy. But this support was promised only as a reward for good behavior—that is, for fulfilling tasks alien to it, and which the democracy itself had just declined to fulfill. The government never knew within what limits it might dare to reveal its semi-contraband sovereignty. The leaders of the Executive Committee could not always advise it, because it was hard for them to guess just where some dissatisfaction would break out in their own midst, expressing the dissatisfaction of the masses. The bourgeoisie pretended that the socialists were deceiving them. The socialists in their turn were afraid that the liberals, with their premature demands, would stir up the masses and complicate a situation difficult enough as it was. *"In so far as"*—that equivocal formula laid its imprint on the whole pre-October period. It became the juridical formulation of the inner lie contained in the hybrid régime of the February revolution.

To bring pressure upon the government, the Executive Committee elected a special commission which it politely but ludicrously named "Contact Commission." The organization of the revolutionary power was thus based upon the principle of mutual persuasion. The mystic writer Merezhkovsky could find a precedent for such a régime only in the Old Testament: the kings of Israel had their prophets. But the prophets of the Bible, like the prophets of the last Romanov, used at least to receive suggestions directly from heaven, and the kings did not dare to contradict. In that way a single sovereignty was assured. It was quite different with the prophets of the Soviet: they prophesied only under the stimulus of their own limited intelligence. The liberal ministers moreover believed that nothing good could come out of the Soviet. Cheidze, Skobelev, Sukhanov and others would run to the government and garrulously try to persuade it to make some concession; the ministers would object; the delegates would return to the Executive Committee, try to influence it with the authority of the government; again get into contact with the ministers; and so begin over again from the beginning. This complicated mill-wheel never did any grinding.

In the Contact Commission everybody complained. Guchkov especially wept over the disorders in the army caused by the connivances of the Soviet. At times the War Minister of the revolution "in the literal sense of the word . . . poured out tears, or at least earnestly wiped his eyes with his handkerchief." He was quite right in thinking that to dry the tears of the anointed is one of the functions of a prophet.

On the ninth of March General Alexeiev, the Chief of Staff, telegraphed the War Minister: "The German yoke is near if only we indulge the Soviet." Guchkov answered him tearfully: "The government, alas, has no real power; the troops, the railroads, the post and telegraph are in the hands of the Soviet. The simple fact is that the Provisional Government exists only so long as the Soviet permits it."

Week followed week, but the situation did not improve in

the least. Early in April when the Provisional Government sent deputies of the Duma to the front, it directed them, gritting its teeth, not to reveal any disagreements with the delegates of the Soviet. Throughout the whole journey the liberal deputies felt as though they were under convoy, but they also knew that without this, notwithstanding their lofty credentials, they not only could not approach the soldiers, but they could not even find seats in the trains. That prosaic detail in the memoirs of Prince Mansyrev excellently supplements Guchkov's correspondence with the staff as to the essence of the February constitution. One of the reactionary wits pretty well characterized the situation thus: "The old government is in prison, and the new one under house arrest."

But did the Provisional Government have no other support but this equivocal one of the Soviet leaders? What had become of the possessing classes? The question is a fundamental one. United by their past with the monarchy, the possessing classes had hastened to group themselves around a new axis after the revolution. On the 2nd of March, the Council of Trade and Industry, representing the united capital of the whole country, saluted the act of the State Duma, and declared itself "wholly at the disposition" of its Committee.

The zemstvos and the town dumas adopted the same course. On March 10, even the Council of the United Nobility, the mainstay of the throne, summoned all the people of Russia in a language of eloquent cowardice "to unite around the Provisional Government as now the sole lawful power in Russia." Almost at the same time the institutions and organs of the possessing classes began to denounce the dual power, and to lay the blame for the disorders upon the Soviet—at first cautiously, but then bolder and bolder. The employers were soon followed by the clerks, the united liberal professions, the government employees. From the army came telegrams, addresses and resolutions of the same character—manufactured in the staff. The liberal press opened a campaign "for a single sovereignty," which in the coming months acquired the character of a hurricane of fire around the heads of the Soviet. All these things together looked exceedingly impressive. The enormous number of institutions, well-known names, resolutions, articles, the decisiveness of tone—it had an indubitable effect upon the suggestible heads of the Committee. And yet there was no serious force behind this threatening parade of the propertied classes. How about the force of property? said the petty bourgeois socialists, answering the Bolsheviks. Property is a relation among people. It represents an enormous power so long as it is universally recognized and supported by that system of compulsion called Law and the State. But the very essence of the present situation was that the old state had suddenly collapsed, and the entire old system of rights had been called in question by the masses. In the factories the workers were more and more regarding themselves as the proprietors, and the bosses as uninvited guests. Still less assured were the feelings of the landlords in the provinces, face to face with those surly vengeful muzhiks, and far from that governmental power in whose existence they did for a time, owing to their distance from the capital, believe. The property-holders, deprived of the possibility of using their property, or protecting it, ceased to be real property-holders and became badly frightened Philistines who could not give any support to the government for the simple reason that they needed support themselves. They soon began to curse the government for its weakness, but they were only cursing their own fate.

In those days the joint activity of the Executive Committee and the ministry seemed to have for its goal to demonstrate that the art of government in time of revolution consists in a garrulous waste of time. With the liberals this was a consciously adopted plan. It was their firm conviction that all measures demanded postponement except one: the oath of loyalty to the Entente.

Miliukov acquainted his colleagues with the secret treaties. Kerensky let them in one ear and out the other. Apparently only the Procuror of the Holy Synod, a certain Lvov, rich in surprises, a namesake of the Premier but not a prince, went into a storm of indignation and even called the treaties "brigandage and swindle"—which undoubtedly provoked a condescending smile from Miliukov ("The everyday man is a fool") and a quiet proposal to return to the order of business. The official Declaration of the government promised to summon a Constituent Assembly at the earliest possible date—which date, however, was intentionally not stated. Nothing was said about the form of government: they still hoped to return to the lost paradise of monarchy. But the real meat of the Declaration lay in its promise to carry the war through to victory, and "unswervingly carry out the agreements made with our Allies." So far as concerned the most threatening problems of the people's existence, the revolution had apparently been achieved only in order to make the announcement: everything remains as before. Since the democrats attributed an almost mystic importance to recognition by the Entente—a small trader amounts to nothing until the bank recognizes his credit—the Executive Committee swallowed in silence the imperialist declaration of March 6.

"Not one official organ of the democracy," grieves Sukhanov a year later, "publicly reacted to the Declaration of the Provisional Government, which disgraced our revolution at its very birth in the eyes of democratic Europe."

At last, on the 8th of March, there issued from the ministerial laboratory a Decree of Amnesty. By that time the doors of the prisons had been opened by the people throughout the whole country, political exiles were returning in a solid stream with meetings, hurrahs, military speeches, flowers. The decree sounded like a belated echo from the government buildings. On the twelfth they announced the abolition of the death penalty. Four months later it was restored in the army. Kerensky promised to elevate justice to unheard-of heights. In a moment of heat he actually did carry out a resolution of the Executive Committee introducing representatives of the workers and soldiers as members of the courts of justice. That was the sole measure in which could be felt the heartbeat of the revolution, and it raised the hair on the heads of the eunuchs of justice. But the matter stopped right there. Lawyer Demianov, an important officer in the ministry under Kerensky, and also a "socialist," decided to adopt the principle of leaving all former officials at their posts. To quote his own words: "The policies of a revolutionary government ought never to offend anybody unnecessarily." That was, at bottom, the guiding principle of the whole Provisional Government, which feared most of all to offend anybody from the circles of the possessing classes, or even the tzarist bureaucracy. Not only the judges, but even the prosecutors of the tzarist régime remained at their posts. To be sure, the masses might be offended. But that was the Soviet's business: the masses did not enter into the field of vision of the government.

The sole thing in the nature of a fresh stream was brought in by the above-mentioned temperamental Procuror, Lvov, who gave an official report on the "idiots and scoundrels" sitting in the Holy Synod. The ministers listened to his juicy characterizations with some alarm, but the synod continued a state institution, and Greek Orthodoxy the state religion. Even the membership of the Synod remained unchanged. A revolution ought not to quarrel with anybody!

The members of the State Council—faithful servants of two or three emperors—continued to sit, or at least to draw their salaries. And this fact soon acquired a symbolic significance. Factories and barracks noisily protested. The Executive Committee worried about it. The government spent two sessions debating the question of the fate and salaries of the members of the State Council, and could not arrive at a decision. Why disturb these respectable people, among whom, by the way, we have many good friends?

The Rasputin ministers were still in prison, but the Provisional Government hastened to vote them a pension. This sounded like mockery, or a voice from another world. But the government did not want to offend its predecessors even though they were locked up in jail.

The senators continued to drowse in their embroidered jackets, and when a left senator, Sokolov, newly appointed by Kerensky, dared to appear in a black frock coat, they quietly removed him from the hall. These tzarist legislators were not afraid to offend the February revolution, once convinced that its government had no teeth.

Karl Marx saw the cause of the failure of the March revolution in Germany in the fact that it "reformed only the very highest political circles, leaving untouched all the layers beneath them—the old bureaucracy, the old army, the old judges, born and brought up and grown old in the service of absolutism." Socialists of the type of Kerensky were seeking salvation exactly where Marx saw the cause of failure. And the Menshevik Marxists were with Kerensky, not Marx.

The sole sphere in which the government showed initiative and revolutionary tempo, was that of legislation on stock holdings. Here the decree of reform was issued on the 17th of March. National and religious limitations were annulled only three days later. There were quite a few people on the staff of the government, you see, who had suffered under the old régime, if at all, only from a lack of business in stocks.

The workers were impatiently demanding an eight-hour day. The government pretended to be deaf in both ears. Besides it is war time, and all ought to sacrifice themselves for the good of the Fatherland. Moreover that is the Soviet's business: let them pacify the workers.

Still more threatening was the land question. Here it was really necessary to do something. Spurred on by the prophets, the Minister of Agriculture, Shingarev, ordered the formation of local land committees—prudently refraining, however, from defining their tasks and functions. The peasants had an idea that these committees ought to give them the land. The landlords thought the committees ought to protect their property. From the very start the muzhik's noose, more ruthless than all others, was tightening round the neck of the February régime.

Agreeably to the official doctrine, all those problems which had caused the revolution were postponed to the Constituent Assembly. How could you expect these irreproachable democrats to anticipate the national will, when they had not even succeeded in seating Mikhail Romanov astride of it? The preparation of a national representation was approached in those days with such bureaucratic heaviness and deliberate procrastination that the Constituent Assembly itself became a mirage. Only on the 25th of March, almost a month after the insurrection—a month of revolution!—the government decided to call a lumbering Special Conference for the purpose of working out an election law. But the conference never opened. Miliukov in his *History of the Revolution*—which is false from beginning to end—confusedly states that as a result of various difficulties "the work of the Special Conference was not begun under the first government." The difficulties were inherent in the constitution of the conference and in its function. The whole idea was to postpone the Constituent Assembly until better times: until victory, until peace, or until the Calends of Kornilov.

The Russian bourgeoisie, which appeared in the world too late, mortally hated the revolution. But its hatred had no strength. It had to bide its time and maneuver. Being unable to overthrow and strangle the revolution, the bourgeoisie counted on starving it out.

Chapter XI

DUAL POWER

What constitutes the essence of a dual power?[1] We must pause upon this question, for an illumination of it has never appeared in historic literature. And yet this dual power is a distinct condition of social crisis, by no means peculiar to the Russian revolution of 1917, although there most clearly marked out.

Antagonistic classes exist in society everywhere, and a class deprived of power inevitably strives to some extent to swerve the governmental course in its favor. This does not as yet mean, however, that two or more powers are ruling in society. The character of a political structure is directly determined by the relation of the oppressed classes to the ruling class. A single government, the necessary condition of stability in any régime, is preserved so long as the ruling class succeeds in putting over its economic and political forms upon the whole of society as the only forms possible.

The simultaneous dominion of the German Junkers and the bourgeoisie—whether in the Hohenzollern form or the republic—is not a double government, no matter how sharp at times may be the conflict between the two participating powers. They have a common social basis, therefore their clash does

[1] *Dual power* is the phrase settled upon in communist literature as an English rendering of *dvoevlastie*. The term is untranslatable both because of its form—twin-powerdom—and because the stem, *vlast*, means *sovereignty* as well as *power*. *Vlast* is also used as an equivalent of *government*, and in the plural corresponds to our phrase *the authorities*. In view of this, I have employed some other terms besides *dual power*: *double sovereignty, two-power régime,* etc. [Trans.]

not threaten to split the state apparatus. The two-power régime arises only out of irreconcilable class conflicts—is possible, therefore, only in a revolutionary epoch, and constitutes one of its fundamental elements.

The political mechanism of revolution consists of the transfer of power from one class to another. The forcible overturn is usually accomplished in a brief time. But no historic class lifts itself from a subject position to a position of rulership suddenly in one night, even though a night of revolution. It must already on the eve of the revolution have assumed a very independent attitude towards the official ruling class; moreover, it must have focussed upon itself the hopes of intermediate classes and layers, dissatisfied with the existing state of affairs, but not capable of playing an independent rôle. The historic preparation of a revolution brings about, in the pre-revolutionary period, a situation in which the class which is called to realize the new social system, although not yet master of the country, has actually concentrated in its hands a significant share of the state power, while the official apparatus of the government is still in the hands of the old lords. That is the initial dual power in every revolution.

But that is not its only form. If the new class, placed in power by a revolution which it did not want, is in essence an already old, historically belated, class; if it was already worn out before it was officially crowned; if on coming to power it encounters an antagonist already sufficiently mature and reaching out its hand toward the helm of state; then instead of one unstable two-power equilibrium, the political revolution produces another, still less stable. To overcome the "anarchy" of this twofold sovereignty becomes at every new step the task of the revolution—or the counter-revolution.

This double sovereignty does not presuppose—generally speaking, indeed, it excludes—the possibility of a division of the power into two equal halves, or indeed any formal equilibrium of forces whatever. It is not a constitutional, but a revolutionary fact. It implies that a destruction of the social equilibrium has already split the state superstructure. It arises where the hostile classes are already each relying upon essentially incompatible governmental organizations—the one outlived, the other in process of formation—which jostle against each other at every step in the sphere of government. The amount of power which falls to each of these struggling classes in such a situation, is determined by the correlation of forces in the course of the struggle.

By its very nature such a state of affairs cannot be stable. Society needs a concentration of power, and in the person of the ruling class—or, in the situation we are discussing, the two half-ruling classes—irresistibly strives to get it. The splitting of sovereignty foretells nothing less than a civil war. But before the competing classes and parties will go to that extreme—especially in case they dread the interference of a third force—they may feel compelled for quite a long time to endure, and even to sanction, a two-power system. This system will nevertheless inevitably explode. Civil war gives to this double sovereignty its most visible, because territorial, expression. Each of the powers, having created its own fortified drill ground, fights for possession of the rest of the territory, which often has to endure the double sovereignty in the form of successive invasions by the two fighting powers, until one of them decisively installs itself.

The English revolution of the seventeenth century, exactly because it was a great revolution shattering the nation to the bottom, affords a clear example of this alternating dual power, with sharp transitions in the form of civil war.

At first the royal power, resting upon the privileged classes or the upper circles of these classes—the aristocrats and bishops—is opposed by the bourgeoisie and the circles of the squirarchy that are close to it. The government of the bourgeoisie is the Presbyterian Parliament supported by the City of London. The protracted conflict between these two régimes is finally settled in open civil war. The two governmental centers—London and Oxford—create their own armies. Here the dual power takes a territorial form, although, as always in civil war, the boundaries are very shifting. Parliament conquers. The king is captured and awaits his fate.

It would seem that the conditions are now created for the single rule of the Presbyterian bourgeoisie. But before the royal power could be broken, the parliamentary army has converted itself into an independent political force. It has concentrated in its ranks the Independents, the pious and resolute petty bourgeoisie, the craftsmen and farmers. This army powerfully interferes in the social life, not merely as an armed force, but as a Praetorian Guard, and as the political representative of a new class opposing the prosperous and rich bourgeoisie. Correspondingly the army creates a new state organ rising above the military command: a council of soldiers' and officers' deputies ("agitators"). A new period of double sovereignty has thus arrived: that of the Presbyterian Parliament and the Independents' army. This leads to open conflicts. The bourgeoisie proves powerless to oppose with its own army the "model army" of Cromwell—that is, the armed plebeians. The conflict ends with a purgation of the Presbyterian Parliament by the sword of the Independents. There remains but the rump of a parliament; the dictatorship of Cromwell is established. The lower ranks of the army, under the leadership of the Levellers—the extreme left wing of the revolution—try to oppose to the rule of the upper military levels, the patricians of the army, their own veritably plebeian régime. But this new two-power system does not succeed in developing: the Levellers, the lowest depths of the petty bourgeoisie, have not yet, nor can have, their own historic path. Cromwell soon settles accounts with his enemies. A new political equilibrium, and still by no means a stable one, is established for a period of years.

In the great French revolution, the Constituent Assembly, the backbone of which was the upper levels of the Third Estate, concentrated the power in its hands—without however fully annulling the prerogatives of the king. The period of the Constituent Assembly is a clearly-marked period of dual power, which ends with the flight of the king to Varennes, and is formally liquidated with the founding of the Republic.

The first French constitution (1791), based upon the fiction of a complete independence of the legislative and executive powers, in reality concealed from the people, or tried to conceal, a double sovereignty: that of the bourgeoisie, firmly entrenched in the National Assembly after the capture by the people of the Bastille, and that of the old monarchy still relying upon the upper circles of the priesthood, the clergy, the bureaucracy, and the military, to say nothing of their hopes of foreign intervention. In this self-contradictory régime lay the germs of its inevitable destruction. A way out could be found only in the abolition of bourgeois representation by the powers of European reaction, or in the guillotine for the king and the monarchy. Paris and Coblenz must measure their forces.

But before it comes to war and the guillotine, the Paris Commune enters the scene—supported by the lowest city layers of the Third Estate—and with increasing boldness contests the power with the official representatives of the national bourgeoisie. A new double sovereignty is thus inaugurated, the first manifestation of which we observe as early as 1790, when the big and medium bourgeoisie is still firmly seated in the administration and in the municipalities. How striking is the picture—and how vilely it has been slandered!—of the efforts of the plebeian levels to raise themselves up out of the social cellars and catacombs, and stand forth in that forbidden arena where people in wigs and silk breeches are settling the fate of the nation. It seemed as though the very foundation of society, tramped underfoot by the cultured bourgeoisie, was stirring and coming to life. Human heads lifted themselves above the solid mass, horny hands stretched aloft, hoarse but courageous voices shouted! The districts of Paris, bastards of the revolution, began to live a life of their own. They were recognized—it was impossible not to recognize them!—and transformed into sections. But they kept continually breaking the boundaries of legality and receiving a current of fresh blood from below, opening their ranks in spite of the law to those with no rights, the destitute Sansculottes. At the same time the rural municipalities were becoming a screen for a peasant uprising against that bourgeois legality which was defending the feudal property system. Thus from under the second nation arises a third.

The Parisian sections at first stood opposed to the Commune, which was still dominated by the respectable bourgeoisie. In the bold outbreak of August 10, 1792, the sections gained control of the Commune. From then on the revolutionary Commune opposed the Legislative Assembly, and subsequently the Convention, which failed to keep up with the problems and progress of the revolution—registering its events, but not performing them—because it did not possess the energy, audacity and unanimity of that new class which had raised itself up from the depths of the Parisian districts and found support in the most backward villages. As the sections gained control of the Commune, so the Commune, by way of a new insurrection, gained control of the Convention. Each of the stages was characterized by a sharply marked double sovereignty, each wing of which was trying to establish a single and strong government—the right by a defensive struggle, the left by an offensive. Thus, characteristically—for both revolutions and counter-revolutions—the demand for a dictatorship results from the intolerable contradictions of the double sovereignty. The transition from one of its forms to the other is accomplished through civil war. The great stages of a revolution—that is, the passing of power to new classes or layers—do not at all coincide in this process with the succession of representative institutions, which march along after the dynamic of the revolution like a belated shadow. In the long run, to be sure, the revolutionary dictatorship of the Sansculottes unites with the dictatorship of the Convention. But with what Convention? A Convention purged of the Girondists, who yesterday ruled it with the hand of the Terror—a Convention abridged and adapted to the dominion of new social forces. Thus by the steps of the dual power the French revolution rises in the course of four years to its culmination. After the 9th Thermidor it begins—again by the steps of the dual power—to descend. And again civil war precedes every downward step, just as before it had accompanied every rise. In this way the new society seeks a new equilibrium of forces.

The Russian bourgeoisie, fighting with and coöperating with the Rasputin bureaucracy, had enormously strengthened its political position during the war. Exploiting the defeat of tzarism, it had concentrated in its hands, by means of the Country and Town unions and the Military-Industrial Committees, a great power. It had at its independent disposition enormous state resources, and was in the essence of the matter a parallel government. During the war the tzar's ministers complained that Prince Lvov was furnishing supplies to the army, feeding it, medicating it, even establishing barber shops for the soldiers. "We must either put an end to this, or give the whole power into his hands," said Minister Krivoshein in

1915. He never imagined that a year and a half later Lvov would receive "the whole power"—only not from the tzar, but from the hands of Kerensky, Cheidze and Sukhanov. But on the second day after he received it, there began a new double sovereignty: alongside of yesterday's liberal half-government —today formally legalized—there arose an unofficial, but so much the more actual government of the toiling masses in the form of the soviets. From that moment the Russian revolution began to grow up into an event of world-historic significance.

What, then, is the peculiarity of this dual power as it appeared in the February revolution? In the events of the seventeenth and eighteenth centuries, the dual power was in each case a natural stage in a struggle imposed upon its participants by a temporary correlation of forces, and each side strove to replace the dual power with its own single power. In the revolution of 1917, we see the official democracy consciously and intentionally creating a two-power system, dodging with all its might the transfer of power into its own hands. The double sovereignty is created, or so it seems at a glance, not as a result of a struggle of classes for power, but as the result of a voluntary "yielding" of power by one class to another. In so far as the Russian "democracy" sought for an escape from the two-power régime, it could find one only in its own removal from power. It is just this that we have called the paradox of the February revolution.

A certain analogy can be found in 1848, in the conduct of the German bourgeoisie with relation to the monarchy. But the analogy is not complete. The German bourgeoisie did try earnestly to divide the power with the monarchy on the basis of an agreement. But the bourgeoisie neither had the full power in its hands, nor by any means gave it over wholly to the monarchy. "The Prussian bourgeoisie nominally possessed the power, it did not for a moment doubt that the forces of the old government would place themselves unreservedly at its disposition and convert themselves into loyal adherents of its own omnipotence" (Marx and Engels).

The Russian democracy of 1917, having captured the power from the very moment of insurrection, tried not only to divide it with the bourgeoisie, but to give the state over to the bourgeoisie absolutely. This means, if you please, that in the first quarter of the twentieth century the official Russian democracy had succeeded in decaying politically more completely than the German liberal bourgeoisie of the nineteenth century. And that is entirely according to the laws of history, for it is merely the reverse aspect of the upgrowth in those same decades of the proletariat, which now occupied the place of the craftsmen of Cromwell and the Sansculottes of Robespierre.

If you look deeper, the twofold rule of the Provisional Government and the Executive Committee had the character of a mere reflection. Only the proletariat could advance a claim to the new power. Relying distrustfully upon the workers and soldiers, the Compromisers were compelled to continue the double bookkeeping—of the kings and the prophets. The twofold government of the liberals and the democrats only reflected the still concealed double sovereignty of the bourgeoisie and the proletariat. When the Bolsheviks displace the Compromisers at the head of the Soviet—and this will happen within a few months—then that concealed double sovereignty will come to the surface, and this will be the eve of the October revolution. Until that moment the revolution will live in a world of political reflections. Refracted through the rationalizations of the socialist intelligentsia, the double sovereignty, from being a stage in the class struggle, became a regulative principle. It was just for this reason that it occupied the center of all theoretical discussions. Everything has its uses: the mirror-like character of the February double government has enabled us better to understand those epochs in history when the same thing appears as a full-blooded episode in a struggle between two régimes. The feeble and reflected light of the moon makes possible important conclusions about the sunlight.

In the immeasurably greater maturity of the Russian proletariat in comparison with the town masses of the older revolutions, lies the basic peculiarity of the Russian revolution. This led first to the paradox of a half-spectral double government, and afterwards prevented the real one from being resolved in favor of the bourgeoisie. For the question stood thus: Either the bourgeoisie will actually dominate the old state apparatus, altering it a little for its purposes, in which case the soviets will come to nothing; or the soviets will form the foundation of a new state, liquidating not only the old governmental apparatus, but also the dominion of those classes which it served. The Mensheviks and the Social Revolutionaries were steering toward the first solution, the Bolsheviks toward the second. The oppressed classes, who, as Marat observed, did not possess in the past the knowledge, or skill, or leadership to carry through what they had begun, were armed in the Russian revolution of the twentieth century with all three. The Bolsheviks were victorious.

A year after their victory the same situation was repeated in Germany, with a different correlation of forces. The social democracy was steering for the establishment of a democratic government of the bourgeoisie and the liquidation of the soviets. Luxemburg and Liebknecht steered toward the dictatorship of the soviets. The Social Democrats won. Hilferding and Kautsky in Germany, Max Adler in Austria, proposed that they should "combine" democracy with the soviet system, including the workers' soviets in the constitution. That would have meant making potential or open civil war a constituent part of the state régime. It would be impossible to imagine a more curious Utopia. Its sole justification on German soil is perhaps an old tradition: the Württemberg democrats of '48 wanted a republic with a duke at the head.

Does this phenomenon of the dual power—heretofore not sufficiently appreciated—contradict the Marxian theory of the state, which regards government as an executive committee of the ruling class? This is just the same as asking: Does the fluctuation of prices under the influence of supply and demand contradict the labor theory of value? Does the self-sacrifice of a female protecting her offspring refute the theory of a struggle for existence? No, in these phenomena we have a more complicated combination of the same laws. If the state is an organization of class rule, and a revolution is the overthrow of the ruling class, then the transfer of power from the one class to the other must necessarily create self-contradictory state conditions, and first of all in the form of the dual power. The relation of class forces is not a mathematical quantity permitting *a priori* computations. When the old régime is thrown out of equilibrium, a new correlation of forces can be established only as the result of a trial by battle. That is revolution.

It may seem as though this theoretical inquiry has led us away from the events of 1917. In reality it leads right into the heart of them. It was precisely around this problem of twofold power that the dramatic struggle of parties and classes turned. Only from a theoretical height is it possible to observe it fully and correctly understand it.

Editor's Summary of Chapters XII–XIV

CHAPTER XII. THE EXECUTIVE COMMITTEE. Unlike The Soviet of Workers' Deputies of the 1905 revolution, which rose out of a general strike and directly represented the masses in struggle, the organization created on February 27, 1917, and named "Executive Committee of the Soviet of Workers' Deputies" was self-constituted, in advance of the Soviet and independently of the factories and regiments, after the victory of the revolution. Its immense authority, and that of the many dependent bodies which sprang up in other Russian communities, rested upon its seeming continuance of the 1905 Soviet. The virtues of the soviet system were considerable. Of all the forms of revolutionary representation developed in past history, this one proved the most flexible, immediate, and transparent. But in the early months following the February revolution the soviets were often unwieldy and indecisive, with a large and indiscriminate membership. The Executive Committee was at first dominated by the Mensheviks (Martov, Dan, Tseretelli, Cheidze) and the Social Revolutionaries (Kerensky, Chernov, Avksentiev, Gotz). The Executive Committee tended to resist the pressure of the masses for full power and generally yielded to them, rather than led them, in such important measures as the arrest of the tzar and his family, the relief of hunger, and the institution of the eight-hour day. Before Lenin's arrival in Petrograd, the Bolsheviks under Kamenev and Stalin were also indecisive.

CHAPTER XIII. THE ARMY AND THE WAR. By 1917 the military was better supplied with guns and ammunition than in the earlier years of the war. Discipline was breaking down, however, even before February; and despair of victory over the Germans was widespread even among the officers. Like all armies, the Russian army was a copy of the society it served, with the difference that it gave social relations a concentrated character, carrying both their negative and their positive features to an extreme. Still largely feudal in organization, the Russian army displayed an antagonism between officer and soldier which was a refraction of the hostility between landlord and peasant in this largely agrarian society. The uprising of the Petrograd garrisons in February took place not only without officers but usually against them, although in some cases the officers were compelled to follow their men, or were killed by their men in revenge for former outrages, or went over more or less willingly to the revolution. At the front and in the fleet, the command delayed informing its forces of the revolution as long as possible. When the news reached them, the various branches of the service reacted in many different ways. While the sailors of the Baltic Fleet responded by executing certain officers, right beside them in the Helsingfors garrison the officers were occupying a leading position in the soldiers' soviet. Military discipline was to be further demoralized by the continuation of the war.

CHAPTER XIV. THE RULING GROUP AND THE WAR. What did the Provisional Government and the Executive Committee intend to do with this war and this army? "Even if there had been no revolution," wrote the Liberal Rodzianko later, "the war would have been lost just the same, and in all probability a separate peace signed." Rodzianko's views typified those of liberally conservative circles. The mutiny of the battalions of the Guard foretold to the possessing classes not victory abroad but defeat at home. The question of war and peace had almost ceased for them to be an independent question. They felt that they would not be able to use the revolution for the purpose of the war, and so much the more imperative became their other task: to use the war against the revolution in order to save the bourgeois régime itself. A war to exhaust the enemy was thus converted into a war to exhaust the militant masses. So, with the support of a majority of the Executive Committee, the Provisional Government restored a measure of discipline in the army, voted a new war loan, and sought to prosecute the war. As a precaution, however, the Executive Committee installed its own commissars in all regiments and institutions of the military to represent the interests of the men and keep watch over the political reliability of the officers.

Chapter XV

THE BOLSHEVIKS AND LENIN

On the 3rd of April Lenin arrived in Petrograd from abroad. Only from that moment does the Bolshevik Party begin to speak out loud, and, what is more important, with its own voice.

For Bolshevism the first months of the revolution had been a period of bewilderment and vacillation. In the "manifesto" of the Bolshevik Central Committee, drawn up just after the victory of the insurrection, we read that "the workers of the shops and factories, and likewise the mutinied troops, must immediately elect their representatives to the Provisional Revolutionary Government." The manifesto was printed in the official organ of the Soviet without comment or objection, as though the question were a purely academic one. But the leading Bolsheviks themselves also regarded their slogans as purely demonstrative. They behaved not like representatives of a proletarian party preparing an independent struggle for power, but like the left wing of a democracy, which, having announced its principles, intended for an indefinite time to play the part of loyal opposition.

Sukhanov asserts that at the sitting of the Executive Committee on March 1 the central question at issue was merely as to the conditions of the handing over of power. Against the thing itself—the formation of a bourgeois government—not one voice was raised, notwithstanding that out of 39 members of the Executive Committee, 11 were Bolsheviks or their adherents, and moreover three members of the Bolshevik center, Zalutsky, Shliapnikov and Molotov, were present at the sitting.

In the Soviet on the next day, according to the report of

Shliapnikov himself, out of 400 deputies present, only 19 voted against the transfer of power to the bourgeoisie—and this although there were already 40 in the Bolshevik faction. The voting itself passed off in a purely formal parliamentary manner, without any clear counter-proposition from the Bolsheviks, without conflict, and without any agitation whatever in the Bolshevik press.

On the 4th of March the Bureau of the Bolshevik Central Committee adopted a resolution on the counter-revolutionary character of the Provisional Government, and the necessity of steering a course towards the democratic dictatorship of the proletariat and the peasantry. The Petrograd committee, rightly regarding this resolution as academic—since it gave no directives for today's action—approached the problem from the opposite angle. "Taking cognizance of the resolution on the Provisional Government adopted by the Soviet," it announces that "it will not oppose the power of the Provisional Government in so far as," etc. . . . In essence this was the position of the Mensheviks and Social Revolutionaries—only moved back to the second line trenches. This openly opportunist resolution of the Petrograd Committee contradicted only in a formal way the resolution of the Central Committee, whose academic character had meant nothing politically but putting up with an accomplished fact.

This readiness to submit silently, or with reservations, to the government of the bourgeoisie did not have by any means the entire sympathy of the party. The Bolshevik workers met the Provisional Government from the first as a hostile rampart unexpectedly grown up in their path. The Vyborg Committee held meetings of thousands of workers and soldiers, which almost unanimously adopted resolutions on the necessity for a seizure of power by the soviets. An active participant in this agitation, Dingelstedt, testifies: "There was not one meeting, not one workers' meeting, which would have voted down such a resolution from us if there had only been somebody to present it." The Mensheviks and Social Revolutionaries were afraid in those first days to appear openly before audiences of workers and soldiers with their formulation of the question of power. A resolution of the Vyborg workers, in view of its popularity, was printed and pasted up as a placard. But the

Petrograd Committee put an absolute ban upon this resolution, and the Vyborg workers were compelled to submit.

On the question of the social content of the revolution and the prospects of its development, the position of the Bolshevik leadership was no less cloudy. Shliapnikov recalls: "We agreed with the Mensheviks that we were passing through the period of the breakdown of feudal relations, and that in their place would appear all kinds of 'freedoms' proper to bourgeois relations." *Pravda* said in its first number: "The fundamental problem is to establish a democratic republic." In an instruction to the workers' deputies, the Moscow Committee announced: "The proletariat aims to achieve freedom for the struggle for socialism, its ultimate goal." This traditional reference to the "ultimate goal" sufficiently emphasizes the historic distance from socialism. Farther than this nobody ventured. The fear to go beyond the boundaries of a democratic revolution dictated a policy of waiting, of accommodation, and of actual retreat before the Compromisers.

It is easy to imagine how heavily this political characterlessness of the center influenced the provinces. We will confine ourselves to the testimony of one of the Saratov organizations: "Our party after taking an active part in the insurrection has evidently lost its influence with the masses, and this has been caught up by the Mensheviks and Social Revolutionaries. Nobody knew what the slogans of the Bolsheviks were. . . . It was a very unpleasant picture."

The left Bolsheviks, especially the workers, tried with all their force to break through this quarantine. But they did not know how to refute the premise about the bourgeois character of the revolution and the danger of an isolation of the proletariat. They submitted, gritting their teeth, to the directions of the leaders. There were various conflicting currents in Bolshevism from the very first day, but no one of them carried its thoughts through to the end. *Pravda* reflected this cloudy and unstable intellectual state of the party, and did not bring any unity into it. The situation became still more complicated toward the middle of March, after the arrival from exile of Kamenev and Stalin, who abruptly turned the helm of official party policy to the right.

Although a Bolshevik almost from the very birth of Bolshevism, Kamenev had always stood on the right flank of the party. Not without theoretical foundations or political instinct, and with a large experience of factional struggle in Russia and a store of political observations made in Western Europe, Kamenev grasped better than most Bolsheviks the general ideas of Lenin, but he grasped them only in order to give them the mildest possible interpretation in practice. You could not expect from him either independence of judgment or initiative in action. A distinguished propagandist, orator, journalist, not brilliant but thoughtful, Kamenev was especially valuable for negotiations with other parties and reconnoiters in other social circles—although from such excursions he always brought back with him a bit of some mood alien to the party. These characteristics of Kamenev were so obvious that almost nobody ever misjudged him as a political figure. Sukhanov remarks in him an absence of "sharp corners." "It is always necessary to lead him on a tow-line," he says. "He may resist a little, but not strongly." Stankevich writes to the same effect: Kamenev's attitude to his enemies "was so gentle that it seemed as though he himself were ashamed of the irreconcilableness of his position; in the committee he was certainly not an enemy but merely an opposition." There is little to add to that.

Stalin was a totally different type of Bolshevik, both in his psychological makeup and in the character of his party work: a strong, but theoretically and politically primitive, organizer. Whereas Kamenev as a publicist stayed for many years abroad with Lenin, where stood the theoretical forge of the party, Stalin as a so-called "practical," without theoretical viewpoint, without broad political interests, and without a knowledge of foreign languages, was inseparable from the Russian soil. Such party workers appeared abroad only on short visits to receive instructions, discuss their further problems, and return again to Russia. Stalin was distinguished among the practicals for energy, persistence, and inventiveness in the matter of moves behind the scenes. Where Kamenev as a natural result of his character felt "embarrassed" by the practical conclusions of Bolshevism, Stalin on the contrary was inclined to defend the practical conclusions which he adopted without any mitigation whatever, uniting insistence with rudeness.

Notwithstanding their opposite characters, it was no accident that Kamenev and Stalin occupied a common position at the beginning of the revolution: they supplemented each other. A revolutionary conception without a revolutionary will is like a watch with a broken spring. Kamenev was always behind the time—or rather beneath the tasks—of the revolution. But the absence of a broad political conception condemns the most willful revolutionist to indecisiveness in the presence of vast and complicated events. Stalin, the empiric, was open to alien influences not on the side of will but on the side of intellect. Thus it was that this publicist without decision, and this organizer without intellectual horizon, carried Bolshevism in March 1917 to the very boundaries of Menshevism. Stalin proved even less capable than Kamenev of developing an independent position in the Executive Committee, which he entered as a representative of the party. There is to be found in its reports and its press not one proposal, announcement, or protest, in which Stalin expressed the Bolshevik point of view in opposition to the fawning of the "democracy" at the feet of liberalism. Sukhanov says in his *Notes of the Revolution:* "Among the Bolsheviks, besides Kamenev, there appeared in the Executive Committee in those days Stalin. . . . During the time of his modest activity in the Executive Committee he gave me the impression—and not only me—of a gray spot which would sometimes give out a dim and inconsequential light. There is really nothing more to be said about him." Although Sukhanov obviously underestimates Stalin as a whole, he nevertheless correctly describes his political characterlessness in the Executive Committee of the Compromisers.

On the 14th of March the manifesto "to the people of the whole world," interpreting the victory of the February revolution in the interests of the Entente, and signifying the triumph of a new republican social patriotism of the French stamp, was adopted by the Soviet *unanimously.* That meant a considerable success for Kamenev and Stalin, but one evidently attained without much struggle. *Pravda* spoke of it as a "conscious compromise between different tendencies represented in the Soviet." It is necessary to add that this compromise involved a direct break with the tendency of Lenin, which was not represented in the Soviet at all.

Kamenev, a member of the emigrant editorial staff of the central organ, Stalin, a member of the Central Committee, and Muranov, a deputy in the Duma who had also returned from Siberia, removed the old editors of *Pravda*, who had occupied a too "left" position, and on the 15th of March, relying on their somewhat problematical rights, took the paper into their own hands. In the program announcement of the new editorship, it was declared that the Bolsheviks would decisively support the Provisional Government "in so far as it struggles against reaction or counter-revolution." The new editors expressed themselves no less categorically upon the question of war: While the German army obeys its emperor, the Russian soldier must "stand firmly at his post answering bullet with bullet and shell with shell." "Our slogan is not the meaningless 'down with war.' Our slogan is pressure upon the Provisional Government with the aim of compelling it . . . to make an attempt to induce all the warring countries to open immediate negotiations . . . and until then every man remains at his fighting post!" Both the idea and its formulation are those of the defensists. This program of pressure upon an imperialist government with the aim of "inducing" it to adopt a peace-loving form of activity, was the program of Kautsky in Germany, Jean Longuet in France, MacDonald in England. It was anything but the program of Lenin, who was calling for the overthrow of imperialist rule. Defending itself against the patriotic press, *Pravda* went even farther: "All 'defeatism,'" it said, "or rather what an undiscriminating press protected by the tzar's censorship has branded with that name, died at the moment when the first revolutionary regiment appeared on the streets of Petrograd." This was a direct abandonment of Lenin. "Defeatism" was not invented by a hostile press under the protection of a censorship, it was proclaimed by Lenin in the formula: "The defeat of Russia is the lesser evil." The appearance of the first revolutionary regiment, and even the overthrow of the monarchy, did not alter the imperialist character of the war. "The day of the first issue of the transformed *Pravda*," says Shliapnikov, "was a day of rejoicing for the defensists. The whole Tauride Palace, from the business men in the committee of the State Duma to the very heart of the revolutionary democracy, the Executive Committee, was brimful of one piece of news: the victory of the moderate and reasonable Bolsheviks over the extremists. In the Executive Committee itself they met us with venomous smiles. . . . When that number of *Pravda* was received in the factories it produced a complete bewilderment among the members of the party and its sympathizers, and a sarcastic satisfaction among its enemies. . . . The indignation in the party locals was enormous, and when the proletarians found out that *Pravda* had been seized by three former editors arriving from Siberia they demanded their expulsion from the party." *Pravda* was soon compelled to print a sharp protest from the Vyborg district: "If the paper does not want to lose the confidence of the workers, it must and will bring the light of revolutionary consciousness, no matter how painful it may be, to the bourgeois owls." These protests from below compelled the editors to become more cautious in their expressions, but did not change their policy. Even the first article of Lenin which got there from abroad passed by the minds of the editors. They were steering a rightward course all along the line. "In our agitation," writes Dingelstedt, a representative of the left wing, "we had to take up the principle of the dual power . . . and demonstrate the inevitability of this roundabout road to that same worker and soldier mass which during two weeks of intensive political life had been educated in a wholly different understanding of its tasks."

The policy of the party throughout the whole country naturally followed that of *Pravda*. In many soviets resolutions about fundamental problems were now adopted unanimously: the Bolsheviks simply bowed down to the Soviet majority. At a conference of the soviets of the Moscow region the Bolsheviks joined in the resolution of the social patriots on the war. And finally at the All-Russian Conference of the representatives of 82 soviets at the end of March and the beginning of April, the Bolsheviks voted for the official resolution on the question of power, which was defended by Dan. This extraordinary political rapprochement with the Mensheviks caused a widespread tendency towards unification. In the provinces the Bolsheviks and Mensheviks entered into united organizations. The Kamenev-Stalin faction was steadily converting itself into a left flank of the so-called revolutionary democracy, and was taking part in the mechanics of parliamentary "pressure" in the *couloirs* upon the bourgeoisie, supplementing this with a similar pressure upon the democracy.

The part of the Central Committee which lived abroad and the Central Organ, *The Social Democrat,* had been the spiritual center of the party. Lenin, with Zinoviev as assistant, had conducted the whole work of leadership. The most responsible secretarial duties were fulfilled by Lenin's wife, Krupskaia. In the practical work this small center relied upon the support of a few score of Bolshevik emigrants. During the war their isolation from Russia became the more unbearable as the military police of the Entente drew its circle tighter and tighter. The revolutionary explosion they had so long and tensely awaited caught them unawares. England categorically refused to the emigrant internationalists, of whom she had kept a careful list, a visa to Russia. Lenin was raging in his Zurich cage, seeking a way out. Among a hundred plans that were talked over, one was to travel on the passport of a deaf-and-dumb Scandinavian. At the same time Lenin did not miss any chance to make his voice heard from Switzerland. On March 6 he telegraphed through Stockholm to Petrograd: "Our tactic; absolute lack of confidence; no support to the new government; suspect Kerensky especially; arming of proletariat the sole guarantee; immediate elections to the Petrograd Duma; no rapprochement with other parties." In this directive, only the suggestion about elections to the Duma instead of the Soviet, had an episodic character and soon dropped out of sight. The other points, expressed with telegraphic incisiveness, fully indicate the general direction of the policy to be pursued. At the same time Lenin begins to send to *Pravda* his *Letters from Afar* which, although based upon fragments of foreign information constitute a finished analysis of the revolutionary situation. The news in the foreign papers soon enabled him to conclude that the Provisional Government, with the direct assistance not only of Kerensky but of Cheidze, was not unsuccessfully deceiving the workers, giving out the imperialist war for a war of defense. On the 17th of March, through friends in Stockholm, he wrote a letter filled with alarm. "Our party would disgrace itself for ever, kill itself politically, if it took part in such deceit. . . .

I would choose an immediate split with no matter whom in our party, rather than surrender to social patriotism. . . ." After this apparently impersonal threat—having definite people in mind however—Lenin adjures: "Kamenev must understand that a world historic responsibility rests upon him." Kamenev is named here because it is a question of political principle. If Lenin had had a practical militant problem in mind, he would have been more likely to mention Stalin. But in just those hours when Lenin was striving to communicate the tensity of his will to Petrograd across smoking Europe, Kamenev with the coöperation of Stalin was turning sharply toward social patriotism.

Various schemes—disguises, false whiskers, foreign or false passports—were cast aside one after the other as impossible. And meanwhile the idea of traveling through Germany became more and more concrete. This plan frightened the majority of emigrants—and not only those who were patriotic, either. Martov and the other Mensheviks could not make up their minds to adopt the bold action of Lenin, and continued to knock in vain on the doors of the Entente. Later on even many of the Bolsheviks repented of their journey through Germany, in view of the difficulties caused by the "sealed train" in the sphere of agitation. From the beginning Lenin never shut his eyes to those future difficulties. Krupskaia wrote not long before the departure from Zurich: "Of course the patriots will raise an outcry in Russia, but for that we must be prepared." The question stood as follows: either stay in Switzerland or travel through Germany. There was no other choice. Could Lenin have hesitated for a moment? Just one month later Martov, Axelrod and the others had to follow in his steps.

In the organization of this unusual trip through hostile territory in war time, the fundamental traits of Lenin as a statesman expressed themselves—boldness of conception and meticulous carefulness in its fulfillment. Inside that great revolutionist there dwelt a pedantic notary—one who knew his function, however, and drew up his paper at the moment when it might help in the overthrow of all such notarial acts for ever. The conditions of the journey through Germany were worked out with extraordinary care in this unique international treaty between the editorial staff of a revolutionary paper and the empire of the Hohenzollerns. Lenin demanded complete extra-territoriality during the transit: no supervision of the personnel of the passengers, their passports or baggage. No single person should have the right to enter the train throughout the journey. (Hence the legend of the "sealed" train.) On their part, the emigrant group agreed to insist upon the release from Russia of a corresponding number of German and Austro-Hungarian civil prisoners.

At the same time a joint declaration was drawn up with several foreign revolutionists. "The Russian internationalists who are now going to Russia in order to serve there the cause of the revolution, will help us arouse the proletariat of other countries, especially of Germany and Austria, against their governments." So speaks the protocol signed by Loriot and Gilbeaux from France, Paul Levy from Germany, Platten from Switzerland, by Swedish left deputies and others. On those conditions and with those precautions, thirty Russian emigrants left Switzerland at the end of March. A rather explosive trainload even among the loads of those war days!

In his farewell letter to the Swiss workers Lenin reminded them of the declaration of the central organ of the Bolsheviks in the autumn of 1915: If the revolution brings to power in Russia a republican government which wants to continue the imperialist war, the Bolsheviks will be against the defense of the republican Fatherland. Such a situation has now arisen. "Our slogan is no support to the government of Guchkov-Miliukov." With those words Lenin now entered the territory of the revolution.

However, the members of the Provisional Government did not see any ground for alarm. Nabokov writes: "at one of the March sessions of the Provisional Government, during a recess, in a long conversation about the increasing propaganda of the Bolsheviks, Kerensky exclaimed with his usual hysterical giggle: 'Just you wait, Lenin himself is coming, then the real thing will begin!'" Kerensky was right. The real thing would begin only then. However the ministers, according to Nabokov, were not greatly disturbed: "The very fact of his having appealed to Germany will so undermine the authority of Lenin that we need not fear him." As was to be expected, the ministers were exceedingly perspicacious.

Friendly disciples went to meet Lenin in Finland. "We had hardly got into the car and sat down," writes Raskolnikov, a young naval officer and a Bolshevik, "when Vladimir Ilych flung at Kamenev: 'What's this you're writing in *Pravda*? We saw several numbers and gave it to you good and proper." Such was their meeting after a separation of several years. But even so it was a friendly meeting.

The Petrograd Committee, with the coöperation of the military organization, mobilized several thousand workers and soldiers for a triumphal welcome to Lenin. A friendly armored car division detailed all their cars to meet him. The committee decided to go to the station with the armored cars. The revolution had already created a partiality for that type of monster, so useful to have on your side in the streets of a city.

The description of the official meeting which took place in the so-called "Tzar's Room" of the Finland station, constitutes a very lively page in the many-volumed and rather faded memoirs of Sukhanov. "Lenin walked, or rather ran, into the Tzar's Room in a round hat, his face chilled, and a luxurious bouquet in his arms. Hurrying to the middle of the room, he stopped still in front of Cheidze as though he had run into a completely unexpected obstacle. And here Cheidze, not abandoning his previous melancholy look, pronounced the following 'speech of greeting,' carefully preserving not only the spirit and letter, but also the tone of voice of a moral instructor: 'Comrade Lenin, in the name of the Petrograd Soviet and the whole revolution, we welcome you to Russia . . . *but* we consider that the chief task of the revolutionary democracy at present is to defend our revolution against every kind of attack both from within and from without. . . . We hope that you will join us in striving towards this goal.' Cheidze ceased. I was dismayed with the unexpectedness of it. But Lenin, it seemed, knew well how to deal with all that. He stood there looking as though what was happening did not concern him in the least, glanced from one side to the other, looked over the surrounding public, and even examined the ceiling of the 'Tzar's Room' while rearranging his bouquet (which harmonized rather badly with his whole figure), and finally, having turned completely away from the delegates of the Executive Committee, 'answered' thus: 'Dear comrades, soldiers, sailors and workers, I am happy to greet in you the victorious Russian revolution, to greet you as the advance guard of the international proletarian army. . . . The hour is not far when, at the summons of our comrade Karl Liebknecht, the people will turn their weapons against their capitalist exploiters. . . . The Russian revolution achieved by you has opened a new epoch. Long live the world-wide socialist revolution!' "

Sukhanov is right—the bouquet harmonized badly with the figure of Lenin, and doubtless hindered and embarrassed him with its inappropriateness to the austere background of events. In general, as it happens, Lenin did not like flowers in a bouquet. But doubtless he was far more embarrassed by that official and hypocritical Sunday school greeting in the parade room of a station. Cheidze was better than his speech of greeting. He was a little timid of Lenin. But they undoubtedly had told him that it was necessary to pull up on the "sectarian" from the very beginning. To supplement Cheidze's speech, which had demonstrated the pitiable level of the leadership, a young naval commander, speaking in the name of the sailors, was brilliant enough to express the hope that Lenin might become a member of the Provisional Government. Thus the February revolution, garrulous and flabby and still rather stupid, greeted the man who had arrived with a resolute determination to set it straight both in thought and in will. Those first impressions, multiplying tenfold the alarm which he had brought with him, produced a feeling of protest in Lenin which it was difficult to restrain. How much more satisfactory to roll up his sleeves! Appealing from Cheidze to the sailors and workers, from the defense of the Fatherland to international revolution, from the Provisional Government to Liebknecht, Lenin merely gave a short rehearsal there at the station of his whole future policy.

And nevertheless that clumsy revolution instantly and heartily took its leader into its bosom. The soldiers demanded that Lenin climb up on one of the armored cars, and he had to obey. The oncoming night made the procession especially impressive. The lights on the other armored cars being dimmed, the night was stabbed by the sharp beam from the projector of the machine on which Lenin rode. It sliced out from the darkness of the street sections of excited workers, soldiers, sailors—the same ones who had achieved the great revolution and then let the power slip through their fingers. The band ceased playing every so often, in order to let Lenin repeat or vary his speech before new listeners. "That triumphal march was brilliant," says Sukhanov, "and even somewhat symbolic."

In the palace of Kshesinskaia, Bolshevik headquarters in the satin nest of a court ballerina—that combination must have amused Lenin's always lively irony—greetings began again. This was too much. Lenin endured the flood of eulogistic speeches like an impatient pedestrian waiting in a doorway for the rain to stop. He felt the sincere joyfulness at his arrival, but was bothered by its verboseness. The very tone of the official greetings seemed to him imitative, affected—in a word borrowed from the petty bourgeois democracy, declamatory, sentimental and false. He saw that the revolution, before having even defined its problems and tasks, had already created its tiresome etiquette. He smiled a good-natured reproach, looked at his watch, and from time to time doubtless gave an unrestrained yawn. The echo of the last greeting had not died away, when this unusual guest let loose upon that audience a cataract of passionate thought which at times sounded almost like a lashing. At that period the stenographic art was not yet open to Bolshevism. Nobody made notes. All were too absorbed in what was happening. The speeches have not been preserved. There remain only general impressions in the memoirs of the listeners. And these have been edited by the lapse of time; rapture has been added to them, and fright washed away. The fundamental impression made by Lenin's speech even among those nearest to him was one of fright. All the accepted formulas, which with innumerable repetition had acquired in the course of a month a seemingly unshakable permanence, were exploded one after another before the eyes of that audience. The short Leninist reply at the station, tossed out over the head of the startled Cheidze, was here developed into a two-hour speech addressed directly to the Petrograd cadres of Bolshevism.

The non-party socialist, Sukhanov, was accidentally present at this meeting as a guest—admitted by the good-natured Kamenev, although Lenin was intolerant of such indulgences. Thanks to this we have a description made by an outsider—

half-hostile and half-ecstatic—of the first meeting of Lenin with the Petersburg Bolsheviks.

"I will never forget that thunderlike speech, startling and amazing not only to me, a heretic accidentally dropped in, but also to the faithful, all of them. I assert that nobody there had expected anything of the kind. It seemed as if all the elements and the spirit of universal destruction had risen from their lairs, knowing neither barriers nor doubts nor personal difficulties nor personal considerations, to hover through the banquet chambers of Kshesinskaia above the heads of the bewitched disciples."

Personal considerations and difficulties—to Sukhanov that meant for the most part the editorial waverings of the *Novy Zhizn* circle having tea with Maxim Gorky. Lenin's considerations went deeper. Not the elements were hovering in that banquet hall, but human thoughts—and they were not embarrassed by the elements, but were trying to understand in order to control them. But never mind—the impression is clearly conveyed.

"On the journey here with my comrades," said Lenin, according to Sukhanov's report—"I was expecting they would take us directly from the station to Peter and Paul. We are far from that, it seems. But let us not give up the hope that it will happen, that we shall not escape it."

For the others at that time the development of the revolution was identical with a strengthening of the democracy; for Lenin the nearest prospect led straight to the Peter and Paul prison-fortress. It seemed a sinister joke. But Lenin was not joking, nor was the revolution joking.

"He swept aside legislative agrarian reform," complains Sukhanov, "along with all the rest of the policies of the Soviet. He spoke for an organized seizure of the land by the peasants, not anticipating . . . any governmental power at all."

"'We don't need any parliamentary republic. We don't need any bourgeois democracy. We don't need any government except the Soviet of workers', soldiers', and farmhands' deputies!'"

At the same time Lenin sharply separated himself from the Soviet majority, tossing them over into the camp of the enemy.

"That alone was enough in those days to make his listeners dizzy!"

"Only the Zimmerwald Left stands guard over the proletarian interests and the world revolution"—thus Sukhanov reports, with indignation, the thoughts of Lenin. "The rest are the same old opportunists, speaking pretty words but in reality betraying the cause of socialism and the worker masses."

Raskolnikov supplements Sukhanov: "He decisively assailed the tactics pursued before his arrival by the ruling party groups and by individual comrades. The most responsible party workers were here. But for them too the words of Ilych were a veritable revelation. They laid down a Rubicon between the tactics of yesterday and today." That Rubicon, as we shall see, was not laid down at once.

There was no discussion of the speech. All were too much astounded, and each wanted a chance to collect his thoughts. "I came out on the street," concludes Sukhanov, "feeling as though on that night I had been flogged over the head with a flail. Only one thing was clear: There was no place for me, a non-party man, beside Lenin!"

Indeed not!

The next day Lenin presented to the party a short written exposition of his views, which under the name of *Theses of April 4* has become one of the most important documents of the revolution. The theses expressed simple thoughts in simple words comprehensible to all: The republic which has issued from the February revolution is not our republic, and the war which it is now waging is not our war. The task of the Bolsheviks is to overthrow the imperialist government. But this government rests upon the support of the Social Revolutionaries and Mensheviks, who in turn are supported by the trustfulness of the masses of the people. We are in the minority. In these circumstances there can be no talk of violence from our side. We must teach the masses not to trust the Compromisers and defensists. "We must patiently explain." The success of this policy, dictated by the whole existing situation, is assured, and it will bring us to the dictatorship of the proletariat, and so beyond the boundaries of the bourgeois régime. We will break absolutely with capital, publish its secret treaties, and summon the workers of the whole world to cast loose from the bourgeoisie and put an end to the war. We are beginning the international revolution. Only its success will confirm our success, and guarantee a transition to the socialist régime.

These theses of Lenin were published in his own name and his only. The central institutions of the party met them with a hostility softened only by bewilderment. Nobody—not one organization, group or individual—affixed his signature to them. Even Zinoviev, arriving with Lenin from abroad, where for ten years his ideas had been forming under the immediate and daily influence of Lenin, silently stepped aside. Nor was this sidestepping a surprise to the teacher, who knew his closest disciple all too well.

Where Kamenev was a propagandist popularizer, Zinoviev was an agitator, and indeed, to quote an expression of Lenin, "nothing but an agitator." He has not, in the first place, a sufficient sense of responsibility to be a leader. But not only that. Lacking inner discipline, his mind is completely incapable of theoretical work, and his thoughts dissolve into the formless intuitions of the agitator. Thanks to an exceptionally quick scent, he can catch out of the air whatever formulas are necessary to him—those which will exercise the most effective influence on the masses. Both as journalist and orator he remains an agitator, with only this difference—that in his articles you usually see his weaker side, and in oral speech his stronger. Although far more bold and unbridled in agitation than any other Bolshevik, Zinoviev is even less capable than Kamenev of revolutionary initiative. He is, like all demagogues, indecisive. Passing from the arena of factional debate to that of direct mass fighting, Zinoviev almost involuntarily separated from his teacher.

There have been plenty of attempts of late years to prove that the April party crisis was a passing and almost accidental confusion. They all go to pieces at first contact with the facts.[1]

[1] In the big collected volume issued under the editorship of Professor Pokrovsky, *Essays on the History of the October Revolution* (vol. II, Moscow, 1927) an apologetic work is devoted to the "April Confusion" by a certain Bayevsky, which for its unceremonious treatment of facts and documents might be called cynical, were it not childishly impotent.

What we already know of the activity of the party in March reveals the deepest possible contradiction between Lenin and the Petersburg leadership. This contradiction reached its highest intensity exactly at the moment of Lenin's arrival. Simultaneously with the All-Russian Conference of representatives of 82 soviets, where Kamenev and Stalin voted for the resolution on sovereignty introduced by the Social Revolutionaries and Mensheviks, there took place in Petrograd a party conference of Bolsheviks assembled from all over Russia. This conference, at the very end of which Lenin arrived, has an exceptional interest for anyone wishing to characterize the mood and opinions of the party and all its upper layers as they issued from the war. A reading of the reports, to this day unpublished, frequently produces a feeling of amazement: is it possible that a party represented by these delegates will after seven months seize the power with an iron hand? A month had already passed since the uprising—a long period for a revolution, as also for a war. Nevertheless opinions were not defined in the party even on the most basic questions of the revolution. Extreme patriots such as Voitinsky, Eliava, and others, participated in the conference alongside of those who considered themselves internationalists. The percentage of outspoken patriots, incomparably less than among the Mensheviks, was nevertheless considerable. The conference as a whole did not decide the question whether to break with its own patriots or unite with the patriots of Menshevism. In an interval between sessions of the Bolshevik conference there was held a united session of Bolsheviks and Mensheviks—delegates to the Soviet conference—to consider the war question. The most furious Menshevik-patriot, Lieber, announced at this session: "We must do away with the old division between Bolshevik and Menshevik, and speak only of our attitude toward the war." The Bolshevik, Voitinsky, hastened to proclaim his readiness to put his signature to every word of Lieber. All of them together, Bolsheviks and Mensheviks, patriots and internationalists, were seeking a common formula for their attitude to the war.

The views of the Bolshevik conference undoubtedly found their most adequate expression in the report of Stalin on relations with the Provisional Government. It is necessary to introduce here the central thought of this speech, which, like the reports as a whole, is not yet published. "The power has been divided between two organs of which neither one possesses full power. There is debate and struggle between them, and there ought to be. The rôles have been divided. The Soviet has in fact taken the initiative in the revolutionary transformation; the Soviet is the revolutionary leader of the insurrectionary people; an organ controlling the Provisional Government. And the Provisional Government has in fact taken the rôle of fortifier of the conquests of the revolutionary people. The Soviet mobilizes the forces, and controls. The Provisional Government, balking and confused, takes the rôle of fortifier of those conquests of the people, which they have already seized as a fact. This situation has disadvantageous, but also advantageous sides. It is not to our advantage at present to force events, hastening the process of repelling the bourgeois layers, who will in the future inevitably withdraw from us."

Transcending class distinctions, the speaker portrays the relation between the bourgeoisie and the proletariat as a mere division of labor. The workers and soldiers achieve the revolution, Guchkov and Miliukov "fortify" it. We recognize here the traditional conception of the Mensheviks, incorrectly modeled after the events of 1789. This superintendent's approach to the historical process is exactly characteristic of the leaders of Menshevism, this handing out of instructions to various classes and then patronizingly criticizing their fulfillment. The idea that it is disadvantageous to hasten the withdrawal of the bourgeoisie from the revolution, has always been the guiding principle of the whole policy of the Mensheviks. In action this means blunting and weakening the movement of the masses in order not to frighten away the liberal allies. And finally, Stalin's conclusion as to the Provisional Government is wholly in accord with the equivocal formula of the Compromisers: "In so far as the Provisional Government fortifies the steps of the revolution, in so far we must support it, but in so far as it is counter-revolutionary, support to the Provisional Government is not permissible."

Stalin's report was made on March 29. On the next day the official spokesman of the Soviet conference, the non-party social democrat Steklov, defending the same conditional support to the Provisional Government, in the ardor of his eloquence painted such a picture of the activity of the "fortifiers" of the revolution—opposition to social reforms, leaning towards monarchy, protection of counter-revolutionary forces, appetite for annexation—that the Bolshevik conference recoiled in alarm from this formula of support. The right Bolshevik Nogin declared: "The speech of Steklov has introduced one new thought: it is clear that we ought not now to talk about support, but about resistance." Skrypnik also arrived at the conclusion that since the speech of Steklov "many things have changed, there can be no more talk of supporting the government. There is a conspiracy of the Provisional Government against the people and the revolution." Stalin, who a day before had been painting an idealistic picture of the "division of labor" between the government and the Soviet, felt obliged to eliminate this point about supporting the government. The short and superficial discussion turned about the question whether to support the Provisional Government "in so far as," or only to support the revolutionary activities of the Provisional Government. The delegate from Saratov, Vassiliev, not untruthfully declared: "We all have the same attitude to the Provisional Government." Krestinsky formulated the situation even more clearly: "As to practical action there is no disagreement between Stalin and Voitinsky." Notwithstanding the fact that Voitinsky went over to the Mensheviks immediately after the conference, Krestinsky was not very wrong. Although he eliminated the open mention of support, Stalin did not eliminate support. The only one who attempted to formulate the question in principle was Krassikov, one of those old Bolsheviks who had withdrawn from the party for a series of years, but now, weighed down with life's experience, was trying to return to its ranks. Krassikov did not hesitate to seize the bull by the horns. Is this then a dictatorship of the proletariat you are about to inaugurate? he asked ironically. But the conference passed over his irony, and along with it passed over this question as one not deserving attention. The resolution of the conference summoned the revolutionary democracy to urge the Provisional Government toward "a most energetic struggle for the complete liquidation of the old régime"—that is, gave the proletarian party the rôle of governess of the bourgeoisie.

The next day they considered the proposal of Tseretelli for a union of Bolsheviks and Mensheviks. Stalin was wholly in favor of the proposal: "We must do it. It is necessary to define our proposal for a basis of union; union is possible on the basis of Zimmerwald-Kienthal." Molotov, who had been removed from the editorship of *Pravda* by Kamenev and Stalin because of the too radical line of the paper, spoke in opposition: Tseretelli wants to unite heterogeneous elements, he himself calls himself a Zimmerwaldist; a union on that basis is wrong. But Stalin stuck to his guns: "There is no use running ahead and trying to forestall disagreements. There is no party life without disagreements. We will live down petty disagreements within the party." The whole struggle which Lenin had been carrying on during the war years against social patriotism and its pacifist disguise, was thus casually swept aside. In September 1916 Lenin had written through Shliapnikov to Petrograd with special insistence: "Conciliationism and consolidation is the worst thing for the workers' party in Russia, not only idiotism, but ruin to the party. . . . We can rely only on those who have understood the whole deceit involved in the idea of unity and the whole necessity of a split with that brotherhood (Cheidze & Co.) in Russia." This warning was not understood. Disagreements with Tseretelli, the leader of the ruling Soviet bloc, seemed to Stalin petty disagreements, which could be "lived down" within a common party. This furnishes the best criterion for an appraisal of the views held by Stalin at that time.

On April 4, Lenin appeared at the party conference. His speech, developing his "theses," passed over the work of the conference like the wet sponge of a teacher erasing what had been written on the blackboard by a confused pupil.

"Why didn't you seize the power?" asked Lenin. At the Soviet conference not long before that, Steklov had confusedly explained the reasons for abstaining from the power: the revolution is bourgeois—it is the first stage—the war, etc. "That's nonsense," Lenin said. "The reason is that the proletariat was not sufficiently conscious and not sufficiently organized. That we have to acknowledge. The material force was in the hands of the proletariat, but the bourgeoisie was conscious and ready. That is the monstrous fact. But it is necessary to acknowledge it frankly, and say to the people straight out that we did not seize the power because we were unorganized and not conscious."

From the plane of pseudo-objectivism, behind which the political capitulators were hiding, Lenin shifted the whole question to the subjective plane. The proletariat did not seize the power in February because the Bolshevik Party was not equal to its objective task, and could not prevent the Compromisers from expropriating the popular masses politically for the benefit of the bourgeoisie.

The day before that, lawyer Krassikov had said challengingly: "If we think that the time has now come to realize the dictatorship of the proletariat, then we ought to pose the question that way. We unquestionably have the physical force for a seizure of power." The chairman at that time deprived Krassikov of the floor on the ground that practical problems were under discussion, and the question of dictatorship was out of order. But Lenin thought that, as the sole practical question, the question of preparing the dictatorship of the proletariat was exactly in order. "The peculiarity of the present moment in Russia," he said in his theses, "consists in the transition from the first stage of the revolution, which gave the power to the bourgeoisie on account of the inadequate consciousness and organization of the proletariat, to its second stage which must give the power to the proletariat and the poor layers of the peasantry." The conference, following the lead of *Pravda,* had limited the task of the revolution to a democratic transformation to be realized through the Constituent Assembly. As against this, Lenin declared that "life and the revolution will push the Constituent Assembly into the background. A dictatorship of the proletariat exists, but nobody knows what to do with it."

The delegates exchanged glances. They whispered to each other that Ilych had stayed too long abroad, had not had time to look around and familiarize himself with things. But the speech of Stalin on the ingenious division of labor between the government and the Soviet, sank out of sight once and forever. Stalin himself remained silent. From now on he will have to be silent for a long time. Kamenev alone will man the defenses.

Lenin had already given warning in letters from Geneva that he was ready to break with anybody who made concessions on the question of war, chauvinism and compromise with the bourgeoisie. Now, face to face with the leading circles of the party, he opens an attack all along the line. But at the beginning he does not name a single Bolshevik by name. If he has need of a living model of equivocation and halfwayness, he points his finger at the non-party men, or at Steklov or Cheidze. That was the customary method of Lenin: not to nail anybody down to his position too soon, to give the prudent a chance to withdraw from the battle in good season and thus weaken at once the future ranks of his open enemies. Kamenev and Stalin had thought that in participating in the war after February, the soldiers and workers were defending the revolution. Lenin thinks that, as before, the soldier and the worker take part in the war as the conscripted slaves of capital. "Even our Bolsheviks," he says, narrowing the circle around his antagonists, "show confidence in the government. Only the fumes of the revolution can explain that. That is the death of socialism. . . . If that's your position, our ways part. I prefer to remain in the minority." That was not a mere oratorical threat; it was a clear path thought through to the end.

Although naming neither Kamenev nor Stalin, Lenin was obliged to name the paper: "*Pravda* demands of the government that it renounce annexation. To demand from the government of the capitalists that it renounce annexation is nonsense, flagrant mockery." Restrained indignation here breaks out with a high note. But the orator immediately takes himself in hand: he wants to say no less than is necessary, but also no more. Incidentally and in passing, Lenin gives incomparable rules for revolutionary statesmanship: "When the masses announce that they do not want conquests, I believe them. When Guchkov and Lvov say they do not want conquests, they are deceivers! When a worker says that he wants the defense of the country, what speaks in him is the instinct of the oppressed." This criterion, to call it by its right name, seems simple as life itself. But the difficulty is to call it by its right name in time.

On the question of the appeal of the Soviet "to the people of the whole world"—which caused the liberal paper *Rech* at one time to declare that the theme of pacifism is developing among us into an ideology common to the Allies—Lenin expressed himself more clearly and succinctly: "What is peculiar to Russia is the gigantically swift transition from wild violence to the most delicate deceit."

"This appeal," wrote Stalin concerning the manifesto, "if it reaches the broad masses (of the West), will undoubtedly recall hundreds and thousands of workers to the forgotten slogan 'Proletarians of all Countries Unite!' "

"The appeal of the Soviet," objects Lenin, "—there isn't a word in it imbued with class consciousness. There is nothing to it but phrases." This document, the pride of the home-grown Zimmerwaldists, is in Lenin's eyes merely one of the weapons of "the most delicate deceit."

Up to Lenin's arrival *Pravda* had never even mentioned the Zimmerwald left. Speaking of the International, it never indicated which International. Lenin called this "the Kautskyanism of *Pravda.*" "In Zimmerwald and Kienthal," he declared at a party conference, "the Centrists predominated. . . . We declare that we created a left and broke with the center. . . . The left Zimmerwald tendency exists in all the countries of the world. The masses ought to realize that socialism has split throughout the world. . . ."

Three days before that Stalin had announced at that same conference his readiness to live down differences with Tseretelli on the basis of Zimmerwald-Kienthal—that is, on the basis of Kautskyanism. "I hear that in Russia there is a trend toward consolidation," said Lenin. "Consolidation with the defensists—that is betrayal of socialism. I think it would be better to stand alone like Liebknecht—one against a hundred and ten." The accusation of betrayal of socialism—for the present still without naming names—is not here merely a strong word; it fully expresses the attitude of Lenin toward those Bolsheviks who were extending a finger to the social patriots. In opposition to Stalin who thought it was possible to unite with the Mensheviks, Lenin thought it was unpermissible to share with them any longer the name of Social Democrat. "Personally and speaking for myself alone," he said, "I propose that we change the name of the party, that we call it the Communist Party." "Personally and speaking for myself alone"—that means that nobody, not one of the members of the conference, agreed to that symbolic gesture of ultimate break with the Second International.

"You are afraid to go back on your old memories?" says the orator to the embarrassed, bewildered and partly indignant delegates. But the time has come "to change our linen; we've got to take off the dirty shirt and put on clean." And he again insists: "Don't hang on to an old word which is rotten through and through. Have the will to build a new party . . . and all the oppressed will come to you."

Before the enormity of the task not yet begun, and the intellectual confusion in his own ranks, a sharp thought of the precious time foolishly wasted in meetings, greetings, ritual resolutions, wrests a cry from the orator: "Have done with greetings and resolutions! It's time to get down to business. We must proceed to practical sober work!"

An hour later Lenin was compelled to repeat his speech at the previously designated joint session of the Bolsheviks and Mensheviks, where it sounded to a majority of the listeners like something between mockery and delirium. The more condescending shrugged their shoulders: This man evidently fell down from the moon; hardly off the steps of the Finland station after a ten-year absence he starts preaching the seizure of power by the proletariat. The less good-natured among the patriots made references to the sealed train. Stankevich testifies that Lenin's speech greatly delighted his enemies: "A man who talks that kind of stupidity is not dangerous. It's a good thing he has come. Now he is in plain sight. . . . Now he will refute himself."

Nevertheless, with all its boldness of revolutionary grasp, its inflexible determination to break even with his former long-time colleagues and comrades-in-arms, if they proved unable to march with the revolution, the speech of Lenin—every part balanced against the rest—was filled with deep realism and an infallible feeling for the masses. Exactly for this reason, it seemed to the democrats a fantastic skimming of the surface.

The Bolsheviks are a tiny minority in the Soviet, and Lenin dreams of seizing the power; isn't that pure adventurism? There was not a shadow of adventurism in Lenin's statement of the problem. He did not for a moment close his eyes to the existence of "honest" defensist moods in the broad masses. He did not intend either to lose himself in the masses or to act behind their backs. "We are not charlatans"—he throws this in the eyes of future objections and accusations—"we must base ourselves only upon the consciousness of the masses. Even if it is necessary to remain in a minority—so be it. It is a good thing to give up for a time the position of leadership; we must not be afraid to remain in the minority." Do not fear to remain in a minority—even a minority of one, like Liebknecht's one against a hundred and ten—such was the leit-motif of his speech.

"The real government is the Soviet of workers' deputies. . . . In the Soviet our party is the minority. . . . What can we do? All we can do is to explain patiently, insistently, systematically the error of their tactics. So long as we are in the minority, we will carry on the work of criticism, in order to free the masses from deceit. We do not want the masses to believe us just on our say so; we are not charlatans. We want the masses to be freed by experience from their mistakes." Don't be afraid to remain in the minority! Not forever, but for a time. The hour of Bolshevism will strike. "Our line will prove right. . . . All the oppressed will come to us, because the war will bring them to us. They have no other way out."

"At the joint conference," relates Sukhanov, "Lenin was the living incarnation of a split. . . . I remember Bogdanov (a prominent Menshevik) sitting two steps away from the orator's tribune. 'Why, that is raving,' he interrupted Lenin, 'that is the raving of a lunatic. . . . You ought to be ashamed to applaud such spouting,' he cried, turning to the audience, white in the face with rage and scorn. 'You disgrace yourselves, Marxists!' "

A former member of the Bolshevik Central Committee, Goldenberg, at that time a non-party man, appraised Lenin's theses in these withering words: "For many years the place of Bakunin has remained vacant in the Russian revolution, now it is occupied by Lenin."

"His program at that time was met not so much with indignation," relates the Social Revolutionary Zenzinov, "as with ridicule. It seemed to everybody so absurd and fantastic."

On the evening of the same day, in the *couloirs* of the Contact Commission, two socialists were talking with Miliukov, and the conversation touched on Lenin. Skobelev estimated him as "a man completely played out, standing apart from the movement." Sukhanov was of the same mind, and added that "Lenin is to such a degree inacceptable to everybody that he is no longer dangerous even to my companion Miliukov here."

The distribution of rôles in this conversation, however, was exactly according to Lenin's formula: the socialists were protecting the peace of mind of the liberal from the trouble which Bolshevism might cause him.

Rumors even arrived in the ears of the British ambassador that Lenin had been declared a bad Marxist. "Among the newly arrived anarchists," wrote Buchanan, "was Lenin, who came through in a sealed train from Germany. He made his first public appearance at a meeting of the Social Democratic Party and was badly received."

The most condescending of all toward Lenin in those days was no other than Kerensky, who in a circle of members of the Provisional Government unexpectedly stated that he must go to see Lenin, and explained in answer to their bewildered questions: "Well, he is living in a completely isolated atmosphere, he knows nothing, sees everything through the glasses of his fanaticism. There is no one around him who might help him orient himself a little in what is going on." Thus testifies Nabokov. But Kerensky never found the time to orient Lenin in what was going on.

The April theses of Lenin not only evoked the bewildered indignation of his opponents and enemies. They repelled a number of old Bolsheviks into the Menshevik camp—or into that intermediate group which found shelter around Gorky's paper. This leakage had no serious political significance. Infinitely more important was the impression which Lenin's position made on the whole leading group of the party. "In the first days after his arrival," writes Sukhanov, "his complete isolation among all his conscious party comrades cannot be doubted in the least." "Even his party comrades, the Bolsheviks," confirms the Social Revolutionary Zenzinov, "at that time turned away in embarrassment from him." The authors of these comments were meeting the leading Bolsheviks every day in the Executive Committee, and had first-hand evidence of what they said.

But there is no lack of similar testimony from among the ranks of the Bolsheviks. "When the theses of Lenin appeared," wrote Tsikhon, softening the colors as much as possible, as do a majority of the old Bolsheviks when they stumble on the February revolution, "there was felt in our party a certain wavering. Many of the comrades argued that Lenin showed a syndicalist deviation, that he was out of touch with Russia, that he was not taking into consideration the given moment," etc. One of the prominent Bolshevik leaders in the provinces, Lebedev, writes: "On Lenin's arrival in Russia, his agitation, at first not wholly intelligible to us Bolsheviks, but regarded as Utopian and explainable by his long removal from Russian life, was gradually absorbed by us, and entered, as you might say, into our flesh and blood."

Zalezhski, a member of the Petrograd Committee and one of the organizers of the welcome to Lenin, expresses it more frankly: "Lenin's theses produced the impression of an exploding bomb." Zalezhski fully confirms the complete isolation of Lenin after that so warm and impressive welcome. "On that day (April 4) Comrade Lenin could not find open sympathizers even in our own ranks."

Still more important, however, is the evidence of *Pravda*. On April 8, after the publication of the theses—when time enough had passed to make explanations and reach a mutual understanding—the editors of *Pravda* wrote: "As for the general scheme of Comrade Lenin, it seems to us unacceptable in that it starts from the assumption that the bourgeois-democratic revolution is ended, and counts upon an immediate transformation of this revolution into a socialist revolution." The central organ of the party thus openly announced before the working class and its enemies a split with the generally recognized leader of the party upon the central question of the revolution for which the Bolshevik ranks had been getting ready during a long period of years. That alone is sufficient to show the depth of the April crisis in the party, due to the clash of two irreconcilable lines of thought and action. Until it surmounted this crisis the revolution could not go forward.

Editor's Summary of Chapters XVI–XXII

CHAPTER XVI. REARMING THE PARTY. The old Bolshevik position limited the revolution to democratic aims. The new position which Lenin first announced in his April 4 theses envisioned an immediate transition to the dictatorship of the proletariat. As this had long been Trotsky's position, Lenin's theses were at first condemned as Trotskyist by certain Old Bolsheviks. Lenin's belatedness forced him to re-educate the party against much opposition from other leaders. But he had considerable support from the rank and file of the party, which in April numbered about 79,000, of whom about 15,000 lived in Petrograd. Would the party have succeeded in making this vital shift in policy if Lenin himself had been unable to reach Russia in time? The rôle of personality in historic events arises before us here on a gigantic scale. Lenin was not a demiurge of the revolutionary process: he merely entered into the chain of objective historic forces. But he was a great link in that chain. It is by no means excluded that, without his presence, a disoriented and split party might have let slip the revolutionary opportunity for many years.

CHAPTER XVII. THE "APRIL DAYS." The entry of the United States into the war on March 23 encouraged the liberal bourgeoisie in the government in its hopes of an Allied victory and of conquests and annexations—especially of Constantinople—for Russia. On March 27, however, the government made public a declaration of policy: Russia proposed to continue the war not in order to achieve conquests but to fulfill her obligations to her allies and in the hope of attaining a peace which would prevent further wars in the future. But as

Miliukov, the foreign minister, had already associated himself publicly with a plan to seize Constantinople and Armenia and to divide Turkey and Austria, the March 27 declaration was interpreted by the Mensheviks and Bolsheviks as a promise "not to rob anyone we don't need to rob." There followed the "April Days," a series of relatively spontaneous street demonstrations by soldiers, sailors, and workers, demanding in some cases the removal of Miliukov and in others the downfall of the entire government. While the former tzarist general, Kornilov, privately urged the government to put down the demonstration by force, and the Executive Committee vacillated, this second upsurge of the revolution played itself out, but not until Miliukov had been forced to resign as foreign minister. Could the Bolsheviks have succeeded in carrying through the proletarian revolution at this time? Lenin proposed to wait until such time as a larger public support was assured, meanwhile insisting that the Bolsheviks must continue to "patiently explain" to the masses the impossibility of the dual power system and the necessity of the Bolshevik slogan: "All Power to the Soviets."

CHAPTER XVIII. THE FIRST COALITION. Two realistic solutions of the problems of dual sovereignty offered: rule by the bourgeoisie or rule by the proletariat. The course now actually adopted was a weak compromise: a coalition government. Invited by the Provisional Government to accept portfolios, encouraged to do so by many visiting socialists from Allied countries as well as by numerous elements in its own ranks, the Executive Committee decided on May 1, by a majority of 41 votes against 18, with 3 abstaining, to enter such a coalition with the Liberals. Only the Bolsheviks and a small group of Menshevik-Internationalists voted against it. Prince Lvov remained premier, Kerensky now became minister of war and marine, and Tereshchenko foreign minister. Altogether the socialists, wanting to be in the minority, appropriated six portfolios out of fifteen. The only new thing in the foreign policy of the Coalition was its hasty rapprochement with America. Supported by the idealistic pronouncements of President Wilson and the hope of American loans, Kerensky agitated for a new military offensive. Meanwhile city dumas were everywhere constituted in the expectation that they would replace the troublesome soviets. They did not, and the rivalry of the soviet system with the formal democracy continued.

CHAPTER XIX. THE OFFENSIVE. The democracy could not resurrect the army for the same reason that it could not take over the power. The military was torn by class tensions as well as national ones. Great Russians composed less than half of it; the remainder was made up of the many different peoples that constituted Russia as a whole. Official reports continued to point to demoralization in the ranks. Fraternization with German soldiers was widespread. French officials feared a contagion of mutiny in their own armed forces and exerted pressure on the Coalition Government to resume the war. Kerensky therefore planned an offensive on the southwestern front and sought to give this proposed action the character of a revolutionary crusade against German autocracy. But the offensive undertaken on June 16 promptly failed. Russian troops made small advances and then refused to go farther. Desertions were common, whole army units simply melted away. It was obvious that a prolongation of the war could give the Russian people nothing but new victims, humiliations, disasters–nothing but an increase of domestic and foreign slavery.

CHAPTER XX. THE PEASANTRY. The basis of the revolution was the agrarian problem: the antique land system, the traditional power of the landlords, the close ties between the landlord and the local administration. But in the first weeks after February the village remained almost inert. The young were at the front; their elders at home remembered too well how attempted revolutions had led to punitive expeditions. But the landlords feared a peasant war with expropriations and began to dispose of their lands to the kulaks, or independent farmers, often in the form of fictitious sales, assuming that private holdings below a certain norm would be spared. The peasants detected these maneuvers and sent delegates to the soviets demanding that all sales be stopped by decree. The gray beseeching figures of the peasant deputies sometimes embarrassed proceedings in the soviets. "I said it would be done, and that means it will be—and you needn't look at me with those suspicious eyes," Kerensky once shouted at such a delegate, as reported by Sukhanov. An act creating land committees as organs for agrarian reform was published by the Provisional Government. But action was slow; there was much theoretical confusion on the subject among the mass parties, with the Social Revolutionaries tending to caution and compromise. Lenin's essential position was that the instruments of the agrarian revolution, and primarily of the seizure of the landed estates, were to be the soviets of peasants' deputies, with the officially appointed land committees subject to them. Between the Bolsheviks and the peasants, however, there was intense suspicion. Lenin feared the peasantry might ultimately line up with the reaction. But soldiers brought home from the front and the city barracks a spirit of initiative and there were some seizures of land and equipment, though on the whole the peasants refrained from acts of violence before July. In time, however, the agrarian movement, from being a prophecy became a fact; and the peasantry as a whole found it possible once more—and for the last time in history—to act as a revolutionary factor.

CHAPTER XXI. SHIFTS IN THE MASSES. Under the pressure of a growing economic breakdown, especially in transport and food supply, the masses were becoming more politically conscious. At first the drift of this awakened populace was overwhelmingly in the direction of the Social Revolutionaries. But the Bolshevik ideas were gaining ground and the Bolshevik party itself increased in membership, despite its association in the public mind with defeatism and German espionage. Between the end of April and the end of June membership in the Petrograd section grew from 15,000 to 32,000. In June the mass discontent emerged in a wave of strikes. To this the industrialists replied by a policy of creeping lockout, often closing factories under the pretense that they were economically ruined. Thus the revolution was disclosing the chief contradiction of capitalism: that between the social character of industry and the private ownership of its tools and equipment. The entrepreneur closes the factory as if it were a mere snuffbox, and not an enterprise necessary to the whole nation. Meanwhile the Liberal press carried on a propaganda campaign against the supposedly irresponsible workers and the too militant sectors of the army and navy. The insurgent sailors of the Kronstadt garrison, virtually a separate republic, were the object of a particularly bitter press attack and of repeated government efforts to subdue the garrison.

CHAPTER XXII. "THE SOVIET CONGRESS AND THE JUNE DEMONSTRATION." The first national congress of the soviets assembled in Petrograd on June 3 with 820 voting delegates, of whom less than one fifth were Bolsheviks. The work of this enormous and flabby assembly was largely confined to passing resolutions and sanctioning the military offensive proposed by Kerensky. In a spirit of protest the Bolsheviks called for a mass street demonstration on June 9. The congress declared this to be a "conspiracy against the revolution" and banned all demonstrations for a period of three days. The Bolsheviks acceded, whereupon the congress appointed a manifestation of its own for Sunday, June 18, in order to demonstrate the unity and strength of the democracy. This had unexpected results for the congress. "Judging by the placards and slogans," declared Gorky's paper, "the Sunday demonstration revealed the complete triumph of Bolshevism among the Petersburg proletariat."

Volume Two

THE ATTEMPTED COUNTER-REVOLUTION

INTRODUCTION TO VOLUMES TWO AND THREE

Russia was so late in accomplishing her bourgeois revolution that she found herself compelled to turn it into a proletarian revolution. Or in other words: Russia was so far behind the other countries that she was compelled, at least in certain spheres, to out-strip them. That seems inconsistent, but history is full of such paradoxes. Capitalist England was so far in advance of other countries, that she had to trail behind them. Pedants think that the dialectic is an idle play of the mind. In reality it only reproduces the process of evolution, which lives and moves by way of contradictions.

The first volume of this work should have explained why that historically belated democratic régime which replaced tzarism proved wholly unviable. The present volumes are devoted to the coming to power of the Bolsheviks. Here too the fundamental thing is the narrative. In the facts themselves the reader ought to find sufficient support for the inferences.

By this the author does not mean to say that he has avoided sociological generalizations. History would have no value if it taught us nothing. The mighty design of the Russian revolution, the consecutiveness of its stages, the inexorable pressure of the masses, the finishedness of political groupings, the succinctness of slogans, all this wonderfully promotes the understanding of revolution in general, and therewith of human society. For we may consider it proven by the whole course of history that society, torn as it is by inner contradictions, conclusively reveals in a revolution not only its anatomy, but also its "soul."

In a more immediate manner the present work should promote an understanding of the character of the Soviet Union. The timeliness of our theme lies not only in that the October revolution took place before the eyes of a generation still living —although that of course has no small significance—but in the fact that the régime which issued from the revolution still lives and develops, and is confronting humanity with ever new riddles. Throughout the whole world the question of the soviet country is never lost sight of for a moment. However, it is impossible to understand any existent thing without a preliminary examination of its origin. For large-scale political appraisals a historic perspective is essential.

The eight months of the revolution, February to October 1917, have required three volumes. The critics, as a general rule, have not accused us of prolixity. The scale of the work is explained rather by our approach to the material. You can present a photograph of a hand on one page, but it requires a volume to present the results of a microscopic investigation of its tissues. The author has no illusion as to the fullness or finishedness of his investigation. But nevertheless in many cases he was obliged to employ methods closer to the miscroscope than the camera.

At times, when it seemed to us that we were abusing the patience of the reader, we generously crossed out the testimony of some witness, the confession of a participant or some secondary episode, but we afterward not infrequently restored much that had been crossed out. In this struggle for details we were guided by a desire to reveal as concretely as possible the very process of the revolution. In particular it was impossible not to try to make the most of the opportunity to paint history from the life.

Thousands and thousands of books are thrown on the market every year presenting some new variant of the personal romance, some tale of the vacillations of the melancholic or the career of the ambitious. The heroine of Proust requires several finely-wrought pages in order to feel that she does not feel anything. It would seem that one might, at least with equal justice, demand attention to a series of collective historic dramas which lifted hundreds of millions of human beings out of non-existence, transforming the character of nations and intruding forever into the life of all mankind.

The accuracy of our references and quotations in the first volume no one has so far called in question: that would indeed be difficult. Our opponents confine themselves for the most part to reflections upon the topic of how personal prejudice *may* reveal itself in an artificial and one-sided selection of facts and texts. These observations, although irrefutable in themselves, say nothing about the given work, and still less about its scientific methods. Moreover we take the liberty to insist firmly that the coefficient of subjectivism is defined, limited, and tested not so much by the temperament of the historian, as by the nature of his method.

The purely psychological school, which looks upon the tissue of events as an interweaving of the free activities of separate individuals or their groupings, offers, even with the best intentions on the part of the investigator, a colossal scope to caprice. The materialist method disciplines the historian, compelling him to take his departure from the weighty facts of the social structure. For us the fundamental forces of the historic process are classes; political parties rest upon them; ideas and slogans emerge as the small change of objective interests. The whole course of the investigation proceeds from the objective to the subjective, from the social to the individual, from the fundamental to the incidental. This sets a rigid limit to the personal whims of the author.

When a mining engineer finds magnetic ore in an uninvestigated region by drilling, it is always possible to assume that this was a happy accident: the construction of a mine is hardly to be recommended. But when the same engineer, on the basis, let us say, of the deviation of a magnetic needle, comes to the conclusion that a vein of ore lies concealed in the earth, and subsequently actually strikes ore at various different points in the region, then the most cavilling sceptic will not venture to talk about accidents. What convinces is the system which unites the general with the particular.

The proof of scientific objectivism is not to be sought in the eyes of the historian or the tones of his voice, but in the inner logic of the narrative itself. If episodes, testimonies, figures, quotations, fall in with the general pointing of the needle of his social analysis, then the reader has a most weighty guarantee of the scientific solidity of his conclusions. To be more concrete: the present author has been true to objectivism in the degree that his book actually reveals the inevitability of the October revolution and the causes of its victory.

The reader already knows that in a revolution we look first of all for the direct interference of the masses in the destinies of society. We seek to uncover behind the events changes in the collective consciousness. We reject wholesale references to the "spontaneity" of the movement, references which in most cases explain nothing and teach nobody. Revolutions take place according to certain laws. This does not mean that the masses in action are aware of the laws of revolution, but it does mean that the changes in mass consciousness are not accidental, but are subject to an objective necessity which is capable of theoretic explanation, and thus makes both prophecy and leadership possible.

Certain official soviet historians, surprising as it may seem, have attempted to criticize our conception as idealistic. Professor Pokrovsky, for example, has insisted that we underestimate the objective factors of the revolution. "Between February and October there occurred a colossal economic collapse." "During this time the peasantry . . . rose against the Provisional Government." It is in these "objective shifts," says Pokrovsky, and not in fickle psychic processes, that one should see the motive force of the revolution. Thanks to a praiseworthy incisiveness of formulation, Pokrovsky exposes to perfection the worthlessness of that vulgarly economic interpretation of history which is frequently given out for Marxism.

The radical turns which take place in the course of a revolution are as a matter-of-fact evoked, not by those episodic economic disturbances which arise during the events themselves, but by fundamental changes which have accumulated in the very foundations of society throughout the whole preceding epoch. The fact that on the eve of the overthrow of the monarchy, as also between February and October, the economic collapse was steadily deepening, nourishing and whipping up the discontent of the masses—that fact is indubitable and has never lacked our attention. But it would be the crudest mistake to assume that the second revolution was accomplished eight months after the first owing to the fact that the bread ration was lowered during that period from one-and-a-half to three-quarters of a pound. In the years immediately following the October revolution the food situation of the masses continued steadily to grow worse. Nevertheless the hopes of the counter-revolutionary politicians for a new overturn were defeated every time. This circumstance can seem puzzling only to one who looks upon the insurrection of the masses as "spontaneous"—that is, as a herd-mutiny artificially made use of by leaders. In reality the mere existence of privations is not enough to cause an insurrection; if it were, the masses would be always in revolt. It is necessary that the bankruptcy of the social régime, being conclusively revealed, should make these privations intolerable, and that new conditions and new ideas should open the prospect of a revolutionary way out. Then in the cause of the great aims conceived by them, those same masses will prove capable of enduring doubled and tripled privations.

The reference to the revolt of the peasantry as a second "objective factor" shows a still more obvious misunderstanding. For the proletariat the peasant war was of course an objective circumstance—insofar as the activity of one class does in general become an external stimulus to the consciousness of another. But the direct cause of the peasant revolt itself lay in changes in the consciousness of the villages; a discovery of the character of these changes makes the content of one chapter of this book. Let us not forget that revolutions are accomplished through people, although they be nameless. Materialism does not ignore the feeling, thinking and acting man, but explains him. What else is the task of the historian?[1]

[1] News of the death of M. N. Pokrovsky, with whom we have had to do battle more than once in the course of these two volumes, arrived after our work was finished. Having come over to Marxism from the liberal camp when already a finished scholar, Pokrovsky enriched the most recent historic literature with precious works and beginnings. But nonetheless he never fully mastered the method of dialectic materialism. It is a matter of simple justice to add that Pokrovsky was a man not only of high gifts and exceptional erudition, but also of deep loyalty to the cause which he served.

Certain critics from the democratic camp, inclined to operate with the help of indirect evidence, have looked upon the "ironic" attitude of the author to the compromise leaders as the expression of an undue subjectivism vitiating the scientific character of his exposition. We venture to regard this criterion as unconvincing. Spinoza's principle, "not to weep or laugh, but to understand" gives warning against inappropriate laughter and untimely tears. It does not deprive a man, even though he be a historian, of the right to his share of tears and laughter when justified by a correct understanding of the material itself. That purely individualistic irony which spreads out like a smoke of indifference over the whole effort and intention of mankind, is the worst form of snobbism. It rings false alike in artistic creations and works of history. But there is an irony deep laid in the very relations of life. It is the duty of the historian as of the artist to bring it to the surface.

A failure of correspondence between subjective and objective is, generally speaking, the fountain-source of the comic, as also the tragic, in both life and art. The sphere of politics less than any other is exempted from the action of this law. People and parties are heroic or comic not in themselves but in their relation to circumstances. When the French revolution entered its decisive stage the most eminent of Girondists became pitiful and ludicrous beside the rank-and-file Jacobin. Jean-Marie Rolland, a respected figure as factory inspector of Lyons, looks like a living caricature against the background of 1792. The Jacobins, on the contrary, measure up to the events. They may evoke hostility, hatred, horror—but not irony.

The heroine of Dickens who tried to hold back the tide with a broom is an acknowledged comic image because of the fatal lack of correspondence between means and end. If we assert that this person symbolizes the policies of the compromise parties in the revolution, it may seem an extravagant exaggeration. And yet Tseretelli, the actual inspiriter of the dual-power régime, confessed to Nabokov, one of the Liberal leaders, after the October revolution: "Everything we did at that time was a vain effort to hold back a destructive elemental flood with a handful of insignificant chips." Those words sound like spiteful satire, but they are the truest words spoken by the Compromisers about themselves. To renounce irony in depicting "revolutionists" who tried to hold back a revolution with chips, would be to plunder reality and betray objectivism for the benefit of pedants.

Peter Struvé, a monarchist from among the former Marxists, wrote as an emigré: "Only Bolshevism was logical about revolution and true to its essence, and therefore in the revolution it conquered." Miliukov, the leader of liberalism, made approximately the same statement: "They knew where they were going, and they went in the direction which they had chosen once for all, toward a goal which came nearer and nearer with every new, unsuccessful experiment of compromisism." And finally, one of the white emigrés not so well known, trying in his own way to understand the revolution, has expressed himself thus: "Only iron people could take this road . . . only people who were revolutionists by their very 'profession' and had no fear of calling into life the all-devouring spirit of riot and revolt." You may say of the Bolsheviks with still more justice what was said above about the Jacobins. They were adequate to the epoch and its tasks; curses in plenty resounded in their direction, but irony would not stick to them —it had nothing to catch hold of.

In the introduction to the first volume it was explained why the author deemed it suitable to speak of himself as a participant of the events in the third person, and not the first. This literary form, preserved also in the second and third volumes, does not in itself of course offer a defense against subjectivism, but at least it does not make subjectivism necessary. Indeed it reminds one of the obligation to avoid it.

On many occasions we hesitated long whether to quote this or that remark of a contemporary, characterizing the rôle of the author in the flow of events. It would have been easy to renounce any such quotation, were nothing greater involved than the rules of correct tone in polite society. The author of this book was president of the Petrograd Soviet after the Bolsheviks won a majority there, and he was afterward president of the Military Revolutionary Committee which organized the October uprising. These facts he neither wishes nor is able to erase from history. The faction now ruling in the Soviet Union has of late years dedicated many articles, and no few books, to the author of this work, setting themselves the task of proving that his activity was steadily directed against the interests of the revolution. The question why the Bolshevik party placed so stubborn an "enemy" during the most critical years in the most responsible posts remains unanswered. To pass these retrospective quarrels in complete silence would be to renounce to some extent the task of establishing the actual course of events. And to what end? A pretense of disinterestedness is needful only to him whose aim is slyly to convey to his readers conclusions which do not flow from the facts. We prefer to call things by their whole name as it is found in the dictionary.

We will not conceal the fact that for us the question here is not only about the past. Just as the enemy in attacking a man's prestige are striking at his program, so his own struggle for a definite program obliges a man to restore his actual position in the events. As for those who are incapable of seeing anything but personal vanity in a man's struggle for great causes and for his place under the banner, we may be sorry for them but we will not undertake to convince them. In any case we have taken measures to see to it that "personal" questions should not occupy a greater place in this book than that to which they can justly lay claim.

Certain of the friends of the Soviet Union—a phrase which often means friends of the present Soviet powers and that only so long as they remain powers—have reproached the author for his critical attitude to the Bolshevik party or its individual leaders. Nobody, however, has made the attempt to refute or correct the picture given of the condition of the party during the events. For the information of these "friends" who consider themselves called to defend against us the rôle of the Bolsheviks in the October revolution, we give warning that our book teaches not how to love a victorious revolution after the event in the person of the bureaucracy it has brought forward, but only how a revolution is prepared, how it develops, and how it conquers. A party is not for us a machine whose sinlessness is to be defended by state measures of repression, but a complicated organism which like all living things develops in contradictions. The uncovering of these contradictions—among them the waverings and mistakes of the general staff—does not in our view weaken in the slightest degree the significance of that gigantic historic task which the Bolshevik party was the first in history to take upon its shoulders.

L. TROTSKY

Prinkipo
May 13, 1932

P.S. The critics have already paid their tribute to Max Eastman's translation. He has brought to his work not only a creative gift of style, but also the carefulness of a friend. I subscribe with warm gratitude to the unanimous voice of the critics.

L. T.

Editor's Summary of Volume Two

VOLUME TWO. THE ATTEMPTED COUNTER-REVOLUTION. Trotsky gives an entire volume to the events of July and August 1917, maintaining that they were crucial in preparing the masses for October and that they had instructive parallels in the history of past revolutions. Kerensky's abortive offensive in June widened the split between bourgeoisie and proletariat, the Provisional Government and the soviets, the right-wing socialists and the Bolsheviks. Early July witnessed angry demonstrations and riots on the part of some of the Petrograd garrisons and especially of the Kronstadt sailors, with several bloody encounters and some loss of life. The Bolsheviks were blamed for what was really a spontaneous movement and one which the Bolsheviks actually sought to restrain, believing the movement immature and insufficiently directed.

These were the "July Days"; and they culminated, so far as the Bolsheviks were concerned, in the sacking of the *Pravda* offices by government troops and in public charges against Lenin. His recent journey to Russia through German territory in the sealed train continued to make trouble; and now forged evidence was produced by one Ermolenko, a former agent of Russian Intelligence, and evidently with the connivance of some elements in the government, to the effect that Lenin was in the pay of the German staff. Convinced that the Bolshevik leaders were about to be arrested and possibly shot, Lenin went into hiding and did not re-emerge until the eve of the October revolution. Trotsky and others were jailed for some weeks. For a time the accusations against Lenin were effective even among the troops and the influence of the Bolsheviks declined sharply. The masses were further demoralized by the prolonged and fruitless conflicts of the dual power régime. No class seemed able or willing to seize power; the deadlock was exhausting the energies of the February revolution; and the whole impossible situation was dramatized on the occasion of a peculiarly futile and embittered State Conference of the various parties held at Moscow beginning August 12.

In the meantime, on July 24, a new Coalition government had been formed with socialists in the majority but still largely subservient to the Liberals. Kerensky and Kornilov were the dominant personalities of this period. Kerensky evidently aimed to put himself at the head of a Bonapartist régime; there is also evidence that he was seeking to use the now thoroughly aroused generals of the army to give his proposed régime something of the character of a military dictatorship. But Kerensky was rapidly losing the support of the masses, and even the Liberals with whom he freely collaborated saw him as an ineffectual and misguided hysteric. Independently of Kerensky and in rivalry with him, Kornilov now attempted a military coup, although he too was a far from gifted leader. Taking advantage of the German capture of Riga, Kornilov withdrew troops from that city and with other forces proposed to march on Petrograd and put down the revolutionary forces there. The march began on August 28 but was firmly opposed by a majority of the troops; Kornilovist officers in the fleet were in some cases summarily executed by the sailors; and Kornilov himself was arrested on September 1. Though quickly put down, the Kornilovist movement had vastly important though opposing results for the revolutionary Russia of the future. The proletariat was unified once more by the victory over him; the slandered Bolsheviks rapidly regained favor with the masses; and the October revolution became possible. On the other hand, the Kornilovist movement was the nucleus out of which grew in 1918 the White Russian attack on Bolshevik Russia, the civil war, the devastation of Russian land and industry, and the Red Terror. Meanwhile, with Trotsky now freed on bail and once more active in the Petrograd Soviet, the Bolsheviks soon captured a majority in that body. On September 24, what was to be the last Coalition Government was formed with Kerensky as president.

Volume Three

THE TRIUMPH OF THE SOVIETS

Editor's Summary of Chapters I–IV

CHAPTER I. THE PEASANTRY BEFORE OCTOBER. In April Lenin had still considered it possible that the main mass of the peasantry might be dragged along the road of compromise with the landlords and the bourgeoisie. For this reason he insisted on the creation of special soviets of farm hands' deputies and on independent organizations of the poorest peasantry. Month by month it became clear that this part of the Bolshevik program would not take root. Indeed the party remained largely isolated from the peasantry, due in part to the agitation against Bolshevism by the Social Revolutionaries. Except in the Baltic state there were no soviets of farm hands' deputies, and the peasant poor also failed to find independent forms of organization. Instead, the peasantry as a whole, despite complex tensions in its own ranks, moved steadily closer to the accomplishment of its historic task: the agrarian revolution. Still relatively patient during the summer, in the early autumn the peasants in many districts embarked on campaigns of land seizure, plunder, and the burning of manor houses. Though the Bolsheviks were blamed for this violence, the peasants were really settling accounts with their oppressors in the ancient manner of all peasant wars. Meanwhile the economic conflict between city and country deepened—a conflict that was to become fundamental in the soviet economy of the future. But in general the peasant and proletarian movements were interdependent. In order that the peasant might clear and fence his land, the worker had to stand at the head of the state: that is the simplest formula for the October revolution.

CHAPTER II. THE PROBLEM OF NATIONALITIES. Whereas in nationally homogeneous states the bourgeois revolutions developed powerfully centripetal tendencies, rallying to the idea of overcoming particularism, as in France, or overcoming national disunion, as in Italy and Germany—in nationally heterogeneous states, on the contrary, such as Turkey, Russia, Austria-Hungary, the belated bourgeois revolution released centrifugal forces. Following the February revolution, separatist movements of various kinds and degrees of intensity started up among the many different peoples who made up Russia and who had hitherto been exploited and deprived of their political rights by the ascendant Great Russians. For these oppressed nations the overthrow of the monarchy inevitably meant their own national revolution. In principle the Provisional Government declared for self-determination of the subject peoples. In practice we observe the same things as in all other departments of the February régime: the official democracy, held in leash by its political dependence on an imperialist bourgeoisie, was incapable of breaking the old fetters. The socialists in the government found themselves united with the liberal bourgeoisie in the effort to discourage separatist movements. In the case of Finland, especially, the parliament of that country was dissolved by decree from Petrograd and Russian soldiers were stationed at its doors.

CHAPTER III. WITHDRAWAL FROM THE PRE-PARLIAMENT AND STRUGGLE FOR THE SOVIET CONGRESS. With the peasant war kindling, the national movements growing bitter, the economic crisis deepening, and the front disintegrating, the Provisional Government sought to stem the flood by calling (for October 7) a Pre-Parliament. This was to be the forerunner of that Constituent Assembly for which all Left parties including the Bolsheviks had long agitated. But in a situation where the bourgeoisie and the proletariat confronted one another in naked and absolute opposition, it was too late for such a lawmaking body. The Bolsheviks boycotted the Pre-Parliament and bent their efforts on capturing the soviets, in which their power was now very much on the rise. (Trotsky was now President of the Petrograd Soviet and, Lenin being still in hiding, was for the time being the chief spirit of Bolshevism.) On September 21, the Petrograd Soviet raised its voice for the prompt calling of a Congress of Soviets. The Executive Committee sought to delay the date of the congress and did succeed in effecting a brief postponement. Meanwhile the Bolsheviks set in motion from below, through the local soviets and organizations of the front, an intensive campaign for the congress. This struggle gave the last impetus in the localities to the Bolshevizing of the soviets. The slogan of the congress gave the revolutionary forces a unity of aim and a date for action, while at the same time partly screening the preparations for an insurrection. This Congress of Soviets was afterwards to sanction the results of the revolution and give the new government a form irreproachable in the eyes of the people.

CHAPTER IV. THE MILITARY-REVOLUTIONARY COMMITTEE. On October 10, the Central Committee of the Bolsheviks adopted in secret session a resolution of Lenin presenting armed insurrection as the practical task of the coming days. But with Lenin still in hiding, Trotsky became the chief organizer of the preparations, while Antonov-Ovseënko and Sverdlov also played vital rôles. The preparations required a careful scrutiny of the military situation in Petrograd and much shrewd maneuvering in the Petrograd Soviet. Rumors of the undertaking circulated widely. The Bolshevik strategy was to take advantage of the psychological crisis created by these rumors, without revealing their actual plans. The various cautionary moves of Kerensky and his supporters in the Soviet all played directly into the Bolsheviks' hands. Kerensky's determination to weaken the Bolshevized Petrograd garrisons by effecting a transfer of troops to and from the front was the decisive move of the anti-Bolsheviks. The Bolshevik counter-move was, in general, to provoke resistance among the troops to what was now clearly Kerensky's counter-revolutionary plan. In particular the Bolsheviks made use of a body created (October 9) in the Soviet by demand of the Mensheviks and named the "Military Revolutionary Committee." As proposed by the Mensheviks, this committee was supposed to gather data on the military situation in Petrograd in order to discover whether Kerensky's transfers were determined by military or political considerations. Getting control of this body, the Bolsheviks converted it into the headquarters of the coming insurrection. In this way they also got over the difficulty of reconciling an instrument of insurrection with an effective and openly functioning Soviet full of hostile elements. The Military Revolutionary Committee created in turn a Garrison Conference among the more important regiments quartered in Petrograd, thus establishing direct liaison with the troops. Trotsky, as President of the Petrograd Soviet, could therefore, with some show of legality, requisition rifles for use of the workers and—in what was probably his most daring and decisive move—enter the Peter and Paul fortress, situated on an island in the Neva commanding the Winter Palace and possessed of an arsenal with 100,000 rifles, and persuade the soldiers of this hitherto doubtful unit to take orders not from the Executive Committee but from Trotsky's own Military Revolutionary Committee. Meanwhile there were psychological preparations. The Soviet designated Sunday, October 22, as a day for a peaceful "review of forces" in Petrograd. The turnout was tremendous. Trotsky and others addressed meetings attended by tens of thousands of enthusiasts; "there was a mood very near to ecstasy," writes Sukhanov. Nevertheless Kerensky remained confident that he had the forces to put down a Bolshevik uprising. He and others in the government evidently wished for such an attempt, expecting that the Bolsheviks would be defeated and disgraced once for all.

Chapter V

LENIN SUMMONS TO INSURRECTION

Besides the factories, barracks, villages, the front and the soviets, the revolution had another laboratory: the brain of Lenin. Driven underground, Lenin was obliged for a hundred and eleven days—from July 6 to October 25—to cut down his meetings even with members of the Central Committee. Without any immediate intercourse with the masses, and deprived of contacts with any organizations, he concentrated his thought the more resolutely upon the fundamental problems of the revolution, reducing them—as was both his rule and the necessity of his nature—to the key problems of Marxism.

The chief argument of the democrats, even the most leftward, against seizing the power, was that the toilers were incapable of mastering the machinery of state. Opportunist elements even within the Bolshevik party cherished the same fears. "The machinery of state!" Every petty bourgeois is brought up in adoration of this mystic principle elevated above people and above classes. And the educated philistine carries in his marrow the same awe that his father did, or his uncle, the shopkeeper or well-off peasant, before these all-powerful institutions where questions of war and peace are decided, where commercial patents are given out, whence issue the whips of the taxes, where they punish and once in a while also pardon, where they legitimize marriages and births, where death itself has to stand in line respectfully awaiting recognition. The machinery of state! Removing in imagination not only his hat but his shoes too, the petty bourgeois comes tiptoeing into the temple of the idol on stocking feet—it matters not what his name is, Kerensky, Laval, MacDonald or Hilferding—that is the way he comes when personal good-luck or the force of circumstances makes him a minister. Such gracious condescension he can answer only with a humble submission before the "machinery of state." The Russian radical intelligentsia, who had never dared crawl into the seats of power even during the revolution except behind the backs of titled landlords and big business men, gazed with fright and indignation upon the Bolsheviks. Those street agitators, those demagogues, think that they can master the machinery of state!

After the Soviet, confronted by the spineless impotence of the official democracy, had saved the revolution in the struggle against Kornilov, Lenin wrote: "Let those of little faith learn from this example. Shame on those who say, 'We have no machine with which to replace that old one which gravitates inexorably to the defense of the bourgeoisie.' For we have a machine. And that is the soviets. Do not fear the initiative and independence of the masses. Trust the revolutionary organizations of the masses, and you will see in all spheres of the state life that same power, majesty and inconquerable will of the workers and peasants, which they have shown in their solidarity and enthusiasm against Kornilovism."

During the first months of his underground life Lenin wrote a book *The State and Revolution,* the principal material for which he had collected abroad during the war. With the same painstaking care which he dedicated to thinking out the practical problems of the day, he here examines the theoretic problems of the state. He cannot do otherwise: for him theory is in actual fact a guide to action. In this work Lenin has not for a minute proposed to introduce any new word into political theory. On the contrary, he gives his work an extraordinarily modest aspect, emphasizing his position as a disciple. His task, he says, is to revive the genuine "teaching of Marxism about the state."

With its meticulous selection of quotations, its detailed polemical interpretations, the book might seem pedantic—to actual pedants, incapable of feeling under the analysis of texts the mighty pulsation of the mind and will. By a mere reestablishment of the class theory of the state on a new and higher historical foundation, Lenin gives to the ideas of Marx a new concreteness and therewith a new significance. But this work on the state derives its immeasurable importance above all from the fact that it constituted the scientific introduction to the greatest revolution in history. This "commentator" of Marx was preparing his party for the revolutionary conquest of a sixth part of the habitable surface of the earth.

If the state could simply reaccommodate itself to the demands of a new historic régime, revolutions would never have arisen. As a fact, however, the bourgeoisie itself has never yet come to power except by way of revolution. Now it is the workers' turn. Upon this question, too, Lenin restored to Marxism its significance as the theoretic weapon of the proletarian revolution.

You say the workers cannot master the machinery of state? But it is not a question—Lenin teaches—of getting possession of the old machine and using it for new aims: that is a reactionary utopia. The selection of personages in the old machine, their education, their mutual relations, are all in conflict with the historic task of the proletariat. After seizing the power our task is not to re-educate the old machine, but to shatter it to fragments. And with what replace it? With the soviets. From being leaders of the revolutionary masses, instruments of education, the soviets will become organs of the new state order.

In the whirlpool of the revolution this work will find few readers; it will be published, indeed, only after the seizure of power. Lenin is working over the problem of the state primarily for the sake of his own inner confidence and for the future. One of his continual concerns was to preserve the succession of ideas. In July he writes to Kamenev: "*Entre nous.* If they bump me off, I ask you to publish my little note-book *Marxism on the State* (stranded in Stockholm). Bound in a blue cover. All the quotations are collected from Marx and Engels, likewise from Kautsky against Pannekoek. There is a whole series of notes and comments. Formulate it. I think you could publish it with a week's work. I think it important, for it is not only Plekhanov and Kautsky who got off the track. My conditions: all this to be absolutely *entre nous.*" The revolutionary leader, persecuted as the agent of a hostile state and figuring on the possibility of attempted assassination by his enemies, concerns himself with the publication of a "blue" note-book with quotations from Marx and Engels. That was to be his secret last will and testament. The phrase "bump me off"[1] was to serve as an antidote against that pathos which he hated, for the commission is pathetic in its very essence.

But while awaiting this blow in the back, Lenin himself was getting ready to deliver a frontal blow. While he was putting in order, between reading the papers and writing letters of instruction, his precious note-book—procured at last from Stockholm—life did not stand still. The hour was approaching when the question of the state was to be decided in practical action.

While still in Switzerland immediately after the overthrow of the monarchy Lenin wrote: "We are not Blanquists, not advocates of the seizure of power by a minority. . . ." This same thought he developed on his arrival in Russia: "We are now in a minority—the masses do not trust us yet. We know how to wait. . . . They will swing to our side, and after explaining the correlation of forces we will then say to them: Our day is come." The question of the conquest of power was presented during those first months as a question of winning a majority in the soviets.

After the July raids Lenin declared: "The power can be seized henceforth only by an armed insurrection; we must obviously rely in this operation not upon the soviets, demoralized by the Compromisers, but on the factory committees; the soviets as organs of power will have to be created anew after the victory." As a matter of fact, only two months after that the Bolsheviks had won over the soviets from the Compromisers. The nature of Lenin's mistake on this question is highly characteristic of his strategic genius: for the boldest designs he based his calculations upon the least favorable premises. Thus in coming to Russia through Germany in April he counted on going straight to prison from the station. Thus on July 5 he was saying: "They will probably shoot us all." And thus now he was figuring: the Compromisers will not let us get a majority in the soviets.

"There is no man more faint-hearted than I am, when I am working out a military plan," wrote Napoleon to General Berthier. "I exaggerate all dangers and all possible misfortunes. . . . When my decision is taken everything is forgotten except

[1] Ukokoshit.

what can assure its success." Except for the pose involved in the inappropriate word faint-hearted, the essence of this thought applies perfectly to Lenin. In deciding a problem of strategy he began by clothing the enemy with his own resolution and far-sightedness. The tactical mistakes of Lenin were for the most part by-products of his strategic power. In the present instance, indeed, it is hardly appropriate to use the word mistake. When a diagnostician arrives at the definition of a disease by a method of successive eliminations, his hypothetical assumptions, beginning with the worst possible, are not mistakes but methods of analysis. As soon as the Bolsheviks had got control of the soviets of the two capitals, Lenin said: "Our day is come." In April and July he had applied the brakes; in August he was preparing theoretically the new step; from the middle of September he was hurrying and urging on with all his power. The danger now lay not in acting too soon, but in lagging. "In this matter it is now impossible to be premature."

In his articles and letters addressed to the Central Committee, Lenin analyzes the situation, always emphasizing first of all the international conditions. The symptoms and the facts of an awakening European proletariat are for him, on the background of the war, irrefutable proof that the direct threat against the Russian revolution from the side of foreign imperialism will steadily diminish. The arrest of the socialists in Italy, and still more the insurrections in the German fleet, made him announce a supreme change in the whole world situation: "We stand in the vestibule of the world-wide proletarian revolution."

The epigone historians have preferred to hush up this starting point of Lenin's thought—both because Lenin's calculation has been refuted by events, and because according to the most recent theories the Russian Revolution ought to be sufficient unto itself in all circumstances. As a matter of fact Lenin's appraisal of the international situation was anything but illusory. The symptoms which he observed through the screen of the military censorship of all countries did actually portend the approach of a revolutionary storm. Within a year it shook the old building of the Central Empires to its very foundation. But also in the victor countries, England and France—to say nothing of Italy—it long deprived the ruling classes of their freedom of action. Against a strong, conservative, self-confident capitalistic Europe, the proletarian revolution in Russia, isolated and not yet fortified, could not have held out even for a few months. But that Europe no longer existed. The revolution in the west did not, to be sure, put the proletariat into power—the reformists succeeded in saving the bourgeois régime—but nevertheless it proved powerful enough to defend the Soviet Republic in the first and most dangerous period of its life.

Lenin's deep internationalism was not expressed solely in the fact that he always gave first place to his appraisal of the international situation. He regarded the very conquest of power in Russia primarily as the impetus for a European revolution, a thing which, as he often repeated, was to have incomparably more importance for the fate of humanity than the revolution in backward Russia. With what sarcasm he lashed those Bolsheviks who did not understand their international duty. "Let us adopt a resolution of sympathy for the German insurrectionists," he mocks, "and reject the insurrection in Russia. That will be a genuinely reasonable internationalism!"

In the days of the Democratic Conference, Lenin wrote to the Central Committee: "Having got a majority in the soviets of both capitals . . . the Bolsheviks can and should seize the state power in their hands. . . ." The fact that a majority of the peasant delegates of the stacked Democratic Conference voted against a coalition with the Kadets, had for him decisive significance: The muzhik who does not want a union with the bourgeoisie has nothing left but to support the Bolsheviks. "The people are tired of the wavering of the Mensheviks and Social Revolutionaries. Only our victory in the capitals will bring the peasants over to us." The task of the party is: "To place upon the order of the day armed insurrection in Petersburg and Moscow, conquest of power, overthrow of the government. . . ." Up to that time nobody had so imperiously and nakedly set the task of insurrection.

Lenin very studiously followed all the elections and votings in the country, carefully assembling those figures which would throw light on the actual correlation of forces. The semi-anarchistic indifference to electoral statistics got nothing but contempt from him. At the same time Lenin never identified the indexes of parliamentarism with the actual correlation of forces. He always introduced a correction in favor of direct action. "The strength of a revolutionary proletariat," he explained, "from the point of view of its action upon the masses and drawing them into the struggle, is infinitely greater in an extra-parliamentary than a parliamentary struggle. This is a very important observation when it comes to the question of civil war."

Lenin with his sharp eye was the first to notice that the agrarian movement had gone into a decisive phase, and he immediately drew all the conclusions from this. The muzhik, like the soldier, will wait no longer. "In the face of such a fact as the peasant insurrection," writes Lenin at the end of September, "all other political symptoms, even if they were in conflict with this ripening of an all-national crisis, would have absolutely no significance at all." The agrarian question is the foundation of the revolution. A victory of the government over the peasant revolt would be the "funeral of the revolution. . . ." We cannot hope for more favorable conditions. The hour of action is at hand. "The crisis is ripe. The whole future of the international workers' revolution for socialism is at stake. The crisis is ripe."

Lenin summons to insurrection. In each simple, prosaic, sometimes angular line, you feel the highest tensity of passion. "The revolution is done for," he writes early in October to the Petrograd party conference, "if the government of Kerensky is not overthrown by proletarians and soldiers in the near future. . . . We must mobilize all forces in order to impress upon the workers and soldiers the unconditional necessity of a desperate, last, resolute struggle to overthrow the government of Kerensky."

Lenin had said more than once that the masses are to the left of the party. He knew that the party was to the left of its own upper layer of "old Bolsheviks." He was too well acquainted with the inner groupings and moods in the Central Committee to expect from it any hazardous steps whatever. On the other hand he greatly feared excessive caution, Fabianism, a letting slip of one of those historic situations which are decades in preparation. Lenin did not trust the Central

Committee—without Lenin. In that lies the key to his letters from underground. And Lenin was not so wrong in his mistrust.

Being compelled in a majority of cases to express himself after a decision had already been reached in Petrograd, Lenin was continually criticizing the policy of the Central Committee from the left. His opposition developed with the question of insurrection as a background. But it was not limited to that. Lenin thought that the Central Committee was giving too much attention to the compromisist Executive Committee, the Democratic Conference, parliamentary doings in the upper soviet circles in general. He sharply opposed the proposal of the Bolsheviks for a coalition praesidium in the Petrograd Soviet. He branded as "shameful" the decision to participate in the Pre-Parliament. He was indignant at the list of Bolshevik candidates for the Constituent Assembly published at the end of September. Too many intellectuals, not enough workers. "To jam up the Constituent Assembly with orators and litterateurs will mean to travel the worn-out road of opportunism and chauvinism. This is unworthy of the Third International." Moreover there are too many new names among the candidates, members of the party not tried out in the struggle! Here Lenin considers it necessary to make an exception: "It goes without saying that . . . nobody would quarrel with such a candidacy for example as that of L. D. Trotsky, for in the first place Trotsky took an internationalist position immediately upon his arrival; in the second place, he fought for amalgamation among the Mezhrayontsi; in the third place, in the difficult July Days he stood at the height of the task and proved a devoted champion of the party of the revolutionary proletariat. It is clear that this cannot be said of a majority of the yesterday's party members who have been introduced into this list. . . ."

It might seem as though the April Days had returned—Lenin again in opposition to the Central Committee. The questions stand differently, but the general spirit of his opposition is the same: the Central Committee is too passive, too responsive to social opinion among the intellectual circles, too compromisist in its attitude to the Compromisers. And above all, too indifferent, fatalistic, not attacking à la Bolshevik the problem of the armed insurrection.

It is time to pass from words to deeds: "Our party has now at the Democratic Conference practically its own congress, and this congress has got to decide (whether it wants to or not) the fate of the revolution." Only one decision is thinkable: Armed overthrow. In this first letter on insurrection Lenin makes another exception: "It is not a question of 'the day' of the insurrection, nor 'the moment' in a narrow sense. This can be decided only by the general voice of those who are in contact with the workers and soldiers, with the masses." But only two or three days later (letters in those days were commonly not dated—for conspirative reasons, not through forgetfulness) Lenin, obviously impressed by the decomposition of the Democratic Conference, insists upon immediate action and forthwith advances a practical plan.

"We ought at once to solidify the Bolshevik faction at the Conference, not striving after numbers. . . . We ought to draw up a short declaration of the Bolsheviks. . . . We ought to move our whole faction to the factories and barracks. At the same time without losing a minute we ought to organize a staff of insurrectionary detachments, deploy our forces, move the loyal regiments into the most important positions, surround the Alexandrinka (the theater where the Democratic Conference was sitting), occupy Peter and Paul, arrest the General Staff and the government, send against the junkers and the Savage Division those detachments which are ready to die fighting, but not let the enemy advance to the center of the city; we ought to mobilize the armed workers, summon them to a desperate, final battle, occupy the telegraph and telephone stations at once, install our insurrectionary staff at the central telephone station, placing in contact with it by telephone all the factories, all the regiments, all the chief points of armed struggle, etc." The question of date is no longer placed in dependence upon the "general voice of those who are in contact with the masses." Lenin proposed an immediate act: To leave the Alexandrinsky theater with an ultimatum and return there at the head of the armed masses. A crushing blow is to be struck not only against the government, but also, simultaneously, against the highest organ of the Compromisers.

"Lenin who in private letters was demanding the arrest of the Democratic Conference,"—such is the accusation of Sukhanov—"in the press, as we know, proposed a 'compromise': Let the Mensheviks and Social Revolutionaries take over the whole power and then see what the Soviet Congress says. . . . The same idea was insistently defended by Trotsky at the Democratic Conference and around it." Sukhanov sees a double game where there was not the slightest hint of it. Lenin proposed an agreement to the Compromisers immediately after the victory over Kornilov—during the first days of September. The Compromisers passed it up with a shrug of their shoulders. They were engaged in converting the Democratic Conference into a screen for a new coalition with the Kadets against the Bolsheviks. With that the possibility of an agreement fell away absolutely. The question of power could henceforth be decided only in open struggle. Sukhanov mixes up two stages, one of which preceded the other by two weeks and politically conditioned it.

But although the insurrection flowed inexorably from the new coalition, nevertheless the sharpness of Lenin's change of front took even the heads of his own party by surprise. To unite the Bolshevik faction at the Conference on the basis of his letter, even without "striving after numbers" was clearly impossible. The mood of the faction was such that it rejected by seventy votes against fifty the proposal to boycott the Pre-Parliament—the first step, that is, on the road to insurrection. In the Central Committee itself Lenin's plan found no support whatever. Four years later at an evening of reminiscences, Bukharin with characteristic exaggerations and witticisms, gave a true account of that episode. "The letter (of Lenin) was written with extraordinary force and threatened us with all sorts of punishments. We all gasped. Nobody had yet posed the question so abruptly. . . . At first all were bewildered. Afterwards, having talked it over, we made a decision. Perhaps that was the sole case in the history of our party when the Central Committee unanimously decided to burn a letter of Lenin. . . . Although we believed unconditionally that in Petersburg and Moscow we should succeed in seizing the power, we assumed that in the provinces we could not yet hold out, that having seized the power and dispersed the Democratic Conference we could not fortify ourselves in the rest of Russia."

The burning of several copies of this dangerous letter, owing to conspirative considerations, was as a matter of fact not unanimously resolved upon, but by six votes against four with six abstaining. One copy, luckily for history, was preserved. But it is true, as Bukharin relates, that all the members of the Central Committee, although for different motives, rejected the proposal. Some opposed an insurrection in general; others thought that the moment of the conference was the least advantageous of all; others simply vacillated and adopted a waiting attitude.

Having run into this direct resistance, Lenin entered into a sort of conspiracy with Smilga, who was also in Finland and as President of the Regional Committee of the Soviets held a tolerable amount of real power in his hands. Smilga stood in 1917 on the extreme left wing of the party and already in July had been inclined to carry the struggle through to the end. At turning points in his policy Lenin always found somebody to rely on. On September 27 Lenin wrote Smilga a voluminous letter: ". . . What are we doing? Only passing resolutions? We are losing time, we are setting 'dates' (October 20–Congress of Soviets–Isn't it ridiculous to postpone this way? Isn't it ridiculous to rely on that?). The Bolsheviks are not carrying on a systematic work of preparing their armed forces for the overthrow of Kerensky. . . . We must agitate in the party for a serious attitude toward armed insurrection. . . . And further, as to your rôle . . . : To create a secret committee of the most loyal military men, talk the thing over on all sides with them, collect (and yourself verify) the most accurate information about the make-up and position of the troops in and around Petrograd, about the transportation of Finland troops to Petrograd, about the movements of the fleet, etc." Lenin demanded "a systematic propaganda among the Cossacks located here in Finland. . . . We must study all information about the attitude of the Cossacks and organize a sending of agitatorial detachments from our best forces of sailors and soldiers of Finland." And finally: "For a correct preparation of minds we must immediately put into circulation a slogan of this kind: The power must immediately pass to the Petrograd Soviet which will hand it over to the Congress of Soviets. For why endure three more weeks of war and of Kornilovist preparations by Kerensky?"

In this letter we have a new plan of insurrection: A secret committee of the more important military men in Helsingfors as a fighting staff, the Russian troops quartered in Finland as fighting forces. "It seems that the only ones we can fully control and who will play a serious military rôle are the Finland troops and the Baltic Fleet." Thus we see that Lenin counted on dealing the chief blow against the government from outside Petrograd. At the same time a "correct preparation of minds" is necessary, so that an overthrow of the government by military forces from Finland shall not fall unexpectedly upon the Petrograd Soviet, which until the Congress of Soviets was to be the inheritor of power.

This new draft of a plan, like the preceding one, was not realized. But it did not go by without effect. The agitation among the Cossack divisions soon gave results: we have heard about this from Dybenko. The participation of Baltic sailors in the chief blow against the government also entered into the plan later adopted. But that was not the chief thing: With his extremely sharp posing of the question Lenin permitted nobody to evade or maneuver. What seemed untimely as a direct tactical proposal became expedient as a test of attitudes in the Central Committee, a support to the resolute against the wavering, a supplementary push to the left.

With all the means at his disposal in his underground isolation Lenin was trying to make the cadres of the party feel the acuteness of the situation and the strength of the mass pressure. He summoned individual Bolsheviks to his hiding-place, put them through partisan cross-questionings, tested out the words and deeds of the leaders, used indirect ways to get his slogans into the party—deep down in it—in order to compel the Central Committee to act in the face of necessity and carry the thing through.

A day after his letter to Smilga Lenin wrote the above quoted document *The Crisis Is Ripe*, concluding it with something in the nature of a declaration of war against the Central Committee. "We must . . . acknowledge the truth that there is in the Central Committee and the upper circles of the party a tendency or an opinion in favor of waiting for the Congress of Soviets, against the immediate seizure of power, against immediate insurrection." This tendency we must overcome at any cost. "Conquer Kerensky first and then summon the Congress." To lose time waiting for the Congress of Soviets is "complete idiotism or else complete treachery. . . ." There remain more than twelve days until the Congress designated for the 20th: "Weeks and even days are now deciding everything." To postpone the show-down means a cowardly renunciation of insurrection, since during the Congress a seizure of power will become impossible: "They will get together the Cossacks for the day of that stupidly 'appointed' insurrection."

The mere tone of the letter shows how ruinous the Fabianism of the Petrograd leadership seemed to Lenin. But this time he is not satisfied with furious criticism; by way of protest he resigns from the Central Committee. He gives his reasons: the Central Committee has made no response since the beginning of the Conference to his insistence in regard to the seizure of power; the editorial board of the party organ (Stalin) is printing his articles with intentional delays, omitting from them his indication of such "flagrant mistakes of the Bolsheviks as their shameful decision to participate in the Pre-Parliament," etc. This procedure Lenin does not consider it possible to conceal from the party: "I am compelled to request permission to withdraw from the Central Committee, which I hereby do, and leave myself freedom of agitation in the lower ranks of the party and at the party congress."

The documents do not show what further formal action was taken in this matter. Lenin in any case did not withdraw from the Central Committee. By announcing his resignation, an act which could not possibly be with him the fruit of momentary irritation, Lenin obviously wanted to make it possible to free himself in case of need from the internal discipline of the Central Committee. He could be quite sure that as in April a direct appeal to the lower ranks would assure him the victory. But the road of open mutiny against the Central Committee required the preparation of a special session; it required time; and time was just what was lacking. Keeping this announcement of his resignation in reserve, but not withdrawing completely beyond the limits of party legality, Lenin now continued with greater freedom to develop his offensive along internal lines. His letter to the Central Committee he not only sent to the Petrograd and Moscow committees, but he also saw to it that copies fell into the hands of the more reliable party workers of the district locals. Early in October—and now over the heads of the Central Committee—Lenin wrote directly to the Petrograd and the Moscow committees: "The Bolsheviks have no right to await the Congress of Soviets. They ought to seize the power *right now*. . . . Delay is a crime. Waiting for the Congress of Soviets is a childish toying with formalities, a shameful toying with formalities, betrayal of the revolution." From the standpoint of hierarchical attitudes towards action, Lenin was by no means beyond reproach, but the question here was of something bigger than considerations of formal discipline.

One of the members of the Vyborg District Committee, Sveshnikov, remembers: "Ilych from underground was writing and writing untiringly, and Nadyezhda Constantinovna (Krupskaia) often read these manuscripts to us in the district committee. . . . The burning words of the leader would redouble our strength. . . . I remember as though it were yesterday the bending figure of Nadyezhda Constantinovna in one of the rooms of the district administration, where the typists were working, carefully comparing the copy with the original, and right alongside stood Uncle and Gene demanding a copy each." "Uncle" and "Gene" were old conspirative pseudonyms for two leaders of the district. "Not long ago," relates the district worker, Naumov, "we got a letter from Ilych for delivery to the Central Committee. . . . We read the letter and gasped. It seems that Lenin had long ago put before the Central Committee the question of insurrection. We raised a row. We began to bring pressure on them." It was just this that was needed.

In the first days of October Lenin appealed to a Petrograd party conference to speak a firm word in favor of insurrection. Upon his initiative the conference "insistently requests the Central Committee to take all measures for the leadership of the inevitable insurrection of the workers, soldiers and peasants." In this phrase alone there are two kinds of camouflage, juridical and diplomatic: It speaks of the leadership of an "inevitable insurrection" instead of the direct preparation of insurrection, in order not to place trump cards in the hands of the district attorney; and it "requests the Central Committee"—it does not demand, and it does not protest—this in obvious deference to the prestige of the highest institution of the party. But in another resolution, also written by Lenin, the speech is more frank: "In the upper circles of the party a wavering is to be observed, a sort of dread of the struggle for power, an inclination to replace this struggle with resolutions, protests, and conferences." This is already almost a direct pitting of the party against the Central Committee. Lenin did not decide lightly upon such steps. But it was a question of the fate of the revolution, and all other considerations fell away.

On October 8, Lenin addressed the Bolshevik delegates of the forthcoming Northern Regional Congress: "We must not await the All-Russian Congress of Soviets which the Central Executive Committee is able to postpone even to November. We must not delay and let Kerensky bring in more Kornilov troops." That Regional Conference, at which Finland, the fleet and Reval were represented, should take the initiative in "an immediate move on Petrograd." The direct summons to immediate insurrection was this time addressed to the representatives of scores of soviets. The summons came from Lenin personally. There was no party decision; the higher institutions of the party had not yet expressed themselves.

It required a mighty confidence in the proletariat, in the party, but also a very serious mistrust of the Central Committee, in order over its head, upon his own personal responsibility, from underground, and by means of a few small sheets of note-paper minutely inscribed, to raise an agitation for an armed revolution, for an armed overthrow of the government. How could it happen that Lenin, whom we have seen at the beginning of April isolated among the leaders of his own party, found himself again solitary in the same group in September and early October? This cannot be understood if you believe the unintelligent legend which portrays the history of Bolshevism as an emanation of the pure revolutionary idea. In reality Bolshevism developed in a definite social milieu undergoing its heterogeneous influences and among them the influence of a petty bourgeois environment and of cultural backwardness. To each new situation the party adapted itself only by way of an inner crisis.

In order that the sharp pre-October struggle in the Bolshevik upper circles may come before us in a true light, it is necessary again to look back at those processes in the party of which we spoke in the first volume. This is the more necessary since exactly at this present time the faction of Stalin is making unheard-of efforts, and that too on an international scale, to wipe out of historic memory every recollection of how the October revolution was in reality prepared and achieved.

In the years before the war the Bolsheviks had described themselves in the legal press as "consistent democrats." This pseudonym was not accidentally chosen. The slogans of revolutionary democracy, Bolshevism and Bolshevism alone carried through to its logical conclusion. But in its prognosis of the revolution it did not go beyond this. The war, however, inseparably binding up the bourgeois democrats with imperialism, proved conclusively that the program of "consistent democracy" could be no otherwise enacted than through a proletarian revolution. Every Bolshevik to whom the war did not make this clear was inevitably destined to be caught unaware by the revolution, and converted into a left fellow-traveler of the bourgeois democracy.

However, a careful study of the materials characterizing the party life during the war and the beginning of the revolution, notwithstanding the extreme and unprecedented scantiness of these materials—and then beginning with 1923 their increasing disingenuousness—reveals more clearly every day the immense intellectual backsliding of the upper stratum of the Bolsheviks during the war when the proper life of the party practically came to an end. The cause of this backsliding is twofold: isolation from the masses and isolation from those abroad—that is primarily from Lenin. The result was a drowning in isolation and provincialism.

Not one of the old Bolsheviks in Russia, left each to himself, formulated throughout the whole war one document which might be looked upon as even the tiniest beacon-light on the road from the Second International to the Third. "The problems of peace, the character of the coming revolution, the rôle of the party in a future Provisional Government, etc."—thus wrote one of the old members of the party, Antonov-Saratovsky, some years ago—"were conceived by us vaguely enough or did not enter into our field of reflection at all." Up to this time there has not been published one article, not one page of a diary, not one letter, in which Stalin, Molotov, or any other of the present leaders, formulated even indirectly, even very hastily, his views upon the perspectives of the war and the revolution. This does not mean, of course, that the "old Bolsheviks" wrote nothing on these questions during the years of the war, of the collapse of the social democracy and the preparation of the Russian revolution. These historic events too insistently demanded an answer; jail and exile, moreover, gave plenty of leisure for meditation and correspondence. But among all that was written on these themes, not one thing has turned up which might even with stretching be interpreted as an approach to the ideas of the October revolution. It is sufficient to remember that the Institute of Party History has been forbidden to print one line from the pen of Stalin during the years 1914–17, and has been compelled to hide carefully the most important documents of March 1917. In the official political biographies of a majority of the present ruling stratum, the years of the war present a vacant space. That is the unadorned truth.

One of the most recent young historians, Bayevsky, specially delegated to demonstrate how the upper circles of the party developed during the war in the direction of proletarian revolution, was unable, in spite of his manifest flexibility of scientific conscience, to squeeze out of the materials anything more than the following meager statement: "It is impossible to follow the course of this process, but certain documents and memoirs indubitably prove that there were subterranean searchings of the party mind in the direction of the April theses of Lenin. . . ." As though it were a question of subterranean searchings, and not of scientific appraisals and political prognoses!

It was possible to arrive *a priori* at the ideas of the October revolution, not in Siberia, not in Moscow, not even in Petrograd, but only at the crossing of the roads of world history. The tasks of a belated bourgeois revolution had to be seen intercrossing with the perspectives of a world proletarian movement, before it could seem possible to advance a program of proletarian dictatorship for Russia. A higher point of observation was necessary—not a national but an international horizon —to say nothing of a more serious armament than was possessed by the so-called Russian "practicals" of the party.

In their eyes the overthrow of the monarchy was to open the era of a "free" republican Russia, in which they intended, following the example of the western countries, to begin a struggle for socialism. Three old Bolsheviks, Rykov, Skvortzov, and Vegman, "at the direction of the social democrats of the Narym district liberated by the revolution," sent a telegram in March from Tomsk: "We send a greeting to the resurrected *Pravda* which has so successfully prepared the revolutionary cadres for the conquest of political liberty. We express our profound confidence that it will succeed in uniting all around its banner for the further struggle in the name of the national revolution." A whole world-philosophy emerges from this collective telegram. It is separated by an abyss from the April theses of Lenin. The February revolution immediately converted the leading layer of the party, with Kamenev, Rykov and Stalin at their head, into democratic defensists—in motion, moreover, toward the right, in the direction of a rapprochement with the Mensheviks. The future historian of the party, Yaroslavsky, the future head of the Central Control Commission, Ordzhonikidze, and the future president of the Ukrainian Central Executive Committee, Petrovsky, published during March in Yakutsk, in close union with the Mensheviks, a paper called the *Social Democrat*, which stood on the borderland of patriotic reformism and liberalism. In recent years the issues of this publication have been carefully collected and destroyed.

The Petersburg *Pravda* tried at the beginning of the revolution to occupy an internationalist position—to be sure, a very contradictory one for it did not transcend the framework of bourgeois democracy. The authoritative Bolsheviks arriving from exile immediately imparted to the central organ a democratical-patriotic policy. Kalinin, in defending himself on the 30th of May against a charge of opportunism, recalled this fact: "Take *Pravda* for example. At the beginning *Pravda* had one policy. Came Stalin, Muranov, Kamenev, and turned the helm of *Pravda* to the other side."

"We must frankly acknowledge," wrote Angarsky, a member of this stratum, when it was still permissible to write such things, "that an enormous number of the old Bolsheviks held fast up to the April party conference to the old Bolshevik views of 1905 as to the character of the revolution of 1917, and that the renunciation of these views, the outgrowing of them, was not so easily accomplished." It would be well to add that those ideas of 1905, having outlived themselves, had ceased in 1917 to be "old Bolshevik views" and had become the ideas of patriotic reformism.

"The April theses of Lenin," says an official historic publication, "just simply had no luck in the Petrograd committee. Only two against thirteen voted for these theses, which created an epoch, and one abstained from the vote." "Lenin's argument seemed too bold even for his most rapturous followers," writes Podvoisky. Lenin's speeches—in the opinion of the Petrograd committee and the Military Organization—"isolated the party of the Bolsheviks, and thus, it goes without saying, damaged the position of the proletariat and the party in the extreme."

"We must say frankly," wrote Molotov some years ago: "The party lacked that clarity and resolution which the revolutionary moment demanded. . . . The agitation and the whole revolutionary party work in general had no firm foundation, since our thoughts had not yet arrived at bold conclusions in regard to the necessity of an immediate struggle for socialism and the socialist revolution." The break began only in the second month of the revolution. "From the time of Lenin's arrival in Russia in April 1917"—so testifies Molotov—"our party felt firm ground under its feet. . . . Up to that moment the party was only weakly and diffidently groping its way."

Stalin at the end of March had spoken in favor of military defense, of conditional support to the Provisional Government and the pacifist manifesto of Sukhanov, and of merging with the party of Tseretelli. "This mistaken position," Stalin himself retrospectively acknowledged in 1924, "I then shared with other party comrades, and I renounced it fully only in the middle of April when I adhered to the theses of Lenin. A new orientation was necessary. Lenin gave the party that new orientation in his celebrated April theses."

Kalinin even at the end of April was still standing for a voting bloc with the Mensheviks. At the Petrograd city conference of the party Lenin said: "I am sharply opposed to Kalinin, because a bloc with . . . chauvinists is unthinkable. . . . That is treason to socialism." Kalinin's attitude was not exceptional even in Petrograd. It was said at the conference: "Under the influence of Lenin the amalgamation fumes are dissipating."

In the provinces the resistance to Lenin's theses lasted considerably longer—in a number of provinces almost to October. According to a Kiev worker, Sivtzov, "The ideas set forth in the theses (of Lenin) were not immediately accepted by the whole Kiev Bolshevik organization. A number of comrades, including G. Piatakov, disagreed with the theses . . ." A railroad worker of Kharkov, Morgunov, says: "The old Bolsheviks enjoyed a great influence among all the railroad workers. . . . Many of the old Bolsheviks remained outside of our faction. After the February revolution a number of them registered as Mensheviks by mistake, a thing at which they themselves afterwards laughed, wondering how it could have happened." There is no lack of this and similar testimony.

In spite of all this, the mere mention of a rearming of the party carried out by Lenin in April, is regarded by the present official historians as blasphemy. These most recent historians have substituted for the historic criterion the criterion of honor to the party uniform. On this theme they are deprived of the right to quote even Stalin himself, who was obliged to acknowledge the great depth of the April change. "The famous April theses of Lenin were necessary," he wrote, "in order that the party should come out with one bold step on a new road." "A new orientation," "a new road"—that means the rearming of the party. Six years later, however, Yaroslovsky, who ventured in his capacity of historian to recall the fact that Stalin had occupied at the beginning of the revolution "a mistaken position upon fundamental questions" was furiously denounced from all sides. The idol of prestige is the most gluttonous of all monsters!

The revolutionary tradition of the party, the pressure of the workers from below, and Lenin's criticism from above, compelled the upper stratum during the months of April and May—employing the words of Stalin—"to come out on a new road." But one would have to be completely ignorant of political psychology to imagine that a mere voting for the theses of Lenin meant an actual and complete renunciation of the "mistaken position on fundamental questions." In reality those crass democratic views, organically fortified during the war, merely accommodated themselves to the new program, remaining in silent opposition to it.

On the 6th of August Kamenev, contrary to the decision of the April conference of the Bolsheviks, spoke in the Executive Committee in favor of participating in the Stockholm conference of the Social Patriots then in preparation. Kamenev's speech met no opposition in the central organ of the party. Lenin wrote a formidable article, which appeared, however, only ten days after Kamenev's speech. The resolute insistence of Lenin himself and other members of the Central Committee was required to induce the editorial staff, headed by Stalin, to publish the protesting article.

A convulsion of doubt went through the party after the July days. The isolation of the proletarian vanguard frightened many leaders, especially in the provinces. During the Kornilov days these frightened ones tried to get in contact with the Compromisers, which again evoked a warning cry from Lenin.

On August 20 Stalin as editor of *Pravda* printed without dissenting comment an article of Zinoviev entitled "What Not to Do," an article directed against the preparation of an insurrection. "We must look the truth in the face: In Petrograd there are now many conditions favorable to the outbreak of an insurrection of the type of the Paris Commune of 1871. . . ." On September 3, Lenin—in another connection and without naming Zinoviev but striking him an indirect blow—wrote: "The reference to the Commune is very superficial and even stupid. For in the first place the Bolsheviks after all have learned something since 1871. They would not fail to seize the banks, they would not renounce the offensive against Versailles, and in these conditions even the Commune might have succeeded. Moreover the Commune could not immediately offer the people what the Bolsheviks can if they come to power, namely, land to the peasants and an immediate proposal of peace. . . ." This was a nameless but unequivocal warning not only to Zinoviev, but also to the editor of *Pravda*, Stalin.

The question of the Pre-Parliament split the Central Committee in half. The decision of the Bolshevik faction of the Conference in favor of participating in the Pre-Parliament was ratified by many local committees, if not a majority of them. It was so for instance in Kiev. "On the question of . . . entering the Pre-Parliament," says E. Bosh in her memoirs, "the majority of the committee voted for participation and elected Piatakov as its delegate." In many cases—as for example Kamenev, Rykov, Piatakov and others—it is possible to trace a succession of waverings: against the theses of Lenin in April, against the boycott of the Pre-Parliament in September, against the insurrection in October. On the other hand, the next lower stratum of the Bolsheviks, standing nearer to the masses and being more fresh politically, easily accepted the slogan of boycott and compelled the committees, including the Central Committee itself, to make an about-face. Under the influence of letters from Lenin, the city conference of Kiev voted with an overwhelming majority against their committee. Similarly at almost all sharp political turning points Lenin relied upon the lower strata of the party machine against the higher, or on the party mass against the machine as a whole.

In these circumstances the pre-October waverings could least of all catch Lenin unawares. He was armed in advance with a sharp-eyed suspicion, was watching for alarming symptoms, was making the worst possible assumptions; and he considered it more expedient to bring excess pressure than to be indulgent.

It was at the suggestion of Lenin beyond a doubt that the Moscow Regional Bureau adopted at the end of September a bitter resolution against the Central Committee, accusing it of irresolution, wavering and introducing confusion into the ranks of the party, and demanding that it "take a clear and definite course toward insurrection." In the name of the Moscow Bureau, Lomov on the 3rd of October reported this decision to the Central Committee. The minutes remark: "It was decided not to debate the question." The Central Committee was still continuing to dodge the question what to do. But Lenin's pressure, brought to bear through Moscow, had its result: After two days the Central Committee decided to withdraw from the Pre-Parliament.

That this step meant entering the road of insurrection was clear to the enemies and opponents. "Trotsky in leading his army out of the Pre-Parliament," writes Sukhanov, "was definitely steering a course towards violent revolution." The report of the Petrograd Soviet on withdrawal from the Pre-Parliament ended with the cry: "Long live the direct and open struggle for revolutionary power in the country!" That was October 9th.

On the following day, upon the demand of Lenin, occurred the famous session of the Central Committee where the question of insurrection was flatly posed. From the beginning of that session Lenin placed his further policy in dependence upon its outcome: either through the Central Committee or against it. "O new jest of the merry muse of history!" writes Sukhanov. "That high-up and decisive session was held in my apartment, still on the same Karpovka (32, Apartment 31). But all this was without my knowledge." The wife of the Menshevik, Sukhanov, was a Bolshevik. "That time special measures were taken to assure my sleeping outside the house: at least my wife made carefully sure of my intention, and gave me friendly and impartial advice—not to tire myself out after my work with the long journey home. In any case the lofty assemblage was completely safe from any invasion from me." What was more important, it proved safe from invasions from Kerensky's police.

Twelve of the twenty-one members of the Central Committee were present. Lenin came in wig and spectacles without a beard. The session lasted about ten hours—deep into the night. In the intervals there were tea with bread and sausage for reinforcement. And reinforcement was needed: it was a question of seizing the power in the former empire of the tzars. The session began, as always, with an organizational report from Sverdlov. This time his communication was devoted to the front—and evidently by previous agreement with Lenin, in order to give him support for the necessary inferences. This was quite in accord with Lenin's methods. Representatives of the army of the northern front gave warning through Sverdlov of preparations by the counter-revolutionary command for some sort of "shady plot involving a withdrawal of troops inland"; from Minsk, the headquarters of the western front, it was reported that a new Kornilov insurrection was in preparation; in view of the revolutionary character of the local garrison, headquarters had surrounded the city with Cossack troops. "Some sort of negotiations of a suspicious character are in progress between headquarters and the general staff"; it is quite possible to seize the headquarters in Minsk: the local garrison is ready to disarm the Cossack ring; they are also in a position to send a revolutionary corps from Minsk to Petrograd; the mood on the front is for the Bolsheviks; they will go against Kerensky.—Such was Sverdlov's report. It was not in every part sufficiently definite, but it was entirely encouraging in character.

Lenin immediately took the offensive: "From the beginning of September there has been a kind of indifference to the question of insurrection." References are made to the cooling off and disappointment of the masses. No wonder. "The masses are tired of words and resolutions." We must take the situation as a whole. Events in the city are now taking place against the background of a gigantic peasant movement. The government would require colossal forces in order to quell the agrarian insurrection. "The political situation is thus ready. We must talk of the technical side. That is the whole thing. Meanwhile in the manner of the defensists we are inclined to regard the systematic preparation of insurrection as something in the nature of a political sin." The speaker was obviously restraining himself: He had too much feeling piled up in him. "We must make use of the northern regional congress and the proposal from Minsk in order to start a decisive action."

The northern congress opened exactly on the day of this session of the Central Committee, and was to close in two or three days. The beginning of "decisive action" Lenin presented as the task of the next days. We must not wait. We must not postpone. On the front—as we have heard from Sverdlov—they are preparing an overturn. Will the Congress of Soviets ever be held? We do not know. We must seize the power immediately and not wait for any congresses. "Never to be communicated or reproduced," wrote Trotsky several years later, "was the general spirit of those tense and passionate impromptu speeches, saturated with a desire to instil into the objecting, the wavering, the doubtful, his thought, his will, his confidence, his courage. . . ."

Lenin expected strong resistance, but his fears were soon dispelled. The unanimity with which the Central Committee had rejected the proposal of immediate insurrection in September had been episodic: The left wing had been against the "surrounding of the Alexandrinka" for temporary reasons; the right for reasons of general strategy, although these were not as yet thoroughly thought out. During the three weeks following, there had been a considerable shift to the left in the Central Committee. Ten against two voted for the insurrection. That was a big victory!

Soon after the revolution, at a new stage in the inner party struggle, Lenin recalled during a debate in the Petrograd committee how up to that session of the Central Committee, he "had fears of opportunism from the side of the internationalist fusionists, but these were dissipated. In our party, however, certain members (of the Central Committee) did not agree. This grieved me deeply." Aside from Trotsky, whom Lenin could hardly have had in mind, the only "internationalists" in the Central Committee were Joffé, the future ambassador in Berlin, Uritzky the future head of the Cheka in Petrograd, and Sokolnikov, the future inventor of the Chervonetz. All three took the side of Lenin. His opponents were two old Bolsheviks, closest of all to Lenin in their past work: Zinoviev and Kamenev. It is to them he referred when he said "this grieved me very much." That session of the 10th reduced itself almost entirely to a passionate polemic against Zinoviev and Kamenev. Lenin led the attack, and the rest joined in one after the other.

The resolution, written hastily by Lenin with the gnawed end of a pencil on a sheet of paper from a child's note-book ruled in squares, was very unsymmetrical in architecture, but nevertheless gave firm support to the course towards insurrection. "The Central Committee recognizes that both the international situation of the Russian revolution (the insurrection in the German fleet, as the extreme manifestation of the growth throughout Europe of a world-wide socialist revolution, and also the threat of a peace between the imperialists with the aim of strangling the revolution in Russia)—and the military situation (the indubitable decision of the Russian bourgeoisie and Kerensky and Co. to surrender Petersburg to the Germans)—all this in connection with the peasant insurrection and the swing of popular confidence to our party (the elections in Moscow), and finally the obvious preparation of a second Kornilov attack (the withdrawal of troops from Petersburg, the importation of Cossacks into Petersburg, the surrounding of Minsk with Cossacks, etc.)—all this places armed insurrection on the order of the day. Thus recognizing that the armed insurrection is inevitable and fully ripe, the Central Committee recommends to all organizations of the party that they be guided by this, and from this point of view consider and decide all practical questions (the Congress of Soviets of the Northern Region, the withdrawal of troops from Petersburg, the coming-out of Moscow and Minsk)."

A remarkable thing here as characterizing both the moment and the author is the very order in which the conditions of the insurrection are enumerated. First comes the ripening of the world revolution; the insurrection in Russia is regarded only as the link in a general chain. That was Lenin's invariable starting-point, his major premise: he could not reason otherwise. The task of insurrection he presented directly as the task of the party. The difficult question of bringing its preparation into accord with the soviets is as yet not touched upon. The All-Russian Congress of Soviets does not get a word. To the northern regional congress and the "coming-out of Moscow and Minsk" as points of support for the insurrection was added, upon the insistence of Trotsky, "the withdrawal of troops from Petersburg." This was the sole hint of that plan of insurrection which was subsequently dictated by the course of events in the capital. Nobody proposed any tactical amendments to the resolution, which defined only the strategical starting-point of the insurrection, as against Zinoviev and Kamenev who rejected the very necessity of insurrection.

The very recent attempt of official historians to present this matter as though the whole guiding stratum of the party except Zinoviev and Kamenev stood for the insurrection, goes to pieces when confronted by facts and documents. Aside from the fact that those voting for insurrection were much of the time inclined to push it off into an indefinite future, the open enemies of the insurrection, Zinoviev and Kamenev, were not alone even in the Central Committee. Rykov and Nogin who were absent at the session of the 10th stood wholly upon their point of view, and Miliutin was close to them. "In the upper circles of the party a wavering is to be observed, a sort of dread of the struggle for power"—such is the testimony of Lenin himself. According to Antonov-Saratovsky, Miliutin, arriving in Saratov after the 10th, "told about the letter of Ilych demanding that we 'begin,' about the waverings in the Central Committee, the preliminary 'failure' of Lenin's proposal, about his indignation, and finally about how the course was taken towards insurrection." The Bolshevik, Sadovsky, wrote later about "a certain vagueness and lack of confidence which prevailed at that time. Even among our Central Committee of those days, as is well known, there were debates and conflicts about how to begin and whether to begin at all."

Sadovsky himself was during that period one of the leaders of the military section of the Soviet and the Military Organization of the Bolsheviks. But it was exactly these members of the Military Organization—as appears from numerous memoirs—who were most exceptionally prejudiced in October against the idea of insurrection. The specific character of the organization inclined its leaders to underestimate the political conditions and overestimate the technical. On the 16th of October Krylenko reported: "The larger part of the bureau (the Military Organization) think that we should not force the issue practically, but the minority think that we can take the initiative." On the 18th, another prominent member of the Military Organization, Lashevich, said: "Ought we not to seize the power immediately? I think that we ought not to speed up the course of events. . . . There is no guarantee that we will succeed in holding the power. . . . The strategic plan proposed by Lenin limps on all four legs." Antonov-Ovseënko tells about a meeting of the chief military workers with Lenin: "Podvoisky expressed doubt; Nevsky at first seconded him, but then fell into the confident tone of Ilych; I described the situation in Finland. . . . Lenin's confidence and firmness had a fortifying effect upon me and cheered up Nevsky, but

Podvoisky remained stubbornly dubious." We must not forget that in all recollections of this kind, the doubts are painted in with water colors and the confidence in heavy oil.

Chudnovsky spoke decisively against the insurrection. The sceptical Manuelsky warningly asserted that "the front is not with us." Tomsky was against the insurrection. Volodarsky supported Zinoviev and Kamenev. Moreover by no means all the opponents of the insurrection spoke openly. At a session of the Petrograd Committee on the 15th, Kalinin said: "The resolution of the Central Committee was one of the best resolutions ever adopted by the Central Committee. . . . We are practically approaching the armed insurrection. But when it will be possible—perhaps a year from now—is unknown." This kind of "agreement" with the Central Committee, although perfectly characteristic of Kalinin, was not peculiar to him. Many adhered to the resolution in order in that way to insure their struggle against the insurrection.

In Moscow least of all was there unanimity among the leaders. The regional bureau supported Lenin. In the Moscow committee there were very considerable hesitations; the prevailing mood was in favor of delay. The provincial committee occupied an indefinite position, but in the regional bureau, according to Yakovleva, they thought that at the decisive moment the provincial committee would swing over to the opponents of insurrection.

Lebedev from Saratov tells how in visiting Moscow not long before the revolution, he took a walk with Rykov, and how the latter, pointing to the stone houses, the rich stores, the businesslike excitement about them, complained of the difficulty of the coming task. "Here in the very center of bourgeois Moscow we really seem to be pygmies thinking of moving a mountain."

In every organization of the party, in every one of its provincial committees, there were people of the same mood as Zinoviev and Kamenev. In many committees they were the majority. Even in proletarian Ivanovo-Voznesensk, where the Bolsheviks ruled alone, the disagreement among the ruling circles took an extraordinarily sharp form. In 1925, when memoirs had already accommodated themselves to the demands of the new course, Kisselev, an old worker Bolshevik, wrote: "The workers' part of the party, with the exception of certain individuals, went with Lenin. Against Lenin, however, was a small group of party intellectuals and solitary workers." In public discussion the opponents of insurrection repeated the same arguments as those of Zinoviev and Kamenev. "But in private arguments," writes Kisselev, "the polemic took a more acute and candid form, and here they went so far as to say that 'Lenin is a crazy man; he is pushing the working-class to certain ruin. From this armed insurrection we will get nothing; they will shatter us, exterminate the party and the working-class, and that will postpone the revolution for years and years, etc.'" Such was the attitude of Frunze in particular, a man of great personal courage but not distinguished by a wide outlook.

Even the victory of the insurrection in Petrograd was far from breaking everywhere the inertia of the waiting policy and the direct resistance of the right wing. The wavering of the leaders subsequently almost shipwrecked the insurrection in Moscow. In Kiev, the committee headed by Piatakov, which had been conducting a purely defensive policy, turned over the initiative in the long run—and afterward the power also—to the Rada. "The organization of our party in Voronezh," says Vrachev, "wavered very considerably. The actual overturn in Voronezh . . . was carried out not by a committee of the party, but by its active minority with Moiseiev at the head." In a whole series of provincial cities the Bolsheviks formed in October a bloc with the Compromisers "against the counter-revolution." As though the Compromisers were not at that moment one of its chief supports! Almost everywhere a push was required both from above and below to shatter the last indecisiveness of the local committee, compel it to break with the Compromisers and lead the movement. "The end of October and the beginning of November were verily days of 'the great turmoil' in our party circles. Many quickly surrendered to moods." Thus reports Shliapnikov, who himself made no small contribution to these waverings.

All those elements which, like the Kharkov Bolsheviks, had found themselves in the Menshevik camp in the beginning of the revolution and afterwards themselves wondered "just how that could have happened," found no place for themselves at all as a general rule in the October Days but merely wavered and waited. These people have now all the more confidently advanced their claims as "old Bolsheviks" in the period of intellectual reaction. In spite of the vast work that has been done in recent years towards concealing these facts, and even without the secret archives which are now inaccessible to the investigator, plenty of testimony has been preserved in the newspapers, memoirs and historic journals of that time, to prove that on the eve of the overturn the official machine even of this most revolutionary party put up a big resistance. Conservatism inevitably finds its seat in a bureaucracy. The machine can fulfill a revolutionary function only so long as it remains an instrument in the service of the party, so long as it remains subordinate to an idea and is controlled by the mass.

The resolution of October 10th became immensely important. It promptly put the genuine advocates of insurrection on the firm ground of party right. In all the party organizations, in all its nuclei, the most resolute elements began to be advanced to the responsible posts. The party organizations, beginning with Petrograd, pulled themselves together, made an inventory of their forces and material resources, strengthened their communications, and gave a more concentrated character to the campaign for an overturn.

But the resolution did not put an end to disagreements in the Central Committee. On the contrary, it only formulated them and brought them to the surface. Zinoviev and Kamenev, who but yesterday had felt surrounded in a certain section of the leading circles by an atmosphere of sympathy, observed with fright how swiftly things were shifting to the left. They decided to lose no more time, and on the very next day distributed a voluminous address to the members of the party. "Before history, before the international proletariat, before the Russian revolution and the Russian working-class," they wrote, "we have no right to stake the whole future at the present moment upon the card of armed insurrection."

Their plan was to enter as a strong opposition party into the Constituent Assembly, which "in its revolutionary work can rely only upon the soviets." Hence their formula: "Constituent Assembly and soviets—that is the combined type of state institution toward which we are traveling." The Constituent

Assembly, where the Bolsheviks, it was assumed, would be a minority, and the soviets where the Bolsheviks were a majority—that is, the organ of the bourgeoisie and the organ of the proletariat—were to be "combined" in a peaceful system of dual power. That had not succeeded even under the leadership of the Compromisers. How could it succeed when the soviets were Bolshevik?

"It is a profound historic error," concluded Zinoviev and Kamenev, "to pose the question of the transfer of power to the proletarian party—either now or at any time. No, the party of the proletariat will grow, its program will become clear to broader and broader masses."

This hope for a further unbroken growth of Bolshevism regardless of the actual course of class conflicts, crashed head on against Lenin's leit-motif in those days: "The success of the Russian and world revolution depends upon a two or three days' struggle."

It is hardly necessary to explain that the truth in this dramatic dialogue was wholly on Lenin's side. A revolutionary situation cannot be preserved at will. If the Bolsheviks had not seized the power in October and November, in all probability they would not have seized it at all. Instead of firm leadership the masses would have found among the Bolsheviks that same disparity between word and deed which they were already sick of, and they would have ebbed away in the course of two or three months from this party which had deceived their hopes, just as they had recently ebbed away from the Social Revolutionaries and Mensheviks. A part of the workers would have fallen into indifferentism, another part would have burned up their force in convulsive movements, in anarchistic flare-ups, in guerrilla skirmishes, in a Terror dictated by revenge and despair. The breathing-spell thus offered would have been used by the bourgeoisie to conclude a separate peace with the Hohenzollern, and stamp out the revolutionary organizations. Russia would again have been included in the circle of capitalist states as a semi-imperialist, semi-colonial country. The proletarian revolution would have been deferred to an indefinite future. It was his keen understanding of this prospect that inspired Lenin to that cry of alarm: "The success of the Russian and world revolution depends upon a two or three days' struggle."

But now, since the 10th of the month, the situation in the party had radically changed. Lenin was no longer an isolated "oppositionist" whose proposals were set aside by the Central Committee. It was the Right Wing that was isolated. Lenin no longer had to gain the right of free agitation at the price of resigning from the Central Committee. The party legality was on his side. Zinoviev and Kamenev, on the other hand, circulating their document attacking a decision adopted by the majority of the Central Committee, were now the violators of discipline. And Lenin in a struggle never left unpunished the oversights of his enemy—even far slighter ones than that!

At the session of the 10th, upon the proposal of Dzerzhinsky, a political bureau of seven men was elected: Lenin, Trotsky, Zinoviev, Kamenev, Stalin, Sokolnikov, Bubnov. This new institution, however, turned out completely impracticable. Lenin and Zinoviev were still in hiding; Zinoviev, moreover, continued to wage a struggle against the insurrection, and so did Kamenev. The political bureau in its October membership never once assembled, and it was soon simply forgotten—as were other organizations created *ad hoc* in the whirlpool of events.

No practical plan of insurrection, even tentative, was sketched out in the session of the 10th. But without introducing the fact into the resolution, it was agreed that the insurrection should precede the Congress of Soviets and begin, if possible, not later than October 15th. Not all eagerly agreed to that date. It was obviously too short for the take-off planned in Petrograd. But to insist on a delay would have been to support the Right Wing and mix the cards. Besides, it is never too late to postpone!

The fact of this preliminary setting of the date at the 15th was first made public in Trotsky's recollections of Lenin in 1924, seven years after the event. The statement was soon disputed by Stalin, and the question has become an acute one in Russian historic literature. As is known, the insurrection actually occurred only on the 25th, and consequently the date originally set was not held to. The epigone historians consider it impossible that there should be a mistake in the policy of the

Central Committee, or even a delay in the matter of a date. "It would follow," writes Stalin upon this theme, "that the Central Committee set the date of the insurrection for October 15th and afterwards itself violated (!) this resolution, delaying the date of the insurrection to October 25th. Is this true? No, it is not true." Stalin comes to the conclusion that "Trotsky's memory has betrayed him." In proof of this he cites the resolution of October 10th which did not set any date.

This debated question of the chronology of the insurrection is very important to an understanding of the rhythm of events and demands clarification. That the resolution of the 10th contained no date is quite true. But this general resolution had to do with an insurrection throughout the whole country, and was destined for hundreds and thousands of leading party workers. To include in it the conspirative date of an insurrection to be carried out in the next few days in Petrograd, would have been unreasonable in the extreme. We must remember that out of caution Lenin did not in those days even put a date on his letters. In the given case it was a question of so important, and withal so simple, a decision that none of the participants could have any difficulty in remembering it—especially seeing that it was a question only of a few days. Stalin's reference to the text of the resolution shows thus a complete failure to understand.

We are prepared to concede, however, that the reference of one of the participants to his own memory, especially when his statement is disputed by another participant, is not sufficient for the historic investigator. Luckily the question is decided beyond possible doubt upon another level—that of an analysis of conditions and documents.

The Congress of Soviets was to open on the 20th of October. Between the session of the Central Committee and the date of the Congress, there remained an interval of ten days. The Congress was not to agitate in favor of power to the soviets but seize it. A few hundred delegates all by themselves, however, were powerless to conquer the power; it was necessary to seize it for the Congress and before the Congress. "First conquer Kerensky and then summon the Congress"—that thought had stood in the center of Lenin's whole agitation since the middle of September. All those agreed with it in principle who stood for the seizure of power in general. Consequently the Central Committee could not help setting itself the task of attempting to carry out an insurrection between the 10th and 20th of October. And since it was impossible to foresee how many days the struggle would last, the beginning of the insurrection was set for the 15th. "About the actual date," wrote Trotsky in his recollections of Lenin, "there was, as I remember, almost no dispute. All understood that the date was approximate, and set, as you might say, merely for purposes of orientation, and that it might be advanced or retarded at the dictation of events. But this could be a question of days only, and not more. The necessity of a date, and that too a near one, was completely obvious."

This testimony of political logic essentially exhausts the question. But there is no lack of supplementary proof. Lenin insistently and frequently proposed that the party avail itself of the Northern Regional Congress of the Soviets for the beginning of military activities. The resolution of the Central Committee adopted this idea. But the Regional Congress, which had opened on the 10th, was to close just before the 15th.

At the conference on the 16th, Zinoviev, while insisting upon the revocation of the resolution adopted six days before, made this demand: "We must say to ourselves frankly that in the next five days we will not make an insurrection." He was referring to the five days still remaining before the Congress of Soviets. Kamenev, arguing at the same conference that "the appointing of an insurrection is adventurism," reminded the conference that "it was said before that the action ought to come before the 20th." Nobody objected to this statement and nobody could object. It was the very delay of the insurrection which Kamenev was interpreting as a failure of Lenin's resolution. According to his words "nothing has been done during this week" towards an insurrection. That is obviously an exaggeration. The setting of the date had compelled all to make their plans more strict and hasten the tempo of their work. But it is indubitable that the five-day interval indicated at the session of the 10th had turned out too short. The postponement was already a fact. It was only on the 17th that the Central Executive Committee transferred the opening of the

Soviet Congress to the 25th. That postponement was as opportune as anything could be.

Lenin, to whom in his isolation all these inner hindrances and frictions inevitably presented themselves in an exaggerated form, was alarmed by the delay, and insisted upon the calling of a new meeting of the Central Committee with representatives from the more important branches of the party work in the capital. It was at this conference, held on the 16th in the outskirts of the city, in Lesnoi, that Zinoviev and Kamenev advanced the arguments quoted above for revoking the old date and against naming a new.

The dispute was reopened with redoubled vigor. Miliutin's opinion was: "We are not ready to strike the first blow. . . . Another prospect arises: Armed conflict. . . . It is growing, its possibility is drawing near. And we ought to be ready for this conflict. But this prospect is a different thing from insurrection." Miliutin occupied that defensive position which was more concisely defended by Zinoviev and Kamenev. Shotman, an old Petrograd worker who lived through the whole history of the party, has asserted that at this city conference, both in the party committee and in the Military Revolutionary Committee, the mood was far less militant than in the Central Committee. "We cannot come out but we ought to get ready." Lenin attacked Miliutin and Shotman for their pessimistic appraisal of the correlation of forces: "It is not a question of a struggle with the army, but a struggle of one part of the army with another. . . . The facts prove that we have the advantage over the enemy. Why cannot the Central Committee begin?"

Trotsky was not present at this meeting. During those same hours he was carrying through the Soviet the resolution on the Military Revolutionary Committee. But the point of view which had firmly crystallized in Smolny during the past days was defended by Krylenko, who had just been conducting hand in hand with Trotsky and Antonov-Ovseënko the Northern Regional Congress of Soviets. Krylenko had no doubt that "the water is boiling hard enough." To take back the resolution in favor of insurrection "would be the greatest possible mistake." He disagreed with Lenin, however, "on the question who shall begin it and how it shall begin?" To set the date of the insurrection definitely now is still inexpedient. "But the question of the removal of the troops is just that fighting issue upon which the struggle is taking place. . . . The attack upon us is thus already a fact, and this we can make use of. . . . It is not necessary to worry about who shall begin, for the thing is already begun." Krylenko was expounding and defending the policy laid down by the Military Revolutionary Committee and the Garrison Conference. It was along this road that the insurrection continued to develop.

Lenin did not respond to the words of Krylenko. The living picture of the last six days in Petrograd had not passed before his eyes. Lenin feared delay. His attention was fixed upon the outright opponents of insurrection. All by-remarks, conditional formulæ, inadequately categorical answers, he was inclined to interpret as an indirect support to Zinoviev and Kamenev, who were opposing him with the determination of people who have burned their bridges behind them. "The week's results," argued Kamenev, "testify that the data for an insurrection are now lacking. We have no machine of insurrection. The enemy's machine is far stronger and has probably grown still greater during this week. . . . Two tactics are in conflict here: the tactic of conspiracy and the tactic of faith in the motive forces of the Russian revolution." Opportunists always believe in those motive forces whenever it becomes necessary to fight.

Lenin replied: "If you consider that an insurrection is right, it is not necessary to argue about conspiracy. If an insurrection is politically inevitable, then we must relate ourselves to insurrection as to an art." It was along this line that the fundamental and really principled dispute in the party took place—the dispute upon whose decision, upon whose resolution one way or the other, depended the fate of the revolution. However, within the general frame of Lenin's formula, which united the majority of the Central Committee, there arose subordinate, but very important, questions: How on the basis of the ripened political situation are we to approach the insurrection? How find a bridge from the politics to the technique of revolution? And how lead the masses along that bridge?

Joffé, who belonged to the left wing, had supported the resolution of the 10th. But he opposed Lenin in one point:

"It is not true that the question is now purely technical. Now too the moment of insurrection must be considered from the political point of view." This very last week has shown that for the party, for the Soviet, for the masses, the insurrection has not yet become a mere question of technique. For that very reason we failed to keep to the date set on the 10th.

Lenin's new resolution summoning "all organizations and all workers and soldiers to an all-sided and most vigorous preparation of armed insurrection," was adopted by 20 voices against 2, Zinoviev and Kamenev, with 3 abstaining. The official historians cite these figures as proof of the complete insignificance of the opposition. But they simplify the matter. The shift to the left in the depths of the party was already so strong that the opponents of insurrection, not daring to come out openly, felt it to their interest to remove any barrier of principle between the two camps. If the overthrow, in spite of the date set before, has not been realized by the 16th, can we not bring it about that in the future, too, the thing will be limited to a platonic "course toward insurrection"? That Kalinin was not so utterly alone, was very clearly revealed in that same session. The resolution of Zinoviev to the effect that "any action before a conference with the Bolshevik section of the Congress of Soviets is inadmissible," was rejected by 15 votes against 6, with 3 abstaining. This is where you find the real test of opinions. Some of the "defenders" of the resolution of the Central Committee really wanted to delay the decision until the Congress of Soviets, and until a new conference with the Bolsheviks of the provinces who were in their majority more moderate. Of these "defenders," counting also those abstaining, there were 9 men out of 24—more, that is, than a third. That, of course, is still a minority, but as a headquarters rather an important one. The hopeless weakness of this headquarters lay in the fact that it had no support in the lower ranks of the party or the working-class.

On the next day Kamenev, in agreement with Zinoviev, gave to Gorky's paper a declaration attacking the decision adopted the night before. "Not only Zinoviev and I, but also a number of practical comrades,"—thus wrote Kamenev—"think that to take the initiative in an armed insurrection at the present moment, with the given correlation of social forces, independently of and several days before the Congress of Soviets, is an inadmissible step ruinous to the proletariat and the revolution. . . . To stake everything . . . on the card of insurrection in the coming days would be an act of despair. And our party is too strong, it has too great a future before it, to take such a step. . . ." Opportunists always feel "too strong" to go into a fight.

Kamenev's letter was a direct declaration of war against the Central Committee, and that too upon a question upon which nobody was joking. The situation immediately became extraordinarily acute. It was complicated by several other personal episodes having a common political source. At a session of the Petrograd Soviet on the 18th, Trotsky, in answer to a question raised by the enemy, declared that the Soviet had not set the date for an insurrection in the coming days, but that if it became necessary to set one, the workers and soldiers would come out as one man. Kamenev, sitting next to Trotsky in the praesidium, immediately arose for a short statement: He wanted to sign his name to Trotsky's every word. That was a cunning ruse. Whereas Trotsky was juridically screening a policy of attack with a speciously defensive formula, Kamenev tried to make use of Trotsky's formula—with which he was in radical disagreement—in order to screen a directly opposite policy.

In order to annul the effect of Kamenev's maneuver, Trotsky said on the same day in a speech to the All-Russian Conference of Factory and Shop Committees: "A civil war is inevitable. We have only to organize it as painlessly as possible. We can achieve this not by wavering and vacillation, but only by a stubborn and courageous struggle for power." All understood that those words about waverings were directed against Zinoviev, Kamenev and their colleagues.

Besides that, Trotsky referred the question of Kamenev's speech in the Soviet to investigation by the next session of the Central Committee. In the interval Kamenev, desiring to free his hands for agitation against the insurrection, resigned from the Central Committee. The question was taken up in his absence. Trotsky insisted that "the situation created is absolutely intolerable," and moved that Kamenev's resignation be accepted.[2]

Sverdlov, supporting Trotsky's motion, read a letter of Lenin branding Zinoviev and Kamenev as strikebreakers for their declaration in Gorky's paper, and demanding their expulsion from the party. "Kamenev's trick at the session of the Petrograd Soviet," writes Lenin, "was something positively vile. He is in complete accord, says he, with Trotsky! But is it hard to understand that Trotsky *could* not, had no right, to say before the enemy any more than he did say? Is it hard to understand that . . . a decision as to the necessity of an armed insurrection, as to the fact that it is fully ripe, as to its all-sided preparation, etc. . . . makes it *necessary* in public speeches to shoulder off not only the blame, but also the initiative, upon the enemy. . . . Kamenev's trick was plain petty cheating. . . ."

When sending his indignant protest through Sverdlov, Lenin could not yet know that Zinoviev, in a letter to the editors of the central organ, had announced that his views "are very far from those which Lenin combats," and that he "subscribes to yesterday's declaration of Trotsky in the Petrograd Soviet." Lunacharsky, a third opponent of insurrection, came out in the press to the same effect. To complete the malicious confusion, a letter of Zinoviev's printed in the central organ on the very day of the session of the Central Committee, the 20th,

[2] In the minutes of the Central Committee for 1917, published in 1929, it says that Trotsky explained his declaration to the Soviet on the ground that "it was forced by Kamenev." Here there is obviously an erroneous record, or the record was subsequently incorrectly edited. The declaration of Trotsky needed no special explanation; it flowed from the circumstances. By a curious accident the Moscow Regional Committee, which wholly supported Lenin, found itself obliged to publish in the Moscow party paper on the same day, the 18th, a declaration almost verbally identical with the formula of Trotsky: "We are not a conspirative party and we do not set the date for our actions secretly. . . . When we decide to come out, we will say so in our printed organ. . . ." It was impossible to reply otherwise to the direct queries of the enemy. But although the declaration of Trotsky was not, and could not have been, forced by Kamenev, it was consciously compromised by Kamenev's false solidarity and that moreover under circumstances which deprived Trotsky of the possibility of putting the missing dots on the i's.

was accompanied with a sympathetic remark from the editors: "We in our turn express the hope that with the declaration made by Zinoviev (and also the declaration of Kamenev in the Soviet) the question may be considered settled. The sharpness of tone of Lenin's article does not alter the fact that in fundamentals we remain of one opinion." That was a new blow in the back, and moreover from a direction from which no one was expecting it. At the time when Zinoviev and Kamenev were coming out in a hostile press with open agitation against the decision of the Central Committee in favor of insurrection, the central organ of the party condemns the "sharpness" of Lenin's tone and registers its solidarity with Zinoviev and Kamenev "in fundamentals." As though at that moment there could be a more fundamental question than the question of insurrection! According to the brief minutes, Trotsky declared at the session of the Central Committee: "The letters of Zinoviev and Lunacharsky to the central organ, and also the remark of the editors are intolerable." Sverdlov supported the protest.

The editors at that time were Stalin and Sokolnikov. The minutes read: "Sokolnikov states that he had no part in the declaration of the editors on the subject of Zinoviev's letter, and considers this declaration an error." It thus became known that Stalin personally and alone—against the other member of the editorial board and a majority of the Central Committee—supported Kamenev and Zinoviev at the most critical moment, four days before the beginning of the insurrection, with a sympathetic declaration. The indignation at this was great.

Stalin spoke against the acceptance of Kamenev's resignation, arguing that "our whole situation is self-contradictory." That is, he took upon himself the defense of that confusion which the members of the Central Committee coming out against the insurrection had introduced into people's minds. Kamenev's resignation was accepted by five votes against three. By six votes, again with Stalin opposing, a decision was adopted forbidding Kamenev and Zinoviev to carry on a struggle against the policy of the Central Committee. The minutes read: "Stalin announces that he withdraws from the editorial board." In order not to complicate an already difficult situation, the Central Committee refused to accept Stalin's resignation.

This conduct on the part of Stalin might seem inexplicable in the light of the legend which has been created around him. In reality it fully corresponds to his spiritual mould and his political methods. When faced by great problems Stalin always retreats—not through lack of character as in the case of Kamenev, but through narrowness of horizon and lack of creative imagination. His suspicious caution almost organically compels him at moments of great decision and deep difference of opinion to retire into the shadow, to wait, and if possible to insure himself against both outcomes. Stalin voted with Lenin for the insurrection; Zinoviev and Kamenev were openly fighting against the insurrection. But nevertheless—aside from the "sharpness of tone" of Lenin's criticism "in fundamentals we remain of one opinion." Stalin made this editorial comment by no means through light-mindedness. On the contrary he was carefully weighing the circumstances and the words. But on the 20th of October he did not think it advisable to burn irrevocably his bridge to the camp of the enemies of the uprising.

The testimony of these minutes, which we are compelled to quote not from the original, but from the official text as worked up by Stalin's secretariat, not only demonstrates the actual position of the figures in the Bolshevik Central Committee, but also, in spite of its brevity and dryness, unfolds before us an authentic panorama of the party leadership as it existed in reality, with all its inner contradictions and inevitable personal waverings. Not only history as a whole, but even its very boldest turns, are accomplished by people to whom nothing human is alien. But does this after all lessen the importance of what is accomplished?

If we were to unfold on a screen the most brilliant of Napoleon's victories, the film would show us, side by side with genius, scope, ingenuity, heroism, also the irresolution of individual marshals, the confusion of generals unable to read the map, the stupidity of officers, and the panic of whole detachments, even down to the bowels relaxed with fright. This realistic document would only testify that the army of Napoleon consisted not of the automatons of legend, but of living

Frenchmen born and brought up during the break between two epochs. And the picture of human weaknesses would only the more plainly emphasize the grandeur of the whole.

It is easier to theorize about a revolution afterward than absorb it into your flesh and blood before it takes place. The approach of an insurrection has inevitably produced, and always will produce, crises in the insurrectionary parties. This is demonstrated by the experience of the most tempered and revolutionary party that history has up to this time known. It is enough that a few days before the battle Lenin found himself obliged to demand the expulsion from the party of his two closest and most prominent disciples. The recent attempts to reduce this conflict to "accidents" of a personal character have been dictated by a purely churchly idealization of the party's past. Just as Lenin more fully and resolutely than others expressed in the autumn months of 1917 the objective necessity of an insurrection, and the will of the masses to revolution, so Zinoviev and Kamenev more frankly than others incarnated the blocking tendencies of the party, the moods of irresolution, the influence of petty bourgeois connections, and the pressure of the ruling classes.

If all the conferences, debates, personal quarrels, which took place in the upper layer of the Bolshevik party during October alone had been taken down by a stenographer, posterity might convince itself with what intense inner struggle the determination necessary for the overthrow was crystallized among the heads of the party. The stenographic report would show at the same time how much a revolutionary party has need of internal democracy. The will to struggle is not stored up in advance, and is not dictated from above—it has on every occasion to be independently renewed and tempered.

Citing the assertion of the author of this book that "the party is the fundamental instrument of proletarian revolution," Stalin asked in 1924: "How could our revolution conquer if its 'fundamental instrument' was no good?" His irony did not conceal the primitive falsity of this objection. Between the saints as the church paints them and the devils as the candidates for sainthood portray them, there are to be found living people. And it is they who make history. The high temper of the Bolshevik party expressed itself not in an absence of disagreements, waverings, and even quakings, but in the fact that in the most difficult circumstances it gathered itself in good season by means of inner crises, and made good its opportunity to interfere decisively in the course of events. That means that the party as a whole was a quite adequate instrument of revolution.

In practice a reformist party considers unshakeable the foundations of that which it intends to reform. It thus inevitably submits to the ideas and morals of the ruling class. Having risen on the backs of the proletariat, the social democrats became merely a bourgeois party of the second order. Bolshevism created the type of the authentic revolutionist who subordinates to historic goals irreconcilable with contemporary society the conditions of his personal existence, his ideas, and his moral judgments. The necessary distance from bourgeois ideology was kept up in the party by a vigilant irreconcilability, whose inspirer was Lenin. Lenin never tired of working with his lancet, cutting off those bonds which a petty bourgeois environment creates between the party and official social opinion. At the same time Lenin taught the party to create its own social opinion, resting upon the thoughts and feelings of the rising class. Thus by a process of selection and education, and in continual struggle, the Bolshevik party created not only a political but a moral medium of its own, independent of bourgeois social opinion and implacably opposed to it. Only this permitted the Bolsheviks to overcome the waverings in their own ranks and reveal in action that courageous determination without which the October victory would have been impossible.

Chapter VI

THE ART OF INSURRECTION

People do not make revolution eagerly any more than they do war. There is this difference, however, that in war compulsion plays the decisive rôle, in revolution there is no compulsion except that of circumstances. A revolution takes place only when there is no other way out. And the insurrection, which rises above a revolution like a peak in the mountain chain of its events, can no more be evoked at will than the revolution as a whole. The masses advance and retreat several times before they make up their minds to the final assault.

Conspiracy is ordinarily contrasted to insurrection as the deliberate undertaking of a minority to a spontaneous movement of the majority. And it is true that a victorious insurrection, which can only be the act of a class called to stand at the head of the nation, is widely separated both in method and historic significance from a governmental overturn accomplished by conspirators acting in concealment from the masses.

In every class society there are enough contradictions so that a conspiracy can take root in its cracks. Historic experience proves, however, that a certain degree of social disease is necessary—as in Spain, for instance, or Portugal, or South America—to supply continual nourishment for a régime of conspiracies. A pure conspiracy even when victorious can only replace one clique of the same ruling class by another—or still less, merely alter the governmental personages. Only mass insurrection has ever brought the victory of one social régime over another. Periodical conspiracies are commonly an expression of social stagnation and decay, but popular insurrections on the contrary come usually as a result of some swift growth which has broken down the old equilibrium of the nation. The chronic "revolutions" of the South American republics have nothing in common with the Permanent Revolution; they are in a sense the very opposite thing.

This does not mean, however, that popular insurrection and conspiracy are in all circumstances mutually exclusive. An element of conspiracy almost always enters to some degree into any insurrection. Being historically conditioned by a certain stage in the growth of a revolution, a mass insurrection is never purely spontaneous. Even when it flashes out unexpectedly to a majority of its own participants, it has been fertilized by those ideas in which the insurrectionaries see a way out of the difficulties of existence. But a mass insurrection can be foreseen and prepared. It can be organized in advance. In this case the conspiracy is subordinate to the insurrection, serves it, smoothes its path, hastens its victory. The higher the political level of a revolutionary movement and the more serious its leadership, the greater will be the place occupied by conspiracy in a popular insurrection.

It is very necessary to understand the relations between insurrection and conspiracy, both as they oppose and as they supplement each other. It is especially so, because the very use of the word conspiracy, even in Marxian literature, contains a superficial contradiction due to the fact that it sometimes implies an independent undertaking initiated by the minority, at others a preparation by the minority of a majority insurrection.

History testifies, to be sure, that in certain conditions a popular insurrection can be victorious even without a conspiracy. Arising "spontaneously" out of the universal indignation, the scattered protests, demonstrations, strikes, street fights, an insurrection can draw in a part of the army, paralyze the forces of the enemy, and overthrow the old power. To a certain degree this is what happened in February 1917 in Russia. Approximately the same picture is presented by the development of the German and Austro-Hungarian revolutions of the autumn of 1918. Since in these events there was no party at the head of the insurrectionaries imbued through and through with the interests and aims of the insurrection, its victory had inevitably to transfer the power to those parties which up to the last moment had been opposing it.

To overthrow the old power is one thing; to take the power in one's own hands is another. The bourgeoisie may win the power in a revolution not because it is revolutionary, but because it is bourgeois. It has in its possession property, education, the press, a network of strategic positions, a hierarchy of institutions. Quite otherwise with the proletariat. Deprived in the nature of things of all social advantages, an insurrectionary proletariat can count only on its numbers, its solidarity, its cadres, its official staff.

Just as a blacksmith cannot seize the red hot iron in his naked hand, so the proletariat cannot directly seize the power; it has to have an organization accommodated to this task. The coordination of the mass insurrection with the conspiracy, the subordination of the conspiracy to the insurrection, the organization of the insurrection through the conspiracy, constitutes that complex and responsible department of revolutionary politics which Marx and Engels called "the art of insurrection." It presupposes a correct general leadership of the masses, a flexible orientation in changing conditions, a thought-out plan of attack, cautiousness in technical preparation, and a daring blow.

Historians and politicians usually give the name of *spontaneous insurrection* to a movement of the masses united by a common hostility against the old régime, but not having a clear aim, deliberated methods of struggle, or a leadership consciously showing the way to victory. This spontaneous insurrection is condescendingly recognized by official historians —at least those of democratic temper—as a necessary evil the responsibility for which falls upon the old régime. The real reason for their attitude of indulgence is that "spontaneous" insurrection cannot transcend the framework of the bourgeois régime.

The social democrats take a similar position. They do not reject revolution at large as a social catastrophe, any more than they reject earthquakes, volcanic eruptions, eclipses and epidemics of the plague. What they do reject—calling it "Blanquism," or still worse, Bolshevism—is the conscious preparation of an overturn, the plan, the conspiracy. In other words, the social democrats are ready to sanction—and that only *ex post facto*—those overturns which hand the power to the bourgeoisie, but they implacably condemn those methods which might alone bring the power to the proletariat. Under this pretended objectivism they conceal a policy of defense of the capitalist society.

From his observations and reflections upon the failure of the many insurrections he witnessed or took part in, Auguste Blanqui derived a number of tactical rules which if violated will make the victory of any insurrection extremely difficult, if not impossible. Blanqui demanded these things: a timely creation of correct revolutionary detachments, their centralized command and adequate equipment, a well calculated placement of barricades, their definite construction, and a systematic, not a mere episodic, defense of them. All these rules, deriving from the military problems of the insurrection, must of course change with social conditions and military technique, but in themselves they are not by any means "Blanquism" in the sense that this word approaches the German "putschism," or revolutionary adventurism.

Insurrection is an art, and like all arts it has its laws. The rules of Blanqui were the demands of a military revolutionary realism. Blanqui's mistake lay not in his direct but his inverse theorem. From the fact that tactical weakness condemns an insurrection to defeat, Blanqui inferred that an observance of the rules of insurrectionary tactics would itself guarantee the victory. Only from this point on is it legitimate to contrast Blanquism with Marxism. Conspiracy does not take the place of insurrection. An active minority of the proletariat, no matter how well organized, cannot seize the power regardless of the general conditions of the country. In this point history has condemned Blanquism. But only in this. His affirmative theorem retains all its force. In order to conquer the power, the proletariat needs more than a spontaneous insurrection. It needs a suitable organization, it needs a plan; it needs a conspiracy. Such is the Leninist view of this question.

Engels' criticism of the fetishism of the barricade was based upon the evolution of military technique and of technique in general. The insurrectionary tactic of Blanquism corresponded to the character of the old Paris, the semi-handicraft proletariat, the narrow streets and the military system of Louis Philippe. Blanqui's mistake in principle was to identify revolution with insurrection. His technical mistake was to identify insurrection with the barricade. The Marxian criticism has been directed against both mistakes. Although at one with Blanquism in regarding insurrection as an art, Engels discovered not only the subordinate place occupied by insurrection in a revolution, but also the declining rôle of the barricade in an insurrection. Engels' criticism had nothing in common with a renunciation of the revolutionary methods in favor of pure parliamentarism, as the philistines of the German Social Democracy, in cooperation with the Hohenzollern censorship, attempted in their day to pretend. For Engels the question about barricades remained a question about one of the technical elements of an uprising. The reformists have attempted to infer from his rejection of the decisive importance of the barricade a rejection of revolutionary violence in general. That is about the same as to infer the destruction of militarism from considerations of the probable decline in importance of trenches in future warfare.

The organization by means of which the proletariat can both overthrow the old power and replace it, is the soviets. This afterwards became a matter of historic experience, but was up to the October revolution a theoretical prognosis—resting, to be sure, upon the preliminary experience of 1905. The soviets are organs of preparation of the masses for insurrection, organs of insurrection, and after the victory organs of government.

However, the soviets by themselves do not settle the question. They may serve different goals according to the program and leadership. The soviets receive their program from the party. Whereas the soviets in revolutionary conditions—and apart from revolution they are impossible—comprise the whole class with the exception of its altogether backward, inert or demoralized strata, the revolutionary party represents the brain of the class. The problem of conquering the power can be solved only by a definite combination of party with soviets—or with other mass organizations more or less equivalent to soviets.

When headed by a revolutionary party the soviet consciously and in good season strives towards a conquest of power. Accommodating itself to changes in the political situation and the mood of the masses, it gets ready the military bases of the insurrection, unites the shock troops upon a single scheme of action, works out a plan for the offensive and for the final assault. And this means bringing organized conspiracy into mass insurrection.

The Bolsheviks were compelled more than once, and long before the October revolution, to refute accusations of conspiratism and Blanquism directed against them by their enemies. Moreover, nobody waged a more implacable struggle against the system of pure conspiracy than Lenin. The opportunists of the international social democracy more than once defended the old Social Revolutionary tactic of individual terror directed against the agents of tzarism, when this tactic was ruthlessly criticized by the Bolsheviks with their insistence upon mass insurrection as opposed to the individual adventurism of the intelligentsia. But in refuting all varieties of Blanquism and anarchism, Lenin did not for one moment bow down to any "sacred" spontaneousness of the masses. He thought out before anybody else, and more deeply, the correlation between the objective and subjective factors in a revolution, between the spontaneous movement and the policy of the party, between the popular masses and the progressive class, between the proletariat and its vanguard, between the soviets and the party, between insurrection and conspiracy.

But if it is true that an insurrection cannot be evoked at will, and that nevertheless in order to win it must be organized in advance, then the revolutionary leaders are presented with a task of correct diagnosis. They must feel out the growing insurrection in good season and supplement it with a conspiracy. The interference of the midwife in labor pains—however this image may have been abused—remains the clearest illustration of this conscious intrusion into an elemental process. Herzen once accused his friend Bakunin of invariably in all his revolutionary enterprises taking the second month of pregnancy for the ninth. Herzen himself was rather inclined to deny even in the ninth that pregnancy existed. In February the question of determining the date of birth hardly arose at all, since the insurrection flared up unexpectedly without centralized leadership. But exactly for this reason the power did not go to those who had accomplished the insurrection, but to those who had applied the brakes. It was quite otherwise with the second insurrection. This was consciously prepared by the Bolshevik party. The problem of correctly seizing the moment to give the signal for the attack was thus laid upon the Bolshevik staff.

Moment here is not to be taken too literally as meaning a definite day and hour. Physical births also present a considerable period of uncertainty—their limits interesting not only to the art of a midwife, but also to the casuistics of the Surrogate's Court. Between the moment when an attempt to summon an insurrection must inevitably prove premature and lead to a revolutionary miscarriage, and the moment when a favorable situation must be considered hopelessly missed, there exists a certain period—it may be measured in weeks, and sometimes in a few months—in the course of which an insurrection may be carried out with more or less chance of success. To discriminate this comparatively short period and then choose the definite moment—now in the more accurate sense of the very day and hour—for the last blow, constitutes the most responsible task of the revolutionary leaders. It can with full justice be called the key problem, for it unites the policy of revolution with the technique of insurrection—and it is needless to add that insurrection, like war, is a continuation of politics with other instruments.

Intuition and experience are necessary for revolutionary leadership, just as for all other kinds of creative activity. But much more than that is needed. The art of the magician can also successfully rely upon intuition and experience. Political magic is adequate, however, only for epochs and periods in which routine predominates. An epoch of mighty historic upheavals has no use for witch-doctors. Here experience, even illumined by intuition, is not enough. Here you must have a synthetic doctrine comprehending the interactions of the chief historic forces. Here you must have a materialistic method permitting you to discover, behind the moving shadows of program and slogan, the actual movement of social bodies.

The fundamental premise of a revolution is that the existing social structure has become incapable of solving the urgent problems of development of the nation. A revolution becomes possible, however, only in case the society contains a new class capable of taking the lead in solving the problems presented by history. The process of preparing a revolution consists of making the objective problems involved in the contradictions of industry and of classes find their way into the consciousness of living human masses, change this consciousness and create new correlations of human forces.

The ruling classes, as a result of their practically manifested incapacity to get the country out of its blind alley, lose faith in themselves; the old parties fall to pieces; a bitter struggle of groups and cliques prevails; hopes are placed in miracles or miracle workers. All this constitutes one of the political premises of a revolution, a very important although a passive one.

A bitter hostility to the existing order and a readiness to venture upon the most heroic efforts and sacrifices in order to bring the country out upon an upward road—this is the new political consciousness of the revolutionary class, and constitutes the most important active premise of a revolution.

These two fundamental camps, however—the big property holders and the proletariat—do not exhaust the population of a country. Between them lie broad layers of the petty bourgeoisie, showing all the colors of the economic and political rainbow. The discontent of these intermediate layers, their disappointment with the policy of the ruling class, their impatience and indignation, their readiness to support a bold revolutionary initiative on the part of the proletariat, constitute the third political premise of a revolution. It is partly passive—in that it neutralizes the upper strata of the petty bourgeoisie—but partly also active, for it impels the lower strata directly into the struggle side by side with the workers.

That these premises condition each other is obvious. The more decisively and confidently the proletariat acts, the better will it succeed in bringing after it the intermediate layer, the more isolated will be the ruling class, and the more acute its demoralization. And, on the other hand, a demoralization of the rulers will pour water into the mill of the revolutionary class.

The proletariat can become imbued with the confidence necessary for a governmental overthrow only if a clear prospect opens before it, only if it has had an opportunity to test out in action a correlation of forces which is changing to its advantage, only if it feels above it a far-sighted, firm and confident leadership. This brings us to the last premise—by no means the last in importance—of the conquest of power: the revolutionary party as a tightly welded and tempered vanguard of the class.

Thanks to a favorable combination of historic conditions both domestic and international, the Russian proletariat was headed by a party of extraordinary political clarity and unexampled revolutionary temper. Only this permitted that small and young class to carry out a historic task of unprecedented proportions. It is indeed the general testimony of history—the Paris Commune, the German and Austrian revolutions of 1918, the soviet revolutions in Hungary and Bavaria, the Italian revolution of 1919, the German crisis of 1923, the Chinese revolution of 1925–27, the Spanish revolution of 1931—that up to now the weakest link in the chain of necessary conditions has been the party. The hardest thing of all is for the working-class to create a revolutionary organization capable of rising to the height of its historic task. In the older and more civilized countries powerful forces work toward the weakening and demoralization of the revolutionary vanguard. An important constituent part of this work is the struggle of the social democrats against "Blanquism," by which name they designate the revolutionary essence of Marxism.

Notwithstanding the number of great social and political crises, a coincidence of all the conditions necessary to a victorious and stable proletarian revolution has so far occurred but once in history: in Russia in October 1917. A revolutionary situation is not long-lived. The least stable of the premises of a revolution is the mood of the petty bourgeoisie. At a time of national crisis the petty bourgeoisie follows that class which inspires confidence not only in words but deeds. Although capable of impulsive enthusiasm and even of revolutionary fury, the petty bourgeoisie lacks endurance, easily loses heart under reverses, and passes from elated hope to discouragement. And these sharp and swift changes in the mood of the petty bourgeoisie lend their instability to every revolutionary situation. If the proletarian party is not decisive enough to convert the hopes and expectations of the popular masses into revolutionary action in good season, the flood tide is quickly followed by an ebb: the intermediate strata turn away their eyes from the revolution and seek a savior in the opposing camp. And just as at flood tide the proletariat draws after it the petty bourgeoisie, so during the ebb the petty bourgeoisie draws after it considerable layers of the proletariat. Such is the dialectic of the communist and fascist waves observable in the political evolution of Europe since the war.

Attempting to ground themselves upon the assertion of Marx that no régime withdraws from the stage of history until it has exhausted all its possibilities, the Mensheviks denied the legitimacy of a struggle for proletarian dictatorship in backward Russia where capitalism had far from exhausted itself. This argument contained two mistakes, both fatal. Capitalism is not a national but a world-wide system. The imperialist war and its consequences demonstrated that the capitalist system had exhausted itself on a world scale. The revolution in Russia was a breaking of the weakest link in the system of world-wide capitalism.

But the falsity of this Menshevik conception appears also from a national point of view. From the standpoint of economic abstraction, it is indeed possible to affirm that capitalism in Russia has not exhausted its possibilities. But economic processes do not take place in the ether, but in a concrete historical medium. Capitalism is not an abstraction, but a living system of class relations requiring above all things a state power. That the monarchy, under whose protection Russian capitalism developed, had exhausted its possibilities is not denied even by the Mensheviks. The February revolution tried to build up an intermediate state régime. We have followed its history: in the course of eight months it exhausted itself completely. What sort of state order could in these conditions guarantee the further development of Russian capitalism?

"The bourgeois republic, defended only by socialists of moderate tendencies, finding no longer any support in the masses . . . could not maintain itself. Its whole essence had evaporated. There remained only an external shell." This accurate definition belongs to Miliukov. The fate of this evaporated system was necessarily, according to his words, the same as that of the tzarist monarchy: "Both prepared the ground for a revolution, and on the day of revolution neither could find a single defender."

As early as July and August Miliukov characterized the situation by presenting a choice between two names: Kornilov or Lenin? But Kornilov had now made his experiment and it had ended in a miserable failure. For the régime of Kerensky there was certainly no place left. With all the varieties of mood, says Sukhanov, "the one thing upon which all united was hate for the Kerensky régime." Just as the tzarist monarchy had toward the end become impossible in the eyes of the upper circle of the nobility and even the grand dukes, so the government of Kerensky became odious even to the direct inspiriters of his régime, the "grand dukes" of the compromisist upper crust. In this universal dissatisfaction, this sharp political nerve-tension of all classes, we have one of the symptoms of a ripe revolutionary situation. In the same way every muscle, nerve and fiber of an organism is intolerably tensed just before an abscess bursts.

The resolution of the July congress of the Bolsheviks, while warning the workers against premature encounters, had at the same time pointed out that the battle must be joined "whenever the general national crisis and the deep mass enthusiasm have created conditions favorable to the going over of the poor people of the city and country to the side of the workers." That moment arrived in September and October.

The insurrection was thenceforth able to believe in its success, for it could rely upon a genuine majority of the people. This, of course, is not to be understood in a formal sense. If a referendum could have been taken on the question of insurrection, it would have given extremely contradictory and uncertain results. An inner readiness to support a revolution is far from identical with an ability clearly to formulate the necessity of it. Moreover, the answer would have depended to a vast degree upon the manner in which the question was presented, the institution which conducted the referendum—or, to put it more simply, the class which held the power.

There is a limit to the application of democratic methods. You can inquire of all the passengers as to what type of car they like to ride in, but it is impossible to question them as to whether to apply the brakes when the train is at full speed and accident threatens. If the saving operation is carried out skilfully however, and in time, the approval of the passengers is guaranteed in advance.

Parliamentary consultations of the people are carried out at a single moment, whereas during a revolution the different layers of the population arrive at the same conclusion one after another and with inevitable, although sometimes very slight, intervals. At the moment when the advanced detachment is burning with revolutionary impatience, the backward layers have only begun to move. In Petrograd and Moscow all the mass organizations were under the leadership of the Bolsheviks. In Tambov province, which has over three million population—that is, a little less than both capitals put together—a Bolshevik faction first appeared in the soviet only a short time before the October revolution.

The syllogisms of the objective development are far from coinciding—day by day—with the syllogisms of the thought process of the masses. And when a great practical decision becomes unpostponable, in the course of events, that is the very moment when a referendum is impossible. The difference in level and mood of the different layers of the people is overcome in action. The advance layers bring after them the wavering and isolate the opposing. The majority is not counted up, but won over. Insurrection comes into being at exactly that moment when direct action alone offers a way out of the contradictions.

Although lacking the power to draw by themselves the necessary political inferences from their war against the landlords, the peasants had by the very fact of the agrarian insurrection already adhered to the insurrection of the cities, had evoked it and were demanding it. They expressed their will not with the white ballot, but with the red cock—a more serious referendum. Within those limits in which the support of the peasantry was necessary for the establishment of a soviet dictatorship, the support was already at hand. "The dictatorship"—as Lenin answered the doubters—"would give land to the peasants and all power to the peasant committees in the localities. How can you in your right mind doubt that the peasant would support that dictatorship?" In order that the soldiers, peasants and oppressed nationalities, floundering in the snow-storm of an elective ballot should recognize the Bolsheviks in action, it was necessary that the Bolsheviks seize the power.

But what correlation of forces was necessary in order that the proletariat should seize the power? "To have at the decisive moment, at the decisive point, an overwhelming superiority of force," wrote Lenin later, interpreting the October revolution, "—this law of military success is also the law of political success, especially in that seething and bitter war of classes which is called revolution. The capitals, or generally speaking, the biggest centers of trade and industry . . . decide to a considerable degree the political fate of the people—that is, of course, on condition that the centers are supported by sufficient local rural forces, although this support need not be immediate." It was in this dynamic sense that Lenin spoke of the majority of the people, and that was the sole real meaning of the concept of majority.

The enemy democrats comforted themselves with the thought that the people following the Bolsheviks were mere raw material, mere historic clay. The potters were still to be these same democrats acting in cooperation with the educated bourgeoisie. "Can't those people see," asked a Menshevik paper, "that the Petrograd proletariat and garrison were never before so isolated from all other social strata?" The misfortune of the proletariat and the garrison was that they were "isolated" from those classes from whom they intended to take the power!

But was it really possible to rely upon the sympathy and support of the dark masses in the provinces and at the front? "Their Bolshevism," wrote Sukhanov scornfully, "was nothing but hatred for the coalition and longing for land and peace." As though that were little! Hatred for the coalition meant a desire to take the power from the bourgeoisie. Longing for land and peace was the colossal program which the peasant and soldier intended to carry out under the leadership of the workers. The insignificance of the democrats, even the most leftward, resulted from this very distrust—the distrust of "educated" sceptics—in those dark masses who grasp a phenomenon wholesale, not bothering about details and nuances. This intellectual, pseudo-aristocratic, squeamish attitude toward the people was foreign to Bolshevism, hostile to its very nature. The Bolsheviks were not lily-handed, literary friends of the masses, not pedants. They were not afraid of those backward strata now for the first time lifting themselves out of the dregs. The Bolsheviks took the people as preceding history had created them, and as they were called to achieve the revolution. The Bolsheviks saw it as their mission to stand at the head of that people. Those against the insurrection were "everybody"—except the Bolsheviks. But the Bolsheviks were the people.

The fundamental political force of the October revolution was the proletariat, and the first place in its ranks was occupied by the workers of Petrograd. In the vanguard of these workers stood the Vyborg district. The plan of the insurrection chose this fundamental proletarian district as the point of departure for its offensive.

Compromisers of all shades, beginning with Martov, attempted after the revolution to portray Bolshevism as a soldier movement. The European social democrats grabbed up this theory with delight. But fundamental historic facts were here ignored: the fact that the proletariat was the first to come over to the Bolsheviks; that the Petrograd workers were showing the road to the workers of all countries; that the garrison and front much longer than the workers remained bulwarks of compromisism; that the Social Revolutionaries and Mensheviks created all kinds of privileges for the soldier at the expense of the worker in the soviet system, struggled against the arming of the workers and incited the soldiers against them; that the break in the troops was brought about only by the influence of workers; that at the decisive moment the leadership of the soldiers was in the hands of the workers; and finally that a year later the social democrats of Germany, following the example of their Russian colleagues, relied on the soldiers in their struggle against the workers.

By autumn the Right Compromisers had ceased even to be able to make speeches in the factories and barracks. But the Lefts were still trying to convince the masses of the madness of insurrection. Martov, who in the struggle against the counter-revolutionary offensive in July had found a path to the minds of the masses, was now again serving a hopeless cause. "We cannot expect"—he himself acknowledged on the 14th of October, at a meeting of the Central Executive Committee—"We cannot expect the Bolsheviks to listen to us." Nevertheless he considered it his duty to "warn the masses." The masses, however, wanted action and not moral admonition. Even where they did patiently listen to their well-known adviser, they "thought their own thoughts as before," as Mstislavsky acknowledges. Sukhanov tells how he made an effort in a drizzling rain to convince the Putilov men that they could fix things up without an insurrection. Impatient voices interrupted him. They would listen for two or three minutes and interrupt again. "After a few attempts I gave it up," he says. "It was no use . . . and the rain was drizzling down on us heavier and heavier." Under that ungracious October sky the poor Left Democrats, even as described in their own writings, look like wet hens.

The favorite political argument of the "Left" opponents of the revolution—and this even among the Bolsheviks—was a reference to the absence of fighting enthusiasm among the lower ranks. "The mood of the laboring and soldier masses," write Zinoviev and Kamenev on October 11th, "is far from comparable even to the mood which existed before the 3rd of July." This assertion was not unfounded: there was a certain depression in the Petrograd proletariat as a result of waiting too long. They were beginning to feel disappointed even in the Bolsheviks: Can it be that they are going to cheat us too? On October 16th Rakhia, one of the fighting Petrograd Bolsheviks, a Finn by birth, said at a conference of the Central Committee: "Our slogan is evidently already getting a little out of date, for there exists a doubt as to whether we will do the thing for which we are calling." But this weariness of waiting, which looked like listlessness, lasted only up to the first fighting signal.

The first task of every insurrection is to bring the troops over to its side. The chief means of accomplishing this are the general strike, mass processions, street encounters, battles at the barricades. The unique thing about the October revolution, a thing never before observed in so complete a form, was that, thanks to a happy combination of circumstances, the proletarian vanguard had won over the garrison of the capital before the moment of open insurrection. It had not only won them over, but had fortified this conquest through the organization of the Garrison Conference. It is impossible to understand the mechanics of the October revolution without fully realizing that the most important task of the insurrection, and the one most difficult to calculate in advance, was fully accomplished in Petrograd before the beginning of the armed struggle.

This does not mean, however, that insurrection had become superfluous. The overwhelming majority of the garrison was, it is true, on the side of the workers. But a minority was against the workers, against the revolution, against the Bolsheviks. This small minority consisted of the best trained elements in the army: the officers, the junkers, the shock battalions, and perhaps the Cossacks. It was impossible to win these elements politically; they had to be vanquished. The last part of the task of the revolution, that which has gone into history under the name of the October insurrection, was therefore purely military in character. At this final stage rifles, bayonets, machine guns, and perhaps cannon, were to decide. The party of the Bolsheviks led the way on this road.

What were the military forces of the approaching conflict? Boris Sokolov, who directed the military work of the Social Revolutionary party, says that in the period preceding the overturn "in the regiments all the party organizations except those of the Bolsheviks had disintegrated, and conditions were not at all favorable to the organization of new ones. The mood of the soldiers was tending definitely toward the Bolsheviks. But their Bolshevism was passive and they lacked any tendency whatever toward active armed movements." Sokolov does not fail to add: "One or two regiments wholly loyal and capable of fighting would have been enough to hold the whole garrison in obedience." Literally all of them, from the monarchist generals to the "socialistic" intelligentsia, wanted only those "one or two regiments" and they would have put down the proletarian revolution! But it is quite true that the garrison, although deeply hostile to the government in its overwhelming mass, was not capable of fighting even on the side of the Bolsheviks. The cause of this lay in the hostile break between the old military structure of the troops, and their new political structure. The backbone of a fighting unit is its commanding staff. The commanding staffs were against the Bolsheviks. The political backbone of the troops was composed of Bolsheviks. The latter, however, not only did not know how to command, but in the majority of cases hardly knew how to handle a gun. The soldier crowd was not homogeneous. The active fighting elements were, as always, a minority. The majority of the soldiers sympathized with the Bolsheviks, voted for them, elected them, but also expected them to decide things. The elements hostile to the Bolsheviks in the troops were too insignificant to venture upon any initiative whatever. The political condition of the garrison was thus exceptionally favorable for an insurrection. But its fighting weight was not large—that was clear from the beginning.

However, it was not necessary to dismiss the garrison entirely from the military count. A thousand soldiers ready to fight on the side of the revolution were scattered here and there among the more passive mass, and for that very reason more or less drew it after them. Certain individual units, more happily constituted, had preserved their discipline and fighting capacity. Strong revolutionary nuclei were to be found even in the disintegrating regiments. In the Sixth Reserve Battalion, consisting of about 10,000 men, out of five companies, the first invariably distinguished itself, being known as Bolshevik almost from the beginning of the revolution and rising to the heights in the October days. The typical regiments of the garrison did not really exist as regiments; their administrative mechanism had broken down; they were incapable of prolonged military effort; but they were nevertheless a horde of armed men a majority of whom had been under fire. All the units were united by a single sentiment: Overthrow Kerensky as soon as possible, disperse, and go home and institute a new land system. Thus that completely demoralized garrison was to rally once more in the October days, and rattle its weapons suggestively, before completely going to pieces.

What force did the Petersburg workers offer from a military point of view? This raises the question of the Red Guard. It is time to speak of this in greater detail, for the Red Guard is soon to come out on the great arena of history.

Deriving its tradition from 1905, the Workers' Guard was

reborn with the February revolution and subsequently shared the vicissitudes of its fate. Kornilov, while Commander of the Petrograd military district, asserted that during the days of the overthrow of the monarchy 30,000 revolvers and 40,000 rifles disappeared from the military stores. Over and above that, a considerable quantity of weapons came into the possession of the people during the disarming of the police and by the hands of friendly regiments. Nobody responded to the demand to restore the weapons. A revolution teaches you to value a rifle. The organized workers, however, had received only a small part of this blessing.

During the first four months the workers were not in any way confronted with the question of insurrection. The democratic régime of the dual power gave the Bolsheviks an opportunity to win a majority in the soviets. Armed companies of workers formed a constituent part of the militia. This was, however, more form than substance. A rifle in the hands of a worker involves a totally different historic principle than the same rifle in the hands of a student.

The possession of rifles by the workers alarmed the possessing classes from the very beginning, since it shifted the correlation of forces sharply to the advantage of the factory. In Petrograd, where the state apparatus supported by the Central Executive Committee was at first an indubitable power, the Workers' Militia was not much of a menace. In the provincial industrial regions, however, a reinforcement of the Workers' Guard would involve a complete change of all relations, not only within the given plant but all around it. Armed workers would remove managers and engineers, and even arrest them. Upon resolutions adopted by a factory meeting the Red Guard would not infrequently receive pay out of the factory exchequer. In the Urals, with their rich tradition of guerrilla fighting in 1905, companies of the Red Guard led by the old veterans established law and order. Armed workers almost unnoticeably dissolved the old government and replaced it with soviet institutions. Sabotage on the part of the property owners and administrators shifted to the workers the task of protecting the plants—the machines, stores, reserves of coal and raw materials. Rôles were here interchanged: the worker would tightly grip his rifle in defense of the factory in which he saw the source of his power. In this way elements of a workers' dictatorship were inaugurated in the factories and districts some time before the proletariat as a whole seized the state power.

Reflecting as always the fright of the property owners, the Compromisers tried with all their might to oppose the arming of the Petrograd workers or reduce it to a minimum. According to Minichev, all the arms in the possession of the Narva district consisted of "fifteen or twenty rifles and a few revolvers." At that time robberies and deeds of violence were increasing in the capital. Alarming rumors were spreading everywhere heralding new disturbances. On the eve of the July demonstration it was generally expected that the district would be set fire to. The workers were hunting for weapons, knocking at all doors and sometimes breaking them in.

The Putilov men brought back a trophy from the demonstration of July 3rd: a machine gun with five cases of cartridge-belt. "We were happy as children," said Minichev. Certain individual factories were somewhat better armed. According to Lichkov, the workers of his factory had 80 rifles and 20 big revolvers. Riches indeed! Through the Red Guard headquarters they got two machine guns. They put one in the dining room, one in the attic. "Our commander," says Lichkov, "was Kocherovsky, and his first assistants were Tomchak, who was killed by White Guards in the October days near Tzarskoe Selo, and Efimov, who was shot by White bands near Hamburg." These scant words enable us to glance into the factory laboratory where the cadres of the October revolution and the future Red Army were forming, where the Tomchaks and Efimovs were being chosen out, tempered, and were learning to command, and with them those hundreds and thousands of nameless workers who won the power, loyally defended it from its enemy, and fell subsequently on all the fields of battle.

The July Days introduced a sudden change in the situation of the Red Guard. The disarming of the workers was now carried out quite openly—not by admonition but by force. However, what the workers gave up as weapons was mostly old rubbish. All the very valuable guns were carefully concealed. Rifles were distributed among the most reliable members of the party. Machine guns smeared with tallow were buried in the ground. Detachments of the Guard closed up shop and went underground, closely adhering to the Bolsheviks.

The business of arming the workers was originally placed in the hands of the factory and district committees of the party. It was only after the recovery from the July Days that the Military Organization of the Bolsheviks, which had formerly worked only in the garrison and at the front, took up the organization of the Red Guard, providing the workers with military instructors and in some cases with weapons. The prospect of armed insurrection put forward by the party gradually prepared the advanced workers for a new conception of the function of the Red Army. It was no longer a militia of the factories and workers' districts, but the cadres of a future army of insurrection.

During August, fires in the shops and factories multiplied. Every new crisis is preceded by a convulsion of the collective mind, sending forth waves of alarm. The factory and shop committees developed an intense labor of defending the plants from attacks of this kind. Concealed rifles came out into the open. The Kornilov insurrection conclusively legalized the Red Guard. About 25,000 workers were enrolled in companies and armed—by no means fully, to be sure—with rifles, and in part with machine guns. Workers from the Schlüsselberg powder factory delivered on the Neva a bargeful of hand grenades and explosives—against Kornilov! The compromisist Central Executive Committee refused this gift of the Greeks! The Red Guards of the Vyborg side distributed the gift by night throughout the district.

"Drill in the art of handling a rifle," says the worker Skorinko, "formerly carried on in flats and tenements, was now brought out into the light and air, into the parks, the boulevards." "The shops were turned into camps," says another worker, Rakitov. . . . "The worker would stand at his bench with knapsack on his back and rifle beside him." Very soon all those working in the bomb factory except the old Social Revolutionaries and Mensheviks were enrolled in the Guard. After the whistle all would draw up in the court for drill. "Side by side with a bearded worker you would see a boy apprentice, and both of them attentively listening to the instructor. . . ."

Thus while the old tzarist army was disintegrating, the foundation of a future Red Army was being laid in the factories.

As soon as the Kornilov danger passed, the Compromisers tried to slow up on the fulfillment of their promises. To the 30,000 Putilov men, for instance, only 500 rifles were given out. Soon the giving out of weapons stopped altogether. The danger now was not from the right, but the left; protection must be sought not among the proletarians but the junkers.

An absence of immediate practical aims combined with the lack of weapons caused an ebbing of workers from the Red Guard, but this only for a short interval. The foundation cadres had been laid down solidly in every plant; firm bonds had been established between the different companies. These cadres now knew from experience that they had serious reserves which could be brought to their feet in case of danger.

The going over of the Soviet to the Bolsheviks again radically changed the position of the Red Guard. From being persecuted or tolerated, it now became an official instrument of the Soviet already reaching for the power. The workers now often found by themselves a way to weapons, asking only the sanction of the Soviet. From the end of September on, and more especially from the 10th of October, the preparation of an insurrection was openly placed on the order of the day. For a month before the revolution in scores of shops and factories of Petrograd an intense military activity was in progress—chiefly rifle practice. By the middle of October the interest in weapons had risen to a new height. In certain factories almost every last man was enrolled in a company.

The workers were more and more impatiently demanding weapons from the Soviet, but the weapons were infinitely fewer than the hands stretched out for them. "I came to Smolny every day," relates the engineer, Kozmin, "and observed how both before and after the sitting of the Soviet, workers and sailors would come up to Trotsky, offering and demanding weapons for the arming of the workers, making reports as to how and where these weapons were distributed, and putting the question: 'But when does business begin?' The impatience was very great. . . ."

Formally the Red Guard remained non-party. But the nearer the final day came, the more prominent were the Bolsheviks. They constituted the nucleus of every company; they controlled the commanding staff and the communications with other plants and districts. The non-party workers and Left Social Revolutionaries followed the lead of the Bolsheviks.

However, even now, on the eve of the insurrection, the ranks of the Guard were not numerous. On the 16th, Uritzky, a member of the Bolshevik Central Committee, estimated the workers' army of Petrograd at 40,000 bayonets. The figure is probably exaggerated. The resources of weapons remained still very limited. In spite of the impotence of the government it was impossible to seize the arsenals without taking the road of open insurrection.

On the 22nd, there was held an all-city conference of the Red Guard, its hundred delegates representing about twenty thousand fighters. The figure is not to be taken too literally—not all those registered had shown any signs of activity. But at a moment of alarm volunteers would pour into the companies in large numbers. Regulations adopted the next day by the conference defined the Red Guard as "an organization of the armed forces of the proletariat for the struggle against counter-revolution and the defense of the conquests of the revolution." Observe this: that twenty-four hours before the insurrection the task was still defined in terms of defense and not attack.

The basic military unit was the ten; four tens was a squad, three squads, a company; three companies, a battalion. With its commanding staff and special units, a battalion numbered over 500 men. The battalions of a district constituted a division.[1] Big factories like the Putilov had their own divisions. Special technical commands—sappers, bicyclers, telegraphers, machine-gunners and artillery men—were recruited in the corresponding factories, and attached to the riflemen—or else acted independently according to the nature of the given task. The entire commanding staff was elective. There was no risk in this: all were volunteers here and knew each other well.

The working women created Red Cross divisions. At the shops manufacturing surgical supplies for the army, lectures were announced on the care of the wounded. "Already in al-

[1] Otryad.

most all the factories," writes Tatiana Graff, "the working women were regularly on duty as nurses with the necessary first-aid supplies." The organization was extremely poor in money and technical equipment. By degrees, however, the factory committees sent material for hospital bases and ambulances. During the hours of the revolution these weak nuclei swiftly developed. An imposing technical equipment was suddenly found at their disposal. On the 24th the Vyborg district soviet issued the following order: "Immediately requisition all automobiles. . . . Take an inventory of all first-aid supplies, and have nurses on duty in all clinics."

A growing number of non-party workers were now going out for shooting drill and maneuvers. The number of posts requiring patrol duty was increasing. In the factories sentries were on duty night and day. The headquarters of the Red Guard were transferred to more spacious rooms. On the 23rd at a pipe foundry they held an examination of the Red Guard. An attempt of a Menshevik to speak against the insurrection was drowned in a storm of indignation: Enough, enough! The time for argument is passed! The movement was irresistible. It was seizing even the Mensheviks. "They were enrolling in the Red Guard," says Tatiana Graff, "participating in all duties and even developing some initiative." Skorinko tells how on the 23rd, Social Revolutionaries and Mensheviks, old and young, were fraternizing with the Bolsheviks, and how Skorinko himself joyfully embraced his own father who was a worker in the same factory. The worker Peskovoi says that in his armed detachment "there were young workers of sixteen and old men of fifty." The variety of ages gave "good cheer and fighting courage."

The Vyborg side was especially fervent in preparing for battle. Having stolen the keys of the drawbridges, studied out the vulnerable points of the district, and elected their military-revolutionary committee, the factory committees established continuous patrols. Kayurov writes with legitimate pride of the Vyborg men: "They were the first to go to battle with the autocracy, they were the first to institute in their district the eight-hour day, the first to come out with a protest against the ten minister-capitalists, the first to raise a protest on July 7th against the persecution of our party, and they were not the last on the decisive day of October 25th." What is true is true!

The history of the Red Guard is to a considerable extent the history of the dual power. With its inner contradictions and conflicts, the dual power helped the workers to create a considerable armed force even before the insurrection. To cast up the general total of the workers' detachments throughout the country at the moment of insurrection is hardly possible, at least at the present moment. In any case, tens and tens of thousands of armed workers constituted the cadres of the insurrection. The reserves were almost inexhaustible.

The organization of the Red Guard remained, of course, extremely far from complete. Everything was done in haste, in the rough, and not always skilfully. The Red Guard men were in the majority little trained; the communications were badly organized; the supply system was lame; the sanitary corps lagged behind. But the Red Guard, recruited from the most self-sacrificing workers, was burning to carry the job through this time to the end. And that was the decisive thing. The difference between the workers' divisions and the peasant regiments was determined not only by the social ingredients of the two—many of those clumsy soldiers after returning to their villages and dividing the landlords' land will fight desperately against the White Guards, first in guerrilla bands and afterwards in the Red Army. Beside the social difference there existed another more immediate one: Whereas the garrison represented a compulsory assemblage of old soldiers defending themselves against war, the divisions of the Red Guard were newly constructed by individual selection on a new basis and with new aims.

The Military Revolutionary Committee had at its disposal a third kind of armed force: the sailors of the Baltic Fleet. In their social ingredients they are far closer to the workers than the infantry are. There are a good many Petrograd workers among them. The political level of the sailors is incomparably higher than that of the soldiers. In distinction from the none too belligerent reserves who have forgotten all about rifles, these sailors have never stopped actual service.

For active operations it was possible to count firmly upon the armed Bolsheviks, upon the divisions of the Red Guard, upon the advanced group of the sailors, and upon the better preserved regiments. The different elements of this collective army supplemented each other. The numerous garrisons lacked the will to fight. The sailor detachments lacked numbers. The Red Guard lacked skill. The workers together with the sailors contributed energy, daring and enthusiasm. The regiments of the garrison constituted a rather inert reserve, imposing in its numbers and overwhelming in its mass.

In contact as they were from day to day with workers, soldiers and sailors, the Bolsheviks were aware of the deep qualitative difference between the constituent parts of this army they were to lead into battle. The very plan of the insurrection was based to a considerable degree upon a calculation of these differences.

The possessing classes constituted the social force of the other camp. This means that they were its military weakness. These solid people of capital, the press, the pulpit—where and when have they ever fought? They are accustomed to find out by telegraph or telephone the results of the battles which settle their fate. The younger generation, the sons, the students? They were almost all hostile to the October revolution. But a majority of them too stood aside. They stood with their fathers awaiting the outcome of the battle. A number of them afterward joined the officers and junkers—already largely recruited from among the students. The property holders had no popular masses with them. The workers, soldiers, peasants had turned against them. The collapse of the compromise parties meant that the possessing classes were left without an army.

In proportion to the significance of railroads in the life of modern states, a large place was occupied in the political calculations of both camps by the question of the railroad workers. Here the hierarchical constitution of the personnel leaves room for an extraordinary political variegation, creating favorable conditions for the diplomats of the Compromisers. The lately formed Vikzhel had kept a considerably more solid root among the clerks and even among the workers than, for instance, the army committees at the front. In the railroads only a minority followed the Bolsheviks, chiefly workers in the stations and yards. According to the report of Schmidt, one of the Bolshevik leaders of the trade union movement, the railroad workers of the Petrograd and Moscow junctions stood closest of all to the party.

But even among the compromisist mass of clerks and workers there was a sharp shift to the left from the date of the railroad strike at the end of September. Dissatisfaction with the Vikzhel, which had compromised itself by talking and wavering, was more and more evident in the lower ranks. Lenin remarked: "The army of railroad and postal clerks continues in a state of sharp conflict with the government." From the standpoint of the immediate tasks of the insurrection that was almost enough.

Things were less favorable in the post and telegraph service. According to the Bolshevik, Boky, "the men in the Post and Telegraph Offices are mostly Kadets." But here too the lower personnel had taken a hostile attitude toward the upper ranks. There was a group of mail carriers ready at a critical moment to seize the Post Office.

It would have been hopeless in any case to try to change the minds of the railroad and postal clerks with words. If the Bolsheviks should prove indecisive, the advantage would remain with the Kadets and the compromisist upper circles. With a decisive revolutionary leadership the lower ranks must inevitably carry with them the intermediate layers, and isolate the upper circles of the Vikzhel. In revolutionary calculations statistics alone are not enough; the coefficient of living action is also essential.

The enemies of the insurrection in the ranks of the Bolshevik party itself found, however, sufficient ground for pessimistic conclusions. Zinoviev and Kamenev gave warning against an underestimation of the enemy's forces. "Petrograd will decide, and in Petrograd the enemy has . . . considerable forces: 5,000 junkers, magnificently armed and knowing how to fight, and then the army headquarters, and then the shock troops, and then the Cossacks, and then a considerable part of the garrison, and then a very considerable quantity of artillery spread out fan-wise around Petrograd. Moreover the enemy with the help of the Central Executive Committee will almost certainly attempt to bring troops from the front. . . ." The list sounds imposing, but it is only a list. If an army as a whole is a copy of society, then when society openly splits, both armies are copies of the two warring camps. The army of the possessors contained the wormholes of isolation and decay.

The officers crowding the hotels, restaurants and brothels had been hostile to the government ever since the break between Kerensky and Kornilov. Their hatred of the Bolsheviks, however, was infinitely more bitter. As a general rule, the monarchist officers were most active on the side of the government. "Dear Kornilov and Krymov, in what you failed to do perhaps with God's help we shall succeed. . . ." Such was the prayer of officer Sinegub, one of the most valiant defenders of the Winter Palace on the day of the uprising. But in spite of the vast number of officers, only single individuals were really ready to fight. The Kornilov plot had already proven that these completely demoralized officers were not a fighting force.

The junkers were not homogeneous in social make-up, and there was no unanimity among them. Along with hereditary fighters, sons and grandsons of officers, there were many accidental elements gathered up under pressure of war-needs even during the monarchy. The head of an engineering school said to an officer: "I must die with you. . . . We are nobles, you know, and cannot think otherwise." These lucky gentlemen, who did after all succeed in evading a noble death, would speak of the democratic junkers as low-breeds, as muzhiks "with coarse stupid faces." This division into the blue blood and the black penetrated deeply into the junker schools, and it is noticeable that here too those who came out most zealously in defense of the republican government were the very ones who most mourned the loss of the monarchy. The democratic junkers declared that they were not for Kerensky but for the Central Executive Committee. The revolution had first opened the doors of the junker schools to the Jews. And in trying to hold their own with the privileged upper circles, the sons of the Jewish bourgeoisie became extraordinarily warlike against the Bolsheviks. But, alas, this was not enough to save the régime—not even to defend the Winter Palace. The heterogeneousness of these military schools and their complete isolation from the army brought it about that during the critical hours the junkers began to hold meetings. They began to ask questions: How are the Cossacks behaving? Is anybody coming out besides us? Is it worth while anyway to defend the Provisional Government? According to a report of Podvoisky, there were about 120 socialist junkers in the Petrograd military schools at the beginning of October, and of these 42 or 43 were Bolsheviks. "The junkers say that the whole commanding staff of the schools is counter-revolutionary. They are being definitely prepared in case anything happens to put down the insurrection. . . ." The number of socialists, and especially Bolsheviks, was wholly insignificant, but they made it possible for Smolny to know everything of importance that went on among the junkers. In addition to that, the location of the military schools was very disadvantageous. The junkers were sandwiched in among the barracks, and although they spoke scornfully of the soldiers, they looked upon them with a great deal of dread.

The junkers had plenty of ground for caution. Thousands of hostile eyes were watching them from the neighboring barracks and the workers' districts. This observation was the more effective in that every school had its soldier group, neutral in words but in reality inclining toward the insurrection. The school storerooms were in the hands of non-combatant soldiers. "Those scoundrels," writes an officer of the Engineering School, "not satisfied with losing the key to the storeroom so that I had to give orders to break in the door, also removed the breech-locks from the machine guns and hid them somewhere." In these circumstances you could hardly expect miracles of heroism from the junkers.

But would not a Petrograd insurrection be threatened from without, from the neighboring garrisons? In the last days of its life the monarchy had never ceased to put its hope in that small military ring surrounding the capital. The monarchy had missed its guess, but how would it go this time? To guarantee conditions excluding every possible danger would have been to make the very insurrection unnecessary. After all, its aim was to break down the obstacles which could not be dissolved politically. Everything could not be calculated in advance, but all that could be, was.

Early in October a conference of the soviets of Petrograd province was held in Kronstadt. Delegates from the garrisons of the environs of the capital—Gatchina, Tzarskoe, Krasnoe,

Oranienbaum, Kronstadt itself—took the very highest note set by the tuning-fork of the Baltic sailors. Their resolution was adhered to by the deputies of Petrograd province. The muzhiks were veering sharply through the Left Social Revolutionaries toward the Bolsheviks.

At a conference of the Central Committee on the 16th, a party worker in the province, Stepanov, drew a somewhat variegated picture of the state of the forces, but nevertheless with a clear predominance of Bolshevik colors. In Sestroretsk and Kolpino the workers are under arms; their mood is militant. In Novy Peterhoff the work in the regiment has fallen off; the regiment is disorganized. In Krasnoe Selo the 176th regiment is Bolshevik (the same regiment which patrolled the Tauride Palace on July 4th), the 172nd is on the side of the Bolsheviks, "and, besides, there is cavalry there." In Luga the garrison of 30,000, after swinging over to the Bolsheviks, is wavering in part; the soviet is still defensist. In Gdov the regiment is Bolshevik. In Kronstadt the mood has declined; the garrison boiled over during the preceding months; the better part of the sailors are in the active fleet. In Schlüsselburg, within 60 versts of Petrograd, the soviet long ago became the sole power; the workers of the powder factory are ready at any moment to support the capital.

In combination with the results of that Kronstadt conference of soviets, this information about the first line reserves may be considered entirely encouraging. The radiation of the February insurrection had been sufficient to dissolve discipline over a wide area. And it was now possible to look with confidence upon the nearby garrisons, their conditions being adequately known in advance.

The troops of Finland and the northern front were among the second line reserves. Here conditions were still more favorable. The work of Smilga, Antonov, Dybenko had produced invaluable results. Along with the garrison of Helsingfors the fleet had become a sovereign in Finnish territory. The government had no more power there. The two Cossack divisions quartered in Helsingfors—Kornilov had intended them for a blow at Petrograd—had come in close contact with the sailors and were supporting the Bolsheviks, or the Left Social Revolutionaries, who in the Baltic Fleet were becoming less and less distinguishable from Bolsheviks.

Helsingfors was extending its hands to the sailors of the Reval naval base, whose attitude up to that time had been indefinite. The Congress of Soviets of the Northern Region, in which also apparently the Baltic Fleet had taken the initiative, had united the soviets of the garrisons surrounding Petrograd in such a wide circle that it took in Moscow on one side and Archangel on the other. "In this manner," writes Antonov, "the idea was realized of armoring the capital of the revolution against possible attacks from Kerensky's troops." Smilga returned from the Congress to Helsingfors to organize a special detachment of sailors, infantry and artillery to be sent to Petrograd at the first signal. The Finland flank of the Petrograd insurrection was thus protected to the last degree. On this side no blow was to be expected, only strong help. On other portions of the front, too, things were wholly favorable—at least far more favorable than the most optimistic of the Bolsheviks in those days imagined. During October committee elections were held throughout the army, and everywhere they showed a sharp swing to the Bolsheviks. In the corps quartered near Dvinsk the "old reasonable soldiers" were completely snowed under in the elections to the regimental and company committees; their places were taken by "gloomy, gray creatures . . . with angry piercing eyes and wolfish snouts." The same thing happened in other sectors. "Committee elections are in progress everywhere, and everywhere only Bolsheviks and defeatists are elected." The governmental commissars began to avoid making trips to their units. "Their situation is now no better than ours." We are quoting Baron Budberg. Two cavalry regiments of his corps, the Hussar and Ural Cossacks, who remained longest of all in the control of the commanders, and had not refused to put down mutinous units, suddenly changed color and demanded "that they be relieved of the function of punitive troops and gendarmes." The threatening sense of this warning was clear to the Baron and to everybody else. "You can't command a flock of hyenas, jackals and sheep by playing on a violin," he wrote. "The only salvation lies in a mass application of the hot iron. . . ." And here follows the tragic confession: ". . . a thing which we haven't got and is nowhere to be gotten."

If we do not cite similar testimony about other corps and divisions, it is only because their chiefs were not so observant as Budberg, or they did not keep diaries, or these diaries have not yet come to light. But the corps standing near Dvinsk was distinguished in nothing but the trenchant style of its commander from the other corps of the 5th Army, which in its turn was but little in advance of the other armies.

The compromisist committee of the 5th Army, which had long been hanging in the air, continued to send telegraphic threats to Petrograd to the effect that it would restore order in the rear with the bayonet. "All that was mere braggadocio and hot air," writes Budberg. The committee was actually living its last days. On the 23rd it failed of re-election. The president of the new Bolshevik committee was Doctor Skliansky, a magnificent young organizer who soon developed his talent widely in the work of creating the Red Army, and who died subsequently an accidental death while canoeing on one of the American lakes.

The assistant of the government Commissar of the Northern Front reports to the War Minister on the 22nd of October that the ideas of Bolshevism are making great headway in the army, that the mass wants peace, and that even the artillery which has held out to the very last moment has become "hospitable to defeatist propaganda." This too is no unimportant symptom. "The Provisional Government has no authority"—reports its own direct agent three days before the revolution.

To be sure, the Military Revolutionary Committee did not then know of all these documents. But what it did know was amply sufficient. On the 23rd, representatives of various units at the front filed past the Petrograd Soviet and demanded peace. Otherwise, they answered, they would march to the rear and "destroy all the parasites who want to keep on fighting for another ten years." Seize the power, the front men said to the Soviet, "the trenches will support you."

In the more remote and backward fronts, the southwestern and Rumanian, Bolsheviks were still rare specimens, curiosities. But the mood of the soldiers here was the same as elsewhere. Evgenia Bosh tells how in the 2nd Corps of the Guards, quartered in the vicinity of Zhmerinka, among 60,000 soldiers there was one young communist and two sympathizers. This did not prevent the corps from coming out in support of the insurrection in the October days.

To the very last hour the government circles rested their hope in the Cossacks. But the less blind among the politicians of the right camp understood that here too things were in a very bad way. The Cossack officers were Kornilovists almost to a man. The rank-and-file were tending more and more to the left. In the government they did not understand this, imagining that the coolness of the Cossack regiments to the Winter Palace was caused by injured feelings about Kaledin. In the long run, however, it became clear even to the Minister of Justice, Maliantovich, that "only the Cossack officers" were supporters of Kaledin. The rank-and-file Cossacks, like all the soldiers, were simply going Bolshevik.

Of that front which in the early days of March had kissed the hands and feet of liberal priests, had carried Kadet ministers on its shoulders, got drunk on the speeches of Kerensky, and believed that the Bolsheviks were German agents—of that there was nothing left. Those rosy illusions had been drowned in the mud of the trenches, which the soldiers refused to go on kneading with their leaky boots. "The denouement is approaching," wrote Budberg on the very day of the Petrograd insurrection, "and there can be no doubt of its outcome. On our front there is not one single unit . . . which would not be in the control of the Bolsheviks."

Chapter VII

THE CONQUEST OF THE CAPITAL

All is changed and yet all remains as before. The revolution has shaken the country, deepened the split, frightened some, embittered others, but not yet wiped out a thing or replaced it. Imperial St. Petersburg seems drowned in a sleepy lethargy rather than dead. The revolution has stuck little red flags in the hands of the cast-iron monuments of the monarchy. Great red streamers are hanging down the fronts of the government buildings. But the palaces, the ministries, the headquarters, seem to be living a life entirely apart from those red banners, tolerably faded, moreover, by the autumn rains. The two-headed eagles with the scepter of empire have been torn down where possible, but oftener draped or hastily painted over. They seem to be lurking there. All the old Russia is lurking, its jaws set in rage.

The slight figures of the militia-men at the street corners remind one of the revolution that has wiped out the old "Pharaohs," who used to stand there like live monuments. Moreover Russia has now for almost two months been called a republic. And the tzar's family is in Tobolsk. Yes, the February whirlwind has left its traces. But the tzarist generals remain generals, the senators senatorialize, the privy councillors defend their dignity, the Table of Precedence is still in effect. Colored hat-bands and cockades recall the bureaucratic hierarchy; yellow buttons with an eagle still distinguish the student. And yet more important—the landlords are still landlords, no end of the war is in sight, the Allied diplomats are impudently jerking official Russia along on a string.

All remains as before and yet nobody knows himself. The

aristocratic quarters feel that they have been moved out into the backyard; the quarters of the liberal bourgeoisie have moved nearer the aristocracy. From being a patriotic myth, the Russian people have become an awful reality. Everything is billowing and shaking under foot. Mysticism flares up with sharpened force in those circles which not long ago were making fun of the superstitions of the monarchy.

Brokers, lawyers, ballerinas are cursing the oncoming eclipse of public morals. Faith in the Constituent Assembly is evaporating day by day. Gorky in his newspaper is prophesying the approaching downfall of culture. The flight from raving and hungry Petrograd to a more peaceful and well-fed province, on the increase ever since the July Days, now becomes a stampede. Respectable families who have not succeeded in getting away from the capital, try in vain to insulate themselves from reality behind stone wall and under iron roof. But the echoes of the storm penetrate on every side: through the market, where everything is getting dear and nothing to be had; through the respectable press, which is turning into one yelp of hatred and fear; through the seething streets where from time to time shootings are to be heard under the windows; and finally through the back entrance, through the servants, who are no longer humbly submissive. It is here that the revolution strikes home to the most sensitive spot. That obstreperousness of the household slaves destroys utterly the stability of the family régime.

Nevertheless the everyday routine defends itself with all its might. School-boys are still studying the old text-books, functionaries drawing up the same useless papers, poets scribbling the verses that nobody reads, nurses telling the fairy-tales about Ivan Tzarevich. The nobility's and merchants' daughters, coming in from the provinces, are studying music or hunting husbands. The same old cannon on the wall of the Peter and Paul fortress continues to announce the noon hour. A new ballet is going on in the Mariinsky theater, and the Minister of Foreign Affairs, Tereshchenko, stronger on choreography than diplomacy, finds time, we may assume, to admire the steel toes of the ballerina and thus demonstrate the stability of the régime.

The remnants of the old banquet are still very plentiful and everything can be had for big money. The Guard officers still click their spurs accurately and go after adventures. Wild parties are in progress in the private dining rooms of expensive restaurants. The shutting-off of the electric lights at midnight does not prevent the flourishing of gambling clubs where champagne sparkles by candlelight, where illustrious peculators swindle no less illustrious German spies, where monarchist conspirators call the bets of Semitic smugglers, and where the astronomical figures of the stakes played for indicate both the scale of debauchery and the scale of inflation.

Can it be that a mere tramcar, run-down, dirty, dilatory, draped with clusters of people, leads from this St. Petersburg in its death-agony into the workers' quarters so passionately and tensely alive with a new hope? The blue-and-gold cupola of Smolny Convent announces from afar the headquarters of the insurrection. It is on the edge of the city where the tramline ends and the Neva describes a sharp turn south, separating the center of the capital from the suburbs. That long gray three-story building, an educative barrack for the daughters of the nobility, is now the stronghold of the soviets. Its long echoing corridors seem to have been made for teaching the laws of perspective. Over the doors of many of the rooms along the corridors little enameled tablets are still preserved: "Teacher's room," "Third Grade," "Fourth Grade," "Grade Supervisor." But alongside the old tablets, or covering them, sheets of paper have been tacked up as best they might, bearing the mysterious hieroglyphics of the revolution: Tz–K P–S–R, S–D Mensheviki, S–D–Bolsheviki, Left S–R, Anarchist–Communists, Despatching Room of the Tz–I–K, etc., etc. The observant John Reed notices a placard on the walls: "Comrades, for the sake of your own health, observe cleanliness." Alas, nobody observes cleanliness, not even nature. October Petrograd is living under a canopy of rain. The streets, long unswept, are dirty. Enormous puddles are standing in the court of Smolny. The mud is carried into the corridors and halls by the soldiers' boots. But nobody is looking down now underfoot. All are looking forward.

Smolny is more and more firmly and imperiously giving commands, for the passionate sympathy of the masses is lifting her up. However, the central leadership grasps directly only the topmost links of that revolutionary system which as a connected whole is destined to achieve the change. The most important processes are taking place below, and somehow of their own accord. The factories and barracks are the chief forges of history in these days and nights. As in February, the Vyborg district focusses the basic forces of the revolution. But it has today a thing it lacked in February—its own powerful organization open and universally recognized. From the dwellings, the factory lunch-rooms, the clubs, the barracks, all threads lead to the house numbered 33 Samsonevsky Prospect, where are located the district Committee of the Bolsheviks, the Vyborg soviet, and the military headquarters. The district militia is fusing with the Red Guard. The district is wholly in the control of the workers. If the government should raid Smolny, the Vyborg district alone could re-establish a center and guarantee the further offensive.

The denouement was approaching close, but the ruling circles thought, or pretended to think, that they had no special cause for anxiety. The British Embassy, which had its own reasons for following events in Petrograd with some attention, received, according to the Russian ambassador in London, reliable information about the coming insurrection. To the anxious inquiries of Buchanan at the inevitable diplomatic luncheon, Tereshchenko replied with warm assurance: "Nothing of the kind" is possible; the government has the reins firmly in hand. The Russian Embassy in London found out about the revolution in Petrograd from the despatches of a British telegraph agency.

The mine owner, Auerbach, paying a visit during those days to the deputy-minister, Palchinsky, inquired in passing—after a conversation about more serious matters—as to the "dark clouds on the political horizon." He received a most reassuring answer: The next storm in a series, and nothing more; it will pass over and all will be clear—"sleep well." Palchinsky himself was going to pass one or two sleepless nights before he got arrested.

The more unceremoniously Kerensky treated the compromise leaders, the less did he doubt that in the hour of danger they would come punctually to his aid. The weaker the Compromisers grew, the more carefully did they surround themselves with an atmosphere of illusion. Exchanging words of mutual encouragement between their Petrograd turrets and their upper-crust organizations in the provinces and the front, the Mensheviks and Social Revolutionaries created a simulacrum of public opinion, and thus disguising their own impotence, fooled not so much their enemy as themselves.

The cumbersome and good-for-nothing state apparatus, representing a combination of March socialist with tzarist bureaucrat, was perfectly accommodated to the task of self-deception. The half-baked March socialist dreaded to appear to the bureaucrat a not wholly mature statesman. The bureaucrat dreaded lest he show a lack of respect to the new ideas. Thus was created a web of official lies, in which generals, district attorneys, newspaper-men, commissars, aides-de-camp, lied the more, the nearer they stood to the seats of power. The commander of the Petrograd military district made comforting reports, for the reason that Kerensky, faced by an uncomforting reality, had great need of them.

The traditions of the dual power worked in the same direction. Were not the current orders of the military headquarters, when countersigned by the Military Revolutionary Committee, implicitly obeyed? The patrolling squads throughout the city were filled out by the troops of the garrison in the usual order —and we must add, it had been long since the troops had done their patrol duty with such zeal as now. Discontent among the masses? But "slaves in revolt" are always discontented. Only the scum of the garrison and the workers' districts will take part in mutinous attempts. The soldiers' sections are against headquarters? But the Military department of the Central Executive Committee is for Kerensky. The whole organized democracy, with the exception of the Bolsheviks, supports the government. Thus the rosy March nimbus had turned into a gray vapor, hiding the actual traits of things.

It was only after the break between Smolny and headquarters that the government tried to adopt a more serious attitude toward the situation. There is of course no immediate danger, they said, but this time we must avail ourselves of the opportunity to put an end to the Bolsheviks. Besides, the bourgeois Allies were bringing every pressure to bear on the Winter Palace. On the night of the 24th the government summoned up its courage and passed a resolution: to institute legal proceedings against the Military Revolutionary Committee; to shut down the Bolshevik papers advocating insurrection; to summon reliable military detachments from the environs and from the front. The proposal to arrest the Military Revolutionary Committee as a body, although adopted in principle, was postponed in execution. For so large an undertaking, they decided, it was necessary to secure in advance the support of the Pre-Parliament.

The rumor of the government's decision spread immediately through the town. In the building of the main headquarters alongside the Winter Palace, the soldiers of the Pavlovsky regiment, one of the most reliable units of the Military Revolutionary Committee, were on sentry duty during the night of the 24th. Conversations went on in their presence about summoning the junkers, about lifting the bridges, about arrests. All that the Pavlovtsi managed to hear and remember they immediately passed on to Smolny. Those in the revolutionary center did not always know how to make use of the communications of this self-constituted Intelligence Service. But it fulfilled an invaluable function. The workers and soldiers of the whole city were made aware of the intentions of the enemy, and reinforced in their readiness to resist.

Early in the morning the authorities began their preparations for aggressive action. The military schools of the capital were ordered to make ready for battle. The cruiser *Aurora* moored in the Neva, its crew favorable to the Bolsheviks, was ordered to put out and join the rest of the fleet. Military detachments were called in from neighboring points: a battalion of shock troops from Tzarskoe Selo, the junkers from Oranienbaum, the artillery from Pavlovsk. The headquarters of the northern front was asked to send reliable troops to the capital immediately. In the way of direct measures of military precaution, the following orders were given: to increase the guard of the Winter Palace; to raise the bridges over the Neva; to have all automobiles inspected by the junkers; to cut Smolny out of the telephone system. The Minister of Justice, Maliantovich, gave an order for the immediate arrest of those Bolsheviks released under bail who had again brought themselves to attention by anti-governmental activity. This blow was aimed primarily at Trotsky. The fickleness of the times is well illustrated by the fact that Maliantovich—as also his predecessor, Zarudny—had been Trotsky's defense counsel in the trial of the St. Petersburg Soviet of 1905. Then too it had been a question of the leadership of the Soviet. The indictments were identical in the two cases, except that the former defenders when they became accusers added the little point about German gold.

Headquarters developed a particularly feverish activity in the sphere of typography. Document followed document. No coming-out will be permitted; the guilty will be held strictly responsible; detachments of the garrison not to leave their barracks without orders from headquarters; "All commissars of the Petrograd Soviet to be removed"; their illegal activities to be investigated "with a view to court martial." In these formidable orders it was not indicated who was to carry them out or how. Under threat of personal liability the commander demanded that owners of automobiles place them at the disposal of headquarters "with a view of preventing unlawful seizures," but nobody moved a finger in response.

The Central Executive Committee was also prolific of warnings and forbiddings. And the peasant executive committee, the city duma, the central committees of the Mensheviks and Social Revolutionaries followed in its steps. All these institutions were sufficiently rich in literary resources. In the proclamations which plastered the walls and fences, the talk was invariably about a handful of lunatics, about the danger of bloody encounters, about the inevitability of counterrevolution.

At five-thirty in the morning a government commissar with a detachment of junkers showed up at the Bolshevik printing-plant, and after manning the exits, presented an order of headquarters for the immediate suppression of the central organ and the soldiers' paper.—What? Headquarters? Does that still exist? No orders are recognized here without the sanction of the Military Revolutionary Committee. But that did not help. The stereotypes were smashed, the building sealed. The government had scored its first success.

A worker and a working-girl from the Bolshevik printing-plant ran panting to Smolny and there found Podvoisky and

Trotsky. If the Committee would give them a guard against the junkers, the workers would bring out the paper. A form was soon found for the first answer to the government offensive. An order was issued to the Litovsky regiment to send a company immediately to the defense of the workers' press. The messengers from the printing-plant insisted that the Sixth Battalion of sappers be also ordered out: these were near neighbors and loyal friends. Telephonograms were immediately sent to the two addresses. The Litovtsi and the sappers came out without delay. The seals were torn from the building, the moulds again poured, and the work went on. With a few hours' delay the newspaper suppressed by the government came out under protection of the troops of a committee which was itself liable to arrest. That was insurrection. That is how it developed.

During this same time the cruiser *Aurora* had addressed a question to Smolny: Shall we go to sea or remain in the Neva? The very same sailors who had guarded the Winter Palace against Kornilov in August were now burning to settle accounts with Kerensky. The government order was promptly countermanded by the Committee and the crew received Order No. 1218: "In case of an attack on the Petrograd garrison by the counter-revolutionary forces, the cruiser *Aurora* is to protect herself with tugs, steam-boats, and cutters." The cruiser enthusiastically carried out this order, for which it had only been waiting.

These two acts of resistance, suggested by workers and sailors, and carried out, thanks to the sympathy of the garrison, with complete impunity, became political events of capital importance. The last remnants of the fetishism of authority crumbled to dust. "It became instantly clear," says one of the participants, "that the job was done!" If not yet done, it was at least proving much simpler than anyone had imagined yesterday.

An attempt to suppress the papers, a resolution to prosecute the Military Revolutionary Committee, an order removing commissars, the cutting-out of Smolny's telephones—these pinpricks were just sufficient to convict the government of preparing a counter-revolutionary *coup d'état*. Although an insurrection can win only on the offensive, it develops better, the more it looks like self-defense. A piece of official sealing-wax on the door of the Bolshevik editorial-rooms—as a military measure that is not much. But what a superb signal for battle! Telephonograms to all districts and units of the garrison announced the event: "The enemy of the people took the offensive during the night. The Military Revolutionary Committee is leading the resistance to the assault of the conspirators." The conspirators—these were the institutions of the official government. From the pen of revolutionary conspirators this term came as a surprise, but it wholly corresponded to the situation and to the feelings of the masses. Crowded out of all its positions, compelled to undertake a belated defense, incapable of mobilizing the necessary forces, or even finding out whether it had such forces, the government had developed a scattered, unthought-out, uncoordinated action, which in the eyes of the masses inevitably looked like a malevolent attempt. The Committee's telephonograms gave the command: "Make the regiment ready for battle and await further orders." That was the voice of a sovereign power. The commissars of the Committee, themselves liable to removal by the government, continued with redoubled confidence to remove those whom they thought it necessary to remove.

The *Aurora* in the Neva meant not only an excellent fighting unit in the service of the insurrection, but a radio-station ready for use. Invaluable advantage! The sailor Kurkov has remembered: "We got word from Trotsky to broadcast . . . that the counter-revolution had taken the offensive." Here too the defensive formulation concealed a summons to insurrection addressed to the whole country. The garrisons guarding the approaches to Petrograd were ordered by radio from the *Aurora* to hold up the counter-revolutionary echelons, and in case admonitions were inadequate to employ force. All revolutionary organizations were placed under obligation "to sit continually, accumulating all possible information as to the plans and activities of the conspirators." There was no lack of proclamations on the part of the Committee also, as you see. In its proclamations, however, the word was not divorced from the deed, but was a comment on it.

Somewhat belatedly the Military Revolutionary Committee undertook a more serious fortification of Smolny. In leaving the building at three o'clock on the night of the 24th, John Reed noticed machine guns at the entrances and strong patrols guarding the gates and the adjacent street corners. The patrols had been reinforced the day before by a company of the Litovsky regiment and a company of machine-gunners with twenty-four machine guns. During the day the guard increased continually. "In the Smolny region," writes Shliapnikov, "I saw a familiar picture, reminding me of the first days of the February revolution around the Tauride Palace." The same multitude of soldiers, workers and weapons of all kinds. Innumerable cords of firewood had been piled up in the court—a perfect cover against rifle-fire. Motor trucks were bringing up foodstuffs and munitions. "All Smolny," says Raskolnikov, "was converted into an armed camp. Cannon were in position out in front of the columns. Machine guns alongside them. . . . Almost on every step those same 'maxims,' looking like toy-cannon. And through all the corridors . . . the swift, loud, happy tramp of workers, soldiers, sailors and agitators." Sukhanov, accusing the organizers of the insurrection—not without foundation—of insufficient military precaution, writes: "Only now, in the afternoon and evening of the 24th, did they begin to bring up armed detachments of Red Guards and soldiers to Smolny to defend the headquarters of the insurrection. . . . By the evening of the 24th the defense of Smolny began to look like something."

This matter is not without importance. In Smolny, whence the compromisist Executive Committee had managed to steal away to the headquarters of the government staff, there were now concentrated the heads of all the revolutionary organizations led by the Bolsheviks. Here assembled on that day the all-important meeting of the Central Committee of the Bolsheviks to take the final decision before striking the blow. Eleven members were present. Lenin had not yet turned up from his refuge in the Vyborg district. Zinoviev also was absent from the session. According to the temperamental expression of Dzerzhinsky, he was "hiding and taking no part in the party work." Kamenev, on the other hand, although sharing the views of Zinoviev, was very active in the headquarters of the insurrection. Stalin was not present at the session. Generally speaking he did not appear at Smolny, spending his time in the editorial office of the central organ. The session, as always, was held under the chairmanship of Sverdlov. The official minutes of the session are scant, but they indicate everything essential. For characterizing the leading participants in the revolution, and the distribution of functions among them, they are irreplaceable.

It was a question of taking full possession of Petrograd in the next twenty-four hours. That meant to seize those political and technical institutions which were still in the hands of the government. The Congress of Soviets must hold its session under the soviet power. The practical measures of the nocturnal assault had been worked out, or were being worked out, by the Military Revolutionary Committee and the Military Organizations of the Bolsheviks. The Central Committee was to underline the final points.

First of all a proposal of Kamenev was adopted: "Today no member of the Central Committee can leave Smolny without a special resolution." It was decided over and above that, to keep on duty here members of the Petrograd Committee of the party. The minutes read further: "Trotsky proposes that they place at the disposal of the Military Revolutionary Committee two members of the Central Committee for the purpose of establishing communications with the postal and telegraph workers and the railroad workers; a third member to keep the Provisional Government under observation." It was resolved to delegate Dzerzhinsky to the postal and telegraph workers, Bubnov to the railroad workers. At first, and obviously at Sverdlov's suggestion, it was proposed to allot the watch over the Provisional Government to Podvoisky. The minutes read: "Objections to Podvoisky; Sverdlov is appointed." Miliutin, who passed as an economist, was appointed to organize the supply of food for the period of the insurrection. Negotiations with the Left Social Revolutionaries were entrusted to Kamenev, who had the reputation of a skilful although too yielding parliamentary. "Yielding," of course only from a Bolshevik criterion. "Trotsky proposes"—we read further—"that a reserve headquarters be established in the Peter and Paul fortress, and that one member of the Central Committee be sent there for that purpose." It was resolved: "To appoint Lashevich and Blagonravov for general observation; to commission Sverdlov to keep in continual touch with the fortress." Further: "to supply all members of the Central Committee with passes to the fortress."

Along party lines all threads were held in the hands of Sverdlov, who knew the cadres of the party as no one else did. He kept Smolny in touch with the party apparatus, supplied the Military Revolutionary Committee with the necessary workers, and was summoned into the Committee for counsel at all critical moments. Since the Committee had a too broad, and to some extent fluid, membership, the more conspirative undertakings were carried out through the heads of the Military Organization of the Bolsheviks, or through Sverdlov, who was the unofficial but all the more real "general secretary" of the October insurrection.

The Bolshevik delegates arriving in those days for the Soviet Congress would come first into the hands of Sverdlov, and would not be left for one unnecessary hour without something to do. On the 24th there were already two or three hundred provincial delegates in Petrograd, and the majority of them were included one way or another in the mechanics of the insurrection. At two o'clock in the afternoon, they assembled at a caucus in Smolny to hear a report from the Central Committee of the party. There were waverers among them who like Zinoviev and Kamenev preferred a waiting policy; there were also newcomers who were merely not sufficiently reliable. There could be no talk of expounding before this caucus the whole plan of the insurrection. Whatever is said at a large meeting inevitably gets abroad. It was still impossible even to throw off the defensive envelope of the attack without creating confusion in the minds of certain units of the garrison. But it was necessary to make the delegates understand that a decisive struggle had already begun, and that it would remain only for the Congress to crown it.

Referring to recent articles of Lenin, Trotsky demonstrated that "a conspiracy does not contradict the principles of Marxism," if objective relations make an insurrection possible and inevitable. "The physical barrier on the road to power must be overcome by a blow. . . ." However, up till now the policy of the Military Revolutionary Committee has not gone beyond the policy of self-defense. Of course this self-defense must be understood in a sufficiently broad sense. To assure the publication of the Bolshevik press with the help of armed forces, or to retain the *Aurora* in the waters of the Neva—"Comrades, is that not self-defense?—It is defense!" If the government intends to arrest us, we have machine guns on the roof of Smolny in preparation for such an event. "That also, comrades, is a measure of defense." But how about the Provisional Government? says one of the written questions. What if Kerensky tries not to submit to the Congress of Soviets? The spokesman replied: If Kerensky should attempt not to submit to the Congress of Soviets, then the resistance of the Government would have created "not a political but a police question." That was in essence almost exactly what happened.

At that moment Trotsky was called out to consult with a deputation just arrived from the city duma. In the capital, to be sure, it was still quiet, but alarming rumors were on foot. The mayor put these questions: Does the Soviet intend to make an insurrection, and how about keeping order in the city? And what will become of the duma itself if it does not recognize the revolution? These respected gentlemen wanted to know too much. The answer was: The question of power is to be decided by the Congress of Soviets. Whether this will lead to an armed struggle "depends not so much upon the soviets as upon those who, in conflict with the unanimous will of the people, are retaining the state power in their hands." If the Congress declines the power, the Petrograd Soviet will submit. But the government itself is obviously seeking a conflict. Orders have been issued for the arrest of the Military Revolutionary Committee. The workers and soldiers can only reply with ruthless resistance. What about looting and violence from criminal gangs? An order of the Committee issued today reads: "At the first attempt of criminal elements to bring about disturbances, looting, knifing or shooting on the streets of Petrograd, the criminals will be wiped off the face of the earth." As to the city duma, it will be possible in case of a conflict to employ constitutional methods—dissolution and a new election. The delegation went away dissatisfied. But what had they as a matter of fact expected?

That official visit of the City Fathers to the camp of the rebels was only too candid a demonstration of the impotence of the ruling groups. "Remember, comrades," said Trotsky upon returning to the Bolshevik caucus, "that a few weeks ago when we won the majority, we were only a trade-name —without a printing press, without a treasury, without departments—and now the city duma sends a deputation to the arrested Military Revolutionary Committee" for information as to the destiny of the city and the state.

The Peter and Paul fortress, won over politically only yesterday, is today completely taken possession of by the Military Revolutionary Committee. The machine gun crew, the most revolutionary unit, is being brought into fighting trim. A mighty work of cleaning the Colt machine guns is in progress —there are eighty of them. Machine guns are set up on the fortress wall to command the quay and the Troitsky bridge. The sentry guard at the gates is reinforced. Patrols are sent out into the surrounding districts. But in the heat of these morning hours it suddenly becomes known that within the fortress itself the situation is not assured. The uncertainty lies in a bicycle battalion. Recruited, like the cavalry, from well-to-do and rich peasants, the bicycle men, coming from the intermediate city layers, constituted a most conservative part of the army. A theme for idealistic psychologists: Let a man find himself, in distinction from others, on top of two wheels with a chain—at least in a poor country like Russia—and his vanity begins to swell out like his tires. In America it takes an automobile to produce this effect.

Brought in from the front to put down the July movement, the bicycle battalion had zealously stormed the Palace of Kshesinskaia, and afterward been installed in Peter and Paul as one of the most reliable detachments. It was learned that at yesterday's meeting which settled the fate of the fortress, the bicycle men had not been present. The old discipline still held in the battalion to such an extent that the officers had succeeded in keeping the soldiers from going into the fortress court. Counting on these bicycle men, the commandant of the fortress held his chin high, frequently got into telephone connection with Kerensky's headquarters, and even professed to be about to arrest the Bolshevik commissar. The situation must not be left indefinite for an extra minute. Upon an order from Smolny, Blagonravov confronts the enemy: the colonel is subjected to house arrest, the telephones are removed from all officers' apartments. The government staff calls up excitedly to know why the commandant is silent, and in general what is going on in the fortress. Blagonravov respectfully reports over the telephone that the fortress henceforward fulfills only the orders of the Military Revolutionary Committee, with which it behooves the government in the future to get in connection.

All the troops of the fortress garrison accepted the arrest of the commandant with complete satisfaction, but the bicycle men bore themselves evasively. What lay concealed behind their sulky silence: a hidden hostility or the last waverings? "We decided to hold a special meeting for the bicycle men," writes Blagonravov, "and invite our best agitational forces, and above all Trotsky, who had enormous authority and influence over the soldier masses." At four o'clock in the afternoon the whole battalion met in the neighboring building of the Cirque Moderne. As governmental opponent, Quartermaster-General Poradelov, considered to be a Social Revolutionary, took the floor. His objections were so cautious as to seem equivocal; and so much the more destructive was the attack of the Committee's representatives. This supplementary oratorical battle for the Peter and Paul fortress ended as might have been foreseen: by all voices except thirty the battalion supported the resolution of Trotsky. One more of the potential bloody conflicts was settled before the fighting and without bloodshed. That was the October insurrection. Such was its style.

It was now possible to rely upon the fortress with tranquil confidence. Weapons were given out from the arsenal without hindrance. At Smolny, in the Factory and Shop Committee room, delegates from the plants stood in line to get orders for rifles. The capital had seen many queues during the war years —now it saw rifle-queues for the first time. Trucks from all the districts of the city were driving up to the arsenal. "You would hardly have recognized the Peter and Paul fortress," writes the worker Skorinko. "Its renowned silence was broken by the chugging automobiles, shouts, and the creak of wagons. There was a special bustle in the storehouses. . . . Here too they led by us the first prisoners, officers and junkers."

The meeting in the Cirque Moderne had another result. The bicycle men who had been guarding the Winter Palace since

July withdrew, announcing that they would no longer consent to protect the government. That was a heavy blow. The bicycle men had to be replaced by junkers. The military support of the government was more and more reducing itself to the officers' schools—a thing which not only narrowed it extremely, but also conclusively revealed its social constitution.

The workers of the Putilov wharf—and not they alone—were insistently urging Smolny to disarm the junkers. If this measure had been taken after careful preparation, in cooperation with the non-combatant units of the schools, on the night of the 25th, the capture of the Winter Palace would have offered no difficulties whatever. If the junkers had been disarmed even on the night of the 26th, after the capture of the Winter Palace, there would have been no attempted counter-insurrection on the 29th of October. But the leaders were still in many directions revealing a "magnanimous spirit"—in reality an excess of optimistic confidence—and did not always listen attentively enough to the sober voice of the lower ranks. In this Lenin's absence, too, was felt. The masses had to correct these omissions and mistakes, with unnecessary losses on both sides. In a serious struggle there is no worse cruelty than to be magnanimous at an inopportune time.

At an afternoon session of the Pre-Parliament, Kerensky sings his swan song. During recent days, he says, the population of Russia, and especially of the capital, has been in a constant state of alarm. "Calls for insurrection appear daily in the Bolshevik papers." The orator quotes the articles of the wanted state criminal, Vladimir Ulianov Lenin. The quotations are brilliant and irrefutably prove that the above-named individual is inciting to insurrection. And when? At a moment when the government is just taking up the question of transferring the land to the peasant committees, and of measures to bring the war to an end. The authorities have so far made no haste to put down the conspirators, wishing to give them the opportunity to correct their own mistakes. "That is just what is wrong!" comes from the section where Miliukov is leader. But Kerensky is unabashed. "I prefer in general," he says, "that a government should act more slowly, and thus more correctly, and at the necessary moment more decisively." From those lips the words have a strange sound! At any rate:

"All days of grace are now past"; the Bolsheviks have not only not repented, but they have called out two companies, and are independently distributing weapons and cartridges. This time the government intends to put an end to the lawlessness of the rabble. "I choose my words deliberately: rabble." This insult to the people is greeted on the right with loud applause. He, Kerensky, has already given orders, he says, for the necessary arrests. "Special attention must be given to the speeches of the President of the Soviet, Bronstein-Trotsky." And be it known that the government has more than adequate forces; telegrams are coming in continually from the front demanding decisive measures against the Bolsheviks. At this point Konovalov hands the speaker the telephonogram from the Military Revolutionary Committee to the troops of the garrison, instructing them to "make the regiment ready for battle and await further orders." After reading the document Kerensky solemnly concludes: "In the language of the law and of judicial authority that is called a state of insurrection." Miliukov bears witness: "Kerensky pronounced these words in the complacent tone of a lawyer who has at last succeeded in getting evidence against his opponent." "Those groups and parties who have dared to lift their hands against the state," he concludes, "are liable to immediate, decisive and permanent liquidation." The entire hall, except the extreme Left, demonstratively applauded. The speech ended with a demand: that this very day, in this session, an answer be given to the question, "Can the government fulfill its duty with confidence in the support of this lofty assemblage?" Without awaiting the vote, Kerensky returned to headquarters—confident, according to his own account, that an hour would not pass before he would receive the needed decision. For what purpose it was needed remains unknown.

However, it turned out otherwise. From two to six o'clock the Mariinsky Palace was busy with factional and interfactional conferences, striving to work out a formula. The conferees did not understand that they were working out a formula for their own funeral. Not one of the compromisist groups had the courage to identify itself with the government. Dan said: "We Mensheviks are ready to defend the Provisional Government with the last drop of our blood; but let the government make it possible for the democracy to unite around it." Towards evening the left faction of the Pre-Parliament, worn out with the search for a solution, united on a formula borrowed by Dan from Martov, a formula which laid the responsibility for insurrection not only on the Bolsheviks, but also on the government, and demanded immediate transfer of the land to the Land Committees, intercession with the Allies in favor of peace negotiations, etc. Thus the apostles of moderation tried at the last moment to counterfeit those slogans which only yesterday they had been denouncing as demagogy and adventurism. Unqualified support to the government was promised by the Kadets and Cossacks—that is, by those two groups who intended to throw Kerensky over at the very first opportunity—but they were a minority. The support of the Pre-Parliament could have added little to the government, but Miliukov is right: this refusal of support robbed the government of the last remnants of its authority. Had not the government itself only a few weeks before determined the composition of the Pre-Parliament?

While they were seeking a salvation formula in the Mariinsky Palace, the Petrograd Soviet was assembling in Smolny for purposes of information. The spokesman considered it necessary to remind the Soviet that the Military Revolutionary Committee had arisen "not as an instrument of insurrection, but on the basis of revolutionary self-defense." The Committee had not permitted Kerensky to remove the revolutionary troops from Petrograd, and it had taken under its protection the workers' press. "Was this insurrection?" The *Aurora* stands today where she stood last night. "Is this insurrection?" We have today a semi-government, in which the people do not believe, and which does not believe in itself, because it is inwardly dead. This semi-government is awaiting that swish of the historic broom that will clear the space for an authentic government of the revolutionary people. Tomorrow the Congress of Soviets will open. It is the duty of the garrison and the workers to put all their forces at the disposal of the Congress. "If, however, the government attempts to employ the twenty-four hours remaining to it in plunging a knife into the back of the revolution, then we declare once more: The vanguard of the revolution will answer blow with blow and iron with steel." This open threat was at the same time a political screen for the forthcoming night attack. In conclusion Trotsky informed the meeting that the Left Social Revolutionary faction of the Pre-Parliament, after today's speech from Kerensky and a mouse-riot among the compromise factions, had sent a delegation to Smolny to express its readiness to enter officially into the staff of the Military Revolutionary Committee. In this shift of the Left Social Revolutionaries the Soviet joyfully welcomed a reflection of deeper processes: the widening scope of the peasant war and the successful progress of the Petrograd insurrection.

Commenting on this speech of the President of the Petrograd Soviet, Miliukov writes: "Probably this was Trotsky's original plan—having prepared for battle, to confront the government with the 'unanimous will of the people' as expressed in the Congress of Soviets, and thus give the new power the appearance of a legal origin. But the government proved weaker than he expected, and the power fell into his hands of its own accord before the Congress had time to assemble and express itself." What is true here, is that the weakness of the government exceeded all expectations. But from the beginning the plan had been to seize the power before the Congress opened. Miliukov recognizes this, by the way, in a different connection. "The actual intentions of the leaders of the revolution," he says, "went much farther than these official announcements of Trotsky. The Congress of Soviets was to be placed before a *fait accompli.*"

The purely military plan consisted originally of guaranteeing a united action of the Baltic sailors and the armed Vyborg workers. The sailors were to come by railroad and detrain at the Finland station, which is in the Vyborg district, and then from this base by way of a further assimilation of the Red Guard and units of the garrison, the insurrection was to spread to other districts of the city, and having seized the bridges, to advance into the center for the final blow. This scheme—naturally deriving from the circumstances, and formulated, it seems, by Antonov—was drawn up on the assumption that the enemy would be able to put up a considerable resistance. It was just this premise that soon fell away. It was unnecessary to start from a limited base, because the government proved open to attack wherever the insurrectionists found it necessary to strike a blow.

The strategic plan underwent changes in the matter of dates also, and that in two directions: the insurrection began earlier and ended later than had been indicated. The morning attacks of the government called out by way of self-defense an immediate resistance from the Military Revolutionary Committee. The impotence of the authorities, thus revealed, impelled Smolny during the same day to offensive actions—preserving, to be sure, a half-way, semi-disguised and preparatory character. The main blow as before was prepared during the night: in that sense the plan held good. It was transgressed, however, in the process of fulfillment—but now in an opposite direction. It had been proposed to occupy during the night all the commanding summits, and first of all the Winter Palace where the central power had taken refuge. But time-calculations are even more difficult in insurrection than in regular war. The leaders were many hours late with the concentration of forces, and the operations against the palace, not even begun during the night, formed a special chapter of the revolution ending only on the night of the 26th—that is, a whole twenty-four hours late. The most brilliant victories are not achieved without duds.

After Kerensky's speech at the Pre-Parliament the authorities tried to broaden their offensive. The railroad stations were occupied by detachments of junkers. Pickets were posted at the big street-crossings and ordered to requisition the private automobiles not turned over to headquarters. By three o'clock in the afternoon the bridges were raised, except for the Dvortsovy which remained open under heavy guard for the movement of the junkers. This measure, adopted by the monarchy at all critical moments and for the last time in the February days, was dictated by fear of the workers' districts. The raising of the bridges was received by the population as an official announcement of the beginning of the insurrection. The headquarters of the districts concerned immediately answered this military act of the government in their own way by sending armed detachments to the bridges. Smolny had only to develop their initiative. This struggle for the bridges assumed the character of a test for both sides. Parties of armed workers and soldiers brought pressure to bear on the junkers and Cossacks, now persuading and now threatening. The guard finally yielded without hazarding a straight-out fight. Some of the bridges were raised and lowered several times.

The *Aurora* received a direct order from the Military Revolutionary Committee: "With all means at your command restore movement on the Nikolaevsky Bridge." The commander of the cruiser at first refused to carry out the order, but after a symbolic arrest of himself and all his officers obediently brought the ship to the bridge. Cordons of sailors spread out along both quays. By the time the *Aurora* had dropped anchor before the bridge, relates Korkov, the tracks of the junkers were already cold. The sailors themselves lowered the bridge and posted guards. Only Dvortsovy bridge remained several hours in the hands of the government patrols.

Notwithstanding the manifest failure of its first experiments, individual branches of the government tried to deal further blows. A detachment of militia appeared in the evening at a big private printing-plant to suppress the newspaper of the Petrograd Soviet, *Worker and Soldier*. Twelve hours before, the workers of the Bolshevik press had run for help in a like case to Smolny. Now there was no need of it. The printers, together with two sailors who happened by, immediately captured the automobile loaded with papers; a number of the militia joined them on the spot; the inspector of militia fled. The captured paper was successfully delivered at Smolny. The Military Revolutionary Committee sent two squads of the Preobrazhentzi to protect the publication. The frightened administration thereupon turned over the management of the printing-plant to the soviet of worker-overseers.

The legal authorities did not even think of penetrating Smolny to make arrests: it was too obvious that this would be the signal for a civil war in which the defeat of the Government was assured in advance. There was made, however, as a kind of administrative convulsion, an attempt to arrest Lenin in the Vyborg district, where, generally speaking, the authorities were afraid even to look in. Late in the evening a certain colonel with a dozen junkers accidentally entered a workers' club instead of the Bolshevik editorial rooms located in the same house. The brave boys had for some reason imagined that Lenin would be waiting for them in the editorial rooms. The club immediately informed the district headquarters of the Red Guard. While the colonel was wandering around from one story to another, arriving once even among the Mensheviks, a detachment of Red Guards, rushing up, arrested him along with his junkers, and brought them to the headquarters of the Vyborg district, and thence to the Peter and Paul fortress. Thus the loudly proclaimed campaign against the Bolsheviks, meeting insuperable difficulties at every step, turned into disconnected jumps and small anecdotes, evaporated, and came to nothing.

During this time the Military Revolutionary Committee was working day and night. Its commissars were on continual duty in the military units. The population was notified in special proclamations where to turn in case of counter-revolutionary attempts or pogroms: "Help will be given on the instant." A suggestive visit to the telephone exchange from the commissar of the Keksgolmsky regiment proved sufficient to get Smolny switched back into the system. Telephone communications, the swiftest of all, gave confidence and regularity to the developing operations.

Continuing to plant its own commissars in those institutions which had not yet come under its control, the Military Revolutionary Committee kept broadening and reinforcing its bases for the coming offensive. Dzerzhinsky that afternoon handed the old revolutionist Pestkovsky a sheet of paper in the form of credentials appointing him to the office of commissar of the central telegraph station. But how shall I get possession of the telegraph station?—asked the new commissar in some surprise. The Keksgolmsky regiment is supplying sentries there and it is on our side! Pestkovsky needed no further illumination. Two Keksgolmtzi, standing by the commutator with rifles, proved sufficient to attain a compromise with the hostile telegraph officials, among whom were no Bolsheviks.

At nine o'clock in the evening another commissar of the Military Revolutionary Committee, Stark, with a small detachment of sailors under the command of the former emigré Savin, also a seaman, occupied the government news agency and therewith decided not only the fate of that institution, but also to a certain degree his own fate: Stark became the first Soviet director of the agency, before being appointed Soviet ambassador to Afghanistan.

Were these two modest operations acts of insurrection, or were they only episodes in the two-power system—transferred, to be sure, from the compromisist to the Bolshevik rails? The question may perhaps reasonably be regarded as casuistic, but for the purpose of camouflaging an insurrection it had a certain importance. The fact is that even the intrusion of armed sailors into the building of the news agency had still a sort of half-way character: it was not yet a question of seizing the institution, but only of establishing a censorship over despatches. Thus right up to the evening of the 24th, the umbilical cord of "legality" was not conclusively severed. The movement was still disguising itself with the remnants of the two-power tradition.

In working out the plans of the insurrection, Smolny rested great hopes on the Baltic sailors as a fighting detachment combining proletarian resolution with strict military training. The arrival of the sailors in Petrograd had been dated in advance to coincide with the Congress of Soviets. To call the Baltic sailors in earlier would have meant to take openly the road of insurrection. Out of this arose a difficulty which subsequently turned into a delay.

During the afternoon of the 24th, two delegates from the Kronstadt soviet, the Bolshevik Flerovsky and the anarchist Yarchuk, who was keeping step with the Bolsheviks, arrived in Smolny for the Congress. In one of the rooms of Smolny they ran into Chudnovsky, who had just returned from the front, and who, alluding to the mood of the soldiers, spoke against insurrection in the near future. "At the height of the argument," relates Flerovsky, "Trotsky came into the room. . . . Calling me aside, he advised me to return immediately to Kronstadt: 'Events are maturing so fast that everyone must be at his post. . . .' In this curt order I felt keenly the discipline of the advancing insurrection." The argument was cut short. The impressionable and hot-headed Chudnovsky laid aside his doubts in order to take part in drawing up the plans of the fight. On the heels of Flerovsky and Yarchuk went a telephonogram: "The armed forces of Kronstadt are to come out at dawn for the defense of the Congress of Soviets."

Through Sverdlov the Military Revolutionary Committee sent a telegram that night to Helsingfors, to Smilga, the president of the regional Committee of the Soviets: "Send regulations." That meant: Send immediately 1500 chosen Baltic sailors armed to the teeth. Although the sailors could reach Petrograd only during the next day, there was no reason to postpone military action; the internal forces were adequate. Yes, and a postponement was impossible. Operations had already begun. If reinforcements should come from the front to help the government, then the sailors would arrive in time to deal them a blow in the flank or rear.

The tactical plans for the conquest of the capital were worked out chiefly by the staff of the Military Organization of the Bolsheviks. Officers of the general staff would have found many faults in them, but military academicians do not customarily take part in the preparation of a revolutionary insurrection. The essentials at any rate were taken care of. The city was divided into military divisions, each subordinate to the nearest headquarters. At the most important points companies of the Red Guard were concentrated in coordination with the neighboring military units, where companies on duty were awake and ready. The goal of each separate operation, and the forces for it, were indicated in advance. All those taking part in the insurrection from top to bottom—in this lay its power, in this also at times its Achilles' heel—were imbued with absolute confidence that the victory was going to be won without casualties.

The main operation began at two o'clock in the morning. Small military parties, usually with a nucleus of armed workers or sailors under the leadership of commissars, occupied simultaneously, or in regular order, the railroad stations, the lighting plant, the munition and food stores, the waterworks, Dvortsovy bridge, the Telephone Exchange, the State Bank, the big printing-plants. The Telegraph Station and the Post Office were completely taken over. Reliable guards were placed everywhere.

Meager and colorless is the record of the episodes of that October night. It is like a police report. All the participants were shaking with a nervous fever. There was no time to observe and record and no one to do it. The information flowing in at headquarters was not always jotted down, and if so it was done carelessly. Notes got lost. Subsequent recollections were dry and not always accurate, since they came for the most part from accidental people. Those workers, sailors, and soldiers who really inspired and led the operation took their places soon after at the head of the first detachments of the Red Army, and the majority laid down their lives in the various theaters of the civil war. In the attempt to determine the sequence of separate episodes, the investigator runs into a vast confusion, which is still more complicated by the accounts in the newspapers. At times it seems as though it was easier to capture Petrograd in the autumn of 1917 than to recount the process fourteen years later.

To the first company of the sapper battalion, the strongest and most revolutionary, was given the task of seizing the nearby Nikolaevsky railroad station. In less than a quarter of an hour the station was occupied by strong guards without a blow. The government squad simply evaporated in the darkness. The keenly cold night was full of mysterious movements and suspicious sounds. Suppressing a sharp alarm in their hearts, the soldiers would conscientiously stop all passers-by, on foot or in vehicles, meticulously inspecting their documents. They did not always know what to do. They hesitated—most often let them go. But confidence increased with every hour. About six in the morning the sappers held up two truckloads of junkers—about sixty men—disarmed them, and sent them to Smolny.

That same sapper battalion was directed to send fifty men to guard the food warehouses, twenty-one to guard the Power Station, etc. Order followed order, now from Smolny, now from the district. Nobody offered a murmur of objection. According to the report of the commissar, the orders were carried out "immediately and exactly." The movement of the soldiers acquired a precision long unseen. However rickety and crumbly that garrison was—good only for scrap-iron in a military sense—on that night the old soldierly drill reawoke, and for one last moment tensed every nerve and muscle in the service of the new goal.

Commissar Uralov received two authorizations: one, to occupy the printing-plant of the reactionary paper *Russkaia*

Volia, founded by Protopopov a little while before he became the last Minister of the Interior of Nicholas II; the other, to get a troop of soldiers from the Semenov Guard Regiment which the government for old times' sake was still considering its own. The Semenovtsi were needed for the occupation of a printing-plant. The printing-plant was needed to issue the Bolshevik paper in large format and with a big circulation. The soldiers had already lain down to sleep. The commissar briefly told them the object of his visit. "I hadn't stopped talking when a shout of 'Hurrah!' went up on all sides. The soldiers were jumping out of their bunks and crowding around me in a close circle." A truck loaded with Semenovtsi approached the printing-plant. The workers of the night-shift quickly assembled in the rotary-press room. The commissar explained why he had come. "And here as in the barracks the workers answered with shouts of 'Hurrah! Long live the Soviets!'" The job was done. In much the same manner the other institutions were seized. It was not necessary to employ force, for there was no resistance. The insurrectionary masses lifted their elbows and pushed out the lords of yesterday.

The commander of the district reported that night to general headquarters and the headquarters of the northern front over the military wire: "The situation in Petrograd is frightful. There are no street demonstrations or disorders, but a regulated seizure of institutions, railroad stations, also arrests, is in progress. . . . The junkers' patrols are surrendering without resistance . . . We have no guarantee that there will not be an attempt to seize the Provisional Government." Polkovnikov was right: they had no guarantee of that.

In military circles the rumor was going round that agents of the Military Revolutionary Committee had stolen from the desk of the Petrograd commandant the password for the sentries of the garrison. That was not at all improbable. The insurrection had many friends among the lower personnel of all institutions. Nevertheless this tale about stealing the password is apparently a legend which arose in the hostile camp to explain the too humiliating ease with which the Bolshevik patrols got possession of the city.

An order was sent out through the garrison from Smolny during the night: Officers not recognizing the authority of the

Military Revolutionary Committee to be arrested. The commanders of many regiments fled of their own accord, and passed some nervous days in hiding. In other units the officers were removed or arrested. Everywhere special revolutionary committees or staffs were formed and functioned hand in hand with the commissars. That this improvised command did not stand very high in a military sense, goes without saying. Nevertheless it was reliable, and the question here was decided primarily in the political court.

It is necessary to add, however, that with all their lack of experience the staffs of certain units developed a considerable military initiative. The committee of the Pavlovsky regiment sent scouts into the Petrograd district headquarters to find out what was going on there. The chemical reserve battalion kept careful watch of its restless neighbors, the junkers of the Pavlovsky and Vladimirsky schools, and the students of the cadet corps. The chemical men from time to time disarmed junkers in the street and thus kept them cowed. Getting into connection with the soldier personnel of the Pavlovsky school, the staff of the chemical battalion saw to it that the keys to the weapons were in the hands of the soldiers.

It is difficult to determine the number of forces directly engaged in this nocturnal seizure of the capital—and this not only because nobody counted them or noted them down, but also because of the character of the operations. Reserves of the second and third order almost merged with the garrison as a whole. But it was only occasionally necessary to have recourse to the reserves. A few thousand Red Guards, two or three thousand sailors—tomorrow with the arrivals from Kronstadt and Helsingfors there will be about treble the number—a score of infantry companies: such were the forces of the first and second order with whose aid the insurrectionists occupied the governmental high points of the capital.

At 3:20 in the morning the chief of the political administration of the War Ministry, the Menshevik Sher, sent the following information by direct wire to the Caucasus: "A meeting of the Central Executive Committee together with the delegates to the Congress of Soviets is in progress with an overwhelming majority of Bolsheviks. Trotsky has received an ovation. He has announced that he hopes for a bloodless victory of the insurrection, since the power is in their hands. The Bolsheviks have begun active operations. They have seized the Nikolaevsky bridge and posted armored cars there. The Pavlovsky regiment has posted pickets on Milliony street near the Winter Palace, is stopping everybody, arresting them, and sending them to Smolny Institute. They have arrested Minister Kartashev and the general administrator of the Provisional Government, Halperin. The Baltic railroad station is also in the hands of the Bolsheviks. If the front does not intervene, the government will be unable to resist with the forces on hand."

The joint session of the Executive Committees about which Lieutenant Sher's communication speaks, opened in Smolny after midnight in unusual circumstances. Delegates to the Congress of Soviets brimmed the hall in the capacity of invited guests. Reinforced guards occupied the entrances and corridors. Trench-coats, rifles, machine guns filled the windows. The members of the Executive Committees were drowned in this many-headed and hostile mass of provincials. The high organ of the "democracy" looked already like a captive of the insurrection. The familiar figure of the president, Cheidze, was absent. The invariable spokesman, Tseretelli, was absent. Both of them, frightened by the turn of events, had surrendered their responsible posts, and abandoning Petrograd, left for their Georgian homeland. Dan remained as leader of the compromise bloc. He lacked the sly good humor of Cheidze, and likewise the moving eloquence of Tseretelli. But he excelled them both in obstinate short-sightedness. Alone in the president's chair the Social Revolutionary, Gotz, opened the session. Dan took the floor amid an utter silence which seemed to Sukhanov languid—to John Reed "almost threatening." The spokesman's hobby was a new resolution of the Pre-Parliament, which had tried to oppose the insurrection with the dying echo of its own slogans. "It will be too late if you do not take account of this decision," cried Dan, trying to frighten the Bolsheviks with the inevitable hunger and the degeneration of the masses. "Never before has the counter-revolution been so strong as at the given moment," he said—that is, on the night before October 25th, 1917. The frightened petty bourgeois confronted by great events sees nothing but dangers and obstacles. His sole recourse is the pathos of alarm. "In the factories and barracks the Black Hundred press is enjoying a far more considerable success than the socialist press." Lunatics are leading the revolution to ruin just as in 1905 "when this same Trotsky stood at the head of the Petrograd Soviet." But no, he cried, the Central Executive Committee will not permit an insurrection. "Only over its dead body will the hostile camps cross their bayonets." Shouts from the benches: "Yes, it's been dead a long time!" The entire hall felt the appropriateness of that exclamation. Over the corpse of Compromisism the bayonets of the bourgeoisie and the proletariat had already crossed. The voice of the orator is drowned in a hostile uproar, his pounding on the table is futile, his appeals do not move, his threats do not frighten. Too late! Too late!

Yes, it is an insurrection! Replying in the name of the Military Revolutionary Committee, the Bolshevik Party, the Petrograd workers and soldiers, Trotsky now throws off the last qualification. Yes, the masses are with us, and we are leading them to the assault! "If you do not weaken there will be no civil war, for the enemy is already capitulating, and you can assume the place of master of the Russian land which of right belongs to you." The astounded members of the Central Executive Committee found no strength even to protest. Up to now the defensive phraseology of Smolny had kept up in them, in spite of all the facts, a glimmering spark of hope. Now that too was extinguished. In those hours of deep night the insurrection lifted its head high.

That session so rich in episodes closed at four o'clock in the morning. The Bolshevik speakers would appear in the tribune only to return immediately to the Military Revolutionary Committee, where from all corners of the city news uniformly favorable was pouring in. The patrols in the streets were doing their work, the government institutions were being occupied one after the other; the enemy was offering no resistance anywhere.

It had been assumed that the central Telephone Exchange would be especially well fortified, but at seven in the morning it was taken without a fight by a company from the Keksgozmsky regiment. The insurrectionists could now not only rest easy about their own communications, but control the telephone connections of the enemy. The apparatus of the

Winter Palace and of central headquarters was promptly cut out.

Almost simultaneously with the seizure of the Telephone Exchange a detachment of sailors from the marine guard, about forty strong, seized the building of the State Bank on the Ekaterininsky Canal. The bank clerk, Ralzevich recalls that the sailors "worked with expedition," immediately placing sentries at each telephone to cut off possible help from outside. The occupation of the building was accomplished "without any resistance, in spite of the presence of a squad from the Semenovsky regiment." The seizure of the bank had to some extent a symbolic importance. The cadres of the party had been brought up on the Marxian criticism of the Paris Commune of 1871, whose leaders, as is well known, did not venture to lay hands on the State Bank. "No, we will not make that mistake," many Bolsheviks had been saying to themselves long before October 25th. News of the seizure of the most sacred institution of the bourgeois state swiftly spread through the districts, raising a warm wave of joy.

In the early morning hours the Warsaw railroad station was occupied, also the printing-plant of the "Stock Exchange News," and Dvortsovy bridge under Kerensky's very windows. A commissar of the Committee presented the soldier patrol from the Volinsky regiment in Kresty prison with a resolution demanding the liberation of a number of prisoners according to the lists of the Soviet. The prison administration tried in vain to get instructions from the Minister of Justice: he was too busy. The liberated Bolsheviks, among them the young Kronstadt leader, Roshal, immediately received military appointments.

In the morning, a party of junkers who had left the Winter Palace in a truck in search of provisions, and been held up by the sappers at Nikolaevsky station, were brought to Smolny. Podvoisky relates the following: "Trotsky told them that they were free on condition that they give a promise not to take further action against the Soviet power, and that they might go back to their school and get to work. The youngsters, who had been expecting a bloody end, were unspeakably surprised at this." To what extent their immediate liberation was wise, remains in doubt. The victory was not yet finally achieved.

The junkers were the chief force of the enemy. On the other hand with the wavering moods in the military schools, it was important to prove by example that a surrender to the mercy of the victor would not threaten the junkers with punishment. The arguments in both directions seemed about equal.

From the War Ministry, not yet occupied by the insurrectionists, General Levitsky sent word by direct wire to General Dukhonin at headquarters: "The troops of the Petrograd garrison . . . have gone over to the Bolsheviks. The sailors and a light-armed cruiser have come from Kronstadt. They have lowered the raised bridges. The whole town is covered with sentry guards from the garrison. But there has been no coming-out. (!) The Telephone Exchange is in the hands of the garrison. The troops in the Winter Palace are defending it only in a formal sense, since they have decided not to come out actively. The general impression is that the Provisional Government finds itself in the capital of a hostile state which has finished mobilization but not yet begun active operations." Invaluable military and political testimony! To be sure, the General anticipates events when he says the sailors have arrived from Kronstadt: they will arrive a few hours later. The bridge was really let down by the crew of the *Aurora.* The hope expressed in conclusion that the Bolsheviks "having long been actually in a position to get rid of us . . . will not dare come into conflict with the opinion of the army at the front," is rather naïve. However, these illusions about the front were about all that the rear generals had left, or the rear democrats either. At any rate that image of the Provisional Government finding itself in the capital of a hostile state will go into the history of the revolution forever as the best possible explanation of the October event.

Meetings were continuous in Smolny. Agitators, organizers, leaders of factories, regiments, districts, would appear for an hour or two, sometimes for a few minutes, to get news, to check up on their own activities and return to their posts. Before room 18, the quarters of the Bolshevik faction of the Soviet, there was an indescribable jam. Tired to death, those arriving would often fall asleep right in the assembly hall, leaning their unbearably heavy heads against a white column, or against the walls in the corridors, with both arms around their rifles—or sometimes they would simply stretch out in piles on the dirty wet floor. Lashevich was receiving the military commissars and giving them their last instructions. In the quarters of the Military Revolutionary Committee on the third floor, reports coming in from all sides would be converted into orders. Here beat the heart of the insurrection.

The district centers reproduced the picture of Smolny on a smaller scale. In the Vyborg district opposite the headquarters of the Red Guard on Samsonevsky Prospect a whole camp was created: the street was jammed full of wagons, passenger-cars and trucks. The institutions of the district were swarming with armed workers. The soviet, the duma, the trade unions, the factory and shop-committees—everything in this district—were serving the cause of the insurrection. In the factories and barracks and various institutions the same thing was happening in a smaller way as throughout the whole capital: they were crowding out some and electing others, breaking the last threads of the old ties, strengthening the new. The backward ones were adopting resolutions of submission to the Military Revolutionary Committee. The Mensheviks and Social Revolutionaries timidly shrank aside along with the factory administrations and the commanding staff of the troops. At continuous meetings fresh information was given out, fighting confidence kept up and ties reinforced. The human masses were crystallizing along new axes; a revolution was achieving itself.

Step by step we have tried to follow in this book the development of the October insurrection: the sharpening discontent of the worker masses, the coming over of the soviets to the Bolshevik banners, the indignation of the army, the campaign of the peasants against the landlords, the flood-tide of the national movement, the growing fear and distraction of the possessing and ruling classes, and finally the struggle for the insurrection within the Bolshevik party. The final act of the revolution seems, after all this, too brief, too dry, too businesslike—somehow out of correspondence with the historic scope of the events. The reader experiences a kind of disappointment. He is like a mountain climber, who, thinking the main difficulties are still ahead, suddenly discovers that he is already on the summit or almost there. Where is the insurrection? There is no picture of the insurrection. The events do not form themselves into a picture. A series of small operations, calculated and prepared in advance, remain separated one from another both in space and time. A unity of thought and aim unites them, but they do not fuse in the struggle itself. There is no action of great masses. There are no dramatic encounters with the troops. There is nothing of all that which imaginations brought up upon the facts of history associate with the idea of insurrection.

The general character of the revolution in the capital subsequently moved Masaryk, among many others, to write: "The October revolution . . . was anything but a popular mass movement. That revolution was the act of leaders working from above and behind the scenes." As a matter of fact it was the most popular mass-insurrection in all history. The workers had no need to come out into the public square in order to fuse together: they were already politically and morally one single whole without that. The soldiers were even forbidden to leave their barracks without permission: upon that point the order of the Military Revolutionary Committee fell in with the order of Polkovnikov. But those invisible masses were marching more than ever before in step with the events. The factories and barracks never lost connection for a minute with the district headquarters, nor the districts with Smolny. The Red Guard detachments felt at their back the support of the factories. The soldier squad returning to the barracks found the new shifts ready. Only with heavy reserves behind them could revolutionary detachments go about their work with such confidence. The scattered government patrols, in contrast, being convinced in advance of their own isolation, renounced the very idea of resistance. The bourgeois classes had expected barricades, flaming conflagrations, looting, rivers of blood. In reality a silence reigned more terrible than all the thunders of the world. The social ground shifted noiselessly like a revolving stage, bringing forward the popular masses, carrying away to limbo the rulers of yesterday.

As early as ten o'clock on the morning of the 25th, Smolny considered it possible to broadcast through the capital and throughout the whole country a triumphant announcement: "The Provisional Government is overthrown. The state power has passed into the hands of the Military Revolutionary Committee." In a certain sense this declaration was very premature. The government still existed, at least within the territory of the Winter Palace. Headquarters existed; the provinces had not expressed themselves; the Congress of Soviets had not yet opened. But the leaders of an insurrection are not historians; in order to prepare events for the historians they have to anticipate them. In the capital the Military Revolutionary Committee was already complete master of the situation. There could be no doubt of the sanction of the Congress. The provinces were awaiting Petrograd's initiative. In order to get complete possession of the power it was necessary to act as a power. In a proclamation to the military organizations of the front and rear, the Committee urged the soldiers to watch vigilantly over the conduct of the commanding staff, to arrest officers not adhering to the revolution, and not to stop at the use of force in case of attempts to throw hostile divisions against Petrograd.

The chief commissar of headquarters, Stankevich, having arrived the night before from the front and not wishing to remain wholly inactive, placed himself at the head of a half company of military engineering students in the morning, and undertook to clean the Bolsheviks out of the Telephone Exchange. It was in this way that the junkers first found out who had possession of the telephone connections. "There is a model of energy for you," exclaimed officer Sinegub, grinding his teeth. "But where did they get such leadership?" The sailors occupying the telephone building could easily have shot down the junkers through the windows. But the insurrectionists were striving with all their might to avoid bloodshed, and Stankevich had given strict orders not to open fire lest the junkers be accused of shooting at the people. The commanding officer thought to himself: "Once order is restored, who will dare to peep?" and concluded his meditations with an exclamation: "Damned clowns!" This is a good formula for the attitude of the officers to the government. On his own initiative Sinegub sent to the Winter Palace for hand grenades and sticks of pyroxyle. In the interval a monarchist lieutenant got into an argument at the gates of the Exchange with a Bolshevik ensign. Like the heroes of Homer they exchanged mighty epithets before the battle. Finding themselves between two fires—for the time only wordy ones—the telephone girls gave free rein to their nerves. The sailors let them go home. "What's this? Women? . . ." They fled with hysterical screams through the gates. "The deserted Morskaia," relates Sinegub, "was suddenly enlivened with running and jumping skirts and hats." The sailors managed somehow to handle the work of the switchboard. An armored car from the Reds soon entered the court of the Exchange, doing no damage to the frightened junkers. They on their side seized two trucks and barricaded the gates of the Exchange from the outside. A second armored car appeared from the direction of the Nevsky, and then a third. It all came down to maneuvers and attempts to frighten each other. The struggle for the Exchange was decided without pyroxyle: Stankevich raised the siege after negotiating a free passage for his junkers.

Weapons in general are still serving merely as an external sign of power: they are not being brought into action. On the road to the Winter Palace a half company of junkers runs into a crew of sailors with rifles cocked. The enemies only measure each other with their eyes. Neither side wants to fight: the one through consciousness of strength, the other of weakness. But where chance offers, the insurrectionists—especially the workers—promptly disarm the enemy. A second half company of those same engineering junkers was surrounded by Red Guards and soldiers, disarmed by them with the help of armored cars, and taken prisoner. Even here, however, there was no conflict; the junkers did not put up a fight. "Thus ended," says the initiator of it—"the sole attempt, so far as I know, at active resistance to the Bolsheviks." Stankevich has in mind, of course, operations outside the Winter Palace region.

By noon the streets around the Mariinsky Palace were occupied by troops of the Military Revolutionary Committee. Members of the Pre-Parliament were just assembling for a meeting. The praesidium made an attempt to get the latest news; their hearts sank when they learned that the telephones of the palace had been cut out. The Council of Elders went into session to decide what to do. The deputies murmured meanwhile in the corners. Avksentiev offered consolation:

Kerensky has gone to the front, and will be back soon and fix everything. An armored car drew up at the entrance. Soldiers of the Litovsky and Keksgolmsky regiments and sailors of the Marine Guard entered the building, formed in line on the staircase, and occupied the first hall. The commander of the detachment suggested to the deputies that they leave the palace at once. "The impression created was appalling," testifies Nabokov. The members of the Pre-Parliament decided to disperse, "temporarily suspending their activities." Forty-eight Right Wing members voted against submitting to violence, quite evidently knowing they would be in a minority. The deputies peacefully descended the magnificent stairway between two rows of rifles. An eye-witness testifies: "in all this there was no attempt at dramatics." "Ordinary, meaningless, obtuse, malicious physiognomies," writes the liberal patriot, Nabokov, of these Russian soldiers and sailors. Down below at the entrance the soldiers inspected their papers and let them all through. "A sorting of members and some arrests had been expected," writes Miliukov, himself let out with the others. "But the revolutionary headquarters had other things to worry about." It was not only that. The revolutionary staff had little experience. The instructions read: Arrest members of the government if found. But none were found. The members of the Pre-Parliament were freely released, among them some who soon became organizers of the civil war.

This parliamentary hybrid, which ended its existence twelve hours in advance of the Provisional Government, had lived in the world for eighteen days. That was the interval between the withdrawal of the Bolsheviks from the Mariinsky Palace to the street and the entry of the armed street forces into the Mariinsky Palace. . . . Of all the parodies of popular representation in which history is so rich, this Council of the Russian Republic was perhaps the most absurd.

After leaving the unlucky building, the Octobrist Shidlovsky went strolling through the town to see the fights—for these gentlemen believed that the people were going to rise in their defense. But no fighting was to be seen. Instead, according to Shidlovsky, the public in the streets—the select crowd, that is, along the Nevsky Prospect—were to the last man laughing. "Have you heard about it? The Bolsheviks have seized the power. Well, that won't last more than three days. Ha ha ha!" Shidlovsky decided to remain in the capital "during the period which social rumor designated for the rule of the Bolsheviks."

The Nevsky public had begun to laugh, it may be remarked, only towards evening. In the morning such a mood of alarm had prevailed that hardly anybody in the bourgeois districts dared go into the streets at all. At about nine o'clock a journalist Knizhnik, ran out on Kamenoöstrovsky Prospect in search of newspapers, but could find no stands. In a little group of citizens he learned that the Bolsheviks had occupied the telephone, the telegraph, and the Bank during the night. A soldier patrol listened to them and asked them not to make so much noise. "But even without that everybody was unusually subdued." Armed detachments of workers were going by. The tramcars moved as usual—that is, slowly. "The scarcity of passers-by oppressed me," writes Knizhnik about the Nevsky. Food could be had in the restaurants, but for the most part in back rooms. At noon the cannon from the walls of Peter and Paul, now safely occupied by the Bolsheviks, thundered out neither louder nor more gently than usual. The walls and fences were pasted over with proclamations warning against insurrection, but other proclamations were already making their way, announcing the victory of the insurrection. There was no time yet to paste them up; they were tossed out from automobiles. Just off the press, these handbills smelled of fresh inks as though of the events themselves.

Companies of the Red Guard had emerged from their districts. The worker with a rifle, the bayonet above hat or cap, the rifle-belt over a civilian coat—that is the essential image of the 25th of October. Cautiously and still diffidently, the armed worker was bringing order into the capital conquered by him.

The tranquillity of the street instilled tranquillity in the heart. The philistines began to dribble down from their houses. Towards evening they felt even less anxious than during the preceding days. Business, to be sure, had come to an end in the governmental and social institutions, but many stores remained open. Others were closed rather through excessive caution than necessity. Can this be insurrection? Is an insurrection like this? The February sentries have merely been replaced by those of October.

By evening the Nevsky was even fuller than usual of that public which was giving the Bolsheviks three days of life. The soldiers of the Pavlovsky regiment, although their patrols were reinforced by armored cars and even anti-aircraft guns, had already ceased to inspire fear. To be sure something serious was going on around the Winter Palace and they would not let you through there, but still an insurrection could not very well all be concentrated on Winter Palace square. An American journalist saw old men in rich fur coats shake their gloved fists at the Pavlovtsi, and handsomely dressed women scream abuse in their faces. "The soldiers argued feebly with embarrassed grins." They were obviously at a loss on that elegant Nevsky, not yet converted into the "Prospect of the Twenty-Fifth of October."

Claude Anet, the official French journalist in Petrograd, was sincerely surprised that these absurd Russians should make a revolution not at all as he had read about it in the old books. "The city is quiet." He calls up his friends on the telephone, receives visitors, and at noon leaves the house. The soldiers who block his road on Moika Street march in perfect order "as under the old régime." There are innumerable patrols on Milliony Street. There is no shooting anywhere. The immense square of the Winter Palace at this noon hour is still almost empty. There are patrols on Morskaia and Nevsky. The soldiers carry themselves in military style, and are dressed irreproachably. At first glance it seems certain that these are government troops. On Mariinsky Square, whence Anet intends to make his way into the Pre-Parliament, he is stopped by soldiers and sailors. "Mighty polite, I assure you." Two streets leading up to the palace are barricaded with automobiles and wagons—here, too, an armored car. These are all under Smolny. The Military Revolutionary Committee has sent out patrols through the town, posted sentries, dissolved the Pre-Parliament, taken command of the capital, and established therein a state of order "unseen since the revolution began." In the evening the janitress informs her French lodger that telephone numbers have been sent over from soviet headquarters, by which at any moment he can summon military help in case of attack, suspicious search parties, etc. "As a fact they never guarded us better."

At 2:35 in the afternoon—the foreign journalists looked at their watches, the Russians were too busy—an emergency session of the Petrograd Soviet was opened with a report by Trotsky, who in the name of the Military Revolutionary Committee announced that the Provisional Government no longer existed. "They told us that an insurrection would drown the revolution in torrents of blood. . . . We do not know of a single casualty." There is no example in history of a revolutionary movement involving such gigantic masses being so bloodless. "The Winter Palace is not yet taken, but its fate will be settled in the course of the next few minutes." The following twelve hours were to show that this prediction was too optimistic.

Trotsky said: "Troops have been moved against Petrograd from the front; it is necessary at once to send commissars of the soviets to the front, and throughout the country, to make known that the revolution has occurred." Voices from the small right sector: "You are anticipating the will of the Congress of Soviets." The speaker answered: "The will of the Congress has been anticipated by the colossal fact of an insurrection of the Petrograd workers and soldiers. It now remains only to develop our victory."

Lenin, who appeared here publicly for the first time after emerging from underground, briefly outlined the program of the revolution: To break up the old governmental apparatus; to create a new system of administration through the soviets; to take measures for the immediate cessation of war, relying upon revolutionary movements in other countries; to abolish the landlords' property rights and thus win the confidence of the peasants; to establish workers' control over production. "The third Russian revolution," he said, "must in the end lead to the victory of socialism."

Chapter VIII

THE CAPTURE OF THE WINTER PALACE

Kerensky was in a great state of excitement when he met Stankevich arriving with his report from the front. He had just returned from a meeting of the Council of the Republic where the insurrection of the Bolsheviks had been conclusively exposed.—Insurrection! Don't you know that we have an armed insurrection?—Stankevich laughed: Why the streets are perfectly quiet; surely that isn't the way a real insurrection ought to look? But anyway we must put an end to these everlasting disturbances.—To this Kerensky heartily agreed; he was only waiting for the resolution of the Pre-Parliament.

At nine in the evening the government assembled in the Malachite Chamber of the Winter Palace to work out methods for a "resolute and final liquidation" of the Bolsheviks. Stankevich, returning from the Mariinsky palace, where he had been sent to hurry things up, reported with indignation the passing of the resolution of semi-non-confidence. Even the struggle against insurrection the resolution of the Pre-Parliament proposed to entrust not to the government, but to a special committee of public safety. Kerensky hotly announced that under those circumstances "he would not remain a minute longer at the head of the government." The compromise leaders were immediately summoned to the palace by telephone. The possibility of Kerensky's resignation surprised them no less than their resolution had surprised Kerensky. Avksentiev presented their excuses: they had, you know, regarded the resolution "as purely theoretical and accidental, and had not believed it would lead to practical steps." Moreover they now themselves saw that the resolution was "perhaps not quite happily worded." Those people never missed an opportunity to show what they were worth.

This nocturnal conversation of the democratic leaders with the head of the State seems absolutely unbelievable on the background of the developing insurrection. Dan, one of the chief grave-diggers of the February régime, demanded that the government immediately, by night, plaster the town with posters announcing that it had proposed immediate peace negotiations to the Allies. Kerensky reported that the government had no need of such counsels. It is quite possible to believe that the government would have preferred a sharp division; but Dan could not offer that. Kerensky, of course, was attempting to throw the responsibility for the insurrection upon his interlocutors. Dan answered that the government was exaggerating events under the influence of its "reactionary staff." At any rate there was no need of resigning: the disagreeable resolution had been necessary in order to break the mood of the masses. The Bolsheviks will be compelled "not later than tomorrow" to dissolve their headquarters, if the government follows Dan's suggestion. "At that very moment," adds Kerensky with legitimate irony in describing this conversation, "the Red Guard was occupying the government buildings one after another."

This so weighty conference with his Left friends had hardly ended when Kerensky's friends from the Right appeared in the form of a delegation from the Council of the Cossack Troops. The officers pretended that the conduct of the three Cossack regiments in Petrograd depended upon their wills, and presented Kerensky with conditions diametrically opposite to those of Dan: no concessions to the Soviet; this time the settlement with the Bolsheviks must be carried through to the end, and not handled as in July when the Cossacks suffered in vain. Kerensky, himself desiring nothing better, promised everything they asked and apologized to his interlocutors for the fact that up to now owing to considerations of prudence he had not arrested Trotsky, the president of the Soviet of Deputies. The delegates departed, assuring him that the Cossacks would do their duty. An order was issued from headquarters to the Cossack regiment: "In the name of freedom, honor and the glory of the homeland, come to the help of the Central Executive Committee, the Provisional Government, and save Russia from ruin." That bigoted government which had so jealously defended its independence of the Central Executive Committee was compelled to hide humbly behind the Committee's back at a moment of danger. Beseeching commands were also sent to the military schools in Petrograd and the environs. The railroads were instructed "to dispatch echelons of troops coming toward Petrograd from the front ahead of all other trains, cutting off passenger traffic if necessary."

When the government dispersed at two o'clock in the morning, having done all it could, there remained with Kerensky in the palace only his vice-minister, the liberal Moscow merchant, Konovalov. The commander of the district, Polkovnikov, came to them with a proposal to organize with the help of the loyal soldiers an immediate expedition for the seizure of Smolny. Kerensky accepted this admirable plan without hesitation, but from the words of the commander it was absolutely impossible to make out upon just what forces he was counting. Only now did Kerensky realize, according to his own confession, that the reports of Polkovnikov during the last ten or twelve days about his complete preparedness for the struggle with the Bolsheviks were "based on absolutely nothing." As though Kerensky had no other sources for an appraisal of the political and military situation but the secretarial reports of a mediocre colonel whom he had placed—nobody knows why—at the head of the district. During the aggrieved meditations of the head of the government the commissar of the city government, Rogovsky, brought a series of communications: A number of ships from the Baltic Fleet have entered the Neva in fighting array; some of them have come as far as the Nikolaevsky Bridge and occupied it; detachments of the insurrectionaries are advancing on Dvortsovy Bridge. Rogovsky called Kerensky's special attention to the circumstance that "the Bolsheviks are carrying out their whole plan in complete order, meeting nowhere the slightest resistance on the part of the government troops." Just what troops were meant by the word "government" was not quite clear, in any case, from the man's report.

Kerensky and Konovalov rushed from the palace to headquarters: "We must not lose another minute," they cried. The impressive red building was brimful of officers. They had come here not on the business of their troops, but to hide from them. "Civilians unknown to anybody were also poking their noses in among this military crowd." A new report from Polkovnikov finally convinced Kerensky that it was impossible to rely upon the commander or his officers. The head of the government decided to gather around his own person "all those loyal to their duty." Remembering that he was the member of a party—as others remember only on their death beds about the church—Kerensky called up the Social Revolutionaries on the telephone and demanded that they send fighting companies immediately. Before this unexpected appeal to the armed forces of the party could give any results, however—supposing it could do so at all—it would inevitably, as Miliukov says, "repel from Kerensky all the Right Wing elements, who even without that were unfriendly enough." Kerensky's isolation, plainly enough exposed already in the Kornilov insurrection, assumed here a more fatal aspect. "The long hours of that night dragged torturingly," says Kerensky, repeating his autobiographic phrase.

Reinforcements arrived from nowhere. The Cossacks held sittings. Representatives of the regiments said that, generally speaking, they might come out—why not?—but for this it was necessary to have machine guns, armored cars, and above all infantry. Kerensky without a thought promised them armored cars which were getting ready to abandon him, and infantry of which he had none. In answer he was told that the regiments would soon decide all questions and "begin to saddle their horses." The fighting forces of the Social Revolutionaries gave no signs of life. Did they indeed still exist? Where in fact was the boundary between the real and the spectral? The officers assembled in headquarters adopted a "more and more challenging" attitude toward the commander-in-chief and head of the government. Kerensky even asserts that there was talk among the officers of arresting him. The headquarters building was, as before, unguarded. Official negotiations were carried on before outsiders in the intervals between excited private conversations. The mood of hopelessness and disintegration soaked through from headquarters into the Winter Palace. The junkers began to get nervous. The armored car crews became excited. There is no support below, there is no head above. In such circumstances can anything but destruction follow?

At five o'clock in the morning Kerensky summoned to headquarters the general director of the War Ministry, Manikovsky. At the Troitsky bridge General Manikovsky was stopped by patrols and taken to the barracks of the Pavlovsky regiment, but there after brief explanation he was set free. The general convinced them, we may assume, that his arrest might upset the whole administrative mechanism and entail damage to the soldiers at the front. At about the same time the automobile of Stankevich was stopped near the Winter Palace, but the regimental committee released him also. "These were insurrectionaries," relates Stankevich, "but they behaved very irresolutely. I telegraphed about it from my house to the Winter Palace, but received tranquilizing assurances that this had been a mistake." The real mistake was the release of Stankevich. In a few hours he will try, as we know, to get the telephone station away from the Bolsheviks.

Kerensky demanded from the headquarters in Moghiliev and from the staff of the northern front at Pskov the immediate dispatch of loyal regiments. Dukhonin assured him over the direct wire that all measures had been taken for the dispatch of troops to Petrograd, and that certain units ought already to be arriving. But the units were not arriving. The Cossacks were still "saddling their horses." The situation in the city was getting worse from hour to hour. When Kerensky and Konovalov returned to the palace to rest a little, a courier handed them an urgent communication: All the palace telephones were cut off; Dvortsovy bridge, under Kerensky's very windows, was occupied by pickets of sailors. The square in front of the Winter Palace remained deserted as before. "Of the Cossacks neither hide nor hair was to be seen." Kerensky again rushed over to headquarters, but here too he got uncomforting news. The junkers had received from the Bolsheviks a demand that they abandon the palace, and were greatly excited. The armored cars had broken order inopportunely exposing the "loss" of certain important units. There was still no news of the echelons from the front. The close approaches to the palace and headquarters were absolutely unguarded. If the Bolsheviks had not yet penetrated this far it was only through lack of information. The building, brimmed with officers since evening, had been rapidly vacated. Everyone was saving himself in his own way. A delegation from the junkers appeared. They were ready to do their duty in the future "only if there is hope of the arrival of some sort of reinforcements." But reinforcements were just exactly what was lacking.

Kerensky hastily summoned his ministers to headquarters. The majority of them had no automobiles. These important instruments of locomotion, which impart a new tempo to modern insurrection, had either been seized by the Bolsheviks or cut off from the ministers by cordons of insurrectionaries. Only Kishkin arrived, and some time later Maliantovich. What should the head of the government do? Go out at once to meet the echelons and bring them forward no matter what the obstacles might be. Nobody could think of anything else.

Kerensky ordered out his "magnificent open touring-car." But here a new factor entered into the chain of events, demonstrating the indestructible solidarity uniting the governments of the Entente in weal and woe. "In what manner I do not know, but the news of my departure had reached the Allied embassies." The representatives of Great Britain and the United States had immediately expressed the desire that with the head of the government in making his get-away from the capital, "there should go an automobile carrying the American flag." Kerensky himself thought the proposal excessive, and was even embarrassed, but accepted it as an expression of the solidarity of the Allies.

The American ambassador, David Francis, gives a different account—not so much like a Christmas story. According to him an automobile containing a Russian officer followed the American automobile to the embassy, and the officer demanded that they turn over the embassy automobile to Kerensky for a journey to the front. Taking counsel together, the officials of the embassy arrived at the conclusion that since the automobile had already been practically "seized"—which was not at all true—there was nothing left but to bow to the force of circumstance. The Russian officer—in spite, they say, of protests from the diplomatic gentlemen—refused to remove the

American flag. And no wonder: it was only that colorful bit which made the automobile inviolable. Francis approved the action of the embassy officials, but told them "to say nothing about it to anybody."

By juxtaposing these two testimonies, which intersect with the line of truth at different angles, a sufficiently clear picture can be made to emerge. It was not the Allies, of course, who imposed the automobile upon Kerensky, but he himself who requested it: but since diplomats are obliged to pay a certain homage to the hypocrisy of non-interference in domestic affairs, it was agreed that the automobile had been "seized," and that the embassy had "protested" against the misuse of the flag. After this delicate matter had been arranged, Kerensky took a seat in his own automobile; the American car followed as a reserve. "It is needless to say," says Kerensky further, "that the whole street—both the passers-by and the soldiers—immediately recognized me. I saluted as always, a little carelessly and with an easy smile." Incomparable picture! Carelessly and smiling—thus the February régime passed into the kingdom of shades. At the gates of the city everywhere stood pickets and patrols of armed workers. At sight of the madly flying automobile the Red Guards rushed into the highway, but did not venture to shoot. In general, shootings were still being avoided. Maybe, too, the little American flag held them back. The automobiles successfully rushed on.

And does this mean that there are no troops in Petrograd prepared to defend the Provisional Government? asked the astonished Maliantovich, who had up to that moment dwelt in the realm of the eternal truths of law. I know nothing, Konovalov answered, shrugging his shoulders. It's pretty bad, he added. And what are these troops that are on their way? insisted Maliantovich. A bicycle battalion, it seems. The minister sighed. There were 200,000 soldiers in Petrograd and in the environs. Things were going badly with the régime, if the head of the government had to fly off with an American flag at his back to meet a bicycle battalion.

The ministers would have sighed deeper if they had known that this third bicycle battalion sent from the front had stopped at Peredolskaia and telegraphed the Petrograd soviet to know for just what purpose it was being sent. The Military

Revolutionary Committee telegraphed the battalion a brotherly greeting and asked them to send their representatives immediately. The authorities sought and did not find the bicycle men, whose delegates arrived that same day in Smolny.

It had been proposed in the preliminary calculations to occupy the Winter Palace on the night of the 25th, at the same time with the other commanding high points of the capital. A special trio had been formed already as early as the 23rd to take the lead in seizing the palace, Podvoisky and Antonov being the central figures. The engineer Sadovsky, a man in military service, was included as a third, but soon fell away, being preoccupied with the affairs of the garrison. He was replaced by Chudnovsky, who had come with Trotsky in May from the concentration camp in Canada, and had spent three months at the front as a soldier. Lashevich also took an important part in the operations—an old Bolshevik who had done enough service in the army to become a non-commissioned officer. Three years later Sadovsky remembered how Podvoisky and Chudnovsky quarrelled furiously in his little room in Smolny over the map of Petrograd and the best form of action against the palace. It was finally decided to surround the region of the palace with an uninterrupted oval, the longer axis of which should be the quay of the Neva. On the river side the circle should be closed up by the Peter and Paul fortress, the *Aurora*, and other ships summoned from Kronstadt and the navy. In order to prevent or paralyze attempts to strike at the rear with Cossacks and junker detachments, it was decided to establish imposing flank defenses composed of revolutionary detachments.

The plan as a whole was too heavy and complicated for the problem it aimed to solve. The time allotted for preparation proved inadequate. Small incoordinations and omissions came to light at every step, as might be expected. In one place the direction was incorrectly indicated; in another the leader came late, having misread the instructions; in a third they had to wait for a rescuing armored car. To call out the military units, unite them with the Red Guards, occupy the fighting positions, make sure of communications among them all and with headquarters—all this demanded a good many hours more than had been imagined by the leaders quarrelling over their map of Petrograd.

When the Military Revolutionary Committee announced at about ten o'clock in the morning that the government was overthrown, the extent of this delay was not yet clear even to those in direct command of the operation. Podvoisky had promised the fall of the palace "not later than twelve o'clock." Up to that time everything had run so smoothly on the military side that nobody had any reason to question the hour. But at noon it turned out that the besieging force was still not filled out, the Kronstadters had not arrived, and that meanwhile the defense of the palace had been reinforced. This loss of time, as almost always happens, made new delays necessary. Under urgent pressure from the Committee the seizure of the palace was now set for three o'clock—and this time "conclusively." Counting on this new decision, the spokesman of the Military Revolutionary Committee expressed to the afternoon session of the Soviet the hope that the fall of the Winter Palace would be a matter of the next few minutes. But another hour passed and brought no decision. Podvoisky, himself in a state of white heat, asserted over the telephone that by six o'clock the palace would be taken no matter what it cost. His former confidence, however, was lacking. And indeed the hour of six did strike and the denouement had not begun. Beside themselves with the urgings of Smolny, Podvoisky and Antonov now refused to set any hour at all. That caused serious anxiety. Politically it was considered necessary that at the moment of the opening of the Congress the whole capital should be in the hands of the Military Revolutionary Committee. That was to simplify the task of dealing with the opposition at the Congress, placing them before an accomplished fact. Meanwhile the hour appointed for opening the Congress had arrived, had been postponed, and arrived again, and the Winter Palace was still holding out. Thus the siege of the palace, thanks to its delay, became for no less than twelve hours the central problem of the insurrection.

The main staff of the operation remained in Smolny, where Lashevich held the threads in his hands. The field headquarters was in the Peter and Paul fortress, where Blagonravov was the responsible man. There were three subordinate headquarters, one on the *Aurora*, another in the barracks of the Pavlovsky regiment, another in the barracks of the sailors. In the field of action the leaders were Podvoisky and Antonov—apparently without any clear order of priority.

In the quarters of the general staff a trio was also bending over the map: the commander of the district Colonel Polkovnikov, the chief of his staff General Bagratuni, and General Alexeiev, especially invited in as a high authority. Notwithstanding this so well qualified commanding staff the plans of the defense were incomparably less definite than those of the attack. It is true that the inexperienced marshals of the insurrection did not know how to concentrate their forces rapidly and deal a punctual blow. But the forces were there. The marshals of the defense had cloudy hopes in place of forces: maybe the Cossacks will make up their minds; maybe loyal units will be found in the neighboring garrison; maybe Kerensky will bring troops from the front. The feelings of Polkovnikov are known from his night telegrams to headquarters: he thought that the game was up. Alexeiev, still less inclined to optimism, soon abandoned the rotten ship.

Delegates from the military schools were brought into headquarters for the purpose of keeping in touch, and an attempt was made to raise their spirits with assurances that troops would soon arrive from Gatchina, Tzarskoe and the front. However they did not much believe in these misty promises, and a depressing rumor began to creep through the schools: "There is a panic in headquarters, nobody is doing anything." And it was so. Cossack officers coming to headquarters to propose that they seize the armored cars in the Mikailovsky Riding Academy found Polkovnikov sitting on the window-seat in a condition of complete prostration. Seize the riding academy? "Seize it. I have nobody. I can't do anything alone."

While this languid mobilization of the schools for the defense of the Winter Palace was going on, the ministers assembled at a meeting. The square before the palace and its adjacent streets were still free from insurrectionists. On the corner of Morskaia and Nevsky armed soldiers were holding up passing automobiles and ejecting their passengers. The crowd was making queries: "Are these soldiers of the government or the Military Revolutionary Committee?" The ministers had for this once the full benefit of their own unpopularity. Nobody was interested in them and hardly anybody recognized them on their way. They all assembled except Prokopovich who was accidentally arrested in a cab—and was, by the way, released again during the day.

The old servants still remained in the palace, having seen much and ceased to be surprised, although not yet cured of fright. Strictly trained, dressed in blue with red collars and gold braids, these relics of the old kept up an atmosphere of order and stability in the luxurious building. They alone perhaps on this alarming morning still gave the ministers an illusion of power.

Not before eleven o'clock in the morning, did the government finally decide to place one of its members at the head of the defense. General Iznikovsky had already refused this honor, offered to him by Kerensky at dawn. Another military man in the staff of the government, Admiral Verderevsky, was still less martially inclined. It thus fell to a civilian to captain the defense—the Minister of Public Charities, Kishkin. An order of the senate confirming his appointment was immediately drawn up and signed by all. Those people had plenty of time to occupy themselves with bureaucratic fandangles. Moreover it never occurred to any of them that Kishkin as a member of the Kadet Party was doubly hated by the soldiers both front and rear. Kishkin in turn selected as his assistants Palchinsky and Ruthenberg. An appointee of the capitalists and protector of lockouts, Palchinsky enjoyed the hatred of the workers. The engineer Ruthenberg was an aide-de-camp of Savinkov, and Savinkov even the all-embracing party of the Social Revolutionaries had expelled as a Kornilovist. Polkovnikov, under suspicion of treason, was discharged. In his place they appointed General Bagratuni who differed from him in nothing.

Although the city telephones of the Winter Palace and headquarters had been cut off, the palace remained in connection with the more important institutions by its own wire—particularly with the War Ministry which had a direct wire to headquarters. Evidently some of the city apparatus also had not been cut out in the hurry of the moment. In a military sense, however, the telephone connections gave nothing to the government, and in a moral sense they damaged rather than improved its situation for they robbed it of its illusions.

From morning on, the leaders of the defense kept demanding local reinforcements while awaiting reinforcements from the front. Certain people in the city tried to help them. A Doctor Feit who took an active part in this, a member of the Central Committee of the Social Revolutionary party, told some years later at a legal proceeding about the "astonishing lightning-like change in the mood of the military units." You would learn, he said, from the most reliable sources of the readiness of this or that regiment to come to the defense of the government, but as soon as you called the barracks directly on the telephone, one unit after another would flatly refuse. "The result is known to you," said the old Narodnik. "Nobody came out and the Winter Palace was captured." The fact of the matter is that no lightning-like changes in the garrison took place, but the remaining illusions of the governmental parties did crumble to the ground with lightning speed.

The armored cars upon which they were especially counting in the Winter Palace and headquarters, were divided into two groups: Bolsheviks and pacifists. None of them were in favor of the government. On the way to the Winter Palace a half-company of engineering junkers ran into two armored cars which they awaited with a feeling of hope and fear: Are they friends or enemies? It turned out that they were neutral, and had come into the street with the purpose of preventing conflicts between the two sides. Out of the six armored cars in the Winter Palace only one remained to guard the palace property; the other five departed. In proportion as the insurrection succeeded the number of Bolshevik armored cars increased, and the neutral army melted away. Such is the fate of pacifism in any serious struggle.

Noon is approaching. The vast square before the Winter Palace is vacant as before. The government has nobody to fill it with. The troops of the Committee do not occupy it, because they are absorbed in carrying out their too complicated plan. Military units, workers' detachments, armored cars, are still assembling for this wide encirclement. The palace district begins to look like a plague spot which is being encircled far away to avoid direct contact with the infection.

The court of the palace opening on the square is piled up with logs of wood like the court of Smolny. Black three-inch field guns are set up to left and right. Rifles are stacked up in several different places. The small guard of the palace clings close to the building. In the court and the first story, two schools of ensigns from Oranienbaum and Peterhoff are quartered—not the whole schools by any means—and a squad from the Constantinovsky Artillery School with six cannon.

During the afternoon a battalion of junkers from the engineering school arrived, having lost half a company on the road. The picture presented when they arrived could in no wise have increased the fighting spirit of the junkers which, according to Stankevich, was inadequate even before. Inside the palace they found a lack of provisions. Even of this nobody had thought in time. A truckload of bread had been seized, it turned out, by patrols of the Committee. Some of the junkers did sentry duty; the rest lay around inactive, uncertain and hungry. No leadership whatever made itself felt. In the square before the palace, and on the quay on the other side, little groups of apparently peaceful passers-by began to appear, and they would snatch the rifles from the junker sentries, threatening them with revolvers.

"Agitators" also began to appear among the junkers. Had they gotten in from the outside? No, these were still evidently internal troublemakers. They succeeded in starting a ferment among the Oranienbaum and Peterhoff students. The committees of the school called a conference in the White Hall, and demanded that representatives of the government come in and make an explanation. All the ministers came in, with Konovalov at their head. The argument lasted a whole hour. Konovalov was heckled and stopped talking. The Minister of Agriculture, Maslov, made a speech as an old revolutionist. Kishkin explained to the junkers that the government had decided to stand firm as long as possible. According to Stankevich one of the junkers was about to express his readiness to die for the government, but "the obvious coolness of the rest of his comrades held him back." The speech of the other ministers produced actual irritation among the junkers, who interrupted, shouted and even, it seems, whistled. The blue-bloods explained the conduct of the majority of the junkers by their low social origin: "They were all from the plow, half-illiterate, ignorant beasts, cattle . . ."

The meeting in the besieged palace ended nevertheless in conciliation. The junkers, after they had been promised active leadership and correct information about what was happening, agreed to stay. The chief of the engineering school, appointed commander of the defense, ran his pencil over the plan of the palace, writing in the names of the units. The forces on hand were distributed in fighting positions. The majority of the junkers were stationed on the first floor where they could train their guns on Winter Palace Square through the windows. But they were forbidden to fire first. A battalion of the Engineering School was brought out into the court-yard to cover the artillery. Squads were appointed for barricade work. A communication squad was formed with four men from each unit. The artillery squad was directed to defend the gate in case of a breach. Fortifications of firewood were laid up in the court and before the gates. Something like order was established. The sentries felt more confident.

A civil war in its first steps, before real armies have been formed and before they are tempered, is a war of naked nerves. As soon as a little activity developed on the side of the junkers—their clearing of the square with gun fire from behind the barricades—the forces and equipment of the defense were enormously overestimated in the attacking camp. In spite of the dissatisfaction of the Red Guard and the soldiers, the leaders now decided to postpone the assault until they had concentrated their reserves; they were chiefly awaiting the arrival of the sailors from Kronstadt.

The delay of a few hours thus created brought some small reinforcements to the besieged. After Kerensky's promise of infantry to the Cossack delegation the Council of the Cossack Troops had gone into session, the regimental committees had gone into session, and the general assembly of the regiments had gone into session. Decision: Two squadrons and the machine gun crew of the Uralsky regiment, brought in from the front in July to crush the Bolsheviks, should immediately enter the Winter Palace, the rest not until the promise was actually fulfilled—that is, not until after the arrival of infantry reinforcements. But even with the two squadrons this was not accomplished without argument. The Cossack youth objected. The "old men" even had to lock the young ones up in the stable, where they could not hinder them from equipping themselves for the march. Only at twilight, when they were no longer expected, did these bearded Uraltsi appear in the palace. They were met like saviors. They themselves, however, looked sulky. They were not accustomed to fight about palaces. Yes, and it was not quite clear which side was right.

Sometime later there arrived unexpectedly forty of the Cavaliers of St. George under command of a staff captain on a cork leg. Patriotic cripples acting as the last reserves of democracy. . . . But even so they felt better. Soon came also a shock company of the Women's Battalion. What encouraged them most of all was that these reinforcements had made their way through without fighting. The cordon of the besieging forces could not, or did not dare, deny them access to the palace. Quite obviously, therefore, the enemy was weak. "Glory be to God, the thing is beginning to pull itself together," said the officers, comforting themselves and the junkers. The new arrivals received their military allotments, replacing those who were tired. However, the Uraltsi glanced with no great approval upon those "wenches" with rifles. Where is the real infantry?

The besiegers were obviously losing time. The Kronstadters were late—not, to be sure, through their own fault. They had been summoned too late. After a tense night of preparation they had begun to embark at dawn. The destroyer *Amur* and the cruiser *Yastreb* had made straight for Petrograd. The old armored cruiser *Zaria Svobodi*, after landing marines at Oranienbaum, where it was proposed to disarm the junkers, was to anchor at the entrance to the Morskoy Canal, in order in case of need to bombard the Baltic railroad. Five thousand sailors and soldiers disembarked early in the morning from the Island of Kotlin in order to embark on the social revolution. In the officers' cabin a solemn silence reigns. These officers are being taken along to fight for a cause which they hate. The commissar of the detachment, the Bolshevik, Flerovsky, announces to them: "We do not count upon your sympathy, but we demand that you be at your posts. . . . We will spare you any unnecessary unpleasantness." He received the brief naval answer: "Aye, aye, sir!" All took their places. The commander ascended the bridge.

Upon arriving in the Neva a triumphal hurrah: the sailors are greeting their own. A band strikes up on the *Aurora,* anchored in midstream. Antonov addresses the new arrivals with a brief greeting: "There is the Winter Palace. . . . We must take it." In the Kronstadt detachment the most resolute and bold choose themselves out automatically. These sailors in black blouses with rifles and cartridge belts will go all the way. The disembarkation on Konnogvardeisky Boulevard takes but a few moments. Only a military watch remains on the ship.

The forces are now more than adequate on the Nevsky. There are strong outposts on the bridge of the Ekaterininsky Canal and on the bridge of the Moika armored automobiles and Zenith guns aimed at the Winter Palace. On this side of the Moika the workers have set up machine guns behind screens. An armored car is on duty on Morskaia. The Neva and its crossings are in the hands of the attackers. Chudnovsky and ensign Dashkevich are ordered to send troops from the Guard regiments to hold Mars Field. Blagonravov from the fortress, after crossing the bridge, is to get into contact with the troops on Mars Field. The sailors just arrived are to keep in contact with the fortress and the crew of the *Aurora.* After artillery fire the storm is to begin.

At the same time five ships of war arrive from the Baltic battle fleet: a cruiser, two destroyers, and two smaller vessels. "However sure we may have been of winning with the forces on hand," writes Flerovsky, "this gift from the navy raised everybody's spirits." Admiral Verderovsky, looking from the windows of the Malachite Hall, could probably see an imposing mutinous flotilla, dominating not only the palace and the surrounding district but also the principal approaches to Petrograd.

About four o'clock in the afternoon Konovalov summoned to the palace by telephone the political leaders standing close to the government. The besieged ministers had need at least of moral support. Of all those invited only Nabokov appeared. The rest preferred to express their sympathy by telephone. Minister Tretiakov complained against Kerensky and against fate: The head of the ministry has fled leaving his colleagues without defense. But perhaps reinforcements will come? Perhaps. However, why aren't they here? Nabokov expressed his sympathy, glancing stealthily at his watch, and hastened to take his farewell. He got out just in time. Shortly after six the Winter Palace was at last solidly surrounded by the troops of the Military Revolutionary Committee. There was no longer any passage either for reinforcements or for individuals.

From the direction of Konnogvardeisky Boulevard, the Admiralty Quay, Morskaia Street, Nevsky Prospect, Mars Field, Milliony Street and Dvortsovy Quay, the oval of the besiegers thickened and contracted. Imposing cordons extended from the iron fences of the Winter Palace garden, still in the hands of the besieged, from the arch between Palace Square and Morskaia Street, from the canal by the Hermitage, from the corners of the Admiralty, and the Nevsky nearby the palace. Peter and Paul fortress frowned threateningly from the other side of the river. The *Aurora* looked in from the Neva with her six-inch guns. Destroyers steamed back and forth patrolling the river. The insurrection looked at that moment like a military maneuver in the grand style.

On Palace Square, cleared by the junkers three hours before, armored automobiles now appeared and occupied the entrances and exits. Their old patriotic names were still visible on the armor under the new designations painted hastily in red. Under the protection of these steel monsters the attackers felt more and more confident on the square. One of the armored cars approached the main entrance of the palace, disarmed the junkers guarding it, and withdrew unhindered.

In spite of the complete blockade now at last established, the besieged still kept in touch with the outside world by telephone. To be sure, as early as five o'clock a company of the Keksgolmsky regiment had already occupied the War Ministry, through which the Winter Palace had kept in touch with headquarters. But even after that an officer still remained apparently for some hours at the apparatus of the southwestern front, located in an attic chamber of the ministry where the captors never thought of looking. However, as before, this contact was of no help. The answers from the northern front had become more and more evasive. The reinforcements had not turned up. The mysterious bicycle battalion never arrived. Kerensky himself seemed to have disappeared like a diver. The city friends confined themselves to briefer and briefer expressions of sympathy. The ministers were sick at heart. There was nothing to talk about, nothing to hope for. The ministers disagreed with each other and with themselves. Some sat still in a kind of stupor, others automatically paced up and down the floor. Those inclined to generalization looked back into the past, seeking a culprit. He was not hard to find: the democracy! It was the democracy which had sent them into the government, laid a mighty burden on them, and at the moment of danger left them without support. For this once the Kadets were fully at one with the socialists. Yes, the democracy was to blame! To be sure, in forming the Coalition both groups had turned their back on an institution as near to them as the Democratic Conference. Independence of the democracy had indeed been the chief idea of the Coalition. But never mind: what does a democracy exist for, if not to rescue a bourgeois government when it gets into trouble? The Minister of Agriculture Maslov, a Right Social Revolutionary, made a note which he himself described as a dying utterance. He solemnly promised to die with a curse to the democracy upon his lips. His colleagues hastened to communicate this fateful intention to the Duma by telephone. His death, to be sure, remained only a project, but there was no lack of curses right on hand.

Up above near the chambers of the commandant there was a dining room where the court servants served the officer gentlemen a "divine dinner and wine." One could forget unpleasantnesses for a time. The officers figured out seniorities, made envious comparisons, and cursed the new power for its slow promotions. They gave it to Kerensky especially: yesterday at the Pre-Parliament he was vowing to die at his post, and today he beats it out of town dressed up as a sister of mercy. Certain of the officers demonstrated to the members of the government the folly of any further resistance. The energetic Palchinsky declared such officers Bolsheviks, and tried even to arrest them.

The junkers wanted to know what was going to happen next, and demanded from the government explanations which it was not in a position to give. During this new conference between the junkers and the ministers, Kishkin arrived from staff headquarters, bringing an ultimatum signed by Antonov and delivered from the Peter and Paul fortress to the Quartermaster-General, Poravelov, by a bicycle man: Surrender and disarm the garrison of the Winter Palace; otherwise fire will be opened from the guns of the fortress and the ships of war; twenty minutes for reflection. This period had seemed small. Poravelov had managed to extract another ten minutes. The military members of the government, Manikovsky and Verderevsky, approached the matter simply. Since it is impossible to fight, they said, we must think of surrendering—that is, accept the ultimatum. But the civilian ministers remained obstinate. In the end they decided to make no answer to the ultimatum, and to appeal to the city duma as the only legal body existing in the capital. This appeal to the duma was the last attempt to wake up the drowsy conscience of the democracy.

Poradelov, considering it necessary to end the resistance, asked for his discharge: he lacked "confidence in the correctness of the course chosen by the Provisional Government." The hesitations of the officer were put an end to before his resignation could be accepted. In about half an hour a detachment of Red Guards, sailors and soldiers, commanded by an ensign of the Pavlovsky regiment, occupied the staff headquarters without resistance, and arrested the faint-hearted Quartermaster General. This seizure of the headquarters might have been carried out some time before since the building was completely undefended from within. But until the arrival of armored cars on the Square, the besiegers feared a sortie of junkers from the palace which might cut them off.

After the loss of headquarters the Winter Palace felt still more orphaned. From the Malachite Room, whose windows opened on the Neva, and seemed, as it were, to invite a few shells from the *Aurora*, the ministers removed themselves to one of the innumerable apartments of the palace with windows on the court. The lights were put out. Only one lonely lamp burned on the table, its light shut off from the windows by newspapers.

What will happen to the palace if the *Aurora* opens fire?

asked the ministers of their naval colleague. It will be a pile of ruins, exclaimed the admiral readily, and not without a feeling of pride in his naval artillery. Verderevsky preferred a surrender, and was not unwilling to frighten these civilians out of their untimely bravery. But the *Aurora* did not shoot. The fortress also remained silent. Maybe the Bolsheviks after all will not dare carry out their threat?

General Bagratuni, appointed in place of the insufficiently steadfast Polkovnikov, considered this the appropriate moment to announce that he refused any longer to occupy the post of commander of the district. At Kishkin's order the general was demoted "as unworthy," and was requested immediately to leave the palace. On emerging from the gates the former commander fell into the hands of the sailors, who took him to the barracks of the Baltic crew. It might have gone badly with the general, but that Podvoisky, making the rounds of his front before the final attack, took the unhappy warrior under his wing.

From the adjacent streets and quays many noticed how the palace which had just been glimmering with hundreds of electric lights was suddenly drowned in darkness. Among these observers were friends of the government. One of the colleagues of Kerensky, Redemeister, has written: "The darkness in which the palace was drowned presented an alarming enigma." The friends did not take any measures toward solving this enigma. We must confess, however, that the possibilities were not great.

Hiding behind their piles of firewood the junkers followed tensely the cordon forming on Palace Square, meeting every movement of the enemy with rifle and machine gun fire. They were answered in kind. Towards night the firing became hotter. The first casualties occurred. The victims, however, were only a few individuals. On the square, on the quays, on Millionу, the besiegers accommodated themselves to the situation, hid behind projections, concealed themselves in hollows, clung along the walls. Among the reserves the soldiers and Red Guards warmed themselves around campfires which they had kindled at nightfall, abusing the leaders for going so slow.

In the palace the junkers were taking up positions in the corridors, on the stairway, at the entrances, and in the court.

The outside sentries clung along the fence and walls. The building would hold thousands, but it held hundreds. The vast quarters behind the sphere of defense seemed dead. Most of the servants had scattered, or were hiding. Many of the officers took refuge in the buffet, where they compelled those servants who had not yet made their getaway to set out continual batteries of wines. This drunken debauch of the officers in the agonizing palace could not remain a secret to the junkers, Cossacks, cripples and women soldiers. The denouement was preparing not only from without but from within.

An officer of the artillery squad suddenly reported to the commandant of the defense: The junkers have left their weapons in the entrance and are going home, in obedience to orders received from the commandant of the Constantinovsky school. That was a treacherous blow! The commandant tried to object: nobody but he could give orders here. The junkers understood this, but nevertheless preferred to obey the commandant of the school, who in his turn was acting under pressure from the commissar of the Military Revolutionary Committee. A majority of the artillery men, with four of the six guns, abandoned the palace. Held up on the Nevsky by a soldier patrol, they attempted to resist, but a patrol of the Pavlovsky regiment, arriving just in time with an armored car, disarmed them and sent them to its barracks with two of the guns. The other two were set up on the Nevsky and the bridge over the Moika and aimed at the Winter Palace.

The two squadrons of the Uraltsi were waiting in vain for the arrival of their comrades. Savinkov, who was closely associated with the Council of the Cossack Troops, and had even been sent by it as a delegate to the Pre-Parliament, attempted with the coöperation of General Alexeiev to get the Cossacks in motion. But the chiefs of the Cossack Council, as Miliukov justly observes "could as little control the Cossack regiment as the staff could the troops of the garrison." Having considered the question from all sides, the Cossack regiment finally announced that they would not come out without infantry, and offered their services to the Military Revolutionary Committee for the purpose of guarding the government property. At the same time the Uralsky regiment decided to send delegates to the Winter Palace to call its two squadrons back to the barracks. This suggestion fell in admirably with the now quite well-defined mood of the Uralsky's "old men." There was nobody but strangers around: junkers—among them a number of Jews—invalid officers—yes, and then these female shock troops. With angry and frowning faces the Cossacks gathered up their saddle bags. No further arguments could move them. Who remained to defend Kerensky? "Yids and wenches . . . but the Russian people has stayed over there with Lenin." It turned out that the Cossacks were in touch with the besiegers, and they got free passes through an exit till then unknown to the defenders. It was about nine o'clock in the evening when the Uraltsi left the palace. Only their machine guns they agreed to leave for the defense of a hopeless cause.

By this same entrance too, coming from the direction of Milliony Street, Bolsheviks had before this got into the palace for the purpose of demoralizing the enemy. Oftener and oftener mysterious figures began to appear in the corridors beside the junkers. It is useless to resist; the insurrectionists have captured the city and the railroad stations; there are no reinforcements; in the palace they "only keep on lying through inertia." . . . What are we to do next? asked the junkers. The government refused to issue any direct commands. The ministers themselves would stand by their old decision; the rest could do as they pleased. That meant free egress from the palace for those who wanted it. The government had neither will nor idea left; the ministers passively awaited their fate. Maliantovich subsequently related: "We wandered through the gigantic mousetrap, meeting occasionally, either all together or in small groups, for brief conversations—condemned people, lonely, abandoned by all. . . . Around us vacancy, within us vacancy, and in this grew up the soulless courage of placid indifference."

Antonov-Ovseënko had agreed with Blagonravov that after the encirclement of the palace was completed, a red lantern should be raised on the flagpole of the fortress. At this signal the *Aurora* would fire a blank volley in order to frighten the palace. In case the besieged were stubborn, the fortress should begin to bombard the palace with real shells from the light guns. If the palace did not surrender even then, the *Aurora* would open a real fire from its six-inch guns. The object of this gradation was to reduce to a minimum the victims and the damage, supposing they could not be altogether avoided. But the too complicated solution of a simple problem threatened to lead to an opposite result. The difficulty of carrying this plan out is too obvious. They are to start off with a red lantern. It turns out that they have none on hand. They lose time hunting for it, and finally find it. However, it is not so simple to tie a lantern to a flagpole in such a way that it will be visible in all directions. Efforts are renewed and twice renewed with a dubious result, and meanwhile the precious time is slipping away.

The chief difficulty developed, however, in connection with the artillery. According to a report made by Blagonravov the bombardment of the capital had been possible on a moment's notice ever since noon. In reality it was quite otherwise. Since there was no permanent artillery in the fortress, except for that rusty-muzzled cannon which announces the noon hour, it was necessary to lift field guns up to the fortress walls. That part of the program had actually been carried out by noon. But a difficulty arose about finding gunners. It had been known in advance that the artillery company—one of those which had not come out on the side of the Bolsheviks in July —was hardly to be relied on. Only the day before it had meekly guarded a bridge under orders from headquarters. A blow in the back was not to be expected from it, but the company had no intention of going through fire for the soviets. When the time came for action the ensign reported: The guns are rusty; there is no oil in the compressors; it is impossible to shoot. Very likely the guns really were not in shape, but that was not the essence of it. The artillerists were simply dodging the responsibility, and leading the inexperienced commissars by the nose. Antonov dashes up on a cutter in a state of fury. Who is sabotaging the plan? Blagonravov tells him about the lantern, about the oil, about the ensign. They both start to go up to the cannon. Night, darkness, puddles in the court from the recent rains. From the other side of the river comes hot rifle fire and the rattle of machine guns. In the darkness Blagonravov loses the road. Splashing through the puddles, burning with impatience, stumbling and falling in the mud, Antonov blunders after the commissar through the dark court.

"Beside one of the weakly glimmering lanterns," relates Blagonravov . . . "Antonov suddenly stopped and peered inquiringly at me over his spectacles, almost touching my face. I read in his eyes a hidden alarm." Antonov had for a second suspected treachery where there was only carelessness.

The position of the guns was finally found. The artillery men were stubborn: Rust . . . compressors . . . oil. Antonov gave orders to bring gunners from the naval polygon and also to fire a signal from the antique cannon which announced the noon hour. But the artillery men were suspiciously long monkeying with the signal cannon. They obviously felt that the commanders too, when not far-off at the telephone but right beside them, had no firm will to resort to heavy artillery. Even under the very clumsiness of this plan for artillery fire the same thought is to be felt lurking: Maybe we can get along without it.

Somebody is rushing through the darkness of the court. As he comes near he stumbles and falls in the mud, swears a little but not angrily, and then joyfully and in a choking voice cries out: "The palace has surrendered and our men are there." Rapturous embraces. How lucky there was a delay! "Just what we thought!" The compressors are immediately forgotten. But why haven't they stopped shooting on the other side of the river? Maybe some individual groups of junkers are stubborn about surrendering. Maybe there is a misunderstanding? The misunderstanding turned out to be good news: not the Winter Palace was captured, but only headquarters. The siege of the palace continued.

By secret agreement with a group of junkers of the Oranienbaum school the irrepressible Chudnovsky gets into the palace for negotiations: this opponent of the insurrection never misses a chance to dash into the firing line. Palchinsky arrests the daredevil, but under pressure from the Oranienbaum students is compelled to release both Chudnovsky and a number of the junkers. They take away with them a few of the Cavaliers of St. George. The unexpected appearance of these junkers on the square throws the cordons into confusion. But there is no end of joyful shouting, when the besiegers know that these are surrendering troops. However, only a small minority surrenders. The remainder continue to fire from behind their cover. The shooting of the attackers has increased. The bright electric light in the court makes a good mark of the junkers. With difficulty they succeed in putting out the light. Some unseen hand again switches on the light. The junkers shoot at the light, and then find the electrician and make him switch off the current.

The Women's Battalion suddenly announce their intention to make a sortie. According to their information the clerks in General Headquarters have gone over to Lenin, and after disarming some of the officers have arrested General Alexeiev—the sole man who can save Russia. He must be rescued at any cost. The commandant is powerless to restrain them from this hysterical undertaking. At the moment of their sortie the lights again suddenly flare up in the high electric lanterns on each side of the gate. Seeking an electrician the officer jumps furiously upon the palace servants: in these former lackeys of the tzar he sees agents of revolution. He puts still less trust in the court electrician: "I would have sent you to the next world long ago if I hadn't needed you." In spite of revolver threats, the electrician is powerless to help. His switch-board is disconnected. Sailors have occupied the electric station and are controlling the light. The women soldiers do not stand up under fire and the greater part of them surrender. The commandant of the defense sends a corporal to report to the government that the sortie of the Women's Battalion has "led to their destruction," and that the palace is swarming with agitators. The failure of the sortie causes a lull lasting approximately from ten to eleven. The besiegers are busied with the preparation of artillery fire.

The unexpected lull awakens some hopes in the besieged. The ministers again try to encourage their partisans in the city and throughout the country: "The government in full attendance, with the exception of Prokopovich, is at its post. The situation is considered favorable. . . . The palace is under fire, but only rifle fire and without results. It is clear that the enemy is weak." In reality the enemy is all-powerful but cannot make up his mind to use his power. The government sends out through the country communications about the ultimatum, about the *Aurora*, about how it, the government, can only transfer the power to the Constituent Assembly, and how the first assault on the Winter Palace has been repulsed. "Let the army and the people answer!" But just how they are to answer the ministers do not suggest.

Lashevich meantime has sent two sailor gunners to the fortress. To be sure, they are none too experienced, but they are at least Bolsheviks, and quite ready to shoot from rusty guns without oil in the compressors. That is all that is demanded of them. A noise of artillery is more important at the moment than a well-aimed blow. Antonov gives the order to begin. The gradations indicated in advance are completely followed out. "After a signal shot from the fortress," relates Flerovsky, "the *Aurora* thundered out. The boom and flash of blank fire are much bigger than from a loaded gun. The curious onlookers jumped back from the granite parapet of the quay, fell down and crawled away. . . ." Chudnovsky promptly raises the question: How about proposing to the besieged to surrender. Antonov as promptly agrees with him. Again an interruption. Some group of women and junkers are surrendering. Chudnovsky wants to leave them their arms, but Antonov revolts in time against this too beautiful magnanimity. Laying the rifles on the sidewalk the prisoners go out under convoy along Milliony Street.

The palace still holds out. It is time to have an end. The order is given. Firing begins—not frequent and still less effectual. Out of thirty-five shots fired in the course of an hour and a half or two hours, only two hit the mark, and they only injure the plaster. The other shells go high, fortunately not doing any damage in the city. Is lack of skill the real cause? They were shooting across the Neva with a direct aim at a target as impressive as the Winter Palace: that does not demand a great deal of artistry. Would it not be truer to assume that even Lashevich's artillerymen intentionally aimed high in the hope that things would be settled without destruction and death? It is very difficult now to hunt out any trace of the motive which guided the two nameless sailors. They themselves have spoken no word. Have they dissolved in the immeasurable Russian land, or, like so many of the October fighters, did they lay down their heads in the civil wars of the coming months and years?

Shortly after the first shots, Palchinsky brought the ministers a fragment of shell. Admiral Verderevsky recognized the shell as his own—from a naval gun, from the *Aurora*. But they were shooting blank from the cruiser. It had been thus agreed, was thus testified by Flerovsky, and thus reported to the Congress of Soviets later by a sailor. Was the admiral mistaken? Was the sailor mistaken? Who can ascertain the truth about a cannon shot fired in the thick of night from a mutinous ship at a tzar's palace where the last government of the possessing classes is going out like an oilless lamp?

The garrison of the palace was greatly reduced in number. If at the moment of the arrival of the Uraltsi, the cripples and the Women's Battalion, it rose to a thousand and a half, or perhaps even two thousand, it was now reduced to a thousand, and perhaps considerably less. Nothing can save the day now but a miracle. And suddenly into the despairing atmosphere of the Winter Palace there bursts—not, to be sure, a miracle, but the news of its approach. Palchinsky announces: "They have just telephoned from the city duma that the citizens are getting ready to march from there for the rescue of the government." "Tell everybody," he gives orders to Sinegub, "that the people are coming." The officer runs up and down stairs and through the corridors with the joyful news. On the way he stumbles upon some drunken officers fighting each other with rapiers—shedding no blood, however. The junkers lift up their heads. Passing from mouth to mouth the news becomes more colorful and impressive. The public men, the merchantry, the people, with the clergy at their head, are marching this way to free the beleaguered palace. The people with the clergy! "That will be strikingly beautiful!" A last remnant of energy flares up: "Hurrah! Long live Russia!" The Oranienbaum junkers, who by that time had quite decided to leave, changed their minds and stayed.

But the people with the clergy come very slowly. The number of agitators in the palace is growing. In a minute the *Aurora* will open fire. There is a whispering in the corridors. And this whisper passes from lip to lip. Suddenly two explosions. Sailors have got into the palace and either thrown or dropped from the gallery two hand grenades, lightly wounding two junkers. The sailors are arrested and the wounded bound up by Kishkin, a physician by profession.

The inner resolution of the workers and sailors is great, but it has not yet become bitter. Lest they call it down on their heads, the besieged, being the incomparably weaker side, dare not deal severely with these agents of the enemy who have penetrated the palace. There are no executions. Uninvited guests now begin to appear no longer one by one, but in groups. The palace is getting more and more like a sieve. When the junkers fall upon these intruders, the latter permit themselves to be disarmed. "What cowardly scoundrels!" says Palchinsky scornfully. No, these men were not cowardly. It required a high courage to make one's way into that palace crowded with officers and junkers. In the labyrinth of an unknown building, in dark corridors, among innumerable doors leading nobody knew where, and threatening nobody knew what, the daredevils had nothing to do but surrender. The number of captives grows. New groups break in. It is no longer quite clear who is surrendering to whom, who is disarming whom. The artillery continues to boom.

With the exception of the district immediately adjoining the Winter Palace, the life of the streets did not cease until late at night. The theaters and moving-picture houses were open. To the respectable and educated strata of the capital it was of no consequence apparently that their government was under fire. Redemeister on the Troitsky bridge saw quietly approaching pedestrians whom the sailors stopped. "There was nothing unusual to be seen." From acquaintances coming from the direction of the People's House Redemeister learned, to the tune of a cannonade, that Chaliapin had been incomparable in *Don Carlos*. The ministers continued to tramp the floors of their mousetrap.

"It is clear that the attackers are weak"; maybe if we hold out an extra hour reinforcements will still arrive. Late at night Kishkin summoned Assistant-Minister of Finance Khrushchev, also a Kadet, to the telephone, and asked him to tell the leaders of the party that the government needed at least a little bit of help in order to hold out until the morning hours, when Kerensky ought finally to arrive with the troops. "What kind of a party is this," shouts Kishkin indignantly, "that can't send us three hundred armed men!" And he is right. What kind of a party is it? These Kadets who had assembled tens of thousands of votes at the elections in Petrograd, could not put out three hundred fighters at the moment of mortal danger to the bourgeois régime. If the ministers had only thought to hunt up in the palace library the books of the materialist Hobbes, they could have read in his dialogues about civil war that there is no use expecting or demanding courage from store-keepers who have gotten rich, "since they see nothing but their own momentary advantage . . . and completely lose their heads at the mere thought of the possibility of being robbed." But after all Hobbes was hardly to be found in the tzar's library. The ministers, too, were hardly up to the philosophy of history. Kishkin's telephone call was the last ring from the Winter Palace.

Smolny was categorically demanding an end. We must not drag out the siege till morning, keep the city in a tension, rasp the nerves of the Congress, put a question-mark against the whole victory. Lenin sends angry notes. Call follows call from the Military Revolutionary Committee. Podvoisky talks back. It is possible to throw the masses against the palace. Plenty are eager to go. But how many victims will there be, and what will be left of the ministers and the junkers? However, the necessity of carrying the thing through is too imperious. Nothing remains but to make the naval artillery speak. A sailor from Peter and Paul takes a slip of paper to the *Aurora*. Open fire on the palace immediately. Now, it seems, all will be clear. The gunners on the *Aurora* are ready for business, but the leaders still lack resolution. There is a new attempt at evasion. "We decided to wait just another quarter of an hour," writes Flerovsky, "sensing by instinct the possibility of a change of circumstances." By "instinct" here it is necessary to understand a stubborn hope that the thing would be settled by mere demonstrative methods. And this time "instinct" did not deceive. Towards the end of that quarter of an hour a new courier arrived straight from the Winter Palace. The palace is taken!

The palace did not surrender but was taken by storm—this, however, at a moment when the power of resistance of the besieged had already completely evaporated. Hundreds of enemies broke into the corridor—not by the secret entrance this time but through the defended door—and they were taken by the demoralized defenders for the Duma deputation. Even so they were successfully disarmed. A considerable group of junkers got away in the confusion. The rest—at least a number of them—still continued to stand guard. But the barrier of bayonets and rifle fire between the attackers and defenders was finally broken down.

That part of the palace adjoining the Hermitage is already filled with the enemy. The junkers make an attempt to come at them from the rear. In the corridors phantasmagoric meetings and clashes take place. All are armed to the teeth. Lifted hands hold revolvers. Hand grenades hang from belts. But nobody shoots and nobody throws a grenade. For they and their enemy are so mixed together that they cannot drag themselves apart. Never mind: the fate of the palace is already decided.

Workers, sailors, soldiers are pushing up from outside in chains and groups, flinging the junkers from the barricades, bursting through the court, stumbling into the junkers on the staircase, crowding them back, toppling them over, driving them upstairs. Another wave comes on behind. The square pours into the court. The court pours into the palace, and floods up and down stairways and through corridors. On the befouled parquets, among mattresses and chunks of bread, people, rifles, hand grenades are wallowing. The conquerors find out that Kerensky is not there, and a momentary pang of disappointment interrupts their furious joy. Antonov and Chudnovsky are now in the palace. Where is the government? That is the door—there where the junkers stand frozen in the last pose of resistance. The head sentry rushes to the ministers with a question: Are we commanded to resist to the end? No, no, the ministers do not command that. After all, the palace is taken. There is no need of bloodshed. We must yield to force. The ministers desire to surrender with dignity, and sit at the table in imitation of a session of the government. The commandant has already surrendered the palace, negotiating for the lives of the junkers, against which in any case nobody had made the slightest attempt. As to the fate of the government, Antonov refuses to enter into any negotiations whatever.

The junkers at the last guarded doors were disarmed. The victors burst into the room of the ministers. "In front of the crowd and trying to hold back the onpressing ranks strode a rather small, unimpressive man. His clothes were in disorder, a wide-brimmed hat askew on his head, eyeglasses balanced uncertainly on his nose, but his little eyes gleamed with the joy of victory and spite against the conquered." In these annihilating strokes the conquered have described Antonov. It is not hard to believe that his clothes and his hat were in disorder: It is sufficient to remember the nocturnal journey through the puddles of the Peter and Paul fortress. The joy of victory might also doubtless have been read in his eyes; but hardly any spite against the conquered in those eyes. I announce to you, members of the Provisional Government, that you are under arrest—exclaimed Antonov in the name of the Military Revolutionary Committee. The clock then pointed to 2:10 in the morning of October 26.—The members of the Provisional Government submit to force and surrender in order to avoid bloodshed—answered Konovalov. The most important part of the ritual was thus observed.

Antonov summoned twenty-five armed men, choosing them from the first detachments to break into the palace, and turned over to them the defense of the ministry. After drawing up a minute of the proceeding, the arrestees were led out into the square. In the crowd, which had made its sacrifice of dead and wounded, there was in truth a flare up of spite against the conquered. "Death to them! Shoot them!" Individual soldiers tried to strike the ministers. The Red Guards quieted the intemperate ones: Do not stain the proletarian victory! Armed workers surrounded the prisoners and their convoy in a solid ring. "Forward!" They had not far to go—through Milliony and across the Troitsky bridge. But the excitement of the crowd made that short journey long and full of danger. Minister Nikitin wrote later very truly that but for the energetic intercession of Antonov the consequences might have been "very serious." To conclude their misadventure, the procession while on the bridge was fired on by accident, and the arrestees and their convoy had to lie down on the pavement. But here too nobody was injured. Somebody was evidently shooting in the air as a warning.

In the narrow quarters of the garrison club of the fortress, lighted with a smoky kerosene lamp because the electricity had refused to function that day, forty or fifty men are crowded. Antonov, in the presence of the commissar of the fortress, calls the roll of the ministers. There are eighteen of them, including the highest assistants. The last formalities are concluded; the prisoners are distributed in the rooms of the historic Trubetskoy Bastion. None of the defenders had been arrested: the officers and junkers were paroled on their word of honor that they would not take any action against the soviet power. Only a few of them kept their word.

Immediately after the capture of the Winter Palace rumors went round in bourgeois circles about the execution of junkers, the raping of the Women's Battalion, the looting of the riches of the palace. All these fables had long ago been refuted when Miliukov wrote this in his History: "Those of the Women's Battalion who had not died under fire were seized by the Bolsheviks, subjected during that evening and night to the frightful attentions of the soldiers, to violence and execution." As a matter of fact there were no shootings and, the mood of both sides being what it was at that period, there could not have been any shootings. Still less thinkable were acts of violence, especially within the palace where alongside of various accidental elements from the streets, hundreds of revolutionary workers came in with rifles in their hands.

Attempts at looting were actually made, but it was just these attempts which revealed the discipline of the victors. John Reed, who did not miss one of the dramatic episodes of the revolution, and who entered the palace on the heels of the first cordons, tells how in the basement stores a group of soldiers were prying drawers open with the butts of their guns and dragging out carpets, linen, china, glassware. It is possible that regular robbers were working in the disguise of soldiers, as they did invariably during the last years of the war, concealing their identity in trenchcoats and *papakhi*. The looting had just begun when somebody shouted: "Comrades, keep your hands off, that is the property of the people." A soldier sat down at a table by the entrance with pen and paper: two Red Guards with revolvers stood behind him. Everyone going out was searched, and every object stolen was taken back and listed. In this way they recovered little statues, bottles of ink, daggers, cakes of soap, ostrich feathers. The junkers were also subjected to a careful search, and their pockets turned out to be full of stolen bric-a-brac. The junkers were abused and threatened by the soldiers, but that was as far as it went. Meanwhile a palace guard was formed with the sailor Prikhodko at the head. Sentries were posted everywhere. The palace was cleared of outsiders. In a few hours Chudnovsky was appointed commandant of the Winter Palace.

But what had become of the people advancing with the clergy at their head to liberate the palace? It is necessary to tell about this heroic attempt, the news of which had for a moment so touched the hearts of the junkers. The city duma was the center of the anti-Bolshevik forces; its building on the Nevsky was boiling like a cauldron. Parties, factions, subfactions, groups, remnants and mere influential individuals were there discussing this criminal adventure of the Bolsheviks. From time to time they would call up the ministry languishing in the palace, and tell them that under the weight of universal condemnation the insurrection must inevitably expire. Hours were devoted to dissertations on the moral isolation of the Bolsheviks. Meanwhile the artillery began to speak. The minister Prokopovich, arrested in the morning but soon released, complained to the duma with a weeping voice that he had been deprived of the possibility of sharing the fate of his comrades. He aroused warm sympathy, but the expression of this sympathy used up time.

From the general confusion of ideas and speeches a practical plan is at last produced, and wins stormy applause from the whole meeting. The duma must march in a body to the Winter Palace in order to die there, if necessary, with the government. The Social Revolutionaries, Mensheviks and Cooperators are all alike seized with a willingness either to save the ministers or fall by their sides. The Kadets, not generally inclined to risky undertakings, this time decide to lay down their heads with the rest. Some provincials accidentally turning up in the hall, the duma journalists, and one man from the general public, request permission in more or less eloquent language to share the fate of the duma. The permission is granted.

The Bolshevik faction tries to offer a prosaic piece of advice: Why wander through the streets in the dark seeking death? Better call up the ministers and persuade them to surrender before blood is shed. But the democrats are indignant: These agents of insurrection want to tear from our hands not only the power, but our right to a heroic death. Meanwhile the members decided, in the interest of history, to take a vote by roll call. After all, one cannot die too late—even though the death be glorious. Sixty-two members of the duma ratify the decision: yes, they are actually going to die under the ruins of the Winter Palace. To this the fourteen Bolsheviks answer that it is better to conquer with Smolny than to die in the Winter Palace, and immediately set off for the meeting of the Soviet Congress. Only three Menshevik-Internationalists decide to remain within the walls of the duma: they have nowhere to go and nothing to die for.

The members of the duma are just on the point of setting out on their last journey when the telephone rings and news comes that the whole of the Executive Committee of the Peasants' Deputies is coming to join them. Unending applause. Now the picture is complete and clear: The representatives of one hundred million peasants, together with the representatives of all classes of the city population are going out to die at the hands of an insignificant gang of thugs. There is no lack of speeches and applause.

After the arrival of the Peasants' Deputies the column finally sets out along the Nevsky. At the head of the column march the burgomaster, Schreider, and the minister Prokopovich. Among the marchers John Reed noticed the Social Revolutionary, Avksentiev, president of the Peasant Executive Committee, and the Menshevik leaders, Khinchuk and Abramovich, the first of whom was considered Right, the second Left. Prokopovich and Schreider each carried a lantern: it had been so agreed by telephone with the ministers, in order that the junkers should not take friends for enemies. Prokopovich carried besides this an umbrella, as did many others. The clergy were not present. The clergy had been created out of misty fragments of the history of the fatherland by the none too opulent imagination of the junkers. But the people also were absent. Their absence determined the character of the whole scheme. Three or four hundred "representatives" and not one man of those whom they represented! "It was a dark night," remembers the Social Revolutionary, Zenzinov, "and the lights on the Nevsky were not burning. We marched in a regular procession and only our singing of the Marseillaise was to be heard. Cannon shots resounded in the distance. That was the Bolsheviks continuing to bombard the Winter Palace."

At the Ekaterininsky Canal a patrol of armed sailors was stretched out across the Nevsky, blocking the way for this column of the democracy. "We are going forward," declared the condemned, "What can you do to us?" The sailors answered frankly that they would use force: "Go home and leave us alone." Someone of the marchers suggested that they die right there on the spot. But in the decision adopted by a roll call vote in the duma this variant had not been foreseen. The minister Prokopovich clambered up on some sort of elevation and "waving his umbrella"—rains are frequent in the autumn in Petrograd—urged the demonstrators not to lead into temptation those dark and deceived people who might actually resort to arms. "Let us return to the duma and talk over methods of saving the country and the revolution."

This was truly a wise proposal. To be sure, the original plan would then remain unfulfilled. But what can you do with armed ruffians who will not permit the leaders of the democracy to die a heroic death? "They stood around for a while, got chilly and decided to go back," writes Stankevich mournfully. He too was a marcher in this procession. Without the Marseillaise now—on the contrary in a glum silence—the procession moved back along the Nevsky to the duma building. There at last it would surely find "methods of saving the country and the revolution."

With the capture of the Winter Palace the Military Revolutionary Committee came into full possession of the capital. But just as the nails and hair continue to grow on a corpse, so the overthrown government continued to show signs of life through its official press. The "Herald of the Provisional Government," which on the 24th had announced the retirement of the Privy Councillors with right to uniform and pension, had suddenly disappeared on the 25th—an event which, to be sure, nobody noticed. But on the 26th it appeared again as if nothing had happened. On the first page it carried a rubric: "In consequence of the shutting off of the electric current the issue of October 25 did not appear." In all other respects except only the electric current, the governmental life was going on in due order, and the "Herald" of a government now located in the Trubetskoy Bastion announced the appointment of a dozen new senators. In its column of "administrative information" a circular of the Minister of the Interior, Nikitin, advised the commissars of the provinces "not to be influenced by false rumors of events in Petrograd where all is tranquil." The minister was not after all so far wrong. The days of the revolution went by peacefully enough, but for the cannonading, whose effect was only acoustic. But just the same the historian will make no mistake if he says that on October 25th not only was the electric current shut off in the government printing-plant, but an important page was turned in the history of mankind.

Chapter IX

THE OCTOBER INSURRECTION

Physical analogies with revolution come so naturally that some of them have become worn-out metaphors: "Volcanic eruption," "birth of a new society," "boiling point." . . . Under the simple literary image there is concealed here an intuitive grasp of the laws of dialectic—that is, the logic of evolution.

Armed insurrection stands in the same relation to revolution that revolution as a whole does to evolution. It is the critical point when accumulating quantity turns with an explosion into quality. But insurrection itself again is not a homogeneous and indivisible act: it too has its critical points, its inner crises and accelerations.

An extraordinary importance both political and theoretical attaches to that short period immediately preceding the "boiling point"—the eve, that is, of the insurrection. Physics teaches that the steady increase of temperature suddenly comes to a stop; the liquid remains for a time at the same temperature, and boils only after absorbing an additional quantity of heat. Everyday language also comes to our aid here, designating this condition of pseudo-tranquil concentration preceding an explosion as "the lull before the storm."

When an unqualified majority of the workers and soldiers of Petrograd had come over to the Bolsheviks, the boiling temperature, it seemed, was reached. It was then that Lenin proclaimed the necessity of immediate insurrection. But it is striking to observe that something was still lacking to the insurrection. The workers, and especially the soldiers, had to absorb some additional revolutionary energy.

The contradiction between word and deed is unknown to

the masses, but the passing over from word to deed—even to a simple strike, and so much the more to insurrection—inevitably calls out inner frictions and molecular regroupings: some move forward, others have to crowd back. Civil war in general is distinguished in its first steps by an extraordinary indecisiveness. Both camps are as though stuck fast in the same national soil; they cannot break away from their own environment with its intermediate groupings and moods of compromise.

The lull before the storm in the lower ranks produced a sudden hesitation among the guiding groups. Those organs and institutions which had been formed in the comparatively tranquil period of preparation—for revolution has like war its peaceful period, its days of calm—proved even in the most tempered party inadequate, or at least not wholly adequate, to the tasks of insurrection. A certain reconstruction and shifting about is unavoidable at the critical moment. Far from all the delegates of the Petrograd Soviet who voted for a soviet government were really imbued with the idea that an armed insurrection had become the task of the day. In order to convert the Soviet into a machine of insurrection, it was necessary with as little disturbance as possible to bring them over to this new course. In the circumstances of a matured crisis this did not require months, or even many weeks. But just in those last days it was most dangerous to fall out of step, to give orders for a jump some days before the Soviet was ready to make it, to bring confusion into one's own ranks, to cut off the party from the Soviet even for 24 hours.

Lenin more than once repeated that the masses are far to the left of the party, just as the party is to the left of the Central Committee. Applied to the revolution as a whole this was perfectly true. But these correlations too have their deep inward oscillations. In April, in June, and especially at the beginning of July, the workers and soldiers were impatiently pushing the party along the path toward decisive action. After the July raids the masses became more cautious. They wanted a revolution as before, and more than before, but having badly burnt themselves once, they feared another failure. Throughout July, August and September, the party was daily holding back the workers and soldiers, whom the Kornilovists on their part were challenging into the streets with all their might.

The political experience of those last months had greatly developed the inhibitory centers not only of the leaders, but of the led. The unbroken success of the agitation had nourished in its turn the inertia of the time-biding attitude. A new political orientation was not enough for the masses: they had need of a psychological readjustment. An insurrection takes in broader masses, the more the commands of the revolutionary party fuse with the command of circumstances.

The difficult problem of passing from the political preparation to the actual technique of insurrection arose throughout the whole country in different forms, but in essence it was everywhere the same. Muralov tells how in the Moscow military organization of the Bolsheviks opinion as to the necessity of a seizure of power was unanimous; however "the attempt to decide concretely how this seizure should be carried out remained unresolved." The last connecting link was lacking.

During those days when Petrograd was full of the transfer of the garrison, Moscow was living in an atmosphere of continual strike conflicts. On the initiative of a factory committee the Bolshevik faction of the soviet put forward a plan to settle economic conflicts by means of decrees. The preparatory steps took a good deal of time. Only on the 23rd of October was "Revolutionary Decree No. 1" adopted by the soviet bodies. It provided that: Workers and clerks in factories and shops shall henceforth be employed and discharged only with the consent of the shop committees. This meant that the soviet had begun to function as a state power. The inevitable resistance of the government would, according to the design of the initiators, unite the masses more closely round the soviet and lead to an open conflict. This idea never came to the test because the revolution in Petrograd gave Moscow, together with all the rest of the country, a far more imperative motive for insurrection—the necessity of coming promptly to the support of the newly formed soviet government.

The attacking side is almost always interested in seeming on the defensive. A revolutionary party is interested in legal coverings. The coming Congress of Soviets, although in essence a Soviet of revolution, was nevertheless for the whole popular mass indubitably endowed, if not with the whole sovereignty, at least with a good half of it. It was a question of one of the elements of a dual power making an insurrection against the other. Appealing to the Congress as the source of authority, the Military Revolutionary Committee accused the government in advance of preparing an attempt against the soviets. This accusation flowed logically from the whole situation. Insofar as the government did not intend to capitulate without a fight it could not help getting ready to defend itself. But by this very fact it became liable to the accusation of conspiracy against the highest organ of the workers, soldiers and peasants. In its struggle against the Congress of Soviets which was to overthrow Kerensky, the government lifted its hand against that source of power from which Kerensky had issued.

It would be a serious mistake to regard all this as juridical hair-splitting of no interest to the people. On the contrary, it was in just this form that the fundamental facts of the revolution reflected themselves in the minds of the masses. It was necessary to make full use of this extraordinarily advantageous tie-up. In thus giving a great political goal to the natural disinclination of the soldier to pass from the barracks to the trenches, and in mobilizing the garrison for the defense of the Soviet Congress, the revolutionary leaders did not bind their hands in the slightest degree regarding the date of the insurrection. The choice of the day and hour depended upon the further course of the conflict. The freedom to maneuver belonged to the strongest.

"First conquer Kerensky and then call the Congress," Lenin kept repeating, fearing that insurrection would be replaced with constitutional by-play. Lenin had obviously not yet appreciated the new factor which had intruded into the preparation of the insurrection and changed its whole character, the sharp conflict between the Petrograd garrison and the government. If the Congress of Soviets was to decide the question of power; if the government wanted to dismember the garrison in order to prevent the Congress from becoming the power; if the garrison without awaiting the Congress of Soviets had refused to obey the government, why this meant that in essence the insurrection had begun, and begun without waiting for the Congress, although under cover of its authority. It would have been wrong politically, therefore, to separate the preparation of the insurrection from the preparation for the Congress of Soviets.

The peculiarities of the October revolution can best be understood by contrasting it with the February revolution. In making this comparison it is not necessary, as in other cases, to assume conditionally the identity of a whole series of circumstances. They are in reality identical. The scene is Petrograd in both cases: the same arena, the same social groupings, the same proletariat, and the same garrison. The victory in both cases was attained by the going over of a majority of the reserve regiments to the side of the workers. But within the framework of these fundamental traits what an enormous difference! The two Petrograd revolutions, historically completing each other in the course of eight months, seem in their contrasting traits almost predestined to promote an understanding of the nature of insurrection in general.

The February insurrection is called spontaneous. We have introduced in their due place all the necessary limitations to this description. But it is true in any case that in February nobody laid out the road in advance, nobody voted in the factories and barracks on the question of revolution, nobody summoned the masses from above to insurrection. The indignation accumulated for years broke to the surface unexpectedly, to a considerable degree, even to the masses themselves.

It was quite otherwise in October. For eight months the masses had been living an intense political life. They had not only been creating events, but learning to understand their connections. After each action they had critically weighed its results. Soviet parliamentarism had become the daily mechanics of the political life of the people. When they were deciding by a vote questions of strikes, of street manifestations, of the transfer of regiments to the front, could the masses forego an independent decision on the question of insurrection?

From this invaluable and sole substantial conquest of the February revolution there arose, however, new difficulties. It was impossible to summon the masses to battle in the name of the Soviet without raising the question formally in the Soviet—that is, without making the problem of insurrection a subject of public debate, and that too with the participation of representatives of the hostile camp. The necessity of creating a special, and to the extent possible a disguised, soviet organ for the leadership of the insurrection was obvious. But this too demanded democratic procedures, with all their advantages and all their delays. The resolution on the Military Revolutionary Committee adopted on the 9th of October was carried out only on the 20th. But that was not the chief difficulty. To take advantage of the majority in the Soviet and compose the Committee of Bolsheviks alone, would have provoked discontent among the non-party men, to say nothing of the Left Social Revolutionaries and certain groups of anarchists. The Bolsheviks in the Military Revolutionary Committee would submit to the decisions of their party—although not always without resistance—but it was impossible to demand discipline of the non-party men and the Left Social Revolutionaries. To get an *a priori* resolution on insurrection at a definite date from them was not to be thought of. And moreover it was extremely imprudent even to put the question to them. By means of the Military Revolutionary Committee, therefore, it was possible only to draw the masses into insurrection, sharpening the situation from day to day and making the conflict irrevocable.

Would it not have been simpler in that case to summon the insurrection directly in the name of the party? This form of action undoubtedly has weighty advantages. But its disadvantages are hardly less obvious. In those millions upon whom the party legitimately counted it is necessary to distinguish three layers: one which was already with the Bolsheviks on all conditions; another, more numerous, which supported the Bolsheviks insofar as they acted through the soviets; a third which followed the soviets in spite of the fact that they were dominated by Bolsheviks.

These three layers were different not only in political level, but to a considerable degree also in social ingredients. Those standing for the Bolsheviks as a party were above all industrial workers, with the hereditary proletarians of Petrograd in the front rank. Those standing for the Bolsheviks insofar as they had a legal soviet cover, were a majority of the soldiers. Those standing for the soviets, independently and regardless of the fact that an overplus of Bolsheviks dominated them, were the more conservative groups of workers—former Mensheviks and Social Revolutionaries, who dreaded to break away from the rest of the masses—the more conservative parts of the army even including the Cossacks, and the peasants who had freed themselves from the leadership of the Social Revolutionary party and were adhering to its left flank.

It would be an obvious mistake to identify the strength of the Bolshevik party with the strength of the soviets led by it. The latter was much greater than the former. However, without the former it would have been mere impotence. There is nothing mysterious in this. The relations between the party and the Soviet grew out of the disaccord inevitable in a revolutionary epoch between the colossal political influence of Bolshevism and its narrow organizational grasp. A lever correctly applied makes the human arm capable of lifting a weight many times exceeding its living force, but without the living arm the lever is nothing but a dead stick.

At a Moscow regional conference of the Bolsheviks at the end of September, one of the delegates reported: "In Yegorevsk the influence of the Bolsheviks is undivided. . . . But the party organization as such is weak. It is in complete neglect; there is neither regular registration nor membership dues." This disproportion between influence and organization, although not everywhere so marked, was a general phenomenon. Broad masses knew of the Bolshevik slogans and the soviet organization. The two fused completely in their minds in the course of September and October. What the people were waiting for was that the soviets should show them when and how to carry out the program of the Bolsheviks.

The party itself systematically educated the masses in this spirit. In Kiev, when the rumor went round that an insurrection was preparing, the Bolshevik Executive Committee immediately came out with a denial: "No action without the summons of the Soviet must take place. . . . Not a step without the Soviet!" In denying on the 18th of October the rumors of an insurrection alleged to have been appointed for the 22nd, Trotsky said: "The Soviet is an elective institution and . . . cannot make a decision which is unknown to the workers and soldiers. . . ." Repeated daily and reinforced by practical action, such formulæ entered into the flesh and blood of the masses.

According to the report of ensign Berzin, at an October

military conference of the Bolsheviks in Moscow the delegates were saying: "It is hard to know whether the troops will come out at the summons of the Moscow committee of the Bolsheviks. At the summons of the Soviet they might all come out." Nevertheless even in September the Moscow garrison had voted 90 per cent Bolshevik. At a conference of October 16th in Petrograd, Boky made this report in the name of the party committee: In the Moscow district "they will come out at the summons of the Soviet, but not of the party"; in the Nevsky district "all will follow the Soviet." Volodarsky thereupon summarized the state of mind in Petrograd in the following words: "The general impression is that nobody is eager to go into the streets, but all will appear at the call of the Soviet." Olga Ravich corrected him: "Some say also at the call of the party." At a Petrograd Garrison Conference on the 18th, delegates reported that their regiments were awaiting the summons of the Soviet to come out. Nobody mentioned the party, notwithstanding that the Bolsheviks stood at the head of many units. Thus unity in the barracks could be preserved only by uniting the sympathetic, the wavering, and the semi-hostile under the discipline of the Soviet. The grenadier regiment even declared that it would come out only at the command of the Congress of Soviets. The very fact that agitators and organizers in estimating the state of mind of the masses always alluded to the distinction between the Soviet and the party, shows what great significance this question had from the standpoint of the summons to insurrection.

The chauffeur Mitrevich tells how in a squad of motor-trucks, where they did not succeed in carrying a resolution in favor of insurrection, the Bolsheviks put through a compromise proposal: "We will not come out either for the Bolsheviks or the Mensheviks, but . . . we will carry out without delay all the demands of the Second Congress of Soviets." These Bolsheviks were applying on a small scale to the motor-truck squad the same enveloping tactics which were being applied at large by the Military Revolutionary Committee. Mitrevich is not arguing but telling a story—the more convincing his testimony!

Attempts to lead the insurrection directly through the party nowhere produced results. A highly interesting piece of testimony is preserved regarding the preparation of the uprising in Kineshma, a considerable center of the textile industry. After insurrection in the Moscow region had been placed on the order of the day, the party committee in Kineshma elected a special trio to take an inventory of the military forces and supplies, and prepare for armed insurrection—calling them for some reason "the Directory." "We must say, however," writes one of the members of this directory, "that little appears to have been done by the elected trio. Events took a somewhat different course. . . . The regional strike wholly took possession of us, and when the decisive events came, the organizational center was transferred to the strike committee and the soviet." On the modest provincial scale the same thing was repeated here which occurred in Petrograd.

The party set the soviets in motion, the soviets set in motion the workers, soldiers, and to some extent the peasantry. What was gained in mass was lost in speed. If you represent this conducting apparatus as a system of cog-wheels—a comparison to which Lenin had recourse at another period on another theme—you may say that the impatient attempt to connect the party wheel directly with the gigantic wheel of the masses —omitting the medium-sized wheel of the soviets—would have given rise to the danger of breaking the teeth of the party wheel, and nevertheless not setting sufficiently large masses in motion.

The opposite danger was, however, no less real—the danger of letting slip a favorable situation as a result of inner frictions in the soviet system. Speaking theoretically, the most favorable opportunity for an insurrection reduces itself to such and such a point in time. There can be no thought of practically lighting upon this ideal point. The insurrection may develop with success on the rising curve approaching this ideal culmination—but also on the descending curve, before the correlation of forces has yet radically changed. Instead of a "moment" we have then a section of time measured in weeks, and sometimes months. The Bolsheviks could have seized the power in Petrograd at the beginning of July. But if they had done so they could not have held it. Beginning with the middle of September they could hope not only to seize the power but also to keep hold of it. If the Bolsheviks had delayed the insurrection beyond the end of October they would probably—although far from surely—have still been able for a certain time to make up for the omission. We may assume conditionally that for a period of three or four months—September to December approximately—the political premises for a revolution were at hand. The thing had ripened but not yet fallen apart. Within these bounds, which are easier to establish after the fact than in the course of action, the party had a certain freedom of choice which gave rise to inevitable and sometimes sharp disagreements of a practical character.

Lenin proposed to raise the insurrection in the days of the Democratic Conference. At the end of September he considered any delay not only dangerous but fatal. "Waiting for the Congress of Soviets," he wrote at the beginning of October, "is a childish toying with formalities—a shameful toying with formalities, betrayal of the revolution." It is not likely, however, that anybody among the Bolshevik leaders was guided in this question by formal considerations. When Zinoviev, for example, demanded a preliminary conference with the Bolshevik faction of the Soviet Congress, he was not seeking a formal sanction, but simply counting on the political support of the provincial delegates against the Central Committee. But the fact is that the dependence of the party on the Soviet—which, in its turn, was appealing to the Congress of Soviets—introduced an element of indefiniteness into the insurrection which greatly and quite justly alarmed Lenin.

The question when to summon the insurrection, was closely bound up with the question who should summon it. The advantages of summoning it in the name of the Soviet were only too clear to Lenin, but he understood sooner than others what difficulties would arise along that road. He could not but fear, especially from a distance, that the hindering elements would prove still stronger in the soviet summits than in the Central Committee, whose policy even without that he considered irresolute. Lenin approached the question who should begin, the Soviet or the party, as a choice between two possible alternatives, but in the first weeks he was decidedly in favor of the independent initiative of the party. In this there was not the shadow of a thought of contrasting the two plans in principle. It was a question of two approaches to an insurrection resting upon one and the same basis, in one and the same situation, for one and the same goal. But nevertheless these were two different approaches.

Lenin's proposal to surround the Alexandrinka and arrest the Democratic Conference flowed from the assumption that the insurrection would be headed not by the soviets, but by the party appealing directly to the factories and barracks. It could not have been otherwise. To carry such a plan through by way of the Soviet was absolutely unthinkable. Lenin was clearly aware that even among the heads of the party his plan would meet resistance; he recommended in advance that they should "not strive after numbers," in the Bolshevik faction of the Conference. With determination up above, the numbers would be guaranteed by the lower ranks. Lenin's bold plan had the indubitable advantages of swiftness and unexpectedness, but it laid the party too bare, incurring the risk that within certain limits it would set itself over against the masses. Even the Petrograd Soviet, taken unawares, might at the first failure lose its still unstable Bolshevik majority.

The resolution of October 10th proposed to the local organizations of the party to decide all questions practically from the point of view of an approaching insurrection. There is not a word in the resolution of the Central Committee about the soviets as organs of the insurrection. At the conference of the 16th, Lenin said: "Facts show that we have the advantage over the enemy. Why cannot the Central Committee begin?" This question on Lenin's lips was by no means rhetorical. It meant: Why lose time accommodating ourselves to the complicated soviet transmission if the Central Committee can give the signal immediately. However, this time the resolution proposed by Lenin concluded with an expression of "confidence that the Central Committee and the Soviet will indicate in good season the favorable moment and expedient methods of action." The mention of the Soviet together with the party, and the more flexible formulation of the question of date, were the result of Lenin's having felt out through the party leaders the resistance of the masses.

The next day in his polemic with Zinoviev and Kamenev, Lenin summed up as follows the debates of the day before: "All agreed that at the summons of the soviets and for the defense of the soviets the workers will come out as one man." This meant: Even if not all are in agreement with him, Lenin, that you can issue the summons in the name of the party, all are agreed that you can do it in the name of the soviets.

"Who is to seize the power?" writes Lenin on the evening of the 24th. "That is now of no importance. Let the Military Revolutionary Committee take it, or 'some other institution,' which will declare that it will surrender the power only to the genuine representatives of the interests of the people." "Some other institution" enclosed in mysterious quotation-marks—that is a conspirative designation for the Central Committee of the Bolsheviks. Lenin here renews his September proposal that action be taken directly in the name of the Central Committee—this time in case soviet legality should hinder the Military Revolutionary Committee from placing the Congress before the accomplished fact of an overthrow.

Although this whole struggle about dates and methods of insurrection continued for a week, not all those who took part in it were clearly aware of its sense and significance. "Lenin proposed the seizure of power through the soviets whether in Leningrad or Moscow, and not behind the back of the soviets," wrote Stalin in 1924. "For what purpose did Trotsky require this more than strange legend about Lenin?" And again: "The party knows Lenin as the greatest Marxist of our times . . . strange to any tinge of Blanquism." Whereas Trotsky "gives us not the great Lenin, but some sort of a dwarf Blanquist. . . ." Not only a Blanquist but a dwarf! In reality the question in whose name to raise an insurrection, and in the hands of what institution to seize the power, is not in the least predetermined by any doctrine. When the general conditions for a revolution are at hand, insurrection becomes a practical problem of art, a problem which can be solved by various methods. This part of the disagreements in the Central Committee was analogous to the quarrel of the officers of a general staff educated in the same military doctrine and appraising alike the strategic situation, but proposing different ways of solving their most immediate—extraordinarily important, to be sure, but nevertheless particular—problem. To mix in here the question of Marxism and Blanquism is only to reveal a lack of understanding of both.

Professor Pokrovsky denies the very importance of the alternative: Soviet or party. Soldiers are no formalists, he laughs: they did not need a Congress of Soviets in order to overthrow Kerensky. With all its wit such a formulation leaves unexplained the problem: Why create soviets at all if the party is enough? "It is interesting," continues the professor, "that nothing at all came of this aspiration to do everything almost legally, with soviet legality, and the power at the last moment was taken not by the Soviet, but by an obviously 'illegal' organization created *ad hoc*." Pokrovsky here cites the fact that Trotsky was compelled "in the name of the Military Revolutionary Committee," and not the Soviet, to declare the government of Kerensky non-existent. A most unexpected conclusion! The Military Revolutionary Committee was an elected organ of the Soviet. The leading rôle of the Committee in the overturn did not in any sense violate that soviet legality which the professor makes fun of but of which the masses were extremely jealous. The Council of People's Commissars was also created *ad hoc*. But that did not prevent it from becoming and remaining an organ of the soviet power, including Pokrovsky himself in its staff as deputy People's Commissar of Education.

The insurrection was able to remain on the ground of soviet legality, and to a certain degree even within the limits of the tradition of the dual power, thanks mainly to the fact that the Petrograd garrison had almost wholly submitted to the Soviet before the revolution. In numberless memoirs, anniversary articles and early historic essays, this fact, confirmed by manifold documents, was taken as indubitable. "The conflict in Petrograd developed about the question of the fate of the garrison," says the first book about October—a book written upon the basis of fresh recollections by the author of the present work in the intervals between sessions of the Brest Litovsk conference, a book which for several years served the party as a text-book of history. "The fundamental question about which the whole movement in October was built up and organized" —this is the still more definite expression of Sadovsky, one of the direct organizers of the uprising—"was the question of the transfer of the Petrograd garrison to the northern front." Not one of the closest leaders of the insurrection then taking part in a collective conversation with the immediate purpose of reviving and establishing the course of events, took it into his head to object to this statement of Sadovsky or correct it. Only after 1924 did it suddenly become known that Trotsky had overestimated the significance of the peasant garrison to the detriment of the Petrograd workers—a scientific discovery which most happily supplements the accusation that he underestimated the peasantry. Scores of young historians with Professor Pokrovsky at their head have explained to us in recent years the importance of the proletariat in a proletarian revolution, have waxed indignant that we do not speak of the workers when we are talking about the soldiers, have arraigned us for analyzing the real course of events instead of repeating copy-book phrases. Pokrovsky condenses the results of this criticism in the following conclusion: "In spite of the fact that Trotsky very well knows that the armed insurrection was decided upon by the party . . . and it was perfectly clear that the pretext to be found for the action was a secondary matter, nevertheless for him the Petrograd garrison stands at the center of the whole picture . . . as though, if it hadn't been for that, there would have been no thought of an insurrection." For our historian the "decision of the party" regarding the insurrection is alone significant, and how the insurrection took place in reality is "a secondary matter." A pretext, he says, can always be found. Pokrovsky gives the name of pretext to the method by which the troops were won over—to the solution, that is, of the very problem which summarizes the fate of every insurrection. The proletarian revolution would undoubtedly have taken place even without the conflict about the transfer of the garrison—in that the professor is right. But that would have been a different insurrection and would have demanded a different exposition. We have in view the events which actually happened.

One of the organizers and afterward a historian of the Red Guard, Malakhovsky, insists that it was the armed workers in distinction to the semi-passive garrison which showed initiative, determination and endurance in the insurrection. "The Red Guard detachments during the October revolution," he writes, "occupied the governmental institutions, the Post Office, the telegraph, and they were in the front rank during the battles, etc. . . ." All that is indubitable. It is not difficult to understand, however, that if the Red Guard was able to simply "occupy" these institutions, that is only because the garrison was at one with them; it supported or at least did not hinder them. This decided the fate of the insurrection.

The very broaching of such a question as who was more important to the insurrection, the soldiers or the workers, shows that we are on so miserably low a theoretic level that there is hardly room for argument. The October revolution was a struggle of the proletariat against the bourgeoisie for power, but the outcome of the struggle was decided in the last analysis by the muzhik. That general schema, which prevailed throughout the country, found its most perfect expression in Petrograd. What here gave the revolution the character of a brief blow with a minimum number of victims, was the combination of a revolutionary conspiracy, a proletarian insurrection, and the struggle of a peasant garrison for self-preservation. The party led the uprising; the principal motive force was the proletariat; the armed detachments of workers were the fist of the insurrection; but the heavy-weight peasant garrison decided the outcome of the struggle.

It is upon just this question that a contrasting of the February with the October revolution is most indispensable. On the eve of the overthrow of the monarchy the garrison represented for both sides a great unknown; the soldiers themselves did not yet know how they would react to an insurrection of the workers. Only a general strike could create the necessary arena for mass encounters of the workers with the soldiers, for the trying-out of the soldiers in action, for the coming over of the soldiers to the side of the workers. In this consisted the dramatic content of the five February days.

On the eve of the overthrow of the Provisional Government the overwhelming majority of the garrison were standing openly on the side of the workers. Nowhere in the whole country was the government so isolated as in its own residence. No wonder it struggled to get away. But in vain: the hostile capital would not let go. With its unsuccessful attempt to push out the revolutionary regiments the government conclusively destroyed itself.

To explain the passive policy of Kerensky before the uprising solely by his personal qualities, is merely to slide over the surface of things. Kerensky was not alone. There were people in the government like Palchinsky not lacking in energy. The leaders of the Executive Committee well knew that the victory of the Bolsheviks meant political death for them. All of them, however, jointly and singly, turned out to be paralyzed, fell like Kerensky into a kind of heavy half-sleep—that sleep in which, in spite of the danger hanging over him, a man is powerless to lift a hand to save himself.

The fraternization of the workers and soldiers in October did not grow out of open street encounters as in February, but preceded the insurrection. If the Bolsheviks did not now call a general strike, it was not because they were unable, but because they did not feel the need. The Military Revolutionary Committee before the uprising already felt itself master of the situation; it knew every part of the garrison, its mood, its inner groupings; it was receiving reports every day—not for show, but expressing the actual facts; it could at any time send a plenipotentiary commissar, a bicycle man with an order, to any regiment; it could summon to its office by telephone the committee of the unit, or give orders to the company on duty. The Military Revolutionary Committee occupied in relation to the troops the position of a governmental headquarters, not the headquarters of conspirators.

To be sure, the commanding summits of the state remained in the hands of the government. But the material foundation was removed from under them. The ministries and the headquarters were hanging over an empty space. The telephones and telegraph continued to serve the government—so did the State Bank. But the government no longer had the military forces to retain possession of these institutions. It was as though the Winter Palace and Smolny had changed places. The Military Revolutionary Committee had placed the phantom government in such a position that it could do nothing at all without breaking up the garrison. But every attempt of Kerensky to strike at the troops only hastened his end.

However, the task of the revolution still remained unachieved. The spring and the whole mechanism of the watch were in the hands of the Military Revolutionary Committee, but it lacked the hands and face. And without these details a clock can not fulfill its function. Without the telegraph and telephone, without the bank and headquarters, the Military Revolutionary Committee could not govern. It had almost all the real premises and elements of power, but not the power itself.

In February the workers had thought, not of seizing the banks and the Winter Palace, but of breaking the resistance of the army. They were fighting not for individual commanding summits, but for the soul of the soldier. Once the victory was won in this field, all remaining problems solved themselves. Having surrendered its guard battalions, the monarchy no longer made an attempt to defend either its court or its headquarters.

In October the government of Kerensky, having irrevocably lost the soul of the soldier, still clung to the commanding summits. In its hands the headquarters, the banks, the telephone, were only the façade of power. When they should come into the hands of the soviets, they would guarantee the conquest of complete power. Such was the situation on the eve of the insurrection, and it decided the forms of activity during the last twenty-four hours.

Demonstrations, street fights, barricades—everything comprised in the usual idea of insurrection—were almost entirely absent. The revolution had no need of solving a problem already solved. The seizure of the governmental machine could be carried through according to plan with the help of comparatively small armed detachments guided from a single center. The barracks, the fortress, the storehouses, all those enterprises in which workers and soldiers functioned, could be taken possession of by their own internal forces. But the Winter Palace, the Pre-Parliament, the district headquarters, the ministries, the military schools, could not be captured from within. This was true also of the telephone, the telegraph, the Post Office and the State Bank. The workers in these institutions, although of little weight in the general combination of forces, nevertheless ruled within their four walls, and these were, moreover, strongly guarded with sentries. It was necessary to penetrate these bureaucratic high points from without. Political conquest was here replaced by forcible seizure. But since the preceding crowding-out of the government from its military bases had made resistance almost impossible, this military seizure of the final commanding heights passed off as a general rule without conflicts.

To be sure, the thing was not after all settled without fighting. The Winter Palace had to be taken by storm. But the very fact that the resistance of the government came down to a defense of the Winter Palace, clearly defines the place occupied by October 25th in the whole course of the struggle. The Winter Palace was the last redoubt of a régime politically shattered during its eight months' existence, and conclusively disarmed during the preceding two weeks.

Conspiratorial elements—understanding by this term, plan and centralized leadership—occupied an insignificant place in the February revolution. This resulted from the mere weakness and scatteredness of the revolutionary groups under the press of tzarism and the war. So much the greater was the task laid upon the masses. The insurrectionaries were not human locusts. They had their political experience, their traditions, their slogans, their nameless leaders. But while the scattered elements of leadership in the insurrection proved adequate to overthrow the monarchy, they were far from adequate to give the victors the fruits of their victory.

The tranquillity of the October streets, the absence of crowds and battles, gave the enemy a pretext to talk of the conspiracy of an insignificant minority, of the adventure of a handful of Bolsheviks. This formula was repeated unnumbered times in the days, months, and even years, following the insurrection. It is obviously with a view to mending the reputation of the proletarian revolution that Yaroslavsky writes of the 25th of October: "Thick masses of the Petrograd proletariat summoned by the Military Revolutionary Committee stood under its banners and overflowed the streets of Petrograd." This official historian only forgets to explain for what purpose the Military Revolutionary Committee had summoned these masses to the streets, and just what they did when they got there.

From the combination of its strong and weak points has grown up an official idealization of the February revolution as an all-national revolution, in contrast to the October one which is held to be a conspiracy. But in reality the Bolsheviks could reduce the struggle for power at the last moment to a "conspiracy," not because they were a small minority, but for the opposite reason—because they had behind them in the workers' districts and the barracks an overwhelming majority, consolidated, organized, disciplined.

The October revolution can be correctly understood only if you do not limit your field of vision to its final link. During the last days of February the chess game of insurrection was played out from the first move to the last—that is to the surrender of the enemy. At the end of October the main part of the game was already in the past. And on the day of insurrection it remained to solve only a rather narrow problem: mate in two moves. The period of revolution, therefore, must be considered to extend from the 9th of October, when the conflict about the garrison began, or from the 12th, when the resolution was passed to create a Military Revolutionary Committee. The enveloping maneuver extended over more than two weeks. The more decisive part of it lasted five to six days—from the birth of the Military Revolutionary Committee to the capture of the Winter Palace. During this whole period hundreds of thousands of workers and soldiers took direct action, defensive in form, but aggressive in essence. The final stage, when the insurrectionaries at last threw off the qualifications of the dual power with its dubious legality and defensive phraseology, occupied exactly twenty-four hours: from 2 o'clock on the night of the 25th to 2 o'clock on the night of the 26th. During this period the Military Revolutionary Committee openly employed arms for the conquest of the city and the capture of the government. In these operations, generally speaking, as many forces took part as were needed to solve the limited problem—hardly more than 25 or 30 thousand at the most.

An Italian author who writes books not only about "The Eunuchs' Nights," but also about the highest problems of state, visited soviet Moscow in 1929, misunderstood what little he learned at second or tenth hand, and upon this basis has created a book: *Coup d'État: The Technique of Revolution.* The name of this writer, Malaparte, makes it easy to distinguish him from a certain other specialist in state insurrections called Bonaparte.

In contrast to "the strategy of Lenin" which was bound up with the social and political conditions of Russia in 1917, "Trotsky's tactics," according to Malaparte, "were not bound up with the general conditions of the country." To Lenin's opinions about the political premises of a revolution the author makes Trotsky reply: "Your strategy demands too many favorable circumstances: an insurrection needs nothing, it is self-sufficient." It would be hard to imagine a more self-sufficient absurdity. Malaparte many times repeats that it was not the strategy of Lenin that won in October, but the tactics of Trotsky. And these tactics still threaten the tranquillity of the European states. "The strategy of Lenin does not constitute an immediate danger to the governments of Europe. The real, and moreover permanent, danger to them is the tactics of Trotsky." And still more concretely: "Put Poincaré in Kerensky's place, and the Bolsheviks' state revolution of October 1917 would succeed just as well." It would be futile to try to find out what is the use of Lenin's strategy, which depends upon historic conditions, if Trotsky's tactics will solve the same problem in any circumstances. It remains to add that this remarkable book has already appeared in several languages. The statesmen are evidently learning from it how to repulse a state revolution. We wish them all success.

A criticism of the purely military operations of October 25th has not yet been made. What exists in soviet literature upon this theme is not critical, but purely apologetic in character. Compared with the writings of the Epigones, even Sukhanov's criticism, in spite of all its contradictions is favorably distinguished by an attentive attitude to facts.

In judging the organization of the October uprising, Sukhanov has presented in the course of two years two views diametrically opposed to each other. In his work on the February revolution he says: "I will write some day, from personal reminiscences a description of the October revolution, which was carried through like a piece of music played from notes." Yaroslavsky repeats this comment of Sukhanov word for word. "The insurrection in Petrograd," he says, "was well prepared and played through by the party as though from notes." Claude Anet, a hostile and not profound, but nevertheless attentive, observer, speaks even more emphatically:

"The state revolution of November 7 permits only ecstatic praise. Not one misstep, not one rift; the government was overthrown before it could say 'ouch!'" On the other hand, in his volume devoted to the October revolution Sukhanov tells how Smolny "stealthily feeling its way, cautiously, and without system" undertook the liquidation of the Provisional Government.

There is exaggeration in both these comments. But from a broader point of view it may be conceded that both appraisals, however they contradict each other, find some support in the facts. The planned character of the October revolution grew chiefly out of objective relations, out of the maturity of the revolution as a whole, the place occupied by Petrograd in the country, the place occupied by the government in Petrograd, out of the whole preceding work of the party, and finally out of the correct political leadership of the revolution. But there remained the problems of military technique. Here there were no few particular failings, and if you join them all together it is possible to create the impression of a job done blindly.

Sukhanov has several times called attention to the military defenselessness of Smolny itself during the last days before the insurrection. It is true that as late as the 23rd the headquarters of the revolution was little better defended than the Winter Palace. The Military Revolutionary Committee assured its inviolability primarily by strengthening its bonds with the garrison, and by thus being able to follow all the military movements of the enemy. More serious measures of a technical military character were undertaken by the Committee approximately twenty-four hours before the government undertook them. Sukhanov feels sure that during the 23rd and the night of the 24th the government, had it shown some initiative, could have captured the Committee. "A good detachment of 500 men," he says, "would have been enough to liquidate Smolny and everybody in it." Possibly. But in the first place, for this the government would have required determination and daring, qualities inconsistent with its nature. In the second place, it would have had to have that "good detachment of 500 men." Where were they to get it? Make it up out of officers? We have observed them towards the end of August in the character of conspirators: they had to be hunted up in the night clubs. The fighting companies of the Compromisers had disintegrated. In the military schools every acute question produced conflicting groups. Things were still worse with the Cossacks. To create a detachment by the method of individual selection from various units would have involved giving oneself away ten times before the thing could be finished.

However, even the existence of such a detachment would still not have settled things. The first shot in the region of Smolny would have resounded in the workers' districts and barracks with a shocking reverberation. Tens of thousands of armed and half-armed men would have run to the help of the threatened center of the revolution at any hour of the day or night. And finally, even the capture of the Military Revolutionary Committee would not have saved the government. Beyond the walls of Smolny there remained Lenin, and in communication with him the Central Committee and the Petrograd committee. There was a second headquarters in the Peter and Paul fortress, a third on the *Aurora,* and each district had its headquarters. The masses would not have been without leadership. And the workers and soldiers in spite of their slowness to move were determined to conquer at any cost.

It is indubitable, however, that supplementary measures of military precaution might and should have been taken some few days earlier. In this respect Sukhanov's criticism is just. The military apparatus of a revolution functions clumsily, with delays and omissions, and the general leadership is too much inclined to put politics in the place of technique. Lenin's eyes were much lacking in Smolny. Others had not yet learned.

Sukhanov is also right in asserting that it would have been infinitely easier to capture the Winter Palace on the night of the 25th, or the morning of that day, than during the second half of it. The palace, and also the neighboring headquarters building, were defended by the usual detachment of junkers: a sudden attack would almost certainly have been successful. Kerensky had got away unhindered that morning in an automobile. This alone proved that there was no serious reconnoitering in progress in regard to the Winter Palace. Here obviously was a bad slip.

The task of keeping watch over the Provisional Government

had been laid upon Sverdlov—too late to be sure, on the 24th! —with Lashevich and Blagonravov as assistants. It is doubtful if Sverdlov, exploding in pieces even without that, ever occupied himself with this additional business at all. It is even possible that the very decision, although inscribed in the minutes, was forgotten in the heat of those hours.

In the Military Revolutionary Committee, in spite of everything, the military resources of the government, and particularly the defenses of the Winter Palace, were overestimated. And even had the direct leaders of the siege known the inner forces of the palace, they might still have feared the arrival of reinforcements at the first alarm: junkers, Cossacks, shock-battalions. The plan for capturing the palace was worked out in the style of a large operation. When civil and semi-civil people undertake the solution of a purely military problem, they are always inclined to excessive strategic ingenuities. And along with their superfluous pedantry, they cannot but prove extraordinarily helpless in carrying them out.

The missteps in the capture of the Palace are explained to a certain degree by the personal qualities of the principal leaders. Podvoisky, Antonov-Ovseënko and Chudnovsky, are men of heroic mould. But after all they are far from being men of system and disciplined thought. Podvoisky, having been too impetuous in the July Days, had become far more cautious and even sceptical about immediate prospects. But in fundamentals he remained true to himself. Confronted with any practical task whatever, he inclined organically to break over its bounds, to broaden out the plan, drag in everybody and everything, give a maximum where a minimum was enough. In the element of hyperbole contained in the plan it is easy to see the impress of his spirit. Antonov-Ovseënko was naturally an impulsive optimist, far more apt at improvisation than calculation. As a former petty officer he possessed a certain amount of military information. An emigré during the Great War, he had conducted in the Paris paper *Nashe Slovo* a review of the military situation, and frequently revealed a gift for guessing out strategy. His impressionable amateurism in this field could not, however, counterbalance the excessive flights of Podvoisky. The third of these military chiefs, Chudnovsky, had spent some months as an agitator on an inactive front—that was the whole of his military training. Although gravitating toward the right wing, Chudnovsky was the first to get into the fight and always sought the place where it was hottest. Personal daring and political audacity are not always, as is well known, in perfect equilibrium. Some days after the revolution Chudnovsky was wounded near Petrograd in a skirmish with Kerensky's Cossacks, and some months later he was killed in the Ukraine. It is clear that the talkative and impulsive Chudnovsky could not make up for what was lacking in the other two leaders. No one of them had an eye to detail, if only for the reason that no one of them had ever learned the secrets of the trade. Feeling their own weakness in matters of reconnoitering, communications, maneuvering, these Red martials felt obliged to roll up against the Winter Palace such a superiority of forces as removed the very possibility of practical leadership. An incongruous grandeur of plan is almost equivalent to no plan at all. What has been said does not in the least mean, however, that it would have been possible to find in the staff of the Military Revolutionary Committee, or around it, any more able military leaders. It would certainly have been impossible to find more devoted and selfless ones.

The struggle for the Winter Palace began with the enveloping of the whole district on a wide circle. Owing to the inexperience of the commanders, the interruption of communications, the unskilfulness of the Red Guard detachments, and the listlessness of the regular units, this complicated operation developed at an extraordinarily slow pace. During those same hours when the detachments were gradually filling up their circle and accumulating reserves behind them, companies of junkers, the Cossack squadrons, the Knights of St. George, and the Women's Battalion made their way into the palace. A resisting fist was being formed simultaneously with the attacking ring. You may say that the very problem arose from the too roundabout way in which it was being solved. A bold attack by night or a daring approach by day would hardly have cost more victims than this prolonged operation. The moral effect of the *Aurora's* artillery might at any rate have been tried out twelve or even twenty-four hours sooner than it was. The cruiser stood ready in the Neva, and the sailors were not complaining of any lack of gun-oil. But the leaders of the operation were hoping that the problem could be solved without a battle, were sending parliamentaries, presenting ultimatums and then not living up to their dates. It did not occur to them to examine the artillery in the Peter and Paul fortress in good season for the simple reason that they were counting on getting along without it.

The unpreparedness of the military leadership was still more clearly revealed in Moscow, where the correlation of forces had been considered so favorable that Lenin even insistently advised beginning there: "The victory is sure and there is nobody to fight." In reality it was in Moscow that the insurrection took the form of extended battles lasting with intervals for eight days. "In this hot work," writes Muralov, one of the chief leaders of the Moscow insurrection, "we were not always and in everything firm and determined. Having an overwhelming numerical advantage, ten to one, we dragged the fight out for a whole week . . . owing to a lack of ability to direct fighting masses, to the undiscipline of the latter, and to a complete ignorance of the tactics of the street fight, both on the part of the commanders and on the part of the soldiers." Muralov has a habit of naming things with their real names: no wonder he is now in Siberian exile. But in the present instance in refusing to load off the responsibility upon others Muralov lays upon the military command a lion's share of the blame which belongs to the political leadership—very shaky in Moscow and receptive to the influence of the compromisist circles. We must not lose sight, either, of the fact that the workers of old Moscow, textile and leather workers, were extremely far behind the Petrograd proletariat. In February no insurrection in Moscow had been necessary: the overthrow of the monarchy had rested entirely with Petrograd. In July again Moscow had remained peaceful. This found its expression in October: the workers and soldiers lacked fighting experience.

The technique of insurrection carries through what politics has not accomplished. The gigantic growth of Bolshevism had undoubtedly weakened the attention paid to the military side of things. The passionate reproaches of Lenin were well founded enough. The military leadership proved incomparably weaker than the political. Could it indeed have been otherwise? For a number of months still, the new revolutionary government will show extreme awkwardness in all those cases where it is necessary to resort to arms.

Even so, the military authorities of the governmental camp in Petrograd gave a very flattering judgment of the military leadership of the revolution. "The insurrectionaries are preserving order and discipline," stated the War Ministry over the direct wire to headquarters immediately after the fall of the Winter Palace. "There have been no cases at all of destruction or pogroms. On the contrary, patrols of insurrectionists have detained strolling soldiers. . . . The plan of the insurrection was undoubtedly worked out in advance and carried through inflexibly and harmoniously." Not altogether "from the notes" as Sukhanov and Yaroslavsky have written, nor yet altogether "without system," as the former has subsequently affirmed. Moreover, even in the court of the most austere critic success is the best praise.

Chapter X

THE CONGRESS OF THE SOVIET DICTATORSHIP

In Smolny on the 25th of October the most democratic of all parliaments in the world's history was to meet. Who knows—perhaps also the most important.

Having got free of the influence of compromisist intellectuals, the local soviets had sent up for the most part workers and soldiers. The majority of them were people without big names, but who had proved themselves in action and won lasting confidence in their own localities. From the active army it was almost exclusively rank-and-file soldiers who had run the blockade of army committees and headquarters and come here as delegates. A majority of them had begun to live a political life with the revolution. They had been formed by an experience of eight months. They knew little, but knew it well. The outward appearance of the Congress proclaimed its make-up. The officers' chevrons, the eye-glasses and neckties of intellectuals to be seen at the first Congress had almost completely disappeared. A gray color prevailed uninterruptedly, in costumes and in faces. All had worn out their clothes during the war. Many of the city workers had provided themselves with soldiers' coats. The trench delegates were by no means a pretty picture: long unshaven, in old torn trench-coats, with heavy *papakhi*[1] on their disheveled hair, often with cotton sticking out through a hole, with coarse, weather-beaten faces, heavy cracked hands, fingers yellowed with tobacco, buttons torn off, belts hanging loose, and long unoiled boots wrinkled and rusty. The plebeian nation had for the first time

[1] Tall fur hats.

sent up an honest representation made in its own image and not retouched.

The statistics of this Congress which assembled during the hours of insurrection are very incomplete. At the moment of opening there were 650 delegates with votes. 390 fell to the lot of the Bolsheviks—by no means all members of the party, but they were of the flesh and blood of the masses, and the masses had no roads left but the Bolshevik road. Many of the delegates who had brought doubts with them were maturing fast in the red-hot atmosphere of Petrograd.

How completely had the Mensheviks and Social Revolutionaries squandered the political capital of the February revolution! At the June Congress of Soviets the Compromisers had a majority of 600 votes out of the whole number of 832 delegates. Now the Compromisist opposition of all shades made up less than a quarter of the Congress. The Mensheviks, with the national group adhering to them, amounted to only 80 members—about half of them "Lefts." Out of 159 Social Revolutionaries—according to other reports, 190—about three-fifths were Lefts, and moreover the Right continued to melt fast during the very sitting of the Congress. Toward the end the total number of delegates, according to several lists, reached 900. But this figure, while including a number of advisory members, does not on the other hand include all those with votes. The registration was carried on intermittently; documents have been lost; the information about party affiliations was incomplete. In any case the dominant position of the Bolsheviks in the Congress remains indubitable.

A straw-vote taken among the delegates revealed that 505 soviets stood for the transfer of all power to the soviets; 86 for a government of the "democracy"; 55 for a coalition; 21 for a coalition, but without the Kadets. Although eloquent even in this form, these figures give an exaggerated idea of the remains of the Compromisers' influence. Those for democracy and coalition were soviets from the more backward districts and least important points.

From early in the morning of the 25th, caucuses of the factions were held in Smolny. Only those attended the Bolshevik caucus who were free from fighting duties. The opening of the Congress was delayed: the Bolshevik leaders wanted to finish with the Winter Palace first. But the opposing factions, too, were in no hurry. They themselves had to decide what to do, and that was not easy. Hours passed. Sub-factions were disputing within the factions. The split among the Social Revolutionaries took place after a resolution to withdraw from the Congress had been rejected by 92 votes against 60. It was only late in the evening that the Right and Left Social Revolutionaries began to sit in different rooms. At 8 o'clock the Mensheviks demanded a new delay: they had too many opinions. Night came on. The operations at the Winter Palace were dragging out. But it became impossible to wait longer. It was necessary to say some clear word to the aroused and watchful nation.

The revolution had taught the art of filling space. Delegates, guests, guards, jammed into the commencement hall of the noble maidens, making room for more and more. Warnings of the danger of the floor's collapsing had no effect, nor did appeals to smoke a little less. All crowded closer and smoked twice as much. John Reed with difficulty fought his way through the noisy crowd around the doors. The hall was not heated, but the air was heavy and hot.

Jamming the entries and the side exits, sitting on all the window sills, the delegates now patiently await the president's gong. Tseretelli, Cheidze, Chernov—none of them is on the platform. Only leaders of the second rank have come to their funeral. A short man in the uniform of a military doctor opens the session at 10:40 in the evening in the name of the Executive Committee. The Congress, he says, assembles in such "exceptional circumstances" that he, Dan, obeying the directions of the Central Executive Committee, will refrain from making a political speech. His party friends are now indeed under fire in the Winter Palace "while loyally fulfilling their duty as ministers." The last thing these delegates are expecting is a blessing from the Central Executive Committee. They look up at the platform with hostility. If those people still exist politically, what have they got to do with us and our business?

In the name of the Bolsheviks a Moscow delegate, Avanessov, moves that the praesidium be elected upon a proportional basis: 14 Bolsheviks, 7 Social Revolutionaries, 3 Mensheviks and 1 Internationalist. The Right immediately declines to enter the praesidium. Martov's group sits tight for the time being; it has not decided. Seven votes go over to the Left Social Revolutionaries. The Congress watches these introductory conflicts with a scowl.

Avanessov announces the Bolshevik candidates for the praesidium: Lenin, Trotsky, Zinoviev, Kamenev, Rykov, Nogin, Skliansky, Krylenko, Antonov-Ovseënko, Riazanov, Muranov, Lunacharsky, Kollontai, Stuchka. "The praesidium," writes Sukhanov, "consisted of the principal Bolshevik leaders and six (in reality seven) Left Social Revolutionaries." Zinoviev and Kamenev were included in the praesidium as authoritative party names in spite of their active opposition to the insurrection; Rykov and Nogin as representatives of the Moscow Soviet; Lunacharsky and Kollontai as popular agitators of that period; Riazanov as a representative of the trade unions; Muranov as an old worker-Bolshevik who had carried himself courageously during the trial of the deputies of the State Duma; Stuchka as head of the Lettish organization; Krylenko and Skliansky as representatives of the army; Antonov-Ovseënko as a leader of the Petrograd battles. The absence of Sverdlov's name is obviously explained by the fact that he himself drew up the list, and in the confusion nobody corrected it. It is characteristic of the party morals of the time that the whole headquarters of the opponents of the insurrection turned up in the praesidium: Zinoviev, Kamenev, Nogin, Rykov, Lunacharsky, Riazanov. Of the Left Social Revolutionaries only the little fragile and courageous Spiridonova, who had served long years at hard labor for assassinating the subduer of the Tombovsk peasants, enjoyed an all-Russian renown. The Left Social Revolutionaries had no other "name." The Rights, on the other hand, had now little or nothing but names left.

The Congress greeted its praesidium with enthusiasm. While the factions had been assembling and conferring, Lenin with his make-up still on, in wig and big spectacles, was sitting in the passage-way in the company of two or three Bolsheviks. On the way to a meeting of their faction Dan and Skobelev stopped still opposite the table where the conspirators were sitting, stared at Lenin, and obviously recognized him. Time, then, to take the make-up off. But Lenin was in no hurry to appear publicly. He preferred to look round a little and gather the threads into his hands while remaining behind the scenes. In his recollections of Lenin published in 1924, Trotsky writes: "The first session of the Second Congress of Soviets was sitting in Smolny. Lenin did not appear there. He remained in one of the rooms of Smolny in which, as I remember, there was for some reason no furniture, or almost none. Later somebody spread blankets on the floor and put two cushions on them. Vladimir Ilych and I took a rest there lying side by side. But in just a few minutes I was called: 'Dan is talking and you must answer him.'[2] Returning after my reply, I again lay down beside Vladimir Ilych, who of course had no thought of going to sleep. Was that indeed possible? Every five or ten minutes somebody would run in from the assembly hall to tell us what was going on."

The president's chair is occupied by Kamenev, one of those phlegmatic types designed by nature herself for the office of chairman. There are three questions, he announces, on the order of the day: organization of a government; war and peace; convocation of the Constituent Assembly. An unusual, dull, alarming rumble breaks into the noise of the meeting from outside. This is Peter and Paul Fortress ratifying the order of the day with artillery fire. A high tension current runs through the Congress, which now suddenly feels and realizes what it really is: the convention of a civil war.

Lozovsky, an opponent of the insurrection, demanded a report from the Petrograd Soviet. But the Military Revolutionary Committee was a little behind hand. Replying artillery testified that the report was not ready. The insurrection was in full swing. The Bolshevik leaders were continually withdrawing to the rooms of the Military Revolutionary Committee to receive communications or give orders. Echoes of the fighting would burst up through the assembly like tongues of flame. When votes were taken hands would be raised among bristling bayonets. A blue-gray acrid tobacco smoke hid the beautiful white columns and chandeliers.

[2] Evidently the name here should be Martov to whom Trotsky did make a reply.

The verbal battles of the two camps were extraordinarily impressive against a background of cannon-shots. Martov demanded the floor. The moment when the balance is still oscillating is his moment—this inventive statesman of eternal waverings. With his hoarse tubercular voice Martov makes instant rejoinder to the metallic voice of the guns: "We must put a stop to military action on both sides. . . . The question of power is beginning to be decided by conspiratorial methods. All the revolutionary parties have been placed before a *fait accompli*. . . . A civil war threatens us with an explosion of counter-revolution. A peaceful solution of the crisis can be obtained by creating a government which will be recognized by the whole democracy." A considerable portion of the congress applauds. Sukhanov remarks ironically: "Evidently many and many a Bolshevik, not having absorbed the spirit of the teachings of Lenin and Trotsky, would have been glad to take just that course." The Left Social Revolutionaries and a group of United Internationalists support the proposal of peace negotiations. The right wing, and perhaps also the close associates of Martov, are confident that the Bolsheviks will reject this proposal. They are wrong. The Bolsheviks send Lunacharsky to the tribune, the most peace-loving, the most velvety of their orators. "The Bolshevik faction," he says, "has absolutely nothing against Martov's proposal." The enemy are astonished. "Lenin and Trotsky in thus giving way a little to their own masses," comments Sukhanov, "are at the same time cutting the ground from under the Right Wing." Martov's proposal is adopted unanimously. "If the Mensheviks and Social Revolutionaries withdraw now," runs the comment in Martov's group, "they will bury themselves." It is possible to hope, therefore, that the congress "will take the correct road of creating a united democratic front." Vain hope! A revolution never moves on diagonals.

The Right Wing immediately violates the just approved initiation of peace negotiations. The Menshevik Kharash, a delegate from the 12th Army with a captain's stars on his shoulders, makes a statement: "These political hypocrites propose that we decide the question of power. Meanwhile it is being decided behind our backs. . . . Those blows at the Winter Palace are driving nails in the coffin of the party which has undertaken such an adventure. . . ." The captain's challenge is answered by the Congress with a grumble of indignation.

Lieutenant Kuchin who had spoken at the State Conference in Moscow in the name of the front, tries here also to wield the authority of the army organizations: "This Congress is untimely and even unauthorized." "In whose name do you speak?" shout the tattered trench-coats, their credentials written all over them in the mud of the trenches. Kuchin carefully enumerates eleven armies. But here this deceives nobody. At the front as at the rear the generals of compromisism are without soldiers. The group from the front, continues the Menshevik lieutenant, "declines to assume any responsibility for the consequences of this adventure." That means a complete break with the revolution. "Henceforth the arena of struggle is transferred to the localities." That means fusion with the counter-revolution against the soviets. And so the conclusion: "The front group . . . withdraws from this congress."

One after another the representatives of the Right mount the tribune. They have lost the parishes and churches, but they still hold the belfries, and they hasten for the last time to pound the cracking bells. These socialists and democrats, having made a compromise by hook and crook with the imperialist bourgeoisie, today flatly refuse to compromise with the people in revolt. Their political calculations are laid bare. The Bolsheviks will collapse in a few days, they are thinking, we must separate ourselves from them as quickly as possible, even help to overthrow them, and thus to the best of our ability insure ourselves and our future.

In the name of the Right Menshevik faction, Khinchuk, a former president of the Moscow soviet and a future soviet ambassador in Berlin, reads a declaration: "The military conspiracy of the Bolsheviks . . . will plunge the country into civil dissension, demolish the Constituent Assembly, threaten us with a military catastrophe, and lead to the triumph of the counter-revolution." The sole way out: "Open negotiations with the Provisional Government for the formation of a power resting on all layers of the democracy." Having learned nothing, these people propose to the Congress to cross off the insurrection and return to Kerensky. Through the uproar, bellowing, and even hissing, the words of the representative of the Right Social Revolutionaries are hardly distinguishable. The declaration of his party announces "the impossibility of work in collaboration" with the Bolsheviks, and declares the very Congress of Soviets, although convoked and opened by the compromisist Central Executive Committee, to be without authority.

This demonstration of the Right Wing does not cow anybody, but causes alarm and irritation. The majority of the delegates are too sick and tired of these bragging and narrow-minded leaders who fed them first with phrases and then with measures of repression. Can it be that the Dans, Khinchuks and Kuchins still expect to instruct and command us? A Lettish soldier, Peterson, with a tubercular flush on his cheeks and burning hatred in his eyes, denounces Kharash and Kuchin as impostors. "The revolution has had enough gab! We want action! The power should be in our hands. Let the impostors leave the congress—the army is through with them!" This voice tense with passion relieves the mind of the Congress, which has received nothing so far but insults. Other front-line soldiers rush to the support of Peterson. "These Kuchins represent the opinions of little gangs who have been sitting in the army committees since April. The army long ago demanded new elections." "Those who live in the trenches are impatiently awaiting the transfer of power to the soviets."

But the Rights still hold the belfries. A representative of the Bund declares that "all that has happened in Petrograd is a misfortune," and invites the delegates to join the members of the duma who have decided to march unarmed to the Winter Palace in order to die with the government." "Gibes were to be heard in the general uproar," writes Sukhanov, "some coarse and some poisonous." The unctuous orator has obviously mistaken his audience. "Enough from you!" "Deserters!" shout the delegates, guests, Red Guards and sentries at the door to the withdrawing delegates. "Join Kornilov!" "Enemies of the people!"

The withdrawal of the Rights did not leave any vacant space. Evidently the rank-and-file delegates had refused to join the officers and junkers for a struggle against the workers and soldiers. Only about 70 delegates—that is, a little more than half of the Right Wing faction—went out. The waverers took their place with the intermediate groups who had decided not to leave the Congress. Whereas before the opening of the Congress the Social Revolutionaries of all tendencies had numbered not over 190 men, during the next few hours the number of Left Social Revolutionaries alone rose to 180. They were joined by all those who had not yet decided to join the Bolsheviks although ready to support them.

The Mensheviks and Social Revolutionaries were quite ready to remain in a Provisional Government or some sort of a Pre-Parliament under any circumstances. Can one after all break with cultured society? But the soviets—that is only the people. The soviets are all right while you can use them to get a compromise with the bourgeoisie, but can one possibly think of tolerating soviets which have suddenly imagined themselves masters of the country? "The Bolsheviks were left alone," wrote the Social Revolutionary, Zenzinov, subsequently, "and from that moment they began to rely only upon crude physical force." Moral Principle undoubtedly slammed the door along with Dan and Gotz. Moral Principle will march in a procession of 300 men with two lanterns to the Winter Palace, only to run into the crude physical force of the Bolsheviks and—back down.

The motion adopted by the Congress in favor of peace negotiations was left hanging in the air. If the Rights had admitted the possibility of compromising with a victorious proletariat, they would have been in no hurry to break with the congress. Martov could not have failed to understand this. Nevertheless he clung to the idea of a compromise—the thing upon which his whole policy always stands or falls. "We must put a stop to the bloodshed . . ." he begins again. "Those are only rumors!" voices call out. "It is not only rumors that we hear," he answers. "If you come to the windows you will hear cannon shots." This is undeniable. When the Congress quiets down, shots are audible without going to the windows.

Martov's declaration, hostile through and through to the Bolsheviks, and lifeless in its arguments, condemns the revolution as "accomplished by the Bolshevik party alone by the method of a purely military plot," and demands that the congress suspend its labors until an agreement has been reached with all the socialist parties. To try to find the resultant of a parallelogram of forces in a revolution is worse than trying to catch your own shadow!

At that moment there appeared in the congress the Bolshevik faction of the city duma, those who had refused to seek a problematic death under the walls of the Winter Palace. They were led by Joffé, subsequently the first soviet ambassador at Berlin. The Congress again crowded up, giving its friends a joyful welcome.

But it was necessary to put up a resistance to Martov. This task fell to Trotsky. "Now since the exodus of the Rights,"—concedes Sukhanov—"his position is as strong as Martov's is weak." The opponents stand side by side in the tribune, hemmed in on all sides by a solid ring of excited delegates. "What has taken place," says Trotsky, "is an insurrection, not a conspiracy. An insurrection of the popular masses needs no justification. We have tempered and hardened the revolutionary energy of the Petersburg workers and soldiers. We have openly forged the will of the masses to insurrection, and not conspiracy. . . . Our insurrection has conquered, and now you propose to us: Renounce your victory; make a compromise. With whom? I ask: With whom ought we to make a compromise? With that pitiful handful who just went out? . . . Haven't we seen them through and through. There is no longer anybody in Russia who is for them. Are the millions of workers and peasants represented in this congress, whom they are ready now as always to turn over for a price to the mercies of the bourgeoisie, are they to enter a compromise with these men? No, a compromise is no good here. To those who have gone out, and to all who make like proposals, we must say, 'You are pitiful isolated individuals; you are bankrupts; your rôle is played out. Go where you belong from now on—into the rubbish-can of history!'"

"Then we will go!"—cries Martov without awaiting the vote of the Congress. "Martov in anger and affectation," regrets Sukhanov, "began to make his way from the tribune towards the door. And I began to gather together my faction for a conference in the form of an emergency session. . . ." It was not wholly a matter of affectation. The Hamlet of democratic socialism, Martov would make a step forward when the revolution fell back as in July; but now when the revolution was ready for a tiger's leap, Martov would fall back. The withdrawal of the Rights had deprived him of the possibility of parliamentary maneuvering, and that put him instantly out of his element. He hastened to abandon the congress and break with the insurrection. Sukhanov replied as best he could. The faction split almost in half: Martov won by 14 votes against 12.

Trotsky introduced a resolution—an act of indictment against the Compromisers: They prepared the ruinous offensive of June 18th; they supported the government of treason to the people; they screened the deception of the peasants on the land question; they carried out the disarming of the workers; they were responsible for the purposeless dragging out of the war; they permitted the bourgeoisie to deepen the economic ruin of the country; having lost the confidence of the masses, they resisted the calling of a soviet congress; and finally, finding themselves in a minority, they broke with the soviets.

Here again the order of the day is suspended for a declaration. Really the patience of the Bolshevik praesidium has no bounds. The president of the executive committee of the peasant soviet has come to summon the peasants to abandon this "untimely" congress, and go to the Winter Palace "to die with those who were sent there to do our will." This summons to die in the ruins of the Winter Palace is getting pretty tiresome in its monotony. A sailor just arrived from the *Aurora* ironically announces that there *are* no ruins, since they are only firing blanks from the cruiser. "Proceed with your business in peace," he says. The soul of the congress finds rest in this admirable black-bearded sailor, incarnating the simple and imperious will of the insurrection. Martov with his mosaic of thoughts and feelings belongs to another world. That is why he breaks with the congress.

Still another special declaration—this time half friendly. "The Right Social Revolutionaries," says Kamkov "have gone out, but we, the Lefts, have remained." The congress welcomes those who have remained. However, even they consider it necessary to achieve a united revolutionary front, and come out against Trotsky's sharp resolution shutting the doors against a compromise with the moderate democracy.

Here too the Bolsheviks make a concession. Nobody ever saw them before, it seems, in such a yielding mood. No wonder: they are the masters of the situation and they have no need to insist upon the forms of words. Again Lunacharsky takes the tribune. "The weight of the task which has fallen upon us is not subject to any doubt," he says. A union of all the genuinely revolutionary elements of the democracy is necessary. But have we, the Bolsheviks, taken any steps whatever to repel the other groups? Did we not adopt Martov's proposal unanimously? For this we have been answered with accusations and threats. Is it not obvious that those who have left the Congress "are ceasing even their compromisist work and openly going over to the camp of the Kornilovists?"

The Bolsheviks did not insist upon an immediate vote on Trotsky's resolution. They did not want to hinder the attempts to reach an agreement on a soviet basis. The method of teaching by object-lesson can be successfully applied even to the accompaniment of artillery! As before with the adoption of Martov's proposal, so now the concession to Kamkov only revealed the impotence of these conciliatory labor pains. However, in distinction from the Left Mensheviks, the Left Social Revolutionaries did not quit the Congress: They were feeling too directly the pressure of the villages in revolt.

A mutual feeling-out has taken place. The primary positions have been occupied. There comes a pause in the evolution of the Congress. Shall we adopt the basic decrees and create a soviet government? It is impossible: the old government is still sitting there in the semi-darkness of a chamber in the Winter Palace, the only lamp on the table carefully barricaded with newspapers. Shortly after two o'clock in the morning the praesidium declares a half-hour recess.

The red marshals employed the short delay accorded to them with complete success. A new wind was blowing in the atmosphere of the Congress when its sitting was renewed. Kamenev read from the tribune a telephonogram just received from Antonov. The Winter Palace has been captured by the troops of the Military Revolutionary Committee; with the exception of Kerensky the whole Provisional Government with the dictator Kishkin at its head is under arrest. Although everybody had already learned the news as it passed from mouth to mouth, this official communication crashed in heavier than a cannon salute. The leap over the abyss dividing the revolutionary class from power has been made. Driven out of the Palace of Kshesinskaia in July, the Bolsheviks have now entered the Winter Palace as rulers. There is no other power now in Russia but the power of the soviets. A complex tangle of feelings breaks loose in applause and shouting: triumph, hope, but also anxiety. Then come new and more confident bursts of applause. The deed is done. Even the most favorable correlation of forces contains concealed surprises, but the victory becomes indubitable when the enemy's staff is made prisoner.

Kamenev impressively reads the list of those arrested. The better known names bring hostile or ironic exclamations from the Congress. Especially bitter is the greeting of Tereshchenko who has guided the foreign destinies of Russia. And Kerensky? Kerensky? It has become known that at ten o'clock this morning he was orating without great success to the garrison of Gatchina. "Where he went from there is not exactly known; rumor says to the front."

The fellow-travelers of the revolution feel bad. They foresee that now the stride of the Bolsheviks will become more firm. Somebody from the Left Social Revolutionaries objects to the arrest of the socialist ministers. A representative of the United Internationalists offers a warning—"lest the Minister of Agriculture, Maslov, turn up in the same cell in which he sat under the monarchy." He is answered by Trotsky, who was imprisoned during the ministry of Maslov in the same "Kresty" as under Nicholas: "Political arrest is not a matter of vengeance; it is dictated . . . by considerations of expediency. The government . . . should be indicted and tried, first of all for its indubitable connection with Kornilov. . . . The socialist ministers will be placed only under house arrest." It would have been simpler and more accurate to say that the seizure of the old government was dictated by the demands of the still unfinished struggle. It was a question of the political beheading of the hostile camp, and not of punishment for past sins.

But this parliamentary query as to the arrests was immediately crowded out by another infinitely more important episode. The third Bicycle Battalion sent by Kerensky against Petrograd had come over to the side of the revolutionary people! This too favorable news seemed unbelievable, but that was exactly what had happened. This selected military unit, the first to be chosen out from the whole active army, adhered to the insurrection before ever reaching the capital. If there had been a shade of restraint in its joy at the arrest of the ministers, the Congress was now seized with unalloyed and irrepressible rapture.

The Bolshevik commissar of Tzarskoe Selo together with a delegate from the bicycle battalion ascended the tribune: They had both just arrived to make a report to the Congress: "The garrison of Tzarskoe Selo is defending the approaches to Petrograd." The defensists withdrew from the soviet. "All the work rested upon us alone." Learning of the approach of the bicycle men, the soviet of Tzarskoe Selo prepared to resist, but the alarm happily turned out to be false. "Among the bicycle men are no enemies of the Congress of Soviets." Another battalion will soon arrive at Tzarskoe, and a friendly greeting is already in preparation there. The Congress drinks down this report in great gulps.

The representative of the bicycle men is greeted with a storm, a whirlwind, a cyclone. This Third Battalion, he reports, was suddenly sent from the southwestern front to the north under telegraphic orders "for the defense of Petrograd." The bicycle men advanced "with eyes blindfolded," only confusedly guessing what was up. At Peredolsk they ran into an echelon of the Fifth Bicycle Battalion, also moving on the capital. At a joint meeting held right there at the station, it became clear that "among all the bicyclers there is not one man to be found who would consent to take action against his brothers." It was jointly decided not to submit to the government.

"I tell you concretely," says the bicycle soldier, "we will not give the power to a government at the head of which stand the bourgeoisie and the landlords!" That word "concretely," introduced by the revolution into the everyday language of the people, sounded fine at this meeting!

How many hours was it since they were threatening the

congress from that same tribune with punishments from the front? Now the front itself had spoken its "concrete" word. Suppose the army committees do sabotage the congress. Suppose the rank-and-file soldier mass only succeeds in getting its delegates there rather as an exception. Suppose in many regiments and divisions they have not yet learned to distinguish a Bolshevik from a Social Revolutionary. Never mind! The voice from Peredolsk is the authentic, unmistakable, irrefutable voice of the army. From this verdict there is no appeal. The Bolsheviks, and they only, had understood in time that the soldier-cook of the bicycle battalion infinitely better represented the front than all the Kharashes and Kuchins with their wilted credentials. A portentous change occurred here in the mood of the delegates. "They began to feel," writes Sukhanov, "that things were going to go smoothly and well, that the horrors promised on the right would not after all be so terrible, and that the leaders might be correct in everything else too."

The unhappy Mensheviks selected this moment to draw attention to themselves. They had not yet, it seems, withdrawn. They had been considering in their faction what to do. Out of a desire to bring after him the wavering groups, Kapelinsky, who had been appointed to inform the congress of the decision adopted, finally spoke aloud the most candid reason for breaking with the Bolsheviks: "Remember that the troops are riding towards Petrograd; we are threatened with catastrophe." "What! Are you still here?"—the question was shouted from all corners of the hall. "Why, you went out once!" The Mensheviks moved in a tiny group towards the entrance, accompanied by scornful farewells. "We went out," grieves Sukhanov, "completely untying the hands of the Bolsheviks, turning over to them the whole arena of the revolution." It would have made little difference if they had stayed. In any case they went to the bottom. The waves of events closed ruthlessly over their heads.

It was time for the Congress to address a manifesto to the people, but the session continued to consist only of special declarations. Events simply refused to fit into the order of the day. At 5:17 in the morning Krylenko, staggering tired, made his way to the tribune with a telegram in his hand: The Twelfth Army sends greetings to the Congress and informs it of the creation of a military revolutionary committee which has undertaken to stand guard on the northern front. Attempts of the government to get armed help have broken against the resistance of the army. The commander-in-chief of the northern front, General Cheremissov, has submitted to the Committee. The commissar of the Provisional Government, Voitinsky, has resigned, and awaits a substitute. Delegations from the echelons moved against Petrograd have one after another announced to the Military Revolutionary Committee their solidarity with the Petrograd garrison. "Pandemonium," says Reed, "men weeping, embracing each other."

Lunacharsky at last got a chance to read a proclamation addressed to the workers, soldiers and peasants. But this was not merely a proclamation. By its mere exposition of what had happened and what was proposed, this hastily written document laid down the foundations of a new state structure. "The authority of the compromisist Central Executive Committee is at an end. The Provisional Government is deposed. The Congress assumes the power. . . ." The soviet government proposes immediate peace. It will transfer the land to the peasant, democratize the army, establish control over production, promptly summon the Constituent Assembly, guarantee the right of the nations of Russia to self-determination. "The Congress resolves: That all power in the localities goes over to the soviets." Every phrase as it is read turns into a salvo of applause. "Soldiers! Be on your guard! Railroad workers! Stop all echelons sent by Kerensky against Petrograd! . . . The fate of the revolution and the fate of the democratic peace is in your hands!"

Hearing the land mentioned, the peasants pricked up their ears. According to its constitution the Congress represented only soviets of workers and soldiers; but there were delegates present from individual peasant soviets. They now demanded that they be mentioned in the document. They were immediately given a right to vote. The representative of the Petrograd peasant soviet signed the proclamation "with both hands and both feet." A member of Avksentiev's Executive Committee, Berezin, silent until now, stated that out of 68 peasant soviets replying to a telegraphic questionnaire, one-half had expressed themselves for a soviet government, the other half for the transfer of power to the Constituent Assembly. If this was the mood of the provincial soviets, half composed of governmental functionaries, could there be any doubt that a future peasant congress would support the soviet power?

While solidifying the rank-and-file delegates, the proclamation frightened and even repelled some of the fellow-travelers by its irrevocableness. Small factions and remnants again filed through the tribune. For the third time a group of Mensheviks, obviously the most leftward now, broke away from the congress. They withdrew, it seems, only in order to be in a position to save the Bolsheviks: "Otherwise you will destroy yourselves and us and the revolution." The president of the Polish Socialist Party, Lapinsky, although he remained at the congress in order to "defend his point of view to the end," gave essential adherence to the declaration of Martov: "The Bolsheviks will not be able to wield the power which they are assuming." The United Jewish Workers Party abstained from the vote—likewise the United Internationalists. How much, though, did all these "uniteds" amount to altogether? The proclamation was adopted by all votes against two, with 12 abstaining! The delegates had hardly strength left to applaud.

The session finally came to an end at about six o'clock. A gray and cold autumn morning was dawning over the city. The hot spots of the campfires were fading out in the gradually lightening streets. The graying faces of the soldiers and the workers with rifles were concentrated and unusual. If there were astrologers in Petrograd, they must have observed portentous signs in the heavens.

The capital awoke under a new power. The everyday people, the functionaries, the intellectuals, cut off from the arena of events, rushed for the papers early to find out to which shore the wave had tossed during the night. But it was not easy to make out what had happened. To be sure, the papers reported the seizure by conspirators of the Winter Palace and the ministers, but only as a passing episode. Kerensky has gone to headquarters; the fate of the government will be decided by the front. Reports of the Soviet Congress reproduce only the declarations of the Right Wing, enumerate those who withdrew, and expose the impotence of those who remained.

The political editorials, written before the seizure of the Winter Palace, exude a cloudless optimism.

The rumors of the street do not wholly coincide with the tone of the newspapers. Whatever you say, the ministers are after all locked up in the fortress. Reinforcements from Kerensky are not yet in sight. Functionaries and officers confer anxiously. Journalists and lawyers ring each other up. Editors try to collect their thoughts. The drawing-room oracles say: We must surround the usurpers with a blockade of universal contempt. Storekeepers don't know whether to do business or refrain. The new authorities give orders to do business. The restaurants open; the tramcars move; the banks languish with evil forebodings; the seismograph of the Stock Exchange describes a convulsive curve. Of course the Bolsheviks will not hold out long, but they may do damage before they tumble.

The reactionary French journalist, Claude Anet, wrote on this day: "The victors are singing a song of victory. And quite rightly too. Among all these blabbers they alone acted. . . . Today they are reaping the harvest. Bravo! Fine work." The Mensheviks estimated the situation quite otherwise. "Twenty-four hours have passed since the 'victory' of the Bolsheviks," wrote Dan's paper, "and the historic fates have already begun to take their cruel revenge. . . . Around them is an emptiness created by themselves . . . They are isolated from all . . . The entire clerical and technical machinery refuses to serve them . . . They . . . are sliding at the very moment of their triumph into the abyss."

The liberal and compromisist circles, encouraged by the sabotage of the functionaries and their own light-mindedness, believed strangely in their own impunity. They spoke and wrote of the Bolsheviks in the language of the July Days. "Hirelings of Wilhelm"—"the pockets of the Red Guard full of German marks"—"German officers in command of the insurrection." . . . The new government had to show these people a firm hand before they began to believe in it. The more unbridled papers were detained already on the night of the 26th. Some others were confiscated on the following day. The socialist press for the time being was spared: It was necessary to give the Left Social Revolutionaries, and also some elements of the Bolshevik party, a chance to convince themselves of the groundlessness of the hope for coalition with the official democracy.

The Bolsheviks developed their victory amid sabotage and chaos. A provisional military headquarters, organized during the night, undertook the defense of Petrograd in case of an attack from Kerensky. Military telephone men were sent to the central exchange where a strike had begun. It was proposed to the armies that they create their own military revolutionary committees. Gangs of agitators and organizers, freed by the victory, were sent to the front and to the provinces. The Central organ of the party wrote: "The Petrograd Soviet has acted; it is the turn of the other soviets."

News came during the day which especially disturbed the soldiers. Kornilov had escaped. As a matter of fact, the lofty captive, who had been living in Bykhov, guarded by Tekintsi, loyal to him, and kept in touch with all events by Kerensky's headquarters, decided on the 26th that things were taking a serious turn, and without the slightest hindrance from anybody abandoned his pretended prison. The connections between Kerensky and Kornilov were thus again obviously confirmed in the eyes of the masses. The Military Revolutionary Committee summoned the soldiers and the revolutionary officers by telegram to capture both former commanders-in-chief and deliver them in Petrograd.

As had the Tauride Palace in February, so now Smolny became the focal point for all functions of the capital and the state. Here all the ruling institutions had their seat. Here orders were issued, and hither people came to get them. Hence a demand went out for weapons, and hither came rifles and revolvers confiscated from the enemy. Arrested people were brought in here from all ends of the city. The injured began to flow in seeking justice. The bourgeois public and its frightened cab-drivers made a great yoke-shaped detour to avoid the Smolny region.

The automobile is a far more genuine sign of present-day sovereignty than the orb and sceptre. Under the régime of dual power the automobiles had been divided between the government, the Central Executive Committee and private owners. Now all confiscated motors were dragged into the camp of the insurrection. The Smolny district looked like a gigantic military garage. The best of automobiles smoked in those days from the low-grade gas. Motorcycles chugged impatiently and threateningly in the semi-darkness. Armored cars shrieked their sirens. Smolny seemed like a factory, a railroad and power station of the revolution.

A steady flood of people poured along the sidewalks of the adjoining streets. Bonfires were burning at the outer and inner gates. By their wavering light armed workers and soldiers were belligerently inspecting passes. A number of armored cars stood shaking with the action of their own motors in the court. Nothing wanted to stop moving, machines or people. At each entrance stood machine guns abundantly supplied with cartridge-belts. The endless, weakly lighted, gloomy corridors echoed with the tramping of feet, with exclamations and shouts. The arriving and departing poured up and down the broad staircase. And this solid human lava would be cut through by impatient and imperative individuals, Smolny workers, couriers, commissars, a mandate or an order lifted high in their hand, a rifle on a cord slung over their shoulder, or a portfolio under their arm.

The Military Revolutionary Committee never stopped working for an instant. It received delegates, couriers, volunteer informers, devoted friends, and scoundrels. It sent commissars to all corners of the town, set innumerable seals upon orders and commands and credentials—all this in the midst of intersecting inquiries, urgent communications, the ringing of telephone bells and the rattle of weapons. People utterly exhausted of their force, long without sleep or eating, unshaven, in dirty linen, with inflamed eyes, would shout in hoarse voices, gesticulate fantastically, and if they did not fall half dead on the floor, it seemed only thanks to the surrounding chaos which whirled them about and carried them away again on its unharnessed wings.

Adventurers, crooks, the worst off-scouring of the old régime, would sniff about and try to get a pass to Smolny. Some of them succeeded. They knew some little secret of administration: Who has the key to the diplomatic correspondence, how to write an order on the treasury, where to get gasoline or a typewriter, and especially where the best court wines are kept. They did not all find their cell or bullet immediately.

Never since the creation of the world have so many orders been issued—by word of mouth, by pencil, by typewriter, by wire, one following after the other—thousands and myriads of orders, not always issued by those having the right, and rarely to those capable of carrying them out. But just here lay the miracle—that in this crazy whirlpool there turned out to be an inner meaning. People managed to understand each other. The most important and necessary things got done. Replacing the old web of administration, the first threads of the new were strung. The revolution grew in strength.

During that day, the Central Committee of the Bolsheviks was at work in Smolny. It was deciding the problem of the new government of Russia. No minutes were kept—or they have not been preserved. Nobody was bothering about future historians, although a lot of trouble was being prepared for them right there. The evening session of the Congress was to create a cabinet of ministers. M-i-n-i-s-t-e-r-s? What a sadly compromised word! It stinks of the high bureaucratic career, the crowning of some parliamentary ambition. It was decided to call the government the Soviet of Peoples Commissars: that at least had a fresher sound. Since the negotiations for a coalition of the "entire democracy" had come to nothing, the question of the party and personal staff of the government was simplified. The Left Social Revolutionaries minced and objected. Having just broken with the party of Kerensky, they themselves hardly knew what they wanted to do. The Central Committee adopted the motion of Lenin as the only thinkable one: to form a government of Bolsheviks only.

Martov knocked at the door of this session in the capacity of intercessor for the arrested socialist ministers. Not so long ago he had been interceding with the socialist ministers for the imprisoned Bolsheviks. The wheel had made quite a sizeable turn. Through one of its members sent out to Martov for negotiations—most probably Kamenev—the Central Committee confirmed the statement that the socialist ministers would be transferred to house arrest. Apparently they had been forgotten in the rush of business, or perhaps had themselves declined privileges, adhering even in the Trubetskoy Bastion to the principle of ministerial solidarity.

The Congress opened its session at nine o'clock in the evening. "The picture on the whole was but little different from yesterday—fewer weapons, less of a jam." Sukhanov, now no longer a delegate, was able to find himself a free seat as one of the public. This session was to decide the questions of peace, land and government. Only three questions: end the war, give the land to the people, establish a socialist dictatorship. Kamenev began with a report of the work done by the praesidium during the day: the death penalty at the front introduced by Kerensky abolished; complete freedom of agitation restored; orders given for the liberation of soldiers imprisoned for political convictions, and members of land committees; all the commissars of the Provisional Government removed from office; orders given to arrest and deliver Kerensky and Kornilov. The Congress approved and ratified these measures.

Again some remnants of remnants took the floor, to the impatient disapproval of the hall. One group announced that they were withdrawing "at the moment of the victory of the insurrection and not at the moment of its defeat." Others bragged of the fact that they had decided to remain. A representative of the Donetz miners urged immediate measures to prevent Kaledin from cutting the north off from coal. Some time must pass, however, before the revolution learns to take measures of such scope. Finally it becomes possible to take up the first point on the order of the day.

Lenin, whom the Congress has not yet seen, is given the floor for a report on peace. His appearance in the tribune evokes a tumultuous greeting. The trench delegates gaze with all their eyes at this mysterious being whom they had been taught to hate and whom they have learned without seeing him to love. "Now Lenin, gripping the edges of the reading-stand, let little winking eyes travel over the crowd as he stood there waiting, apparently oblivious to the long-rolling ovation, which lasted several minutes. When it finished, he said simply, 'We shall now proceed to construct the socialist order.'"

The minutes of the Congress are not preserved. The parliamentary stenographers, invited in to record the debates, had abandoned Smolny along with the Mensheviks and Social Revolutionaries. That was one of the first episodes in the campaign of sabotage. The secretarial notes have been lost without a trace in the abyss of events. There remain only the hasty and tendential newspaper reports, written to the tune of the artillery or the grinding of teeth in the political struggle. Lenin's speeches have suffered especially. Owing to his swift delivery and the complicated construction of his sentences, they are not easily recorded even in more favorable conditions. That initial statement which John Reed puts in the mouth of Lenin does not appear in any of the newspaper accounts. But it is wholly in the spirit of the orator. Reed could not have made it up. Just in that way Lenin must surely have begun his speech at the Congress of Soviets—simply, without unction, with inflexible confidence: "We shall now proceed to construct the socialist order."

But for this it was first of all necessary to end the war. From his exile in Switzerland Lenin had thrown out the slogan: Convert the imperialist war into a civil war. Now it was time to convert the victorious civil war into peace. The speaker began immediately by reading the draft of a declaration to be published by the government still to be elected. The text had not been distributed, technical equipment being still very weak. The Congress drank in every word of the document as pronounced.

"The workers' and peasants' government created by the revolution of October 24–25, and resting upon the soviets of workers', soldiers' and peasants' deputies, proposes to all the warring peoples and their governments to open immediate negotiations for a just, democratic peace." Just conditions exclude annexations and indemnities. By annexations is to be understood the forceful accession of alien peoples or the retention of them against their will, either in Europe or in remote lands over the seas. "Herewith the government declares that it by no means considers the above indicated conditions of peace ultimative—that is, it agrees to examine any other conditions," demanding only the quickest possible opening of negotiations and the absence of any secrecy in their conduct. On its part the soviet government abolishes secret diplomacy and undertakes to publish the secret treaties concluded before October 25, 1917. Everything in these treaties directed toward the accruing of profit and privilege to the Russian landlords and capitalists, and the oppression of other peoples by the Great Russians, "the government declares unconditionally and immediately annulled." In order to enter upon negotiations, it is proposed to conclude an immediate armistice, for not less than three months at least. The workers' and peasants' government addresses its proposals simultaneously to "the governments and peoples of all warring countries . . . especially the conscious workers of the three most advanced countries," England, France and Germany, confident that it is they who will "help us successfully carry through the business of peace and therewith the business of liberating the toilers and the exploited masses of the population from all slavery and all exploitation."

Lenin limited himself to brief comments on the text of the declaration. "We cannot ignore the governments, for then the possibility of concluding peace will be delayed . . . , but we have no right not to appeal at the same time to the people. The people and the governments are everywhere at variance, and we ought to help the people interfere in the matter of war and peace." "We will, of course, defend in all possible ways our program of peace without annexations or indemnities," but we ought not to present our conditions in the form of an ultimatum, as that will make it easier for the governments to refuse to negotiate. We will consider also every other proposal. "*Consider* does not mean that we will accept it."

The manifesto issued by the Compromisers on March 14th proposed to the workers of other countries to overthrow the bankers in the name of peace; however the Compromisers themselves not only did not demand the overthrow of their own bankers, but entered into a league with them. "Now we have overthrown the government of the bankers." That gives us a right to summon the other peoples to do the same. We have every hope of victory. "It must be remembered that we live not in the depths of Africa, but in Europe where everything can become quickly known." The guarantee of victory Lenin sees, as always, in converting the national into an international revolution. "The workers' movement will get the upper hand and lay down the road to peace and socialism."

The Left Social Revolutionaries sent up a representative to present their adherence to the declaration. Its "spirit and meaning are close and understandable to us." The United Internationalists were for the declaration, but only on condition that it be issued by a government of the entire democracy. Lapinsky, speaking for the Polish Left Mensheviks, welcomed "the healthy proletarian realism" of the document. Dzerzhinsky for the social democracy of Poland and Lithuania, Stuchka for the social democracy of Latvia, Kapsukass for the Lithuanian social democracy, adhered to the declaration without qualification. The only objection was offered by the Bolshevik, Eremeev, who demanded that the peace conditions be given the character of an ultimatum—otherwise "they may think that we are weak, that we are afraid."

Lenin decisively, even fiercely, objected to the ultimative presentation of the conditions: In that way, he said, we will only "make it possible for our enemies to conceal the whole truth from the people, to hide the truth behind our irreconcilability." You say that "our not presenting an ultimatum will show our impotence." It is time to have done with bourgeois falsities in politics. "We need not be afraid of telling the truth about our weariness. . . ." The future disagreements of Brest Litovsk gleam out for a moment already in this episode.

Kamenev asked all who were for the proclamation to raise their delegates' cards. "One delegate," writes Reed, "dared to raise his hand against, but the sudden sharp outburst around him brought it swiftly down." The appeal to the peoples and governments was adopted unanimously. The deed was done! And it impressed all the participants by its close and immediate magnitude.

Sukhanov, an attentive although also prejudiced observer, noticed more than once at that first session the listlessness of the Congress. Undoubtedly the delegates—like all the people, indeed—were tired of meetings, congresses, speeches, resolutions, tired of the whole business of marking time. They had no confidence that this Congress would be able and know how to carry the thing through to the end. Will not the gigantic size of the task and the insuperable opposition compel them to back down this time too? An influx of confidence had come with the news of the capture of the Winter Palace, and afterward with the coming over of the bicycle men to the insurrection. But both these facts still had to do with the mechanics of insurrection. Only now was its historic meaning becoming clear in action. The victorious insurrection had built under this congress of workers and soldiers an indestructible foundation of power. The delegates were voting this time not for a resolution, not for a proclamation, but for a governmental act of immeasurable significance.

Listen, nations! The revolution offers you peace. It will be accused of violating treaties. But of this it is proud. To break up the leagues of bloody predation is the greatest historic service. The Bolsheviks have dared to do it. They alone have dared. Pride surges up of its own accord. Eyes shine. All are on their feet. No one is smoking now. It seems as though no one breathes. The praesidium, the delegates, the guests, the sentries, join in a hymn of insurrection and brotherhood. "Suddenly, by common impulse,"—the story will soon be told by John Reed, observer and participant, chronicler and poet of the insurrection—"we found ourselves on our feet, mumbling together into the smooth lifting unison of the Internationale. A grizzled old soldier was sobbing like a child. Alexandra Kollontai rapidly winked the tears back. The immense sound rolled through the hall, burst windows and doors and soared into the quiet sky." Did it go altogether into the sky? Did it not go also to the autumn trenches, that hatchwork upon unhappy, crucified Europe, to her devastated cities and villages, to her mothers and wives in mourning? *"Arise ye prisoners of starvation! Arise ye wretched of the earth!"* The words of the song were freed of all qualifications. They fused with the decree of the government, and hence resounded with the force of a direct act. Everyone felt greater and more important in that hour. The heart of the revolution enlarged to the width of the whole world. "We will achieve emancipation. . . ." The spirit of independence, of initiative, of daring, those joyous feelings of which the oppressed in ordinary conditions are deprived—the revolution had brought them now. ". . . with our own hand!" The omnipotent hand of those millions who had overthrown the monarchy and the bourgeoisie would now strangle the war. The Red Guard from the Vyborg district, the gray soldier with his scar, the old revolutionist who had served his years at hard labor, the young black-bearded sailor from the *Aurora*—all vowed to carry through to the end this "last and deciding fight." "We will build our own new world!" We will build! In that word eagerly spoken from the heart was included already the future years of the civil war and the coming five-year periods of labor and privation. "Who was nothing shall be all!" All! If the actualities of the past have often been turned into song, why shall not a song be turned into the actuality of the future? Those trench-coats no longer seemed the costumes of galley-slaves. The *papakhi* with their holes and torn cotton took a new aspect above those gleaming eyes. "The race of man shall rise again!" Is it possible to believe that it will not rise from the misery and humiliation, the blood and filth of this war?

"The whole praesidium, with Lenin at its head, stood and sang with excited enraptured faces and shining eyes." Thus testifies a sceptic, gazing with heavy feelings upon an alien triumph. "How much I wanted to join it," confesses Sukhanov, "to fuse in one feeling and mood with that mass and its leaders! But I could not." The last sound of the anthem died away, but the Congress remained standing, a fused human mass enchanted by the greatness of that which they had experienced. And the eyes of many rested on the short, sturdy figure of the man in the tribune with his extraordinary head, his high cheekbones and simple features, altered now by the shaved beard, and with that gaze of his small, slightly Mongol eyes which looked straight through everything. For four months he had been absent. His very name had almost separated itself from any living image. But no. He was not a myth. There he stood among his own—how many now of "his own"!—holding the sheets of a message of peace to the peoples of the world in his hand. Even those nearest, those who knew well his place in the party, for the first time fully realized what he meant to the revolution, to the people, to the peoples. It was he who had taught them; it was he who had brought them up. Somebody's voice from the depth of the hall shouted a word of greeting to the leader. The hall seemed only to have awaited the signal. Long live Lenin! The anxieties endured, the doubts overcome, pride of initiative, triumph of victory, gigantic hopes—all poured out together in one volcanic eruption of gratitude and rapture. The sceptical observer dryly remarks: "Undoubted enthusiasm of mood . . . They greeted Lenin, shouted hurrah, threw their caps in the air. They sang the

Funeral March in memory of the victims of the war—and again applause, shouts, throwing of caps in the air."

What the Congress experienced during those minutes was experienced on the next day, although less compactly, by the whole country. "It must be said," writes Stankevich, in his memoirs, "that the bold gesture of the Bolsheviks, their ability to step over the barbed-wire entanglements which had for four years divided us from the neighboring peoples, created of itself an enormous impression." Baron Budberg expresses himself more crudely but no less succinctly in his diary: "The new government of Comrade Lenin went off with a decree for immediate peace. . . . This was now an act of genius for bringing the soldier masses to his side: I saw this in the mood of several regiments which I made the rounds of today; the telegram of Lenin on an immediate three months' armistice and then peace, created a colossal impression everywhere, and evoked stormy joy. We have now lost the last chance of saving the front." By saving the front which they had ruined, those men had long ceased to mean anything but saving their own social positions.

If the revolution had had the determination to step over the barbed-wire entanglements in March and April, it might still have soldered the army together for a time—provided the army was at the same time reduced to a half or a third its size—and thus created for its foreign policy a position of exceptional force. But the hour of courageous action struck only in October, when to save even a part of the army for even a short period was unthinkable. The new government had to load upon itself the debt, not only for the war of tzarism, but also for the spendthrift light-mindedness of the Provisional Government. In this dreadful, and for all other parties hopeless, situation, only Bolshevism could lead the country out on an open road—having uncovered through the October revolution inexhaustible resources of national energy.

Lenin is again in the tribune—this time with the little sheets of a decree on land. He begins with an indictment of the overthrown government and the compromisist parties, who by dragging out the land question have brought the country to a peasant revolt. "Their talk about pogroms and anarchy in the country rings false with cowardly deceit. Where and when have pogroms and anarchy been caused by reasonable measures?" The draft of the decree has not been multigraphed for distribution. The speaker has the sole rough draft in his hands, and it is written so badly—Sukhanov remembers—"that Lenin stumbles in the reading, gets mixed up, and finally stops entirely. Somebody from the crowd jammed around the tribune comes to his help. Lenin eagerly yields his place and the undecipherable paper." These rough spots did not, however, in the eyes of that plebeian parliament diminish by an iota the grandeur of what was taking place.

The essence of the decree is contained in two lines of the first point: "The landlord's property in the land is annulled immediately and without any indemnity whatever. The landlord, appanage, monastery and church estates with all their goods and chattels are given in charge of the town land committees and county soviets of peasant deputies until the Constituent Assembly. The confiscated property is placed as a national possession under the protection of the local soviets. The land of the rank-and-file peasants and rank-and-file Cossacks is protected against confiscation. The whole decree does not come to more than thirty lines. It smashes the Gordian knot with a hammer. To the fundamental text certain broader instructions are adjoined, borrowed wholly from the peasants themselves. In *Izvestia of the Peasant Soviet* there had been printed on August 19th a summary of 242 instructions given by the electors to their representatives at the First Congress of Peasant Deputies. Notwithstanding that it was the Social Revolutionaries who prepared these collated instructions, Lenin did not hesitate to attach the document in its entirety to his decree "for guidance in carrying out the great land transformation."

The collated instructions read: "The right to private property in the land is annulled forever." "The right to use the land is accorded to all citizens . . . desiring to cultivate it with their own labor." "Hired labor is not permitted." "The use of the land must be equalized—that is, the land is to be divided among the toilers according to local conditions on the basis of standards either of labor or consumption."

Under a continuation of the bourgeois régime, to say nothing of a coalition with the landlords, these Social Revolutionary instructions remained a lifeless Utopia, where they did not become a conscious lie. Even under the rule of the proletariat, they did not become realizable in all their sections. But the destiny of the instructions radically changed with a change in the attitude toward them of the governmental power. The workers' state gave the peasants a period in which to try out their self-contradictory program in action.

"The peasants want to keep their small properties," wrote Lenin in August, "standardize them on a basis of equality, and periodically re-equalize them. Let them do it. No reasonable socialist will break with the peasant poor on that ground. If the lands are confiscated, that means that the rule of the banks is undermined—if the equipment is confiscated, that means that the rule of capital is undermined. The rest . . . with a transfer of political power to the proletariat . . . will be suggested by practice."

A great many people, and not only enemies but friends, have failed to understand this far-sighted, and to a certain extent pedagogical, approach of the Bolshevik party to the peasantry and its agrarian program. The equal distribution of the land—objected Rosa Luxemburg for example—has nothing in common with socialism. The Bolsheviks, it goes without saying, had no illusion upon this point. On the contrary, the very construction of the decree bears witness to the critical vigilance of the legislator. Whereas the collated instructions say that all the land, both that of the landlords and the peasants, "is converted into national property," the basic decree does not commit itself at all as to the new form of property in the land. Even a none too pedantic jurist would be horrified at the fact that the nationalization of the land, a new social principle of world-historic importance, is inaugurated in the form of a list of instructions adjoined to a basic law. But there was no reactionary slovenliness here. Lenin wanted as little as possible to tie the hands of the party and the soviet power *a priori* in a still unexplored historic realm. Here again he united unexampled audacity with the greatest caution. It still remained to determine in experience how the peasants themselves would understand the conversion of the land into "the property of the whole people." Having made so long a dash forward, it was necessary to fortify the positions also in case a retreat should become necessary. The distribution of the landlord's land among the peasants, while not in itself a guarantee against bourgeois counter-revolution, made impossible in any case a feudal-monarchic restoration.

It would be possible to speak of socialist perspectives only after the establishment and successful preservation of the proletarian power. And this power could preserve itself only by giving determined coöperation to the peasant in carrying out his revolution. If the distribution of the land would strengthen the socialist government politically, it was then wholly justified as an immediate measure. The peasant had to be taken as the revolution found him. Only a new régime could re-educate him—and not at once, but in the course of a generation, with the help of new technique and a new organization of industry. The decree together with the instructions meant that the dictatorship of the proletariat assumed an obligation not only to take an attentive attitude toward the interests of the land laborer, but also to be patient of his illusions as a petty proprietor. It was clear in advance that there would be a number of stages and turning-points in the agrarian revolution. The collated instructions were anything but the last word. They represented merely a starting-point which the workers agreed to occupy while helping the peasants to realize their progressive demands, and warning them against false steps.

"We must not ignore," said Lenin in his speech, "the resolutions of the lower ranks of the people, even though we are not in agreement with them. . . . We must give full freedom to the creative capacity of the popular masses. The essence of the thing is that the peasantry should have full confidence that there are no more landlords in the country, and let the peasants themselves decide all questions and build their own life." Opportunism? No, it was revolutionary realism.

Before even the applause was over, a Right Social Revolutionary, Pianykh, arrived from the Peasants' Executive Committee and took the floor with a furious protest on the subject of the socialist ministers being under arrest. "During the last days," cried the orator pounding the table as though beside himself, "a thing is on foot which has never happened in any revolution. Our comrades, members of the Executive Committee, Maslov and Salazkin, are locked up in prison. We demand their immediate release!" "If one hair falls from their heads . . ." threatened another messenger in a military coat. To the Congress they both seemed like visitors from another world.

At the moment of the insurrection there were about 800 men in prison in Dvinsk, charged with Bolshevism, in Minsk about 6000, in Kiev 535—for the most part soldiers. And how many members of the peasant committees were under lock and key in various parts of the country! Finally a good share of the delegates to this very Congress, beginning with the praesidium, had passed through the prisons of Kerensky since July. No wonder the indignation of the friends of the Provisional Government could not pluck at any heart-strings in this assembly. To complete their bad-luck a certain delegate, unknown to anybody, a peasant from Tver, with long hair and a big sheepskin coat, rose in his place, and having bowed politely to all four points of the compass, adjured the Congress in the name of his electors not to hesitate at arresting Avksentiev's executive committee as a whole: "Those are not peasants' deputies, but Kadets. . . . Their place is in prison." So they stood facing each other, these two figures: The Social Revolutionary Pianykh, experienced parliamentarian, favorite of ministers, hater of Bolsheviks, and the nameless peasant from Tver who had brought Lenin a hearty salute from his electors. Two social strata, two revolutions: Pianykh was speaking in the name of February, the Tver peasant was fighting for October. The Congress gave the delegate in a sheepskin coat a veritable ovation. The emissaries of the Executive Committee went away swearing.

"The resolution of Lenin is greeted by the Social Revolutionary faction as a triumph of their ideas," announces Kalegaev, but in view of the extraordinary importance of the question we must take it up in caucus. A Maximilist, representative of the extreme left wing of the disintegrated Social Revolutionary party, demands an immediate vote: "We ought to give honor to a party which on the very first day and without any blabber brings such a measure to life." Lenin insisted that the intermission should be at any rate as short as possible. "News so important to Russia should be in print by morning. No filibustering!" The decree on land was not only, indeed, the foundation of the new régime, but also a weapon of the revolution, which had still to conquer the country. It is not surprising that Reed records at that moment an imperative shout breaking through the noise of the hall: "Fifteen agitators wanted in room 17 at once! To go to the front!" At one o'clock in the morning a delegate from the Russian troops in Macedonia enters a complaint that the Petersburg governments one after the other have forgotten them. Support for peace and land from the soldiers in Macedonia is assured! Here is a new test of the mood of the army—this time from a far corner of southeastern Europe. And here Kamenev announces: The Tenth Bicycle Battalion, summoned by the government from the front, entered Petrograd this morning, and like its predecessors has adhered to the Congress of Soviets. The warm applause testifies that no amount of these confirmations of its power will seem excessive to the Congress.

After the adoption, unanimously and without debate, of a resolution declaring it an affair of honor of the local soviets not to permit Jewish or any other pogroms on the part of the criminal element, a vote is taken on the draft of the land law. With one vote opposed and eight abstaining, the congress adopts with a new burst of enthusiasm the decree putting an end to serfdom, the very foundation stone of the old Russian culture. Henceforth the agrarian revolution is legalized, and therewith the revolution of the proletariat acquires a mighty basis.

A last problem remains: the creation of a government. Kamenev reads a proposal drawn up by the Central Committee of the Bolsheviks. The management of the various branches of the state life is allotted to commissions who are to carry into action the program announced by the Congress of Soviets "in close union with the mass organizations of working men and women, sailors, soldiers, peasants and clerical employees." The governmental power is concentrated in the hands of a collegium composed of the presidents of these commissions, to be called the Soviet of Peoples Commissars. Control over the activities of the government is vested in the Congress of Soviets and its Central Executive Committee.

Seven members of the Central Committee of the Bolshevik party were nominated to the first Council of Peoples Commissars: Lenin as head of the government, without portfolio; Rykov as Peoples' Commissar of the Interior; Miliutin as head of the Department of Agriculture; Nogin as chief of Commerce and Industry; Trotsky as head of the Department of Foreign Affairs; Lomov of Justice; Stalin, president of a Commission on the Affairs of the Nationalities; Military and naval affairs were allotted to a committee consisting of Antonov-Ovseënko, Krylenko and Dybenko; the head of the Commissariat of Labor is to be Shliapnikov; the chief of the Department of education, Lunacharsky; the heavy and ungrateful task of Minister of Provisions is laid upon Theodorovich; the Posts and Telegraph upon the worker, Glebov; the position of Peoples Commissar of Communications is not yet allotted, the door being left open here for an agreement with the organizations of the railroad workers.

All fifteen candidates, four workers and eleven intellectuals have behind them years of imprisonment, exile and emigrant life. Five of them had been imprisoned even under the régime of the democratic republic. The future prime-minister had only the day before emerged from the democratic underground. Kamenev and Zinoviev did not enter the Council of Peoples Commissars. The former was selected for president of the new Central Executive Committee, the latter for editor of the official organ of the soviets. "As Kamenev read the list of Commissars," writes Reed, there were "bursts of applause after each name, Lenin's and Trotsky's especially." Sukhanov adds also that of Lunacharsky.

A long speech against the proposed staff of the government was made by a representative of the United Internationalists, Avilov, once a Bolshevik, litterateur from Gorky's paper. He conscientiously enumerated the difficulties standing before the revolution in the sphere of domestic and foreign politics. We must "clearly realize . . . whither we are going. . . . Before the new government stand all the old questions: of bread and of peace. If it does not solve these problems it will be overthrown." There is little grain in the country; it is in the hands of the well-to-do peasants; there is nothing to give in exchange for grain; industry is on the decline; fuel and raw material are lacking. To collect the grain by force is a difficult, long and dangerous task. It is necessary, therefore, to create a government which will have the sympathy not only of the poor but also of the well-to-do peasantry. For this a coalition is necessary.

"It will be still harder to obtain peace." The governments of the Entente will not answer the proposal of the congress for an immediate armistice. Even without that the Allied ambassadors are planning to leave. The new government will be isolated; its peace initiative will be left hanging in the air. The popular masses of the warring countries are still far from revolution. The consequences may be two: either extermination of the revolution by the troops of the Hohenzollern or a separate peace. The peace terms in both cases can only be the worst possible for Russia. These difficulties can be met only by "a majority of the people." The unfortunate thing is the split in the democracy: the left half wants to create a purely Bolshevik government in Smolny, and the right half is organizing in the city duma a Committee of Public Safety. To save the revolution it is necessary to form a government from both groups.

A representative of the Left Social Revolutionaries, Karelin, spoke to the same effect. It is impossible to carry out the program adopted without those parties which have withdrawn from the Congress. To be sure "the Bolsheviks are not to blame for their withdrawal." But the program of the congress ought to unite the entire democracy. "We do not want to take the road of isolating the Bolsheviks, for we understand that with the fate of the Bolsheviks is bound up the fate of the whole revolution. Their ruin will be the ruin of the revolution. If they, the Left Social Revolutionaries, have nevertheless declined the invitation to enter the government, their purpose is a good one: to keep their hands free for mediation between the Bolsheviks and the parties which have abandoned the Congress. In such mediations . . . the Left Social Revolutionaries see their principal task at the present moment." The Left Social Revolutionaries will support the work of the new government in solving urgent problems. At the same time they vote against the proposed government.—In a word the young party has got mixed up as badly as it knows how.

"Trotsky rose to defend a government of Bolsheviks only," writes Sukhanov, himself wholly in sympathy with Avilov and having inspired Karelin behind the scenes. "He was very clear, sharp, and in much absolutely right. But he refused to understand in what consisted the center of the argument of his opponents. . . ." The center of the argument consisted of an ideal diagonal. In March they had tried to draw it between the bourgeoisie and the compromisist soviets. Now Sukhanov dreamed of a diagonal between the compromisist democracy and the dictatorship of the proletariat. But revolutions do not develop along diagonals.

"They have tried to frighten us more than once with a possible isolation of the Left Wing," said Trotsky. "Some days back when the question of insurrection was first openly raised, they told us that we were headed for destruction. And in reality if you judged the grouping of forces by the political press, then insurrection threatened us with inevitable ruin. Against us stood not only the counter-revolutionary bands, but also the defensists of all varieties. The Left Social Revolutionaries, only one wing of them, courageously worked with us in the Military Revolutionary Committee. The rest occupied a position of watchful neutrality. And nevertheless even with these unfavorable circumstances and when it seemed that we were abandoned by all, the insurrection triumphed. . . .

"If the real forces were actually against us, how could it happen that we won the victory almost without bloodshed. No, it is not we who are isolated, but the government and the so-called democrats. With their wavering, their compromisism, they have erased themselves from the ranks of the authentic democracy. Our great superiority as a party lies in the fact that we have formed a coalition with the class forces, creating a union of the workers, soldiers and poorest peasants.

"Political groupings disappear, but the fundamental interests of the classes remain. That party conquers which is able to feel out and satisfy the fundamental demands of a class. . . . We pride ourselves upon the coalition of our garrison, chiefly composed of peasants, with the working class. This coalition has been tried by fire. The Petrograd garrison and proletariat went hand in hand into that great struggle which is the classic example in the history of revolutions among all peoples.

"Avilov has spoken of the vast difficulties which stand before us. To remove those difficulties he proposes that we form a coalition. But he makes no attempt to lay bare his formula and tell us what coalition. A coalition of groups, or classes, or simply a coalition of newspapers? . . .

"They tell us the split in the democracy is a misunderstanding. When Kerensky is sending shock troops against us, when with the consent of the Central Executive Committee we are deprived of the telephone at the most critical moment of our struggle with the bourgeoisie, when they deal us blow after blow—is it possible to talk of misunderstanding?

"Avilov says to us: There is little bread, we must have a coalition with the defensists. Do you imagine that this coalition will increase the quantity of bread? The problem of bread is the problem of a program of action. The struggle with economic collapse demands a definite system from below, and not political groupings on top.

"Avilov speaks of a union with the peasantry: But again of what peasantry is he talking? Today and right here, a representative of the peasants of Tver province demanded the arrest of Avksentiev. We must choose between this Tver peasant and Avksentiev who has filled the prisons with members of the peasant committees. A coalition with the kulak elements of the peasantry we firmly reject in the name of a coalition of the working class and the poorer peasant. We are with the Tver peasants against Avksentiev. We are with them to the end and inseparably.

"Whoever now chases the shadow of coalition is totally cutting himself off from life. The Left Social Revolutionaries will lose support among the masses to the extent that they venture to oppose our party. Every group which opposes the party of the proletariat, with whom the village poor have united, cuts himself off from the revolution.

"Openly and before the face of the whole people we raised the banner of insurrection. The political formula of this insurrection was: All power to the soviets—through the Congress of Soviets. They tell us: You did not await the Congress with your uprising. We thought of waiting, but Kerensky would not wait. The counter-revolutionists were not dreaming. We as a party considered this our task: to make it genuinely possible for the Congress of Soviets to seize the power. If the

Congress had been surrounded with junkers, how could it have seized the power? In order to achieve this task, a party was needed which would wrench the power from the hands of the counter-revolution and say to you: 'Here is the power and you've got to take it!' (Stormy and prolonged applause.)

"Notwithstanding that the defensists of all shades stopped at nothing in their struggle against us, we did not throw them out. We proposed to the Congress as a whole to take the power. How utterly you distort the perspective, when after all that has happened you talk from this tribune of our irreconcilability. When a party surrounded with a cloud of gunpowder smoke, comes up to them and says, 'Let us take the power together!' they run to the city duma and unite there with open counter-revolutionists! They are traitors to the revolution with whom we will never unite!

"For the struggle for peace, says Avilov, we must have a coalition with the Compromisers. At the same time he acknowledges that the Allies do not want to make peace. . . . The Allied imperialists laughed, says Avilov, at the oleomargarine delegate Skobelev. Nevertheless if you form a bloc with the oleomargarine democrats, the cause of peace is assured!

"There are two roads in the struggle for peace. One road is to oppose to the Allied and enemy governments the moral and material force of revolution. The other is a bloc with Skobelev, which means a bloc with Tereshchenko and complete subjection to Allied imperialism. In our proclamation on peace we address ourselves simultaneously to the governments and the peoples. That is a purely formal symmetry. Of course we do not think to influence the imperialist governments with our proclamations, although as long as they exist we cannot ignore them. We rest all our hope on the possibility that our revolution will unleash the European revolution. If the revolting peoples of Europe do not crush imperialism, then we will be crushed—that is indubitable. Either the Russian revolution will raise the whirlwind of struggle in the west, or the capitalists of all countries will crush our revolution. . . ."

"There is a third road," says a voice from the benches.

"The third road," answers Trotsky, "is the road of the Central Executive Committee—on the one hand sending delegates to the west European workers, and on the other forming a union with the Kishkins and Konovalovs. That is a road of lies and hypocrisy which we will never enter.

"Of course we do not say that only the day of insurrection of the European workers will be the day that the peace treaty is signed. This also is possible: that the bourgeoisie, frightened by an approaching insurrection of the oppressed, will hasten to make peace. The dates are not set. The concrete forms cannot be foretold. It is important and it is necessary to define the method of struggle, a method identical in principle both in foreign and domestic politics. A union of the oppressed here and everywhere—that is our road."

The delegates of the Congress, says John Reed, "greeted him with an immense crusading acclaim, kindling to the daring of it, with the thought of championing mankind." At any rate it could not have entered the mind of any Bolshevik at that time to protest against placing the fate of the Soviet Republic, in an official speech in the name of the Bolshevik party, in direct dependence upon the development of the international revolution.

The dramatic law of this Congress was that each significant act was concluded, or even interrupted, by a short intermission during which a figure from the other camp would suddenly appear upon the stage and voice a protest, or a threat, or present an ultimatum. A representative of the Vikzhel, the executive committee of the railroad workers' union, now demanded the floor immediately and on the instant. He must needs throw a bomb into the assembly before the vote was taken on the question of power. The speaker—in whose face Reed saw implacable hostility—began with an accusation. His organization, "the strongest in Russia" had not been invited to the Congress. . . . "It was the Central Executive Committee that did not invite you," was shouted at him from all sides. But he continued: And be it known that the original decision of the Vikzhel to support the Congress of Soviets has been revoked. The speaker hastened to read an ultimatum already distributed by telegraph throughout the country: The Vikzhel condemns the seizure of power by one party; the government ought to be responsible before the "entire revolutionary democracy"; until the creation of a democratic government only the Vikzhel will control the railroad lines. The speaker adds that counter-revolutionary troops will not be admitted to Petrograd; but in general the movements of troops will henceforth take place only at the direction of the old Central Executive Committee. In case of repressions directed against the railroad workers, the Vikzhel will deprive Petrograd of food.

The Congress bristled under the blow. The chiefs of the railroad union were trying to converse with the representatives of the people as one government with another! When the workers, soldiers, and peasants take the administration of the state into their hands, the Vikzhel presumes to give commands to the workers, soldiers, and peasants! It wants to change into petty cash the overthrown system of dual power. In thus attempting to rely not upon its numbers, but upon the exceptional significance of railroads in the economy and culture of the country, these democrats of the Vikzhel exposed the whole frailty of the criterion of formal democracy upon the fundamental issues of a social struggle. Truly revolution has a genius for education!

At any rate the moment for this blow was not badly chosen by the Compromisers. The faces of the praesidium were troubled. Fortunately the Vikzhel was by no means unconditional boss on the railroads. In the local districts the railroad workers were members of the city soviets. Even here at the Congress the ultimatum of the Vikzhel met resistance. "The whole mass of the railroad workers of our district," said the delegate from Tashkent, "have expressed themselves in favor of the transfer of power to the soviets." Another delegate from railroad workers declared the Vikzhel a "political corpse." That doubtless was exaggerated. Relying upon the rather numerous upper layers of railroad clerks, the Vikzhel had preserved more life force than the other higher-up organizations of the Compromisers. But it belonged indubitably to the same type as the army committees or the Central Executive Committee. Its star was swiftly falling. The workers were everywhere distinguishing themselves from the clerical employees; the lower clerks were opposing themselves to the higher. The impudent ultimatum of the Vikzhel would undoubtedly hasten these processes. No, the station masters can't hold back the locomotive of the October revolution!

"There can be no questioning the legal rights of this congress," declared Kamenev with authority. "The quorum of the Congress was established not by us, but by the old Central Executive Committee. . . . The Congress is the highest organ of the worker and soldier masses." A simple return to the order of the day!

The Council of Peoples Commissars was ratified by an overwhelming majority. Avilov's resolution, according to the excessively generous estimate of Sukhanov, got 150 votes, chiefly Left Social Revolutionaries. The Congress then unanimously confirmed the membership of the new Central Executive Committee: out of 101 members–62 Bolsheviks, 29 Left Social Revolutionaries. The Central Executive Committee was to complete itself in the future with representatives of the peasant soviets and the re-elected army organizations. The factions who had abandoned the Congress were granted the right to send their delegates to the Central Executive Committee on the basis of proportional representation.

The agenda of the Congress was completed! The soviet government was created. It had its program. The work could begin. And there was no lack of it. At 5:15 in the morning Kamenev closed the Constituent Congress of the soviet régime. To the stations! Home! To the front! To the factories and barracks! To the mines and the far-off villages! In the decrees of the Soviet, the delegates will carry the leaven of the proletarian revolution to all corners of the country.

On that morning the central organ of the Bolshevik party, again under the old name *Pravda,* wrote: "They wanted us to take the power alone, so that we alone should have to contend with the terrible difficulties confronting the country. . . . So be it! We take the power alone, relying upon the voice of the country and counting upon the friendly help of the European proletariat. But having taken the power, we will deal with the enemies of revolution and its saboteurs with an iron hand. They dreamed of a dictatorship of Kornilov. . . . We will give them the dictatorship of the proletariat. . . ."

CONCLUSION

A remarkable consecutiveness of stages is to be observed in the development of the Russian revolution—and this for the very reason that it was an authentic popular revolution, setting in motion tens of millions. Events succeeded each other as though obeying laws of gravitation. The correlation of forces was twice verified at every stage: first the masses would demonstrate the might of their assault, then the possessing classes, attempting revenge, would reveal only the more clearly their isolation.

In February the workers and soldiers of Petrograd rose in insurrection—not only against the patriotic will of all the educated classes, but also contrary to the reckonings of the revolutionary organizations. The masses demonstrated that they were inconquerable. Had they themselves been aware of this, they would have become the government. But there was not yet a strong and authoritative revolutionary party at their head. The power fell into the hands of the petty bourgeois democracy tinted with a protective socialist coloration. The Mensheviks and Social Revolutionaries could make no other use of the confidence of the masses but to summon to the helm the liberal bourgeoisie, who in their turn could only place the power slipped to them by the Compromisers at the service of the interests of the Entente.

In the April days the indignation of the regiments and factories—again without the summons of any party—brought them out on the streets of Petrograd to resist the imperialist policy of the government wished on them by the Compromisers. This armed demonstration attained an appearance of success. Miliukov, the leader of Russian imperialism, was removed from the government. The Compromisers entered the government, superficially as plenipotentiaries of the people, in reality as call-boys of the bourgeoisie.

Without having decided one of the problems which had evoked the revolution, the coalition government violated in June the *de facto* armistice that had been established on the front, throwing the troops into an offensive. By this act the February régime, already characterized by the declining trust of the masses in the Compromisers, dealt itself a fatal blow. The period opened of direct preparation for a second revolution.

At the beginning of July the government, having all the possessing and educated classes behind it, was prosecuting every revolutionary manifestation whatever as treason to the fatherland and aid to the enemy. The official mass organizations—the soviets, the social-patriotic parties—were struggling against a coming-out with all their power. The Bolsheviks for tactical reasons were trying to restrain the workers and soldiers from coming into the streets. Nevertheless the masses came out. The movement proved unrestrainable and universal. The government was nowhere to be seen. The Compromisers hid. The workers and soldiers proved masters of the situation in the capital. Their offensive went to pieces, however, owing to the inadequate readiness of the provinces and the front.

At the end of August all the organs and institutions of the possessing classes stood for a counter-revolutionary overturn: the diplomats of the Entente, the banks, the leagues of landed proprietors and industrialists, the Kadet party, the staffs, the officers, the big press. The organizer of the overturn was no other than the supreme commander-in-chief with the officer-apparatus of an army of millions to rely on. Military detachments specially selected from all fronts were thrown against Petrograd under pretense of strategic considerations and by secret agreement with the head of the government.

In the capital everything, it seemed, was prepared for the success of the enterprise: the workers had been disarmed by the authorities with the help of the Compromisers; the Bolsheviks were under a steady rain of blows; the more revolutionary regiments had been removed from the city; hundreds of specially selected officers were concentrated in shock brigades—with the officer schools and Cossack detachments they should constitute an impressive force. And what happened? The plot, patronized it would seem by the gods themselves, barely came in contact with the revolutionary people when it scattered in dust.

These two movements, at the beginning of July and the end of August, relate to each other as a theorem and its converse. The July days demonstrated the might of the self-dependent movement of the masses. The August days laid bare the complete impotence of the ruling groups. This correlation signalized the inevitability of a new conflict. The provinces and the front were meanwhile drawing closer to the capital. This predetermined the October victory.

"The ease with which Lenin and Trotsky overthrew the last coalition government of Kerensky," wrote the Kadet, Nabokov, "revealed its inward impotence. The degree of this impotence was an amazement at that time even to well-informed people." Nabokov himself seems hardly aware that it was a question of his impotence, that of his class, of his social structure.

Just as from the armed demonstration of July the curve rises to the October insurrection, so the movement of Kornilov seems a dress-rehearsal of the counter-revolutionary campaign undertaken by Kerensky in the last days of October. The sole military force against the Bolsheviks found at the front by the democratic commander-in-chief after his flight under cover of the little American flag, was that same Third Cavalry Corps which two months before had been designated by Kornilov for the overthrow of Kerensky himself. The commander of the corps was still the Cossack General, Krasnov, militant monarchist placed in this post by Kornilov. A more appropriate commander for the defense of democracy was not to be found.

Moreover nothing was left of the corps but its name. It had been reduced to a few Cossack squadrons, who after an unsuccessful attempt to take the offensive against the Reds near Petrograd, fraternized with the revolutionary sailors and turned Krasnov over to the Bolsheviks. Kerensky was obliged to take flight—both from the Cossacks and the sailors. Thus eight months after the overthrow of the monarchy the workers stood at the head of the country. And they stood firmly.

"Who would believe," wrote one of the Russian generals,

Zalessky, expressing his indignation at this, "that the janitor or watchman of the court building would suddenly become Chief Justice of the Court of Appeals? Or the hospital orderly, manager of the hospital; the barber a big functionary; yesterday's ensign, the commander-in-chief; yesterday's lackey or common laborer, burgomaster; yesterday's train oiler, chief of division or station superintendent; yesterday's locksmith, head of the factory?"

"Who would believe it?" They had to believe it. It was impossible not to believe it, when ensigns routed the generals, when burgomasters from the ranks of common labor put down the resistance of yesterday's lords, train oilers regulated transport, and locksmiths as directors revived industry.

The chief task of a political régime, according to an English aphorism, is to put the right people in the right positions. How does the experiment of 1917 look from this point of view? During the first two months Russia was ruled, through right of monarchic succession, by a man inadequately endowed by nature who believed in saints' mummies and submitted to Rasputin. During the next eight months the liberals and democrats attempted from their governmental high places to prove to the people that the revolution had been accomplished in order that all should remain as before. No wonder those people passed over the country like wavering shadows leaving no trace. From the 25th of October the man at the head of Russia was Lenin, the greatest figure in Russian political history. He was surrounded by a staff of assistants who, as their most spiteful enemies acknowledge, knew what they wanted and how to fight for their aims. Which of these three systems, in the given concrete conditions, proved capable of putting the right people in the right positions?

The historic ascent of humanity, taken as a whole, may be summarized as a succession of victories of consciousness over blind forces—in nature, in society, in man himself. Critical and creative thought can boast of its greatest victories up to now in the struggle with nature. The physico-chemical sciences have already reached a point where man is clearly about to become master of matter. But social relations are still forming in the manner of the coral islands. Parliamentarism illumined only the surface of society, and even that with a rather artificial light. In comparison with monarchy and other heirlooms from the cannibals and cave-dwellers, democracy is of course a great conquest, but it leaves the blind play of forces in the social relations of men untouched. It was against this deeper sphere of the unconscious that the October revolution was the first to raise its hand. The soviet system wishes to bring aim and plan into the very basis of society, where up to now only accumulated consequences have reigned.

Enemies are gleeful that fifteen years after the revolution the soviet country is still but little like a kingdom of universal well-being. Such an argument, if not really to be explained as due to a blinding hostility, could only be dictated by an excessive worship of the magic power of socialist methods. Capitalism required a hundred years to elevate science and technique to the heights and plunge humanity into the hell of war and crisis. To socialism its enemies allow only fifteen years to create and furnish a terrestrial paradise. We took no such obligation upon ourselves. We never set these dates. The process of vast transformations must be measured by an adequate scale.

But the misfortunes which have overwhelmed living people? The fire and bloodshed of the civil war? Do the consequences of a revolution justify in general the sacrifices it involves? The question is teleological and therefore fruitless. It would be as well to ask in face of the difficulties and griefs of personal existence: Is it worth while to be born? Melancholy reflections have not so far, however, prevented people from bearing or being born. Even in the present epoch of intolerable misfortune only a small percentage of the population of our planet resorts to suicide. But the people are seeking the way out of their unbearable difficulties in revolution.

Is it not remarkable that those who talk most indignantly about the victims of social revolutions are usually the very ones who, if not directly responsible for the victims of the world war, prepared and glorified them, or at least accepted them? It is our turn to ask: Did the war justify itself? What has it given us? What has it taught?

It will hardly pay now to pause upon the assertions of injured Russian proprietors that the revolution led to the cultural decline of the country. That aristocratic culture overthrown by the October revolution was in the last analysis only a superficial imitation of higher western models. Remaining inaccessible to the Russian people, it added nothing essential to the treasure-store of humanity. The October revolution laid the foundation of a new culture taking everybody into consideration, and for that very reason immediately acquiring international significance. Even supposing for a moment that owing to unfavorable circumstances and hostile blows the soviet régime should be temporarily overthrown, the inexpugnable impress of the October revolution would nevertheless remain upon the whole future development of mankind.

The language of the civilized nations has clearly marked off two epochs in the development of Russia. Where the aristocratic culture introduced into world parlance such barbarisms as *tzar, pogrom, knout,* October has internationalized such words as *Bolshevik, soviet* and *piatiletka.* This alone justifies the proletarian revolution, if you imagine that it needs justification.

CHRONOLOGICAL TABLE

1774

Pugachev Rebellion of Cossacks and peasants.

1825

DECEMBER Dekabrist (Decembrist) uprising against tzarism led by liberal officers.

1848

The Communist Manifesto published by Karl Marx and Friedrich Engels—the foundation of revolutionary socialism or communism.

1861

Peasant Reform; abolition of serfdom in Russia.

1864

"The International" (first international organization of socialist workers) established by Marx and others.

1871

The Paris Commune.

1882

Plekhanov publishes first pamphlet introducing Marxian socialism into Russia.

1905

The Revolution of 1905 in Russia. First organization of soviets by Russian workers.

JANUARY 9* "Bloody Sunday"—workers led by Father Gapon and carrying a petition to the tzar, are mowed down by the tzar's troops.

1914

AUGUST 1 World War begins.
Germany declares war against Russia.

NOVEMBER 4 Bolshevik deputies in the State Duma arrested and sent to Siberia.

1915

APRIL Russian revolutionary internationalist paper, *Nashe Slovo*, appears in Paris with Trotsky on the editorial staff.

SEPTEMBER International socialist congress in Zimmerwald, Switzerland.

1916

MAY Second Congress of socialist internationalists at Kienthal.

1917

JANUARY 9 Street meetings and a printers' strike celebrate the anniversary of "Bloody Sunday."

FEBRUARY 14 The last State Duma assembles.

FEBRUARY 23 Celebration of International Women's Day begins the revolution.

FEBRUARY 24 Two hundred thousand workers on strike in Petrograd.

FEBRUARY 25 General strike in Petrograd. Shootings and arrests of revolutionists.

FEBRUARY 26 Duma dissolved by the tzar. The deputies disperse but decide not to leave town.
Tens of thousands of workers in the streets.

FEBRUARY 27 Mutiny of the Guard regiments.
Formation of the Soviet of Workers' deputies.
Formation of Provisional Committee of the Duma.

* Russian dates are given according to the old calendar. Add 13 days to find the date according to the calendar that is now international.

FEBRUARY 28 Arrest of the tzar's ministers.
Capture of Schlüsselburg Prison.
First issue of *Izvestia*—"The News of the Soviet."

MARCH 1 "Order No. 1" is issued to the soldiers.
Formation of the soldiers' section of the Soviet.
First session of the Moscow Soviet.

MARCH 2 The tzar abdicates in favor of the Grand Duke Mikhail.
The Provisional Government is formed by the Provisional Committee of the Duma, with the support of the Soviet and with Kerensky as Minister of Justice.

MARCH 3 The Grand Duke Mikhail abdicates.
The Provisional Government announces the revolution to the world by radio.

MARCH 5 The first issue of *Pravda*, central organ of the Bolshevik Party.

MARCH 6 The Provisional Government declares amnesty for political prisoners.

MARCH 8 The tzar arrested at Moghiliev.

MARCH 14 Address of the Soviet "to the people of the whole world" declaring for peace without annexations or indemnities.

MARCH 23 Funeral of the martyrs of the revolution.

MARCH 29 All-Russian conference of the soviets.

APRIL 3 Lenin, Zinoviev and other Bolsheviks arrive from Switzerland.

APRIL 4 Lenin's "April Theses" outlining his policy of proletarian revolution.

APRIL 18 Celebration of the international socialist holiday of May 1.
Foreign Minister Miliukov sends a note to the Allies promising war to victory on the old terms.

APRIL 20 Armed demonstrations of protest against the note of Miliukov—the "April Days."

APRIL 24 Beginning of an All-Russian conference of the Bolshevik party.

MAY 1 The Petrograd Soviet votes for a coalition government.

MAY 2 Miliukov resigns.

MAY 4 Trotsky arrives from America, seconding the policies of Lenin.
An All-Russian Congress of Peasants' Deputies opens in Petrograd.

MAY 5 Coalition government is organized with Kerensky as Minister of War.

MAY 17 The Kronstadt Soviet declares itself the sole governing power in Kronstadt.

MAY 25 All-Russian congress of the Social Revolutionary party.

MAY 30 First conference of factory and shop committees opens in Petrograd.

JUNE 3 First All-Russian congress of soviets.

JUNE 16 Kerensky orders Russian armies to take the offensive.

JUNE 18 A demonstration called by the Mensheviks and Social Revolutionaries turns out to be a Bolshevik demonstration.

JUNE 19 Patriotic demonstration on Nevsky Prospect, carrying portraits of Kerensky.

JULY 3–5 "July Days"—semi-insurrection followed by attempted stamping out of Bolshevism in Petrograd.

JULY 6 Kerensky offensive collapses as Germans smash Russian lines at Tarnopol on southern front.

JULY 7 Socialist Government of Salvation of the Revolution is formed with Kerensky as president.

JULY 12 Restoration of the death penalty in the army.

JULY 16 Kornilov replaces Brussilov as commander-in-chief of the army.

JULY 23 Trotsky and Lunacharsky imprisoned; Lenin in hiding.

JULY 24 New Coalition Government with Kadets replaces Government of Salvation of the Revolution.

JULY 26 Sixth Congress of the Bolshevik party; fusion with Mezhrayontzi; Central Committee elected which is to lead party through October revolution.

AUGUST 12 State Conference in Moscow provokes general strike of Moscow workers. Conference hails Kornilov, who secretly sets August 27th for counter-revolutionary insurrection.

AUGUST 18–21 Germans break through northern front, take Riga, threaten Petrograd.

AUGUST 26 Government doubles price of grain. Ministers resign to give Kerensky free hand.

AUGUST 27 Kerensky tries to remove Kornilov, who ignores his orders and begins march on Petrograd. Soviet Committee for Struggle against Counter-Revolution formed.

AUGUST 28, 29, 30 Kornilov coup collapses as workers sabotage his advance and his troops desert.

SEPTEMBER 1 Kornilov arrested at General Headquarters in Moghilev.
Bolshevik resolution carries the Petrograd Soviet for the first time.

SEPTEMBER 4 Trotsky freed on bail by Provisional Government.

SEPTEMBER 5 Bolshevik resolution carries Moscow Soviet.

SEPTEMBER 9 Bolshevik majority of the Petrograd Soviet formally ratified. Compromise praesidium resigns.

SEPTEMBER 14 Democratic Conference opens in Petrograd.

SEPTEMBER 21 Democratic Conference closes after electing a Council of the Republic, or Pre-Parliament. Petrograd Soviet sends out call for All-Russian Soviet Congress on October 20th.

SEPTEMBER 24 Last Coalition Government formed, with Kerensky as president.

OCTOBER 7 Bolsheviks withdraw from the Council of the Republic.

OCTOBER 9 Petrograd Soviet votes to form the Committee for Revolutionary Defense.

OCTOBER 10 Bolshevik Central Committee adopts Lenin's resolution on armed insurrection as an immediate task.

OCTOBER 13 Petrograd Soldiers' Soviet votes to transfer military authority from Headquarters to the Military Revolutionary Committee. Northern Regional Soviet Congress endorses coming All-Russian Congress and declares for Soviet power.

OCTOBER 15 Kiev Soviet declares for Soviet power.

OCTOBER 16 Southwest Regional Soviet Congress at Minsk declares for Soviet power. Meeting of the Bolshevik Central Committee reaffirms Lenin's resolution on the insurrection against the opposition of Zinoviev and Kamenev.

OCTOBER 17 Rumored Bolshevik uprising fails to materialize. Zinoviev and Kamenev attack insurrectionary policy of Bolshevik Central Committee in the public press. All-Russian Soviet Central Executive Committee postpones All-Russian Soviet Congress from October 20th to October 25th.

OCTOBER 19 Ural Regional Soviet Congress declares for Soviet power.

OCTOBER 20 Committee for Revolutionary Defense, known as the Military Revolutionary Committee, begins active preparations for the insurrection.

OCTOBER 22 Enormous meetings throughout Petrograd as Soviet forces are mobilized for review.

OCTOBER 23 Peter and Paul Fortress, the last military obstacle of any importance in Petrograd, comes over to the Soviets.

OCTOBER 24 Provisional Government issues orders to take legal steps against the Military Revolutionary Committee, to suppress the Bolshevik papers, and to bring loyal troops into the capital, orders which were never carried out. Kerensky makes his last speech to the Council of the Republic. Left Social Revolutionaries indicate willingness to participate in the Military Revolutionary Committee.

OCTOBER 25 Insurrection begins at 2:00 A.M. Council of the Republic closed by troops at 12:00 noon. Lenin makes his first public appearance at a session of the Petrograd Soviet at 3:00 P.M. Operations against the seat of the Provisional Government at the Winter Palace begin at 9:00 P.M. Second All-Russian Congress of the Soviets opens at the Smolny at 11:00 P.M.

OCTOBER 26 Winter Palace falls and the Provisional Government is arrested at 2:00 A.M.

OCTOBER 26 AND 27 Second All-Russian Soviet Congress passes decrees on peace and land and sets up the new government of the Council of People's Commissars. Congress adjourns at 5:00 A.M., October 27th.

A SHORT LIST OF PRINCIPAL PERSONS

GENERAL ALEXEIEV Monarchist and active counter-revolutionary, commander-in-chief of the armies of the Provisional Government from April 1st to May 22nd.

ANTONOV-OVSEËNKO Bolshevik military leader, active in the 1905 revolution, associated with the Mensheviks during the years of reaction, internationalist during the war, joined the Bolsheviks after his return to Russia, one of the organizers of the October insurrection in Petrograd.

AVKSENTIEV School-teacher and leader of the Social Revolutionary party. President of the Executive Committee of the Peasants' Congress, Minister of the Interior in various coalition governments, President of the Council of the Republic.

BLAGONRAVOV Bolshevik corporal, who was Commissar of Peter and Paul Fortress at the time of the October insurrection.

GENERAL BRUSSILOV Tzarist general who subsequently gave his allegiance to the Soviet Government.

BUCHANAN British Ambassador to Russia during the revolution.

BUKHARIN Bolshevik theoretician and leader, active in Moscow, member of the Central Committee of the Bolshevik party in October.

CHEIDZE Social Democrat (Menshevik), first president of the Petrograd Soviet.

CHERNOV A leader of the Social Revolutionaries standing between the Rights and Lefts, Minister of Agriculture in the Coalition Government.

CHUDNOVSKY Bolshevik military leader, returned from America with Trotsky, one of the organizers of the October insurrection.

DAN Menshevik leader, active in the Soviets, member of the All-Russian Soviet Executive Committee until the insurrection.

GENERAL DENIKIN Tzarist general who later commanded anti-Bolshevik forces in southern Russia.

DYBENKO Bolshevik sailor and leader of the Soviet of the Baltic Fleet.

DZERZHINSKY Polish Social Democrat freed from prison by the February revolution, joined the Bolsheviks, later became first president of the Cheka.

FATHER GAPON Priest who led the working people carrying a petition to the tzar on "Bloody Sunday," January 9, 1905.

PRINCE GOLYTSIN A septuagenarian who headed the last tzarist ministry.

GOREMYKIN Premier of Russia immediately before Prince Golytsin.

GORKY The great Russian short-story writer and novelist.

GOTZ Terrorist and leader of the Social Revolutionary party. Member of the All-Russian Soviet Executive Committee until October.

GUCHKOV The first Minister of War and Marine under the Provisional Government, a moderate conservative and imperialist, one of the founders of the Octobrist party.

GENERAL IVANOV Russian commander who tried to bring his forces to Petrograd to crush the February revolution. Eleven years earlier he had subdued an uprising in Kronstadt.

IZVOLSKY Russian Minister of Foreign Affairs (1906–1910) and Ambassador to France (1910–1917).

JOFFÉ Joined the Bolshevik party with the Mezhrayontzi at the July fusion congress, member of the October Central Committee of the Bolshevik party. First Soviet Ambassador to Germany.

GENERAL KALEDIN Cossack general and counter-revolutionary leader, elected Ataman of the Don Cossack Army in July, supporter of the Kornilov insurrection.

KAMENEV A prominent member of the Central Committee of the Bolshevik party, subsequently a diplomat of the Soviet Government and president of the Council of Labor and Defense.

KERENSKY A Trudovik in the Duma—after the revolution a Social Revolutionary, first Minister of Justice, then of War and Marine, and finally "Minister-President" of the Provisional Government, fled from Russia when the Bolsheviks triumphed.

GENERAL KHABALOV Tzarist general, military commander of the troops of the Petrograd district during the first days of the revolution.

ADMIRAL KOLCHAK Russian naval officer, subsequently leader of anti-Bolshevik forces in Siberia.

KONOVALOV Moscow industrialist, Minister of Trade and Industry in the first coalition, resigned after two weeks, joined the Kadet party, Vice-President of the last (September) Coalition Government.

GENERAL KORNILOV Russian general who succeeded Khabalov in command of the Petrograd district—subsequently tried to establish a military dictatorship.

GENERAL KRASNOV Commander of the Third Cavalry, monarchist leader of the Kornilov march on Petrograd, later active in the counter-revolution.

KRYLENKO Bolshevik ensign and leader at the front, commander-in-chief of the armies after the insurrection, later Attorney General of the Soviet Republic.

KROPOTKIN Anarchist leader who became a patriot during the war and an anti-Bolshevik during the revolution.

LASHEVICH Bolshevik non-commissioned officer, prominent military leader in Petrograd.

LENIN Head of the Bolshevik party, leader of the Russian revolution and first head of the Soviet Government.

LIEBKNECHT German Socialist Reichstag Deputy, one of the few who held an internationalist position during the war, imprisoned, later a leader of the Spartacus Bund, killed during the revolution of 1919.

LOMOV Member of the October Central Committee of the Bolshevik party, first People's Commissar of Justice.

LUNACHARSKY Joined the Bolsheviks with the Mezhrayontzi in July, first People's Commissar of Education in the Soviet Government.

LUXEMBURG Polish Socialist leader, internationalist during the war, imprisoned, leader of the Spartacus Bund, killed on the same day as Liebknecht during the German revolution of 1919.

PRINCE LVOV A Constitutional Democrat (Kadet), first Prime Minister after the February revolution.

MARTOV Theoretician and leader of the Menshevik party, lifelong opponent of Lenin, an internationalist during the war; he tried to play the rôle of loyal opposition after the October revolution.

MILIUKOV Head of the Kadet party, Minister of Foreign Affairs and actual boss of the Provisional Government.

MILIUTIN Economist and member of the October Central Committee of the Bolshevik party, first People's Commissar for Agriculture.

NABAKOV Kadet leader, Minister without Portfolio in the Provisional Government, author of memoirs of the Provisional Government.

NOGIN Member of the October Central Committee of the Bolshevik party, first People's Commissar of Commerce and Industry.

PALCHINSKY Kadet engineer, Minister of Trade and Industry in the Provisional Government, Governor General of Petrograd.

PLEKHANOV Veteran Russian Social Democrat, translator of Karl Marx and regarded as the father of Russian Marxism, took a patriotic and conservative position during the World War and the revolution.

PODVOISKY Bolshevik military leader, one of the organizers of the Petrograd insurrection.

PROTOPOPOV A leader of the Progressive bloc in the last Duma, later broke with it, joined the court camarilla and became Minister of the Interior under the tzar.

RASKOLNIKOV Bolshevik leader in the Baltic Fleet and at Kronstadt.

GREGORY RASPUTIN An illiterate Siberian monk who exercised a great influence over the tzar and the tzarina and was assassinated in December, 1916, by members of the court.

REED American revolutionary journalist in Petrograd, later one of the founders of the Communist party of the United States.

RODZIANKO A great landowner, Lord Chamberlain under the tzar and conservative President of the Duma.

RYKOV Member of the October Central Committee of the Bolshevik party, first People's Commissar of the Interior.

SAVINKOV Social Revolutionary terrorist during the revolution of 1905 and after, patriot during the war, active in the Kornilov counter-revolutionary conspiracy, led counter-revolutionary uprisings after the October revolution, died in a Soviet prison.

SAZONOV Minister of Foreign Affairs in Russia after 1910, dismissed by the tzar in 1917.

PRINCE SHERBATOV Russian Minister of the Interior during the World War.

SKOBELEV One of the leaders of the Menshevik party, became Minister of Labor in the Coalition Government.

STALIN A prominent member of the Central Committee of the Bolshevik party, editor with Kamenev of the official organ *Pravda* until Lenin's arrival in Russia, became general secretary of the party in 1922 and is at present virtual head of the Soviet Government.

STANKEVICH Compromise Socialist, Political Commissar for the Provisional Government to the Army Supreme Command, author of memoirs of the revolution.

STÜRMER Premier of Russia during most of 1916.

SUKHANOV A social democrat belonging to Gorky's group, one of the leaders of the Petrograd Soviet in the early days of the revolution, author of *Notes of the Revolution* in seven volumes.

SVERDLOV Bolshevik since 1903, released from exile by the February revolution, one of the most talented organizers of the Bolshevik party, active in Petrograd, President of the All-Russian Soviet after the October revolution, died in 1919.

TERESHCHENKO Kadet–Minister of Foreign Affairs in the reconstructed Provisional Government following Miliukov's resignation.

TSERETELLI A leader of the Menshevik party and principal leader of the Soviet until the Bolsheviks won a majority.

URITSKY Joined the Bolshevik party in July with the Mezhrayontzi, member of the October Central Committee, assassinated in 1918.

VERKHOVSKY Military Commander of the Moscow District, Minister of War in Kerensky's last coalition government.

COUNT WITTE Russian statesman of the old régime, champion of industrial development, died in 1915.

GENERAL YUDENICH Tzarist general who subsequently led anti-Bolshevik forces in an attempt to capture Petrograd.

PRINCE YUSSUPOV One of the assassins of Rasputin.

ZINOVIEV Prominent member of the Central Committee of the Bolshevik party, came to Russia with Lenin on April 3rd from Switzerland, subsequently first President of the Third (Communist) International.

A SHORT LIST OF PRINCIPAL PLACES

ALEXANDRINSKY THEATER Petrograd theater where the Democratic Conference met.

CIRQUE MODERNE Auditorium near Peter and Paul Fortress.

GATCHINA Southern suburb of Petrograd, where Kornilov march on the capital expired.

HELSINGFORS Seaport capital of Finland, about 120 miles west of Petrograd on the Gulf of Finland.

KIEV Capital of the Ukraine, about 600 miles south of Petrograd.

KRASNOE SELO Southern suburb of Petrograd.

KRONSTADT An island fortress in the Gulf of Finland guarding Petrograd.

KSHESINSKAIA'S PALACE Palace of a former favorite dancer of the tzar, located near Peter and Paul Fortress. Headquarters of the Bolshevik party until the "July Days."

MARIINSKY PALACE Palace in Petrograd where the ministry of the Provisional Government held its meetings.

MOGHILEV Small city about 400 miles south of Petrograd where the High Command was established.

MOONSUND ISLANDS Strategic naval base in the Baltic, near Riga.

NEVSKY PROSPECT The main avenue of Petrograd.

ORANIENBAUM, PETERHOF Western suburbs of Petrograd, where military academies were located.

PETER AND PAUL FORTRESS Formidable prison fortress on an island in Petrograd.

RIGA Capital of the former tzarist province of Latvia, a Baltic seaport.

SCHLÜSSELBURG Eastern suburb of Petrograd, location of a munitions factory and a prison.

SMOLNY INSTITUTE Former school for the daughters of the nobility, occupied by the Soviet when it moved from the Tauride Palace.

TAURIDE PALACE Palace in Petrograd in the right wing of which the Duma met. The Soviet was formed and held its meetings during the first months of the revolution in the left wing of the same palace.

TZARSKOE SELO A town near Petrograd where one of the tzar's palaces was located.

VYBORG The principal industrial district of Petrograd.

WINTER PALACE The tzar's official residence in Petrograd.

A BRIEF GLOSSARY OF UNFAMILIAR TERMS OR TERMS USED THROUGHOUT THIS BOOK IN A SPECIAL SENSE

Ataman Elected chief of the Cossacks.

Blanquism A theory of insurrection by a select clique of conspirators, usually contrasted to the Marxian conception of mass insurrection. The name is taken from Louis Auguste Blanqui, French revolutionist, 1805–1881.

Bonapartism In the Marxian sense: a transitional government based on military force during a period when class rule is not secure.

bourgeoisie Used in feudal times to designate city people as opposed to those who lived in the country, this word came to mean the representatives of capital as opposed to the landowning nobility and to wage labor. Where the landowning nobility ceases to play a separate class rôle, the word often means much the same thing as "propertied classes."

petty bourgeoisie Small proprietors, peasants, artisans, and tradesmen—people, broadly speaking, who employ labor but also labor themselves.

camarilla A company of advisers, a clique—the author's name for that small group surrounding the tzar and tzarina and Rasputin who ruled Russia just before the revolution.

commissar Commissioner. In the central government equivalent to minister; but the name was applied also to the representatives of the government in the provinces who replaced the tzarist governors, and to those special representatives in the various units of the army—"Commissar of the Western Front," "Commissar of General Headquarters," etc.

communal land Land owned in common by the peasants of a village.

The Commune The revolutionary régime established by the proletarian uprising in Paris in 1871, when the power was seized and held for seventy-two days.

compradors Native agents of foreign business concerns in China.

Constituent Assembly The assembly elected by universal suffrage which, it was promised, should determine the permanent constitution of the Russian state.

Convention Revolutionary government of France elected by universal suffrage to replace the Legislative Assembly. The Convention lasted from 1792 to 1795, when it was overthrown by the Directory.

cooperatives Consumers' cooperative societies founded by liberals and moderate socialists throughout Russia.

Cossacks Cavalry soldiers who formed a caste and almost a nationality in tzarist Russia, since they enjoyed special privileges (exemption from taxes and land allotments) in return for obligatory military service, and since the land allotments were consigned to special territories.

dumas Municipal elective governing bodies.

The Duma The Russian Parliament, limited in power and based upon a greatly restricted suffrage.

epigones Disciples who corrupt the doctrines of their teacher—applied by the author to the present leaders, historians, and theoreticians of the Bolshevik party in Russia.

Frondeurs Members of the Fronde, a faction of the French nobility who opposed the government during the minority of Louis XIV, and made war on the Court party. Also a general term for an opposition arising within the ruling nobility, and sometimes also for an opposition arising out of mere "contrariness."

Georgian A native of Georgia, a province in the southeastern part of European Russia.

Girondists Members of the Gironde, a party in the French Revolution, which expressed the interests of the big bourgeoisie of southern and western France (most of its leaders coming from the Gironde province). They wanted to overthrow the old régime which stood in the way of economic development, but feared the city poor and the peasant masses who could alone overthrow it, and therefore perpetually wavered between the revolution and the counter-revolution, finally going over to the latter.

Hansa The Hanseatic League of northern German commercial cities during the Middle Ages.

"Izvestia" "The News," official organ of the Soviet. Its full title was "The News of the Soviet."

Jacobins Left wing of the French Convention, composed of petty bourgeois and worker delegates. The Jacobins overthrew the Girondists in 1792–93 and ruled supreme until the execution of the Jacobin leader, Robespierre, in July, 1794.

Jacquerie Name given to a revolt of the French peasants in 1358 and since applied to any spontaneous armed peasant uprising.

Junkers Students of the officers' schools.

kulak "Fist"—nickname for a wealthy peasant.

Kuomintang Chinese bourgeois nationalist party, led by Chiang Kai-shek.

Legislative Assembly A predominately monarchist and big bourgeois congress created by the French National Assembly in October, 1791. The Legislative Assembly was forced to dissolve in favor of the revolutionary Convention in 1792.

muzhik Nickname for the Russian peasant in general.

National Assembly The first representative body of the French Revolution. Composed of the delegates to the States General, who were elected by classes, the National Assembly ruled France from 1789 to 1791, when it was superseded by the Legislative Assembly.

palace revolution Deposition and, if necessary, assassination, of a reigning monarch by members and associates of the court.

political strike A strike in which workers have a political objective—frequently a protest against some government policy.

pogrom Raid on and massacre of the Jewish population, and on rare occasions of other minorities.

"Pravda" "The truth"—official newspaper of the Bolshevik party, first published in 1912.

Rada The Ukrainian national congress.

Seim The Finnish national congress.

soviet The Russian word for *council*. It is used in this translation only to designate the councils of workers' and soldiers' (and later also peasants') deputies. In other cases the Russian word "soviet" is translated "council."

Holy Synod The highest governing body of the Greek Orthodox church in Russia.

Thermidor On the 9th of Thermidor (July 27), 1794, Robespierre was deposed and executed, and the revolutionary power came into the hands of opportunists under whom it gradually passed over to the reaction.

verst A Russian measure of distance, about two-thirds of a mile.

Vikzhel Abbreviated name for the Russian Railroad Workers' Union.

zemstvo Provincial and county council, elected on the basis of a franchise limited by a rather high property qualification, and having only economic and cultural functions.

A LIST OF PARTIES AND POLITICAL GROUPS

ANARCHISTS People who thought that the cooperative commonwealth could be introduced by abolishing the political state.

BLACK HUNDREDS Popular name for the Union of the Russian People—a league of the most reactionary monarchists and nationalists who employed methods of criminal terror against the revolutionaries and were the chief instigators of pogroms.

BOLSHEVIKS Revolutionary Marxist party, who believed that the working class should unite with the poor peasants, taking the lead in a struggle against all bourgeois society, not only for the overthrow of tzarism, but for the inauguration of a labor republic and a socialist state.

THE BUND An organization of Russian Jewish workers, led by Lieber, Menshevik in policy.

THE COMPROMISERS General name for the leaders of the Menshevik and Social Revolutionary parties in the Soviet, who, although professing socialist principles, compromised with the Kadets upon essential points, voluntarily handing over the power to them.

DEFENSISTS Those who believed in prosecuting the war as a war in defense of the fatherland.

DEKABRISTS Participants in the unsuccessful uprising against the tzar Alexander I in December (Dekabr) 1825.

KADETS Popular name for the Constitutional Democrats (K.D.'s)—subsequently also called Party of the People's Freedom—the great liberal party favoring a constitutional monarchy or even ultimately a republic, the party of the progressive landlords, middle bourgeoisie and bourgeois intelligentsia, headed by Miliukov, a professor of history.

LEFT MENSHEVIKS Extreme left wing of the Mensheviks, led by Larin, joined the Bolsheviks in July.

LEFT SOCIAL REVOLUTIONARIES Left wing of the Social Revolutionary party. As a separate party they participated for a brief time in the government set up by the Bolsheviks, but a few months after the October Revolution were organizing anti-Bolshevik uprisings.

MAXIMALISTS An extremist tendency which split off from the Social Revolutionaries in the Revolution of 1905.

MENSHEVIKS Moderate socialist party claiming allegiance to Karl Marx, but believing that the working class must combine with the liberal bourgeoisie to overthrow tzarism and establish a democratic republic.

MENSHEVIK-INTERNATIONALISTS A group of left Mensheviks led by Martov, closely associated with Maxim Gorky's radical socialist paper *Novaia Zhizn* and on many issues friendly to the Bolsheviks.

MEZHRAYONTZI The so-called Inter-City Group, an organization of about 4000 workers and revolutionists, including Trotsky, Joffé, Uritsky, Riazanov, Manuilsky, Lunacharsky, etc., which fused with the Bolsheviks at the July Congress.

NARODNIKS General name for those revolutionists with socialist ideals who, not knowing or accepting the Marxian theory, looked to the peasants rather than the working class to take the lead in overthrowing tzarism and transforming Russia. The name (from *narod,* meaning people) includes the Terrorists who hoped to destroy tzarism and rouse the peasants by the "propaganda of the deed," as well as the mildest of evangelical socialists who hoped to transform Russia by "going to the people."

OCTOBRISTS A party named for its support of the imperial Manifesto of October 1905, establishing a Duma—monarchist and imperialist, the party of the big commercial, industrial and landowning bourgeoisie, headed by Guchkov, a Moscow capitalist.

PROGRESSIVE BLOC An alliance of most of the deputies in the Duma during the war, striving for a strong government.

THE REACTION The old churchly, tzarist, and aristocratic landlord opposition to democratic progress even of the kind represented by the Kadet party.

SECOND INTERNATIONAL Founded in 1889, the Second International embraced all the working class parties. After its political failure during the war, the Third (Communist) International was formed by the left wing of the Second International, in 1919. Both Internationals exist today.

SOCIAL DEMOCRATS Party based upon the theories of Karl Marx, which were translated into Russian during the last two decades of the 19th century by Plekhanov. They looked to the development of industrial capitalism and the creation of a revolutionary working class for the overthrow of tzarism and the transformation of Russia into a socialist state. The party split in 1903 into the Mensheviks (minority men) and Bolsheviks (majority men).

SOCIAL PATRIOTS Socialists who abandoned the principle of internationalism and other revolutionary principles in the interest of war time patriotism.

SOCIAL REVOLUTIONARIES Peasant socialist party, formed at the beginning of the century from a fusion of several tendencies of the Narodniks. Representing the wavering interests of the small peasant proprietor in the revolution, this party soon split into a group of Left Social Revolutionaries, anarchist in their leanings but participating for a time in the Bolshevik government, and the Right Social Revolutionaries who supported Kerensky.

TRUDOVIKS A party composed of cautious Narodnik intellectuals who defended the peasants as against the landlords, but did not venture too far to the left of the Kadets—the party to which Kerensky belonged when in the Duma.

ZIMMERWALDISTS Socialists loyal to the principle of internationalism during the war—so named for their adherence to the program of the International Socialist Congress held in Zimmerwald, Switzerland, in 1915.

INDEX